Cotton Mather's Spanish Lessons

Cotton Mather's Spanish Lessons

A Story of Language, Race, and Belonging in the Early Americas

Kirsten Silva Gruesz

THE BELKNAP PRESS OF HARVARD UNIVERSITY PRESS

CAMBRIDGE, MASSACHUSETTS

LONDON, ENGLAND

2022

Printed in the United States of America

First printing

Library of Congress Cataloging-in-Publication Data is available from loc.gov

ISBN: 978-0-674-97175-2 (cloth)

To Teodoro & Elias, my little birds grown:

no olviden que tienen dos alas

Contents

Note on Style

I have retained Mather's idiosyncratic spelling and capitalization and, when possible, his enthusiastic use of underlines, italics, and punctuation to highlight certain words and phrases in his printed works. Texts for reading aloud made use of these different styles to indicate emphasis and breath marks. They are the equivalent of performance scripts, and allow the reader to imagine the sonic qualities of Mather's oral delivery. In some cases, I have had to rely on printed transcriptions of these works that do not indicate such authorial preferences. One exception to this general fidelity to seventeenth- and eighteenth-century orthography is that I have spelled out his scribal abbreviations for common terms like "which" and "the." For example, the thorn character, which looks like a y with a superscript e, was used as an abbreviation for "the" but is often represented as "ye" and thus confused with the second-person plural pronoun "ye" (you-all).

I have also followed period style in citations from Spanish. Today's orthography was standardized beginning in the early eighteenth century by the newly founded Real Academia Española, so earlier texts may use different spellings, as in "Christiano": this is not an error on Mather's part. Citations of books in Spanish do not routinely capitalize most words in a title, as they do in English, but I hew to Mather's own usage in capitalizing *Fe* and *Christiano*, as his bibliographer Thomas Holmes and most library records have also done.

Mather, who lived on the cusp of the transition from the Julian to the Gregorian calendar, generally recorded both Old and New Style dates in letters and diaries. I follow most modern editions of his works in giving only the Gregorian dates to avoid confusion.

Unless otherwise indicated, all translations are mine, and are given in brackets in the text.

Introduction

The First Spanish Imprint in English America

———————

Flocks of tourists each year walk the red-painted lines that mark Boston's Freedom Trail, a secular pilgrim's route of historical markers and monuments. Visitors with strong calves might hike along the steep incline leading to Copp's Hill Burying Ground to view the graves of the city's early free Black activists and of the "fire-and-brimstone preachers Cotton and Increase Mather, two Puritan ministers closely associated with the Salem witch trials," as the interpretive materials describe them. Larger crowds throng the less strenuous route toward the iconic Old North Church, associated with Paul Revere's ride. Near that building stood an even older, now-vanished landmark of North Square: the Second Church, presided over for seventy-five years by members of those same Mathers, who lived nearby. Less than a mile from here, the red sidewalk lines lead—across solid ground that had been water before the city's seventeenth-century founders filled it in—to Boston Common, where a sign proclaims, "The Revolution begins here." In pointing out such connections between colony and nation, the Freedom Trail does its interpretive work: to induct visitors into a narrative of national becoming that centers this English settlement as the Puritan seed that would grow into the republic of the United States. But just a few steps off the marked path, a visitor might catch the sounds of something different: people singing, praying, and preaching in Spanish.[1]

The sounds emanate from the Tremont Temple adjacent to Boston Common. Established in the nineteenth century as a racially integrated Baptist church, it was once an important site of abolitionist activity. Now the building's basement houses a different congregation, the Iglesia Bautista Hispanoamericana de Boston. At first glance, these two congregations—the imposing North

Square churches of the past that housed some of the first Christian settlers and the Spanish-speaking evangelical church hidden from street view today—appear to have no connection with one another. Yet in many ways, the Tremont congregation represents the fulfillment of a vision that Cotton Mather had in the 1690s, when he set out to learn Spanish and to write tracts in that language. *La Fe del Christiano* (The Faith of the Christian) was the first Spanish-language publication in what would become the United States. Mather imagined these words on paper as "a little Fire" that would kindle a blaze of Protestant conviction across the vast zones of the Americas to the south of the little English town he barely ventured out of during his lifetime. That "little Fire" took only three hundred years to arrive at his front door.

If entering the old buildings along the Freedom Trail is a kind of public pedagogy that encourages visitors to feel a sense of continuity with the past, studying New England's first books does the same in American history and literature classrooms. Both educational projects have been importantly revised in recent years to center other people besides English settlers. The popular Boston Black Heritage Trail leads by the nation's oldest surviving church and school established by and for African Americans, while the *Mamusse Wunneet-upanatamwe Up-Biblum God* (1663) is a rare and prized possession of many libraries: as the first complete Bible printed in British North America, a stunning technical and intellectual achievement of Wampanoag translator-printers, it proves that there was once a will to embrace languages other than English within the colony. By taking back the living, spoken language from these books, centuries later, the Wampanoag community has turned them into powerful symbols of cultural survival and persistence. Claiming a part in these foundational stories is a different matter for Latinos like the ones gathered in the Tremont Temple basement. Most identify as having a mixed-race ancestry that is captured by neither a US Black/white racial binary nor Native tribal enrollment standards. Their families' residency in the United States may stretch back a few generations, but it is more likely to be recent. If Mather's *La Fe del Christiano* is the first Spanish-language imprint within the nation's current borders, should it be considered the first Latino text? What manner of thread connects this fragile artifact to the present?

Mather understood the world in terms of a contest between his God's revealed truth and an array of other religious faiths he regarded as false, chief among them Roman Catholicism. Any gratification he might feel to know that Latinos make up the fastest-growing demographic of evangelical Protestants in the country today would be tempered by the fact that the archdiocese of Boston maintains a robust Apostolado Hispano (Hispanic ministry), which seeks to keep this same population within the Catholic fold. For most US Americans, however, the competition among different sects of Christianity long ago ceded its importance to a different kind of struggle, one waged over the way the nation remembers its collective past, its distribution of rights and opportunities in the present, and its openness to making new citizens through immigration in the future. This is a struggle about inclusion and belonging, pitting those who claim longstanding or ancestral presence in the country against those who are perceived as outsiders and strangers. So contentious is the question that it has kept immigration policy paralyzed for decades, leaving some eleven million US residents stranded in the legal limbo of the undocumented: semivisible participants in the nation's social, economic, and religious life without enjoying the full rights of citizenship. Millions of other would-be immigrants are detained and deported at its borders and from within its cities. Although these persons come from all over the globe, more than 80 percent are from Latin America. Thus, in the media's nuance-flattening way, the prototypically undesirable migrant comes from "south of the border," speaks Spanish, and looks Brown.[2]

With this last characteristic in particular, Latinx migrants are shepherded into an already-existing system of racialization: the social use of a false correlate between outward appearance and biological difference to harm some humans and benefit others. US histories of race and of migration are different but they cross-hatch at many points. Successive groups of immigrants have navigated the shoals of a profound anti-Blackness, the erasure and denigration of Indigenous Americans, and a host of biases about their ethnicity and religion to assimilate into whiteness—and thus into an affiliation with the European "founder" peoples celebrated in places like Boston's Freedom Trail—when they could. Others, especially Latinx, Asian, and Muslim and Jewish Americans (no matter how acculturated) remain vulnerable to outbursts of a racially tinged nativism. At a moment when US institutions of historical memory are being called upon to reckon with the overdue accounts of the African slavery and settler-colonial appropriation of land that were necessary to build the nation, assessing claims from the past in the form of tribal land-restoration claims and reparations for descendants of the enslaved, the place of these "other Others" in such racial reckonings is not clear.[3]

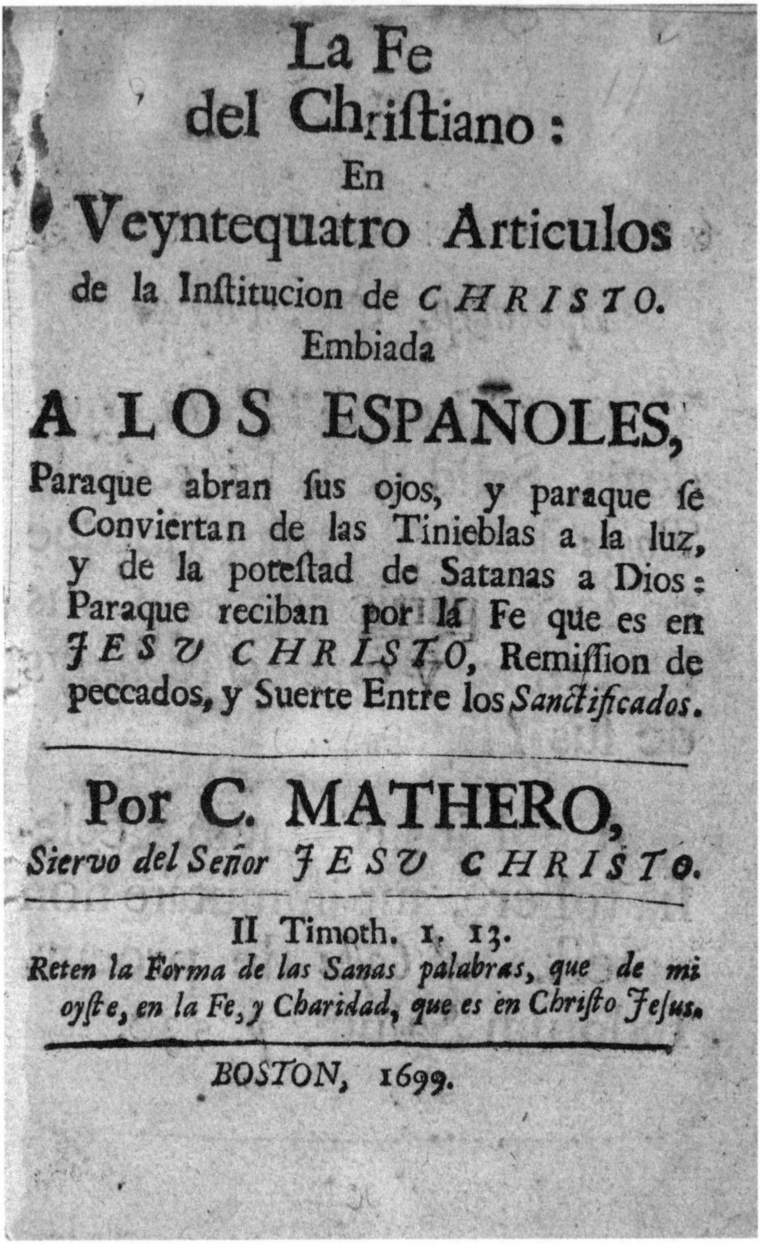

La Fe
del Chriſtiano:
En
Veyntequatro Articulos
de la Inſtitucion de *CHRISTO.*
Embiada
A LOS ESPAÑOLES,
Paraque abran ſus ojos, y paraque ſe
Conviertan de las Tinieblas a la luz,
y de la poteſtad de Satanas a Dios:
Paraque reciban por la Fe que es en
JESV CHRISTO, Remiſſion de
peccados, y Suerte Entre los *Sanctificados.*

Por C. MATHERO,
Siervo del Señor JESV CHRISTO.

II Timoth. 1. 13.
*Reten la Forma de las Sanas palabras, que de mi
oyſte, en la Fe, y Charidad, que es en Chriſto Jeſus.*

BOSTON, 1699.

Figure 1: Cotton Mather, *La Fe del Christiano: En veyntequatro articulos de la institucion de Christo.*
Title page recto. *AC7.M4208.699f Lobby VI.3.33, Houghton Library, Harvard University.

And this is where, unexpectedly, Cotton Mather and his little Spanish book come in.

The thread that links *La Fe del Christiano* to the present is not one of ancestral descent or an unbroken tradition, but of a *language problem* extending from the colonial to the national period. The long title of Mather's work addresses it "A LOS ESPANOLES" (without the *virgulilla*, or tilde), a plural noun we might translate as "the Spanish people." But what exactly did he mean by that? Was ESPANOLES used as a demonym (indicating where a person is from), an ethnonym (indicating their genealogical or chosen family or tribe), or what we might call a loquonym (indicating the speech community to which they belong)? Prior to the normalization of modern notions of citizenship and race, these categories—along with those that designated religious belief—strongly determined the boundaries of insider and outsider, belonging and nonbelonging to a community. Such onomastic terms can often carry more than one of these three meanings, as with "English," calling for careful untangling (the casual "I'm Irish" spoken by an English-speaking American would be accurate only as an ethnonym, for example). But as English became the dominant language in the United States, the potential function of the word "English" to describe *people* has become less ambiguous, while in contrast the word "Spanish" and its associated morphemes continue to mark human difference in a way that ethnologist Jonathan Rosa refers to as "raciolinguistic." Mather's ESPANOLES, as we will see, fluctuates between demonym, ethnonym, and loquonym in an unstable way, just as the categorical boundaries of "Latinx," the latest of a long series of names that attempt to represent this highly diverse population, do today.[4]

Cotton Mather's Spanish Lessons uses the unlikely existence of *La Fe del Christiano* to tell two intertwined stories. The first is a group biography that situates Mather within the household that enabled his copious textual production: the supporting framework of his family and a multiracial group of servants assigned different degrees of freedom, including people he referred to paternalistically as "Negroes" and "Spanish Indians." The second narrative line traces the life history of *La Fe del Christiano* itself—beginning with the evangelical writings by Spanish Catholics that inspired it, continuing with the library of Spanish-language instructional works that Mather and a companion assembled in order to prepare to write it, and culminating in the mechanics of its composition, printing, and distribution. In attributing a kind of life to this material text, imagining its copresence with prior and contemporary intertexts and its withering away as it loses readers, I follow Joanna Brooks's insight about the fragile survival rate of early Black publications and libraries: "Books, like people, have life chances." This story takes us from Boston to Mexico, Florida, and Barbados, among other places. It makes the case that a hemispheric, translational framework, attuned to the many nuances of spoken and written language proficiency and to the evolution of linguistically expressed concepts over time, can illuminate both the historical and the contemporary contexts of US Latina/o/x belonging, in all its ethnoracial ambiguity.[5]

Cotton Mather and the New Puritan Studies

If that leap from twenty-first-century *latinidad* back to the turn of the eighteenth century seems implausible, it may be because US national memory has been so invested in colonial New England. Pilgrims and Puritans have played an outsized role in American Studies since that field's beginnings, with the founding, in the early nineteenth century, of the historical societies and archives that preserved cultural materials and interpreted them retroactively. These filiopietistic amateur historians (among them Mather's granddaughter Hannah Mather Crocker) found precedents among the early Puritans for ideological arguments about the national "type": variously self-reliant, pioneering, faith-centered. Under the influence of Harvard-trained historians like Vernon Parrington in the 1920s, the Calvinist Puritan heritage became a foundation not only of the field of US history, but the origin point of a distinctly *American* literary canon within English departments. At the intersection of those two disciplines arose the field-formation of American Studies, strongly tied to New England universities as well. Incorporating scholars of radical as well as liberal-centrist orientations, the Puritan Studies of midcentury often reached an ambivalent to negative judgment regarding that inheritance (as in the towering work of Perry Miller), but it hardly questioned the nineteenth-century consensus about the centrality of English settlers. As Bryce Traister puts it, the field neatly "assumed a certain continuity with everything that came after: 'from colony to province,' to borrow one well-known phrase; from evangelicalism to democracy; from liberty of conscience to political liberty; from dissent to consent." Abram van Engen's recent study of the periodic revivals of John Winthrop's figure of the "City on a Hill," summoning visions of a shining, sanctified America dating back to 1630, proves that point.[6]

The challenge to scholarly narratives of American exceptionalism that percolated in the 1990s (prompted by, among other things, the Native and Latino response to the Columbian quincentenary in 1992) aimed to displace this long tradition of seeing the New England settlements as the primal scene of national origins. Their once-outsized presence in the canon shrank to make way for other voices. Yet the rise of postnational and multiethnic American Studies also made for a liberating divorce that reenergized the field into what has variously been called the "New" or "Post-" Puritan Studies. The past decade in particular has seen an extraordinary renaissance of scholarship that focuses less on those assumed temporal continuities between colony and nation than on the perspectives of New England's Native populations as they fought for political and spiritual sovereignty; on interrelationships between the English colonies along the Eastern seaboard with those in the West Indies; on transatlantic and global exchanges of scientific knowledge and market commodities, including the rising trade in African souls; on material and social histories of literacy, media, and print technologies; and on the reconception of foundational categories such as gender, the body, emotion and affect, modernity, and secularism. *Cotton Mather's Spanish Lessons* is indebted to this groundbreaking work, as well as to the equally dynamic recent production in multiple languages among scholars of colonial Latin America and the Caribbean. Perhaps more than the New Puritan Studies, that field has stressed ethnogenesis: the making of new peoples and communities who struggled against colonial circumstances to claim degrees of freedom over their own lives and bodies.[7]

Turning to Cotton Mather to contribute to this new scholarly current may seem, at first, retrogressive. Few families in colonial New England have been as scrutinized as the Mathers, in part because the patriarchs held positions of power and in part because they left such a wealth of documents. It is precisely because previous writers have constructed so many different versions of this figure that he bears revisitation, so a brief recap of how Mather has been useful to past critics is in order. In the older continuity narratives, scholars noted that Cotton Mather was one of the principal instigators of the New England Revolt of 1689, likely authoring the collective manifesto that some have seen as a forerunner of the Declaration of Independence. Adding to that protonationalist portrait is biographer Kenneth Silverman's assessment that "no other person born in America between the time of Columbus and of Franklin strove to make himself so conspicuous—strove, more accurately, to become conspicuous as an American." Mather was the first Englishman to give himself that label in print. The original sense of "American" as noun and adjective signified Native peoples; only in the later eighteenth century did its default meaning shift to mean settlers. Mather also used the term frequently in the Neo-Latin titles of his many English-language publications: his chronicle of New England church history was *Magnalia Christi Americana* (The Great Works / Annals of Christ in America, 1702); an important missive to Boston's secular leaders, *Theopolis Americana* (The American City of God, 1710), and a hymnal-commentary *Psalterium Americana* (The American Book of Psalms, 1718). This last was one of the only sections published during his lifetime of a massive commentary titled *Biblia Americana* (The American Bible), an encyclopedic attempt to reconcile all known science and history with the Bible: consisting of more than 4,500 folio-sized manuscript pages in Mather's cramped cursive, it is only now being issued in print, one volume at a time. As Reiner Smo-linski, Jan Stievermann, and other religious historians have shown, the *Biblia* makes a powerful case for Mather as one of the foremost theologians of his time, and a surprisingly ecumenical Christian as well.[8]

As that tiny sampling of his titles indicates, "American" literature has also leaned hard on Mather—even as that discipline, too, has come to reject the continuity narrative that once put his work near the front of the typical anthology. William Spengemann, who has influentially challenged the periodization of "early" American literature and its retroactive identification of colonial writers as forerunners of a nation they could not have anticipated, groused about his prose style: "Cotton Mather's hard work on behalf of the American Renaissance did not make him a Melville." Spengemann refers to the field's use of *Magnalia Christi Americana* as a foundational literary work—although it is a history, Mather's strong personal voice in it seems in some ways novelistic—but his Melville comparison, even in the negative, is apt in terms of scale as well. Nearly four hundred printed objects, from small tracts like *La Fe del Christiano* to sermons to almanacs, bear Mather's name. Although his father, Increase, was also a prolific writer, that total number of titles accounts for half of the entire production of the Boston press in a three-decade span. Unmatched as a patron of the early colonial press, he was the most conspicuous experimenter of his period into what an author could be: as I will argue here, his notion of authorship involved being a particularly dedicated *reader* who absorbed and reassembled both the divine and mortal words of others. Mitchell Breitweiser has described the herculean *Biblia* as an endlessly branching hypertext, "a single vast demonstration of the Bible's prototypical centrality among books by revealing other textualities—science, mythology, history, philosophy, Judaica—as more or less corrupt variants on the prototype." The omnivorous note-taking that Mather poured into the *Magnalia* and the *Biblia Americana* came from sources in multiple languages, and a major intention behind this book's attention to Spanish is to push against the default assumption that American literature must necessarily be written in English. Mather's aesthetics was translational.[9]

Thanks in part to the recent publication of the first volumes of the *Biblia Americana*, scholarship on the history of science has also returned to Mather, who had once intended to be a medical doctor instead of a minister. As the first North American chosen as a Fellow of the Royal Society (the "F.R.S." that garnishes the author's name in his later publications), Mather avidly consumed the philosophical and scientific literature that England and Europe produced. He corresponded not only with British interlocutors but with individuals in present-day Germany, India, and France. His theologically structured view of the world did not preclude his intellectual curiosity, his participation in what historian of medicine Sari Altschuler calls the "imaginative experimentation" of early eighteenth-century science, a viewpoint that embraced, rather than denied, the presence of the observer's own mind and body in experimental practice. This nascent empiricism of the body coexisted with spiritual treatments in Mather's medical manual *The Angel of Bethesda*, written in 1724 but not published until the 1970s. During the smallpox epidemic that struck Boston in 1721, Mather acted on information about African inoculation practices that he had learned, years earlier, from a man known as Onesimus who had bought his freedom from the minister. With Zabdiel Boylston, Mather began an inoculation campaign that was ultimately successful in curbing the epidemic. This episode, periodically recalled during moments of anxiety about the safety of vaccination protocols, is one of the two contexts in which the general public learns about Cotton Mather (and sometimes about Onesimus as well).[10]

The other context, of course, is the Salem witch trials. The Freedom Trail's marker at the Mather gravesite, as we saw, reduces both father and son to their roles in this event. Although he was neither a judge nor a direct participant in the proceedings and executions, Cotton Mather was seen to have intellectually abetted the case of the court against the accused witches, to have failed to exert the family's political influence to stop the proceedings immediately. This had fatal ramifications for the son's reputation, even more than the father's.

Wonders of the Invisible World, with its discussion of spectral evidence, is the one Mather title—among those hundreds—still consistently read by students and witch-history buffs. Possessed of an unforgettable name, this single person more than any other stands in metonymically for a "puritanical" worldview, as that adjective was later turned into a synonym for zealotry and intolerance. "Cotton Mather" indexes a superstitious witch-burner in a Marvel comics series, and the sexually tortured paragon of Puritan intolerance in a Gothic television drama called *Salem.* To make caricature even easier, the single, widely circulated portrait of him is dominated by a massive, now ridiculous-looking, powdered and crimped hairpiece. The image cements popular memory of Mather as a "prig in a periwig." (Actually, Robert E. Brown argues, Mather was unperturbed by the gender anxiety felt by many around men's wearing of long wigs: he wrote that hair length was simply a matter of custom, not inborn nature.)[11]

Against the tide of that popular memory, this is a book featuring Cotton Mather that contains only glancing references to the Salem witch trials. Salem was consequential to Mather mainly in its aftermath, several years later, when Robert Calef succeeded in publishing an incendiary pamphlet blaming Increase and Cotton Mather for the deaths at Salem and the two unwisely and unsuccessfully tried to censor the pamphlet, creating even more of a scandal. And as Jane Kamensky has argued from a historian's perspective, the enduring popularity of the Salem interlude has had the unfortunate effect of drawing attention away from more consequential processes unfolding in New England at the time: the dramatic exclusion and punishment of Native peoples, even those allied with the English, following King Philip's War; the scaffolding of new forms of structural violence around the nascent slave economy Boston was entering; and the waning of theocratic authority in this new mercantile world. These developments in the English settlement project toward the end of the seventeenth century have led to new scrutiny of a third dimension of Mather's legacy: his views about intrahuman hierarchies, including the presumed dominion of men over women and Europeans over Amerindians and people of African descent.[12]

Building on Lorenzo Greene's foundational *The Negro in Colonial New England* (1942), these scholarly conversations have galvanized around Mather's sermon, *The Negro Christianized* (1706). That text accommodated Christian slaveholding while also insisting on monogenesis and the equality of African souls and minds. These two strands of the sermon's argument pulled in different directions, and Mather's words would be echoed, contradictorily, both by proponents of a biblical defense of Southern slavery and by champions of Black emancipation in the nineteenth century. Crossing over from academic to popular history, Ibram X. Kendi's *Stamped from the Beginning,* a study that won the National Book Award in 2017, identified Mather unambiguously as the first in a historical line of American racist thinkers: the first of five key figures on a trajectory that Kendi traces from segregationist hate toward antiracist love. A bestselling young-adult version and an adaptation for children of Kendi's history of American racism and belonging are both bringing a new generation of students back to the table of the Puritan-origins idea. And Cotton Mather, it appears, continues to sit at its head.[13]

"Spaniard Dr. Mather's Negro"

An anecdote will illustrate the need to think complexly about how theories and practices of racism can cluster around anti-Blackness without being reducible to it. In 1714, Samuel Sewall—one of the most important men in Boston, remembered today for convicting some of the accused Salem witches (and later repenting)—received a messenger. The name the man went by, reiterated enough times in Sewall's diary to suggest they were on familiar terms, was "Spaniard." A longtime bondservant to the elderly Increase Mather, this man Spaniard delivered a printed broadside containing an updated version of the governing rules of Boston's Society of Negroes. In a social world where African-descended persons were rarely allowed to be called by the names meaningful to them or to their ancestors, a single name and a possessive often went together in a formulation such as Sewall noted on the broadside with the date: "Delivered to me by Spaniard Dr. Mather's Negro."[14]

Relations between the Sewall and Mather households, between which Spaniard walked that day, were both intimate and fraught. Samuel Sewall, himself a former printer, had been the younger Mather's tutor at Harvard and, as we shall see, his collaborator on the Spanish project. He used the Boston press to make an early case for abolition in 1700 with his tract *The Selling of Joseph,* receiving more criticism than approval for taking that stand and for advocating successfully that two Black people in different homes, one bonded and one enslaved, should be allowed to marry. Mather's *The Negro Christianized,* which shared Sewall's condemnation of sinfully cruel masters but came to the opposite policy recommendation, has often been read as a response to *The Selling of Joseph,* with the result that Sewall seems the "good" Puritan and Mather the "bad." However, *The Selling of Joseph* is likewise a product of its time: Sewall's diaries show him wrangling the theoretical commitment to equality he expresses there against the affective, irrational fear of dark-skinned others that one finds nearly across the board in European writing from the period. Sewall had inherited considerable property, including a grand estate no minister could afford, through his father-in-law, whose wealth derived in part from West Indian plantations and the control of Spanish silver. Cotton Mather, of more modest means, directed some of his salary to hire a master to teach Black Christians to read—the first such school in New England—and founded what he called the Society of Negroes in 1693 as a safe place for Black men in his church to gather. It was a reprint of that society's rules that Spaniard delivered to the Sewall mansion some years later. Dividing Sewall against Mather in a binary of anti- and proslavery thinkers is an oversimplification, as is understanding questions of race and slavery during the colonial period according to a black-white definition of racism such as Kendi's.[15]

The man named Spaniard also illustrates the limits of such a binary. The name given to him suggests that he was *both* "Negro" and in some way "Spanish," in the way the label "Afro-Latin" tries to capture today. Was he a Senegambian or Kongolese man, kidnapped and brought to the Spanish West Indies, then transshipped to English colonies? Or was he of the second, third, or even fourth generation to live in the western hemisphere, his lineage already intermingled with that of other African peoples, Europeans, or Amerindians? If the latter, did he get his name because he knew Spanish before he learned English, perhaps speaking with an accent? Was "Spaniard" a demonym, ethnonym, loquonym, or some combination? While the historical record does not say, Spaniard did outlive the possessive case discursively attached to him here as "Dr. Mather's Negro." When Increase Mather wrote his will, Cotton either did not want to or did not try to inherit Spaniard from him: no Mather legated a human being as property to their heirs (a low bar of virtue, to be sure, but not one that the president of Harvard College at the time was able to pass). When he walked out of the Hanover Street house—and perhaps into a new name lost to history—Spaniard joined the company of the free Black folk of Boston who would, by the time of the revolution, outnumber the city's enslaved population, comprising the activist core of African Americans who would launch the long, unfinished struggle for liberation and equality. This community, and others elsewhere, founded its own institutions of mutual aid such as the African Masonic Lodge, the African Meeting House, and the Abiel Smith School, sites on the Black Heritage Trail. Sewall's and Mather's overtures of benevolence toward that population admixed philanthropic sympathy with paternalistic control, evident in the strict rules of godly conduct for the Society of Negroes. But the through-line from the seventeenth and early eighteenth centuries to the later eighteenth-century emergence of free Black Boston is mostly obscure, and it is tempting to think about how Spaniard might have made use of the master's tools to begin dismantling the master's house. Presumably he had been a member of that society, whose goals included literacy so that members could read the Bible—and everything beyond.[16]

Further complicating the question of how to imagine Spaniard's mind and body is the presence of persons that both Sewall and Mather referred to, in their copious personal writings, as "Spanish Indians." In the 1680s, 1690s, and 1710s, respectively, two men and a woman described in this way were brought into the Mather household as servants. Their precise legal status—whether bonded to labor for a number of years, a status that English people also routinely accepted, or enslaved for their lifetimes—is likewise unknown, but each of those labor options had precedent in the New England settlements. As Margaret Newell has shown, Indigenous people lent their labor to settler households in many different capacities, but outright enslavement began to be more common in the later seventeenth century. English law allowed the incarceration, enslavement, and in some cases deportation of peoples they considered belligerents; the regional resistance that became known as King Philip's War resulted in hundreds of captives being sent into slavery locally or, to intensify the punishment, to the Caribbean. The modifier *Spanish* Indian, then, marks these individuals as not belonging to one of the tribal groups known to settlers in the region: the Wampanoag, Abenaki, Mohegan, Pequot, and other Native peoples.[17]

If Spaniard was considered phenotypically "Negro," how did these "Spanish Indians" appear to Englishmen? Demonymic use (meaning "from the Spanish Indies") is possible, but "Spanish Indies" was not a common English term for the West Indies. If it referred to phenotype and assumptions about ethnicity, could it have attempted to describe mixed Afro-Indian *castas* from the Spanish-controlled sectors of the hemisphere that extended beyond the Caribbean islands proper to New Spain, including the Yucatan and Central America? Or was it a reference to a more proximate part of New Spain, the "shatter zone" of the post-Mississippian world along the southeastern Atlantic seaboard, where some Indigenous peoples had made alliances with the Spanish for over a century already? As later chapters explore, refugees from the fading Timucua-Guale-Appalachee mission system in Florida and Georgia were sold north into slavery during Mather's time as a result of interimperial and intra-Indigenous struggles along the Carolina-Florida border. There is evidence that some, perhaps many, spoke Spanish as a second language. If the "Spanish" in "Spanish Indians" described a lingua franca rather than an ethnicity, these members of his household could have been uncredited collaborators on Mather's Spanish language-learning project.

These people are—to use a phrase with a weighty meaning in the context of Latina/o/x migration today—undocumented. Unlike the case of Spaniard, no English use-names for these three people were even recorded. Their presence in the archive is mediated by others and unrecoverable except through what Saidiya Hartman calls critical fabulation: using the archive against itself in order to restore agency to those people. The lessons that enabled Mather to write in Spanish—the linguistic encounters, both oral and written, that he glancingly mentions—are mostly undocumented as well. But these lessons link the micronarrative this book tells about his household and about *La Fe del Christiano* with an important macronarrative: the geopolitical and religious struggles between and among European-American settler cultures, Indigenous, Black, and mixed-race peoples throughout the hemisphere that set in place structures of belonging and nonbelonging. As the Coda argues, those contexts are crucial for understanding *latinidad* in the United States today, nearly three hundred years after Mather's death.[18]

How Great a Little Fire: The Scale of "America"

Mather wrote near the end of his life that he had yet to see any direct effects of *La Fe del Christiano,* but hoped optimistically that in later years others might see "how Great a little Fire may kindle." If he had imagined the work as a cupped flame, for a long time it was more like an ember forgotten in the corner of a cold hearth. The American Studies discipline that evolved in the twentieth century, with its strong focus on the New England Puritans as the nation's cultural progenitors, lavished books and articles on Mather's production but largely ignored the material not in English, with one significant exception. In 1955, Yale professor Stanley T. Williams (interestingly, also a Melvillean) published his two-volume *The Spanish Origins of American Literature*, which opens with a long section on *La Fe del Christiano*. Williams hoped to spur further research into Spanish—principally meaning, to him, Peninsular Castilian—"contributions" to US American culture. But this idea, too, was slow to spark. With the exception of a translation of the tract published in a scholarly newsletter in the 1960s, no Americanists followed Williams's lead until the late 1980s, when the combined energies of multiculturalism, postnationalism, and the disavowal of the Puritan origins thesis resulted in new methodological approaches variously described as comparative, hemispheric, transamerican, or borderlands.[19]

In their landmark collection *Reinventing the Americas: Comparative Studies of Literature of the United States and Spanish America* (1986), Bell Gale Chevigny and Gari Laguardia revived Williams's study to mark *La Fe del Christiano* as a point on which the old and new intellectual currents in American Studies could converge by tracing "the history of literary contacts in the Americas": "Such a study might begin with the Puritans' anxious interest in the reported opulence of Mexico City . . . and Cotton Mather's decision in 1699 to study Spanish in order to prepare such a text to aid the evangelization of Latin America and the creation of a Puritan continent." The generation of Latina/o/x scholars who followed this directive, including myself, savored the irony of this tidbit: that it was a Boston Puritan—*of all people!*—who had authored the nation's first Spanish imprint. As new migration patterns created a spike in the resident population of Latinos during the final decades of the twentieth century, the number of Spanish speakers rose to previously unimaginable levels: staggeringly, the United States now contains more Spanish speakers than there are in Spain itself. The time seemed ripe for a more multilingual and transnational approach to American Studies, with some commentators calling for Spanish proficiency and/or field study outside the United States as requirements for PhDs in the field. Carlos Alonso, later president of the Modern Language Association, influentially wrote that "Spanish should no longer be regarded as a foreign language in this country."[20]

That utopian vision has not come to pass. US-based scholars barely noted the only substantial scholarly commentary on Mather's hemispheric eye since Williams: *Dos Américas, Dos Pensamientos: Carlos de Sigüenza y Góngora y Cotton*

Mather (1998), an archivally rich book by Mexican historian Alicia Mayer González. Spanish may be the "second national language" of the United States, as Alonso put it, but monolingual citation practices underscore how marginalized it remains as a language of scholarship. With all respect to Mayer's work, however, it rests—like that of Chevigny and Laguardia—on a limited comparative method. Mayer treats these two thinkers as heirs and promoters of the distinctive intellectual legacies of Loyola and Calvin, each bearing one pole of a Reformation / Counter-Reformation division born in Europe that "se transplantó con la colonización a un nuevo escenario histórico, al continente americano, donde tuvo y quizá tiene todavía, una vigencia extraordinaria" (was transplanted, with colonization, to the new historical stage of the American continent, where it had and perhaps still has tremendous staying power). This sense of a fundamental North-South split—religious, intellectual, cultural—between the Anglo and Latin Americas, I argue in the Coda, is an invention of the nineteenth and twentieth centuries that does not serve us well today.[21]

In place of comparison as method, this book follows the lead of recent scholarship that has argued for a vision of *entangled* histories. The rise of Atlantic history as an alternative to nation-based models emphasized how people, commodities, and ideas moved across and between oceanic and settled coastal spaces. Whereas the comparative method gives two objects equal weight, pluralistic models attend to the imbalance of the scales. As Eliga Gould points out, English America in the seventeenth century (and well into the eighteenth) sat on the periphery of a maritime world that "was deeply asymmetric, with the balance of power for much of the colonial era in Spain's favor." Jorge Cañizares-Esguerra, likewise, has urged historians "to place the Spanish Atlantic at the center of U.S. colonial history." Caribbeanists, in particular, have led the way in developing multiracial—and of necessity multilingual—archives and models for these entangled histories of the Americas, which have outgrown the efforts of national academies to contain them. While Paul Gilroy's spatial model of the "Black Atlantic" has centered the transformative consequences of the African slave trade, attention to continental spaces has emphasized that during this same period, North America was still dominated by sovereign Indian nations. Nor are the spatial constructs of ocean and continent mutually exclusive, as formulations such as Jace Weaver's "Red Atlantic" suggest. The effect of all these models has been to scale back the exaggerated significance of the early settler towns to what Katherine Grandjean, neatly suturing metaphors of land and sea, describes as an "English archipelago" separated by Native-controlled space. The Omohundro Institute, a venerable research center founded in the distinctly English-centered space of the College of William and Mary campus, now promotes "Vast Early America" as its motto, encouraging research involving the other languages, including Indigenous ones, of the colonial hemisphere. Within the Mather households, Spaniard the "Negro" and the three "Spanish Indians" hint at deep connections between Black and Indigenous lives.[22]

The "Vast Early America" concept also allows for movement into the interior, beyond the oceanic contexts of Atlantic studies. During the three decades emphasized in this book, roughly 1695–1725, the Spanish Crown redoubled its efforts to secure territorial claims farther inward on the North American continent. It reinforced the crumbling Franciscan missions in La Florida, a territory encompassing present-day Georgia and South Carolina. Mather followed events closely in the southerly colonies, including those in the West Indies, alert for evangelizing possibilities. While the Florida-Carolina border may have seemed far from Boston, frequent intracontinental traffic between the other coastal cities with English settlements—Philadelphia, New York, Charles Town—brought fresh news about the approach of Spanish military forces and their Indigenous allies during Queen Anne's War (1702–1713). Mather may also have heard about Popé's Rebellion, in which the Pueblo peoples in New Mexico ejected Spanish colonizers and missionaries from their dominions in 1680. He made notes about places at the edges of the province of New Spain such as Florida and California: it was in one of his publications that the word "California" appears in print in the English colonies for the first time. Mather did not have the opportunity to venture far from greater Boston during his lifetime; he never crossed the Atlantic himself. But he was the quintessential armchair traveler, and likely the best-informed person in New England about Spanish, French, Portuguese, and Dutch accounts of the Americas—as limited and limiting as those written accounts were. Taking the method of entangled history and the vantage point of a vast early América not only illuminates Mather's world, it also undermines the linked binary oppositions of Anglo/Latin, English/Spanish, Protestant/Catholic, and North/South. From the perspective of Amerindians and Africans, the Englishman and the Spaniard—each professing a Christian God who had endowed white men with his patriarchal authority—were much more alike than different.[23]

As an interdisciplinary study, this book cannot pretend to be a comprehensive history of the vast or entangled early Americas during those three decades, nor a theologically deep study on the religious beliefs of Mather and his contemporaries. Rather, it plucks out certain threads from those rich bodies of scholarship to try to bring into view a pattern that can help us better understand discourse and multiple meaning: the domain of language and literature. Although written materials from Mexico, Peru, and elsewhere are incorporated into this book, I make no pretense at an evenly balanced *comparison* between the enormous textual production in the Spanish Americas and the relatively scanty corpus produced by English settlers by the dawn of the eighteenth century. My intent instead is to show how this wider Americas context informed Mather's writing and enabled his view of the world from his homes near the wharf in Boston. When he wrote, "I that am an *American* must needs be Lothe to allow all *America* still unto the Devils Possession, when our Lord shall possess all the rest of the *World*," I argue that he envisioned a hemispheric meaning to that word, using it in its old sense as Europe's conceptual fourth continent. Underscoring that Cotton Mather's "America" was not coextensive in shape or size with the continental area that would later become identified with the United States (most of which was claimed at the time as New Spain, though not controlled by it) has implications for the national literary tradition that has acknowledged him as the first English settler to call himself an American in print.[24]

The Matter of the Text

Cotton Mather's Spanish Lessons is a literary history insofar as it explores *La Fe del Christiano* with reference to sources, intertexts, and sibling works of its time, but it also leans on two other disciplinary methodologies to which literary criticism is indebted. The first is the bibliographic and the material analysis of printing and printed objects; the second, the theory and practice of language learning and translation, which cross applied linguistics and sociolinguistics. The first practice, book history, links socioeconomic contexts to the history of ideas: ideas about human language difference, about the value of symbolic substitution through metonymy and metaphor, and about the way body, mind, and spirit are understood. One belief that united Spanish and English colonizers was the unchallenged assumption of alphabetic literacy as the highest order of human civilization. Learning to read, and sometimes also to write—alphabetization and literacy training—served multiple purposes. In seventeenth- and eighteenth-century New England, literacy was essential for the practice of individual Bible reading that was elevated by the preferred state religion, and thus its records are a particularly rich site for studies of everyday self-making through language. In short, the methods of book and print culture analysis deemphasize the author and turn literary production into a collective enterprise. I use the term "literary" in a catholic sense: intentional language use, addressed to an audience of one or many, with a purpose that is more than instrumental (if, for these settlers, rarely limited to pleasure for its own sake, since their cosmological and religious beliefs prescribed other uses for the word). In moving back and forth between Mather and the household servants, family members, and interlocutors who enabled him to perform his titanic feat of authorship, I am trying to keep these individual and collective axes of literary production in this readerly Reformed Protestant colony productively dialectical.

Mather's body of published work cannot be understood without foregrounding the category of scale. As a writer, a propagandist through and for print, Mather relished the challenge of scaling the same truths to different magnitudes. If the *Biblia Americana*, with its virtually unpublishable one million words, represents one extreme of length, his "Maxims of Piety" stand at the other extreme: these three statements, repeated in and attached to many different tracts over the years, distill the Protestant faith into its barest essentials. We might imagine his corpus as an accordion bellows. Whether extended to its full breadth (as in the *Biblia*) or compressed into the maxims, it remained the same tool: God's revealed truth, expressed through Mather's humble human breaths. (One of his catechisms was actually called "Much in a Little.") Of the 350 or so imprints that bear his name, very few seem as book-like as *Magnalia Christi Americana*, published in England because of the limitations of the local press—which perhaps explains why literary scholars apparently read it more often than the rest of his surprisingly diverse work. The vast majority are chapbooks: printed sermons, elaborated histories like the *Decennium Luctuosum* (1688), and advice manuals on doctrine and family life. *La Fe del Christiano* is one of these shorter chapbooks. Mather himself used the term "Small Book" to refer to his local, which is to say Boston, imprints. In his manuscript autobiography *Paterna*, Mather writes that "While I gave away *Small Books* unto others, God gave *Great Books* unto me," referring to his famous library. However, he continues, "While I was giving away *Good Books* Written by *other men*, I had all along a Secret Perswasion, That a Time would Come, when

I should have as many *Books* written by *myself* Like-wise to give away. And I have Lived Since to see this Perswasion most Remarkably Accomplished."[25]

Whatever their genre, and regardless of whether one labels their form as tracts, chapbooks, or simply texts, Small Books like *La Fe del Christiano* were imagined as everyday objects for common use. Under fifty pages, portable, and user-friendly, they were designed to be sold inexpensively or to be given away: Mather brought sheaves of them on pastoral visits and sent them by the rudimentary mail system. Many contained the sermons he preached at Second Church and on civic occasions, often rewritten and recycled to advise and admonish specific audiences: parents, children, women, sailors, prisoners on the gallows (he was particularly drawn to convicted pirates), drunkards, or followers of the (to him, misguided) Anglican, Quaker, Catholic, or Jewish faiths. Despite constituting a majority of Mather's publications, the Small Books have generally been neglected in favor of the larger ones by literary scholars. Relatively little of his print production falls into the two best-known genres of Puritan writing, the jeremiad (a sermon aimed at terrifying people into recognizing the error of their ways and changing paths) and devotional poetry, such as that of Anne Bradstreet or Edward Taylor (Mather's few poems tend toward doggerel). Little of his work that is not what we think of as "book-length" is available in any printed edition. To read the vast majority of these smaller-scale works, one has to click laboriously through digital windows that reproduce microforms made in the 1960s. The transcription and translation provided at the end of this book aim to make Mather's Spanish tracts newly accessible in a way he could not have dreamed of.

The illustrations gathered here allow us to take a closer look at the document in question. Compared to the charmingly off-kilter, fancifully decorated title page of the *Bay Psalm Book,* well known to scholars and rare-book collectors as the first North American imprint in English, *La Fe del Christiano* is not an impressive-looking product of the colonial printer's art. If you folded four sheets of office paper in half and stitched them together in the middle—say, to create a little sheaf of poems—it would look similar: a bit smaller, more squared-off in proportion, but only slightly more professional-looking. As Figure 1 shows, the title page of *La Fe del Christiano* bears an imprint of Boston, 1699, below the author's name, disguised by the pseudo-Spanish "C. Mathero." The page was typeset sloppily: the "Ch" is canted upward, the rules are crooked, and the "O" droops noticeably off the end of "Mathero," as if to expose the tacked-on ending of the pseudonym. Lacking special characters to express non-English sounds or accentuation, the tilde in the word "ESPAÑOLES" is hand-inked in this copy, missing in others. *La Fe del Christiano* is actually the title of only one of the two tracts, written separately, that are published here together. *La Religion Pura*, the other, begins on the verso (or left-hand side) of page eight, violating the custom—one that Boston printers followed even during paper shortages—of beginning a new chapter or section on the recto, or right-hand side. These flaws all suggest an unusually hurried job, a journeyman's work, a project struggling to justify the time and expense it cost: this object was made to give away, not to sell. Perhaps a few hundred copies were printed, and at least three have survived, while many of Mather's other "Little Books," as he called them, have vanished altogether.

Book history prompts other questions about this enterprise. Is it significant that *La Fe* is one of only a handful, among Mather's nearly four hundred small and large "books," that does not reveal the name of its printer, as required by English law? What features of its manufacture, such as paper and the way it was cut and folded into signatures, are distinctive compared to similar works? What is the relationship of this Spanish work to other early North American imprints in languages other than English—most famously the tracts, textbooks, and partial and complete Bibles in the Natick Wampanoag language issued by the Cambridge Press, but also in French, Dutch, and Spanish North America? How many readers among the audience of "ESPANOLES"—whether understood as Spanish speakers, people in Spain, people of partially Spanish descent anywhere—did Mather's work ever reach? Have more copies survived somewhere beyond the three housed in US libraries? Did any others escape the fire of censorship or the damp mold of apathy? These are all questions raised by book history, covering different points along what Robert Darnton called the "communications circuit" that follows a printed object's life from creators to producers, distributors, consumers, and conservators. In the case of *La Fe del Christiano*, we need to add a precondition for Mather to write in a language not one's own: the invisible language instructors he consulted as books, as bodies, or in a combination of both.[26]

Linguistics and the Embodiment of Human Difference

Along with the question of how, exactly, Mather imagined his readership among LOS ESPANOLES—with its overlapping senses as demonym, ethnonym, loquonym—lie other questions about the conditions of possibility that enabled this text to come into material being. Chief among these is language acquisition itself. From what source, exactly, did Mather learn enough Spanish to write it? Was his method strictly self-study or did he have tutors of some kind, as my introduction of the possible loquonymic meaning of "Spanish Indians" meant to suggest? Did Mather ever speak Spanish aloud during or after the project, and if so with whom? What textual aids (grammars, dictionaries, other Spanish books) did he possess? How did he get them and what happened to them afterward? In particular, how did he come by a copy of the rare Spanish Protestant translation of the Bible from which, I argue below, he abridged and copied his citations?

Book historians are particularly interested in what may be thought of as metaliterary materials: textbooks, from children's hornbooks and primers to catechisms, grammars, and anthologies of selected readings; and manuals for handwriting, composing letters, and for conducting oneself in general. These pedagogical works help reveal how individuals were taught the rules, made into proper subjects of their society. Textbooks for learning a second language, however, have been relatively neglected among such studies. If pedagogies are inherently social, then the question of what grammars, exercises, and reference works Mather used in his learning can reconstruct what assumptions he inherited from his English sources about the Spanish language, its origin, and its speakers. Language ideologies include beliefs about which uses are appropriate in public or private, or which languages best reflect transcendent values like beauty, rationality, purity, traditionalism, or logical consistency. Language *attitudes,* on the other hand, are individually held but shaped with or against these wider-circulating and shifting beliefs. This book tracks both through Mather's Spanish learning and writing.[27]

Mather once wrote (speaking about himself coyly, as a third-person other) that he had published works in "Seven Languages." A handful of the "Small Books" included Latin alongside English text; others inserted Hebrew and Greek characters. Mather's principal motive for learning modern spoken languages was to keep up with the Spanish, French, and Portuguese missionary priests of various Catholic orders who had preceded the English Protestants to America by a century and more. In addition to *La Fe del Christiano,* he arranged to publish three tracts in French: two apparently addressed to Catholics, the other to Protestant Huguenots. Two other publications appeared under Mather's imprimatur in Indigenous American languages: one in the written Natick dialect that was comprehensible to some speakers of other Algonquian languages; the other in Iroquoian, with a Dutch translation on the side. Both were translated from his English original by other collaborators. Rather than take Mather and his son at their word about the seven languages he "mastered," I attempt to measure his fluency using the tools of applied linguistics. Thinking about linguistic proficiency as a multiscalar phenomenon rather than a simple question of mastery is important for understanding the inexact conjunction of loquonym and ethnonym among Latinos in the United States today, as the Coda explores. How has *being Spanish-speaking* come to be a kind of onto-logical definition of *latinidad,* despite the many degrees of proficiency, regional varieties of Spanish, and expressive possibilities of bilingualism observable in this population?

The Mathers were closely connected to a linguistic-religious project that had begun a generation earlier: the Algonquian publication project launched by John Eliot and his Indigenous collaborators from the "Praying Indian" town of Natick. The first printing press in New England, the Cambridge Press, was financed for this purpose. Indigenous tongues and Native informants were vi-tally important in the development of print cultures and of linguistic research in North America. The desire to convert these people also produced early lin-guistic researchers, including some like Roger Williams who raved about the structural beauties and capacities of Indigenous languages. But both the indi-vidual contributions of Native speakers and their status as equally human were often erased in this knowledge production, for ideas about the visible, embodied differences that would come to be called "race" were linked through biblical rationales to linguistic difference. The Algonquian and Iroquoian language families, to which most dialects of Indigenous people in the region belonged, featured a very different phonology and syntax than the Latinate, Germanic, and Semitic languages known to the settlers. Their sounds were sometimes de-scribed as "babble" or "slabber" by settlers who encountered them as enemies in war. These histories of Euro-Indigenous language exchange are thus impor-tant for contextualizing the place of Spanish and the way it, too, would even-tually take on racialized aspects.[28]

Some of these English missionaries, such as the family of Experience Mayhew and Mather's own cousin Josiah Cotton, crossed over to live perma-nently within the Algonquian language-world in a context not so unlike today's dual-immersion programs among the Diné / Navajo or in heavily Spanish-speaking Latino communities. What, though, did it do to a person to learn to speak a language not their natal tongue, to conform their body to an alien sound? As I show below, learning to read and to compose in another language was not to Mather a drily intellectual process but a combination of bodily effort, reasoned research, and divine spiritual aid. It involved what he described as the "turning" of his mind to an alien pitch: a *becoming-other* that was not unlike the kind of conversion evangelizers sought to inspire in those who spoke their target language. Mouths and tongues were not only metaphors for language practices, they were organs that could be taken over by forces external to the individual will. Producing unintelligible sounds was a sign of demonic possession, and as Kamensky suggests, women were disproportionately accused of witchcraft because powerful men believed their tongues (like other parts of their bodies) were more physically vulnerable to being occupied by demonic forces. Language was not only produced by the mind but performed by the body.[29]

Shifting the biographical gaze away from the Mather men to the household as the unit of microanalysis recognizes that the structure of inheritance requires the bodies of women, the institution of marriage, and certain customs of hierarchized labor to secure it. Heteropatriarchy, a system of distributing social power according to the alignment of biological sex with gender roles, was so profoundly at the heart of the Christian social system that it was invisible to nearly all these English settlers *as* a system—one among many possible ways of organizing a society. Like another "Wonder of the Invisible World," heteropatriarchy presented itself as the God-given truth that men were ordained by the divine Father to lead, instruct, and hold dominion over the women, children, and servants in their household. The stories of Mather's three wives and his several daughters remind us that this system hinged upon the observation at birth of differences in the genitalia of infants. Visible bodily difference was also what would eventually consign millions to hereditary chattel slavery. In the early colonial period there were varieties of law and practice governing servitude, enslavement, and possibilities for freedom that cut across ethnic groups. Scopic biases based on skin color and physiognomy were certainly activated during Mather's time, and bodies did shape a person's life chances—but the link between race and slavery was not nearly as absolute as would become the case by the late eighteenth century.

But Christian doctrine also taught that redemption came to the *souls* of the faithful, regardless of such bodily differences. Key to Calvinist theology was the notion of election: that some persons had been predestined for eternal salvation and others for damnation. Good works and outward piety were signs of likely status among the Elect, and New England Congregationalist churches limited full membership to those who professed their individual encounter with God and who behaved like "visible saints." A believer never knew for certain. That potential self-doubt and self-scrutiny engendered uncertainty: it called for humility and never-ending (even self-deconstructing) critique, which is one element that continues to draw many literary scholars to the writing. However, so long as the possibility existed that non-English people were *also* among the Elect, embodiment—or what would become in the following centuries a false notion of race as a set of essential biological differences—was theoretically unimportant. Thus Mather wrote about the potential for reaching readers in Spanish America: "Who can tell, but the Great God may bring some of His Elect in your way! Oh! How Blesssed are you, if you may be the instruments of bringing any such home unto the Lord!" Rather than a sign of elitism, the idea of spiritual election contained a potential alternative to the biopolitics of racial and gender difference as the dominant form of governance. I am not arguing that the Puritan male leadership of the colony *enacted* tolerance and open-mindedness to the lifeways and beliefs of others—but that the kinds of visible bodily differences that would come to be called "racial" were, to them, theologically and intellectually on a par with audible linguistic differences.

A Brief Summary of Mather's Book, and This One

Cotton Mather's Spanish Lessons will not proceed through a reading, page by page, of the two Spanish tracts bound together as *La Fe del Christiano*. They are not narratives or poems. They are doctrinal tracts intended for persuasion, and in that sense invite surface reading. They are, however, witness to Mather's selection processes—what he thought important to address to LOS ESPANOLES—and to the accomplishment and limitations of his language proficiency. They engage with intertexts including, but hardly limited to, the Bible, which itself not a singular text but a repeatedly, significantly, translated one. A summary of what's in the text will thus be helpful up front.

Each tract is crafted in a numerologically significant way: there are twelve articles in *La Religion Pura*, twenty-four in *La Fe del Christiano*. Mather refers to twelve, the number of the Apostles of Christ, as a "Sacred Number." The genre is that of a list of articles of faith, a credo. Yet neither set reproduces the Westminster Confession or follows other commonly accepted Reform Protestant catechisms. The articles are instead carefully chosen to sway his target audience of Roman Catholics. *La Fe del Christiano* begins with a trumpet for Protestant bibliocentrism, asserting the divine inspiration of Scripture before launching into the more traditional beginning-places for a catechism (the concept of the Trinity, the history of creation, the doctrine of original sin, the divinity of Jesus). It prioritizes Reformist points of disagreement with the Roman church, describing arcana such as the nature of angelic beings even before it gets to important topics like what one must do to be saved or how to organize a church. The twenty-four articles in *La Fe* are condensed from the Bible verses referenced in the margin glosses, including the Ten Commandments and the Lord's Prayer.

La Religion Pura, the first of the two tracts to be written, reveals even more than its companion about the level of proficiency Mather reached in writing Spanish, for it contains complex sentences that he did not copy or compress from his Spanish Bible. Mather's key messages to Catholics here are that Christ, not the Pope, is the rightful head of the church (Articles III, IV); that prayers should not be directed at saints or other intercessors (V); that neither works nor indulgences but grace alone can bring about the forgiveness of sins (VI); that the only true sacraments are baptism and the Lord's Supper, but the bread and wine are not the transubstantiated body of Christ (VII, VIII, IX); and that priestly celibacy and the proscription of meat eating on certain days are not dictated by God but are mere Catholic customs (XI). Spanish readers could use these simple articles either to learn the basic tenets of the Christian faith or to *unlearn* the way they had been taught them.[30]

In imitation of Mather's numerological conceit, this book contains twelve chapters indexed by Roman numerals; this introduction constitutes the first of the twelve. Rather than Articles of Faith such as Mather's, Chapters II to X explore the multiple contexts and conditions of possibility within which *La Fe del Christiano* came to be. They are followed by the Coda, which reflects on the conditions of US *latinidad* today. Chapter II begins by describing the winter of the writing of *La Fe del Christiano* within the context of Mather's multigenerational family. Although the burden of inheritance from fathers to sons is an old theme in Puritan studies, this chapter emphasizes the hemispheric context by reaching back to Increase Mather with a particular eye on his involvement in the "Western Design" to establish a Protestant empire across the Americas. Some of Cotton Mather's earliest public sermons invoked that mission, which was revived during his mid-thirties, an important transitional period in his life. He had a divine vision of the importance of learning Spanish, and wrote *La Fe del Christiano* after backing away from a more local participation in New England's governance. Mather embarked on this project at the same time as he began writing the *Biblia,* and while that volume was intended for publication, another long-term writing project born at the turn of the eighteenth century was private. *Paterna,* his little-read manuscript autobiography, was meant for a readership of just one: Increase, the first of his male children to survive infancy, named after Mather's own famous father and known in the family as Creasy. While awaiting Creasy's birth, Mather acted on his pledge to learn Spanish, a task that seemed mysteriously connected to accidents befalling his daughters at the same time. This theme of leaving a patrimony will return in Chapters IX and X, where I look at the adolescence and young adulthood of that same son. These chapters may be thought of us as bookends for readers primarily interested in the family biography and its connections to the macrohistorical transformation of Boston.

Chapters III and IV form another pair that shows how Indigenous evangelization in the English and Spanish colonies shaped Mather's decision to learn Spanish. Chapter III opens with Mather's research into the earlier Catholic missions in Peru and New Spain, particularly his reading of the sixteenth-century Jesuit José de Acosta. Sewall, who learned news of Mexico from mariners passing through Boston, went further to envision the Second Coming of Christ occurring in what he called "America Mexicana." Christian eschatologists after 1492 had often speculated that Amerindians were a lost tribe of Israel whose conversion would hasten the end times; Acosta's millennialism turned in a different direction than the later Wampanoag ministries of John Eliot and the Mayhews. But the puzzle of mapping the history of the ancient Hebrews onto the Americas persisted, as Mather and Sewall enlisted two Ladino-speaking Sephardic Jews to aid their understanding both of Biblical Hebrew and of Spanish.

The story turns in Chapter IV from eschatology to missionary linguistics: the fostering of Indigenous evangelization through written works. Acosta's convictions about the right to hear the Gospel in one's own tongue helped launch bilingual print cultures not only in Lima, but in Mexico City and, eventually, in Boston, leaving their mark on *La Fe del Christiano.* The Cambridge Press's

"Indian Library," which had halted production by the time Mather came of age, nonetheless influenced his thinking about how Spanish and French, the imperial languages, might be used to de-Catholicize *castas* and creoles elsewhere in the Americas. Apparently unbeknown to either Eliot or Mather, another major Indigenous print project had already been underway on the southern edge of the English colonial empire in North America: a library of books in the Timucua language undertaken by Francisco Pareja and his collaborators. These addresses to missionized Amerindians in La Florida, although printed in Mexico City, offer an alternative origin point for North American print culture to the Cambridge Press.

Chapter V returns to the Mather household to tell a speculative "history from below" about one of the servants he described as Spanish Indian. Piecing together fragmentary evidence from Mather's diary, it suggests that this man's uncertain legal status as either free-born or enslavable may indicate an origin in Spanish Florida and an ability to speak Spanish. The loquonymic function of "Spanish" next to "Indian" occurs in other seventeenth-and eighteenth-century texts. This man's story updates the earlier thread about the Spanish Franciscan missions in the Timucua-Guale-Appalachee region with the beginnings of the cross-continental trade in Native bodies, as the frontier between the English Carolinas and Spanish Florida became increasingly violent. This chapter sets up an argument about the manifold meanings of race in this period that will come to fruition in the Coda.

The cluster of Chapters V, VI, VII, and VIII focus on the relationship between language learning and material book culture. Chapter VI is devoted to pedagogical genres: catechisms, grammars, dialogues, and confessionals. Similarities in genre link the teaching of language to the teaching of religion, as well as natural philosophy or science. As textbooks meant to be used dialogically, between a master and a student, the works of missionary linguistics produced in New Spain and New England represent more than visual texts, they address bodies speaking and acting on the instructions they offer. The chapter reaches back to Mather's childhood and youth, and to the bodily practices he used to acquire a second language—Latin in its Classical and Neo-Latin varieties—for the first time. It was for him a spoken tongue in addition to a written one, acquired with the help of catechisms and grammars. Chapter VII adopts a perspective from applied linguistics to analyze vocabulary and usage clues in *La Fe del Christiano* in order to judge the degree of written proficiency in Spanish that Mather reached. Tracing the history of Renaissance and early modern handbooks that were available for English speakers wanting to learn Spanish, I speculate on textbooks he could have used and on their underlying language ideologies—broad-based assumptions about the relative value of the spoken and written registers, regional and dialectal variations, of a particular language system. Concluding the explorations of earlier chapters on Indigenous-language learning in the Americas, it assesses the shifting values that Mather placed on various biblical, classical, and modern spoken languages.

Chapter VIII takes a deep dive into *La Fe del Christiano* as a material text. Following traces of different translations and editions of Spanish-language Bibles, it shows how Mather, with Sewall's help, sourced the biblical citations that he abridged for the tracts. It plays on the dual meaning of composition as an authorial and typesetting practice to suggest that Mather's extraordinary output was enabled by his ability to pragmatically reuse materials. It then considers how the unnamed Boston printer might have crafted an approximation of the *enye* [ñ] in 1699, when no equivalent was available in the English-language case and no type foundry existed in the colonies. With this reimagining of the scene of the text's production comes the inevitable question: how and where were the copies distributed, and who preserved them?

Turning back again from books to persons, Chapters IX and X take us into the first quarter of the eighteenth century, tracing shifts in the balance of power between Spain, France, England, and Native nations during Queen Anne's War as they illustrate questions of racial and linguistic ideologies. A decade after writing *La Fe del Christiano,* Mather adapted it into a French version, *La Vrai Patron des Saines Paroles,* thinking about New England's northern border with the French rather than its southern one with the Spanish. At the same time, Boston's economy and society became even more oriented toward the West Indies trade, relying increasingly on African rather than Indian labor and raising the specter of French piracy coming from that space. As Sewall puzzled through the status of "Spanish Negroes" in the courts, Mather wrote *The Negro Christianized.* He was rewarded by his congregation with the title of master to the African-born man called Onesimus. He tried to catechize Onesimus, who then transformed the top-down hierarchy of servant and master into a dialogue by revising Mather's terms for his freedom. Chapter IX weighs the contradictions within Mather's protoracial arguments and actions over time.

Chapter X returns to the smaller constellation of English bodies within Mather's household: his wives and children. Tracking the expansion and contraction of that family through various epidemics, it links Mather's inherited ideas about patrimony to his decision about the occupation of his elder son, Creasy, born the same year as this "Little Book" and the first audience for *Paterna,* returning to these group-biographical threads. Creasy became not a minister but a trader in Caribbean commodities. Mather's daughters were well educated, but their life opportunities were likewise constrained by Boston's newly dominant mercantile class. Mather's fraught relationship with Creasy colored the years before his own death in 1728. Carrying the story beyond his grave, the chapter ends with Mather's granddaughter, Hannah Mather Crocker, taking on the masculine pseudonym of Increase in her pro-Revolutionary and abolitionist writings. As the collector who chose to preserve the family's library and papers with the American Antiquarian Society, she helped shape the nationalist narrative of US history and literature.

The Coda, a more personal chapter, looks backward upon Mather's Spanish lessons to ask how Latinos fit into the contemporary racial reckonings called for by Black and Indigenous American activists and intellectuals. Bridging the disciplines of early American and Latinx Studies, it argues that the confusion of ethnicity and race inherent in various terms for *latinidad* arose during the national period. Thus, frameworks based either on individual nation-states or on contrasts between "two Americas," North and South, will miss the most important elements of the hemispheric substrate of colonialism and race. Returning to the distinction introduced here between demonym, ethnonym, and loquonym, this concluding meditation considers the range of Spanish proficiencies among US Latina/o/x residents, including recent communities of Mesoamerican Indigenous people, and shows that linguistic performance remains a feature by which Latinos in particular are racialized. Despite obstacles to our full citizenship and belonging, I argue that Latinos have a profound claim on American memory as well as futurity.

The final chapter presents a full transcription and a facing-page, annotated English translation of *La Fe del Christiano.* As a headnote on translation theory explains, this version does not attempt theological accuracy. Rather, it illustrates how Mather's intermediate proficiency in Spanish, along with his limited available sources, moved him to make specific compositional choices in the sections he wrote himself, as well as the sections he abridged from the Bible. By back-translating his seventeenth-century Spanish into twenty-first-century English, resisting the urge to turn his occasional awkward usages into more fluent phrases, this translation seeks to give a sense of how *La Fe del*

Christiano might have read to native Spanish speakers in Mather's time. With detailed notes that demonstrate where Mather amended his sources, this section provides supporting evidence for several of the chapters and may be consulted at any point.

Like Mather's own "Articles," these chapters draw from many sources and disciplines but do not pretend to exhaust any of them. They may be thought of as a *continua* on the main text of *La Fe del Christiano*, turning toward and away from it from many angles. As Meredith Neuman explains, the *continua* (a Latin noun, but *continuar* is also a verb in Spanish) was the steady thread of a single biblical passage that a minister would embroider, in different interpretive veins, over the course of several Thursday lectures or Sunday sermons; congregants discussed them in the interim. In her study of ordinary parishioner's sermon notes, Neuman suggests that those listeners deauthorized the preacher himself, building community through their own commentaries. Hers is a horizontal vision of where interpretive power and communal attachment reside. With the final turn to shared contemporary conditions, I invite the reader to participate in a *continua que continua.*[31]

· II ·

The Global Designs of a Creole Family

During the year in which *La Fe del Christiano* was completed, Cotton Mather began a private autobiographical notebook. While the Spanish tracts were meant to be strewn like seeds throughout the Americas, *Paterna* was intended for an audience of just one: it is addressed and dedicated "To my SON" (Figure 2). Dividing his life's chronology into phases of Before and After, the very structure of *Paterna* suggests the momentousness of the event that inspired it. After her sixth pregnancy, his wife, Abigail Philips Mather, delivered a healthy male child in the summer of 1699. The couple's three young girls were alive and well, but this notebook was for masculine eyes only: it was conceived on the premise that having a son launched Mather into a different order of parenthood. Mather and his co-religionists organized their mortal lives around patriarchy as both social system and religious metaphor. Brought up to revere his distinguished forefathers as the very type of the godly man, he took as a sign of personal blessing the birth of this son, whom he named Increase Mather in honor of his own father. To distinguish the two, the boy was called Creasy (also spelled Cresy, Cressy) throughout his life. Creasy's birth was not the root cause of Cotton Mather's decision to learn to write in Spanish and to evangelize the Spanish Americas later in the same year, yet the events coincide in meaningful ways that dissolve boundaries between public and private, and the confessional notebook that Mather began on this occasion contains thoughts about the Spanish language that are found nowhere else. This chapter argues that Mather's conviction about missionizing in the Spanish Americas presented itself as another form of patriarchal succession: it would continue the Western Design to turn all the peoples of the Americas toward the Reformed way. If fathering a son fulfilled the corporeal, tribal aspect of this devotional duty, accomplishing this unfinished work of his forebears fulfilled the political one.

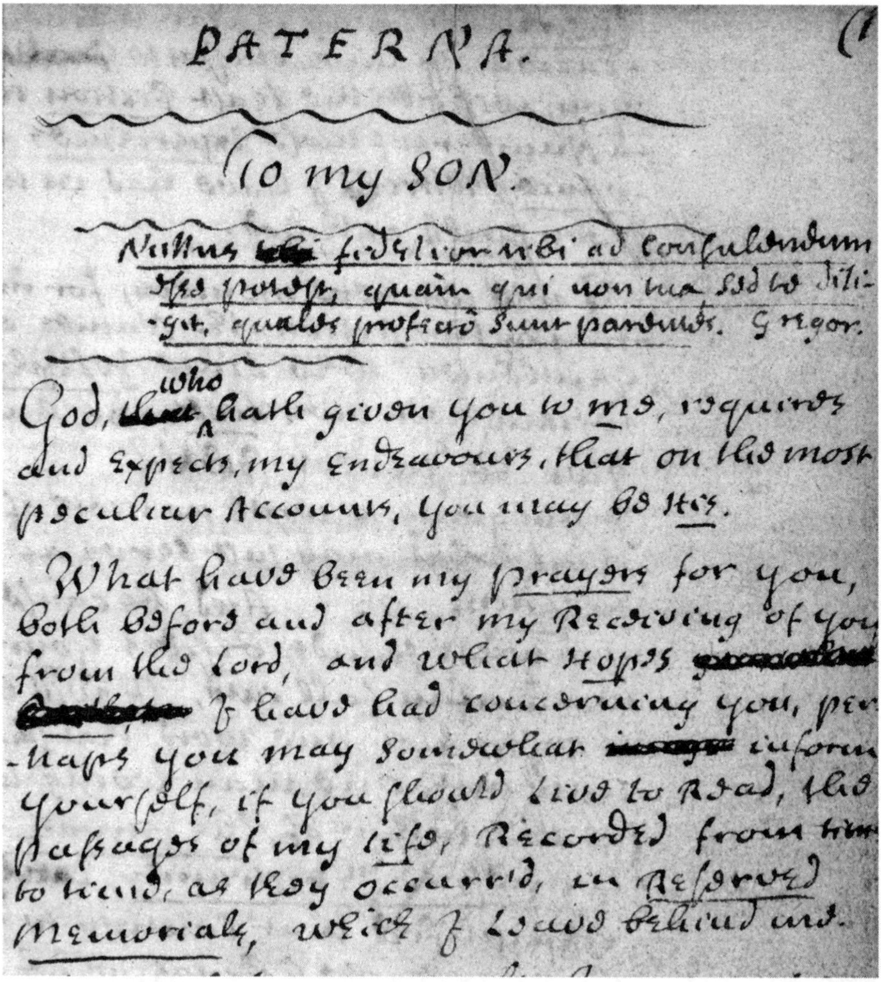

Figure 2: Opening page of *Paterna: To my SON,* showing Mather's handwriting and his dedication of this autobiographical work to Creasy. The dedication beneath the Latin epigraph reads: "GOD, who hath given you to *me,* requires and expects, my endeavours, that on the most peculiar Accounts, you may be *His.* What have been my *prayers* for you, both before and after my Receiving of you from the Lord, and what *Hopes* [deletion] I have had concerning you, perhaps you may somewhat [deleted] inform yourself, if you should live to Read, the passages of my *life,* recorded from time to time, as they occurred, in *Reserved Memorials,* which I leave behind writ." Cotton Mather, *Paterna,* Accession #3860, Special Collections, University of Virginia Library, University of Virginia, Charlottesville, Virginia.

The indissoluble link between the patriarchal family structure and the governance of the Massachusetts Bay Colony was a bedrock of New England Puritanism. Mather's grandfathers, John Cotton and Richard Mather, had been prominent Nonconforming ministers who arrived in the Great Migration, the first major wave of English settlers, and who joined forces to banish dissenters from Boston. When John Cotton died, his widow, Sarah, married Richard Mather, making Increase Mather and Maria Cotton stepsiblings; they later wed. Increase Mather wielded even more influence over local affairs than his father: he presided not only over the pulpit of the powerful Second Church (North Church), but over Harvard, the colony's only college. While scholars have argued vigorously over interpretations of the Puritan legacy, they converge on this: Cotton Mather both lived through and emblematized the transition from the founding vision of a pious, peaceable community (however violated that vision was) to the ascendant order of a capital-driven, socially stratified eighteenth-century city. Mather came to adulthood just as the theocratic model of governance propped up by Reverend Cotton and Reverend Mather was waning; he retreated to the pulpit and the pen rather than attempting to dominate town meetings in person. Given his unique privileges of inheritance, many interpreters have found the father-son theme irresistible and have psychologized the relationship among the Mather men in various ways—usually without pausing to question the naturalness of patriarchy as a form of social organization. My attention to Mather's biological family, as the core of a home-world that included a more diverse slice of the colony's population, emphasizes instead how the microstory of this household represents the American hemisphere on a macro scale, one more vast than the reduction of "American" origins to the Massachusetts colony has allowed.[1]

Well before 1699, when Creasy's birth, *Paterna,* and *La Fe del Christiano* coincided, Mather had absorbed family stories about the West Indies and the Spanish Main, and speculated on a question of natural philosophy that likewise occupied contemporary Christian thinkers such as Carlos Sigüenza de Góngora: what it meant for living beings—and for Man, God's seed, in particular—to grow in American places. Mather's horizon was directed not toward the sun's rise in the direction of England but toward Europe's American settlements, including those of the Spanish, French, and Dutch, to the north and south of him. He grasped the reality of ethnogenesis—the making of new peoples, behaviors, and social forms—as part of the hemisphere's historical unfolding, in a way that his English forefathers had not. This is not to claim absurdly that he thought from the perspective of non-Christian Indigenous, Black, or mixed-race *castas,* but that he thought about them as essential parts of the ambient world into which his own descendants would be born as Creoles. In adopting this Latin American historical term to apply to settler families like the Mathers, I follow a more recent strain of comparatist Atlantic history that has challenged the old Puritan Studies consensus based in New England exceptionalism. But I also follow Mather himself. He appears to be the first of the settler tribe in America to use an English-language version of the Afro-Portuguese term to describe such ethnogenesis, a term that would eventually settle as *creole/criollo.* How would that notion of creolization inform both the Spanish project and his conduct as a father (the Latin adjective *paterna* means "in a fatherly way") within the constrained Christian circle of the family, including daughters as well as this seemingly anointed son?

The Western Design as Family Inheritance

For Mather's immediate forebears, Catholic Spain was the "anti" to Protestant England, but also its "ante," its predecessor in the project of colonizing the American hemisphere. The first half-century of contact—persistently labeled an age of "conquest" but more accurately viewed as a time of acute ecological, social, biological, and cosmological chaos—had settled into something like a new order by the middle of the sixteenth century. Asserting hegemony over much of the Caribbean and a good deal of the Amerindian mainland, especially in the areas previously organized under the Aztec and Incan empires, Spain had built structures and spaces for extracting labor and natural resources from the "Indies." The massive influx of American-mined silver and gold created a new form of global capitalism built on extraction and slave labor, a "modern world-system organized along the axis of coloniality/modernity," in the influential formulation of Emanuel Wallerstein and Aníbal Quijano. Other European powers carved out their niches within this system, looking to the Spanish for vital information and for lessons to emulate or improve upon. England was a slow starter in this colonization contest, largely because of the turbulent uncertainty of its commitment to Protestantism as the sole state religion following the death of Henry VIII. The sixteenth-century relationship between England and Spain, so ambivalently adversarial, gave birth to two powerful ideas important to this story, each boosted by the new technology of the printed book.[2]

One is the rationale for the reciprocal learning of English and Castilian through user-friendly modern language manuals, as Chapter VII in this book will later explore. The first such manual celebrated the occasion of Mary Tudor's 1554 marriage to Felipe II of Spain, an alliance that briefly re-Catholicized England and introduced a flood of positive rhetoric around all things Spanish, as Christopher Heaney has shown. But as the state religion shifted again under Queen Elizabeth I, this brief flowering of English Hispanism withered under the force of the Black Legend: a habitual depiction of Catholic Spain as corrupt, degenerate, and cruel. *La leyenda negra* had been stoked by the translation and dissemination of the *Brevísima relación de la destrucción de las Indias* of Bartolomé de las Casas (written 1542, published 1552) into Dutch, English, and other European languages. The Black Legend proved an enduring influence not only on English colonials but later in the United States, where it drove anti-Catholic, anti-Mexican, and anti-Latino sentiment well through the nineteenth century and arguably to the present day. Protestant commentators echoed the *Brevísima relación*'s condemnation of the conquistadors' cruelty to Amerindians, citing Las Casas selectively while ignoring his steadfast adherence to Catholic theological tradition. They also adopted his early suggestion that the importation of African laborers could remedy the evils of Indian slavery—a notion Las Casas later retracted.[3]

The world-shaping significance of that first century of encounter between the Americas and Europe was graven into Cotton Mather's consciousness from birth—for the Puritan movement itself was an outgrowth of the violent, erratic years of contest between Protestants and Catholics in sixteenth- and early seventeenth-century England. By retaining some familiar-feeling practices and forms, the Anglican Church softened the sense of an absolute divide between the old religion and the new. But the Puritans (the name, originally an insult, had been repurposed) sought to purge such lingering Catholic tendencies, forging ties with fellow Calvinists in other countries. Whether Separatists like most of the Plymouth settlers of 1620 or Non-Separatists and Dissenters like the Winthrop fleet that established Boston in 1630, the first waves of English Protestants in Massachusetts sought to reestablish an absolute clarity between those who belonged to God's light and those who lived in the darkness of depravity, and to enforce that clarity through their living arrangements, expelling those whose dissenting and questioning powers threatened their own consensus. Such a Manichean moral tendency could map neatly onto a geopolitical situation where Catholic Spain represented both dark enemy and rival.[4]

The overthrow of the Catholic-friendly Charles I and the installation of Oliver Cromwell, a fellow Puritan, as Lord Protector of the Commonwealth during the English Civil War not only cheered the New England settlers, it lent them real geopolitical importance, through a new instantiation of the Black Legend. Thomas Gage, an English Catholic who had been ordained as a Dominican priest in Spain and lived for years in Mexico and Guatemala, returned in disillusionment to England and converted to Anglicanism. His exposé of Spanish missionizing, *The English–American, His Travail by Sea and Land: Or, A New Survey of the West-Indies* (1648), was a sensational turncoat's story of greed and corruption. In the outrage-provoking mode of Las Casas, Gage argued that Spain had squandered its mandate to organize the New World after a European Christian model, hinting at the riches and glory that could fall to better masters. Cromwell took great interest, and with Gage's help crafted England's Western Design, a plan to drive the Spanish and French out of the New World by taking over their Caribbean trading posts and fledgling plantations, settling more Puritans into planned settlements from Central America northward, where they could eventually link in a solid English chain. Both Richard Mather and his young son Increase were loosely involved in the plans. But the most important New England player was John Cotton, whom Cromwell consulted about how to interpret the allegorical items in the Book of Revelation, such as the seven seals and books, that promised to reveal the present moment's relation to the end times. Cotton concluded that the culmination of human history would take the form of a battle between the Spanish and English, the forces of the Antichrist-Pope and of Christ, respectively, somewhere in the Americas.[5]

Despite English military superiority, Cromwell's squadron failed at its first attempt to take over Santo Domingo. Then its little settlement off the coast of Nicaragua, Providence Island, was ousted by the Spanish, and the Western Design folded. The only real gain from Cromwell's adventuring was the sparsely populated island of Jamaica. The cost may have been the political viability of the Puritan Protectorate: a Stuart king was restored to the throne in 1660, to the consternation of the New England ministerial elites. But the enormous financial investment that went into Cromwell's Western Design had long-term resonance, for it conjoined the Massachusetts elite's aims of religious purification for the colony with broader imperial-economic goals. Gage had planted the idea that Puritans could stage a redo of Spain's history of contact with the Americas a century and a half later. This time they would get it morally right, paving the way for the glorious millennial reign of Christ in the New Jerusalem. From his two powerful grandfathers Cotton Mather inherited not only a privileged social standing, a church, and a library, but also a way of understanding their God's plan for the only place he had ever called home.

Local Sovereignty and Criolian Degeneracy

The first- and second-generation settlers could place hopes on Cromwell's promise to bring greater purity to England's state religion, but Cotton Mather was born after the Restoration, in a phase of renewed murmurs about Catholic influences on the Anglican Stuart kings. His young adulthood was bound up with the slow-burning dissent that resulted in the New England Revolt. First, James II revoked the Charter of Massachusetts, which contained generous provisions for home rule, and installed the hugely unpopular governor Edmund Andros, who ended town meetings and promoted Anglicans to power in the newly named Dominion of New England. A group of clergymen sent Increase Mather, slipping out of Boston in the dark of night in 1688, on a secret mission to London, but the anti-Andros sentiment was widespread among less powerful settlers as well. Emboldened by news of the installation of the new Protestant monarchs, Mary II and William III of Orange, local leaders helped organize a militia to overthrow his government in April 1689. An anonymous "Declaration of Gentlemen and Merchants," which Cotton Mather likely had a hand in writing, made a case for self-rule that many historians have seen as a landmark expression of political philosophy, giving hints of declarations of independence to come. While Increase Mather stayed on in England negotiating a new charter, the son enjoyed what would turn out to be a rare moment out of his father's shadow.[6]

Shortly after Andros was deposed, the twenty-three-year-old was chosen for a considerable honor: to preach the first Election Sermon in three years. By suspending the legislative assembly, Andros had also ended this annual custom of addressing current political matters through a Biblical lens, often in the chastening form later described as a jeremiad. With this choice the colony's elder elites, bound by intricate family ties, affirmed their own internalized norm of patriarchal succession, for John Cotton had delivered the first Election Sermon in 1634. In the sermon, Mather both honors that tradition and departs from it. He takes up the very familiar Puritan theme of degeneration: the notion that the intentional community of believers has lost its way. By falling off in its piety (often blamed on younger generations or newer arrivals), the whole settlement has risked the loss of God's favor, as evidenced by some fresh experience with disease or violence. Mather's twist on this evergreen theme is twofold: first, he is visibly himself one of the youthful "rising generation" that is supposedly at fault; and second, he coins a word for a particularly American backsliding from the faith of the fathers. With it, he implicates the problem as the colony's lack of attention to its worldly competition: what the Spanish and French are doing in the rest of the hemisphere.

Pointing out that the colony's college, Harvard, can produce only a small number of learned Reformed ministers, Mather worries that "the seminaries of Canada or Mexico" are churning out many more Catholic priests. He laments

> the too general want of education in the rising generation, which if not prevented will gradually but speedily dispose us to that sort of Criolian degeneracy observed to deprave the children of the most noble and worthy Europeans when transplanted into America.

The educational race goes beyond producing ministers, for the American challenge requires lay evangelists as well. Without more education, "if our youth be permitted to run wild in our woods, we shall soon be forsaken by the God whom our fathers followed hither when it was a land not sown," and Christianity will not flourish there in its last days heading toward the promised millennium of Christ. The English settlers had imagined their walled towns as "plantations" of "a land not sown," embracing the rationale of *terra nullius* at the terrible expense of Indigenous lives and livelihoods. The metaphor of the breeding, growth, and decay of plant life informed a longstanding fear that one's descendants would become progressively less vigorous. Speaking as a Criolian himself, one of the "rising generation" still in his twenties, Mather does not reject the identity but provides, through his performance, counterevidence to the fear of degeneracy. This was not a new theme, but "Criolian" was a new contribution of this, Mather's breakout public address.[7]

Mather's "Criolian" is an early use by an English North American of a word engendered by the postcontact world system: *creole*. The idea of creolization as involving an organism that alters its nature after being displaced into a new environment and hybridized with natives of that system is distinctly of the New World. (The term's distinctive use in linguistics to describe the genesis of new languages through intensive contact also originates in this context.) Portugal was the first European power to cruise the African coast for captives to trade as slaves, and the word first surfaced among Black Portuguese speakers in the sixteenth-century *crioulo:* an enslaved person born in the master's household. By the early seventeenth century, the word had seeded itself in multiple tongues to designate a native-born person—but the sense of racial caste that accompanied it differed according to locale. The Spanish *criollo* came to signify American-born but culturally and (at least by claim) genealogically Europeans. This is clearly Mather's sense here, using an offshoot Anglicization that was rarely used until the more popular variant *creole* replaced it later in the eighteenth century. "Criolian" was an intellectual inheritance of the Western Design, borrowed first in Thomas Gage's *The English-American* from José de Acosta's Latin rendition of *criollo* as *cariollo:* as subsequent chapters will show, Acosta was a key source for Mather and for *La Fe del Christiano* in particular. Why does this nomenclature matter?[8]

Unlike Gage and others, who referred specifically to Spaniards, Mather extends the meaning of *Criolian* to mean all American-born Europeans. But he would later substitute a different word to indicate the subtype of European Christian naturalized to the New World: *American,* once a term for Indigenous people and then inverted to stand for their antagonists, as had occurred to *crioulo.* English writers had begun to experiment with hyphenated terms for this category (witness Gage's self-descriptive title, *The English-American*), but it would be Mather who proudly proliferated its use and wore as a personal badge: "I that am an *American.*" One of my key assumptions throughout this book is that Mather thought of America as comprising the entire hemisphere. It was the work of later commentators to shrink his sense of "American" into the narrow confines of English settler descendants only, as those commentators shaped a canon and a narrative for US literary and intellectual history for which he served as forefather. Mather's experimental use of "Criolian" as early as 1689 is a reminder of this amplitude. He was not making common cause with Iberian Catholic fellow Criolians, but rather recognizing the usefulness of the concept. He placed English settler descendants into the emergent historical category these *criollos* had already carved out: despite being latecomers to American colonization, he imagined that these Protestant Creoles would shine by comparison. The Coda (XI) briefly traces how Anglo-Americans later disavowed their similarity to Spanish *criollos* through a binary of two Americas North and South, painting them (in the palette of the Black Legend) as the degenerate heirs of a suspect imperial religion and as a racially impure people at best "off-white."[9]

By referring to Cotton Mather as a Creole, as one of a tribe of settlers, this book joins a chorus of scholarship that has challenged the exceptionalist view of US historiography to draw out the common pillars of colonial practice in the Americas: the African slave trade and the eradication of Native peoples. Resisting, as Stephanie Smallwood puts it, "the pull of a teleology that figures the colonial as merely a period in the temporal unfolding of American nationhood" offers the possibility of "a counternarrative that is an account of the entanglements of dispossession and slavery as colonialism's twin tools of domination." Emphasizing that the idea of European descent was central to Criolian / *criollo* identity also relativizes those people into one of many tribes who found themselves in the same space as other peoples, inevitably comingling but in a very uneven way that James Sidbury and Jorge Cañizares-Esguerra capture in the term *ethnogenesis*. Ethnogenesis in the Americas came about through migrations, economic contacts, and acts of violence "within the panhemispheric and pan-Atlantic processes that linked them to one another." Adopting this nonbinary perspective of a complex colonial system, this book explores how Mather's efforts to interpret God's design for the destiny of the Western hemisphere were informed not only by the prior presence of the Spanish but also by the ongoing fact of ethnogenesis across the Americas.[10]

A Creole Knight, Demonic Fright, and the Launching of an Author

The *OED* refuses to pass judgment on which Romance tongue loaned Criolian / creole to English. It's not impossible that young Mather heard some oral form of *crioulo / criollo / créole* spoken aloud by one of the seafarers who passed through Boston—perhaps even his most famous parishioner and patron, Sir

William Phips. Phips had seen more of the Americas than most anyone else in Mather's circle, and he was responsible for bringing into Mather's household the "Spanish Indian" whose story is told in Chapter V. Of humble New England origins, Phips had formed a successful expedition to recover a sunken Spanish treasure ship off the coast of Hispaniola, receiving in return fame, fortune, and a knighthood. He too turned against Andros during the events of the 1689 New England Revolt, and Cotton Mather—heading the Second Church congregation while his father was away in London—hastily baptized Phips into membership to give him status as a freeman (citizen) so that Phips could lead the colony's military expedition against French strongholds in Canada. Then Phips went to England, where Increase Mather and others were negotiating the new charter for an enlarged Province of Massachusetts Bay. They leveraged his recognition value to have him appointed governor. Phips returned to Boston in May 1692, in time to be tasked with convening magistrates to hear the charges against dozens of people brought into custody in Salem, the small port a half-day's journey to the north, as suspected witches.[11]

Returning from adventuring some years earlier, Phips had brought in his retinue some household servants from the West Indies. The racial fears that swirled around other non-English outsiders such as Tituba and John Indian soon materialized as rumors about whether Phips's own wife might be among those in the demonic snare. The Salem hysteria subsided when Phips finally shut down the court trials, but the controversy did not. Cotton Mather was not one of the Salem magistrates, and visited only once during the 1692–1693 proceedings and executions. Both the influential, just-returned father and the young Creole son lent their intellectual support to the prosecution. At the least, they failed to slow the executions while debating procedure, and the accusations that Robert Calef launched against them—Cotton in particular—would become the subterranean talk of Boston. The events of the Salem witch trials and their aftermath have been ably told and debated elsewhere. The Mathers' writings on demonic possession have inspired some of the deepest comparative research on the Americas today by showing how Indigenous, Catholic, and Protestant belief met on the contested terrain of invisible spirits: what Ralph Bauer terms ethnodemonology. Three aspects of the Salem episode are directly relevant, however, to the story of the Spanish project. One is familial, about the influence of spirits on Mather's wife's body; the second is vocational, about its impact on his writing career; and the third metaphysical, about his experiences with supernatural beings.[12]

The familial connection was his closest call with the purported epidemic of diabolical activity throughout New England. In May 1693, Mather was trying to heal or exorcise a young woman named Mercy Short, a former captive among the French-allied Wabanaki, who seemed possessed by demons. While Mather was working with her in his study, the very pregnant Abigail saw a "Fright," a malevolent specter, on the porch. When she gave birth some weeks later to their firstborn son, the infant was born with an imperforate anus and soon died: the result, Mather suspected, of his wife's close encounter with the demonic. This loss of his son, who had also been named Increase, was a setback to his hopes for the line of patriarchal succession, revived only by the arrival of Creasy in the midst of the Spanish project in 1699.[13]

The vocational shift resulted from the blow of Salem's aftermath to political power of the Mathers, as well as Phips—who was recalled to England to address challenges to his administration and then died. Cotton Mather afterward separated his "personal and spiritual life from the political life of Congregationalist New England," as biographer David Levin puts it, and devoted the final decade of the seventeenth century to writing and publishing at a frenetic pace. By *La Fe del Christiano* in 1699, his thirty-sixth year, he had published over seventy titles—sermons and hortatory works, an almanac, and reflections on the meaning of recent events in New England—but he had also begun working on his longest, most ambitious work to date, a historical work titled *Magnalia Christi Americana* [Annals of Christ in America]: *Or, the Ecclesiastical History of New-England, From Its First Planting in 1620, Unto the Year of our LORD, 1698*, which did not find a London publisher until 1702. Integrated into this work was the lionizing biography of Phips, *Pietas in Patriam* (Piety in the service of the country, 1697). The two volumes of *Magnalia* suture together previously published and new writing to narrate Boston's early governance under John Winthrop, its battles against enemies seen and unseen, and the spread of Reformed churches into other towns, culminating in the final section that makes Phips out to be a "second Winthrop," a "New-England Knight."[14]

Magnalia is a deeply biased work of history, but an influential work of ideology that elevated New England, above all colonies, as having "a Singular Prospect of Churches erected in an *American* Corner of the World, on purpose to express and pursue the Protestant *Reformation.*" With epic sweep, the first book of *Magnalia*, "Antiquities," positions this American hemisphere (one of four continental parts or "corners") within biblical, classical, and Western history so as to claim a triumphant place for it in the coming millennium, as Chapter III explores. On the first page of the introduction, he praises—harkening back to the Election Sermon—the generation of ministers that had been educated at Harvard, those "*Criolians*, in our *Biography*, provoking the *whole World*, with vertuous [*sic*] Objects of Emulation." "Provoking" has the sense here of inspiring others to follow, and his diaries in the late 1690s are peppered with hopeful visions of a "mighty Revolution" he hoped to be looming "upon France and Great Britain" (France persecuted its Huguenot Protestants, and even after the ascent of William and Mary in 1688, English Puritans suspected residual Catholicism among those in power). The word *revolution* already possessed its contemporary meaning of a sweeping political change from below (as in the Glorious Revolution that had brought those Protestant monarchs to power), but it also carried the sense of a widespread spiritual renewal, what the Great Awakenings of later centuries would call *revival.* Mather, as his father had trained him, associated these "mighty Convulsions, mighty changes at hand," with observable phenomena such as earthquakes and fires. In 1696, as we shall see, this seemed to include for the first time portents about the Spanish Americas, as well as France, England, and the other familiar places he habitually prayed for.[15]

You Must Be an Angel

The final connection between the post-Salem turn of Mather's career and the Spanish project is his relationship at this time to the world of spirit-beings. Mather had long been attentive to potential signs of such "revolutions" that might manifest not as earthquakes or comets but as visions and intuitive convictions from God. As David D. Hall's transformative scholarship on the Puritans has shown, their lived religious practice was not only intellectual but affective and embodied. Mather's athletic prayer sessions often involved prostration and fasting, and occasionally would result in what he called "Particular Faiths": tangible, ecstatic feelings of conviction that a future outcome was promised by God. Mather experienced relatively few of these Particular Faiths and tested them empirically as he went back recursively through his diaries. Sometime in his mid to late twenties, Mather had experienced a Particular Faith so important that it was delivered in a full-fledged optical vision. A beardless, "comely" male angel appeared to him, with wings, a tiara, and glowing white robes belted in an exotic "Oriental" design:

> this angel talked of the influence his reason would have, and of the books that this youth would publish. And he added certain special prophecies of the great work this youth would do for the Church of Christ in the coming revolutions.

These "special prophecies" promise a brilliant writerly career in the "coming revolutions," but curiously the passage refers to Mather in the third person, in case *Paterna* should get into the wrong hands. It appears here, in the notebook destined for Creasy, in Latin to cloak it better from prying eyes; it is not mentioned in the diary, which he reread and redacted on a regular basis. Why the secrecy?[16]

Both prophecy and the existence of angels existed in a disputed theological zone for Puritans. Reformation belief rejected the intercession of saints and argued that the age of miracles was over; at the same time, the Holy Spirit might still on occasion grant suprahuman insights or healing powers to the faithful. Disagreements about the disposition of such revelatory visions, prophecies, and gifts caused or deepened rifts among Protestant sects. The dominant Congregationalist ministers of Boston, notoriously suspicious of claims to gifts of the Spirit such as those made by Anne Hutchinson or by Quakers, nonetheless believed—as did most every inhabitant of the Americas in the seventeenth century—that nonhuman spirits were omnipresent, if unseen. The title of Mather's major treatise on witchcraft, *Wonders of the Invisible World*, conveys that belief: "wonders" was a descriptive term, and not necessarily a positive one. As Mather rehearses there, Satan worked through oppositions and inversions of sacred practices, so if demons could manifest themselves in visions to people (as many had claimed in Salem), so in theory could angels. But this was not to be dwelt on in public, lest it approach the rejected Catholic cosmovision. Increase Mather wrote two treatises on the theory of angelology; however, he urged congregants that they might easily mistake a message from the Lord's adversaries for one from his emissaries, and steered them away from entertaining such convictions. Thus, the visions that Cotton Mather labeled as Particular Faiths walked a fine theological line in claiming the power of foresight. He gave them a kind of empirical test by tracking them over time as he later reread his Reserved Memorials (diaries and other personal writings). In that transformative period following Salem, he followed up on the angel's private prophecy by embarking on a public work of extraordinary ambition: the massive Bible commentary he would title, in similar fashion to *Magnalia,* his *Biblia Americana.*[17]

The Way for Our Communication Opens

The angel's prophecy may have weighed on Mather in the years immediately following Salem, the shock of the first infant son's mortal disability, and the eclipse of the temporal power that had been seemingly promised by his central role in the New England Revolt and his connection to William Phips. During the latter half of the 1690s, he recounts a particular attention to the spiritual state of the known world, devoting hours in the prayer closet "to wrestle with the Lord, prostrate in the Dust before Him, on the behalf, of *whole* Nations." The first hint of a focus on the Spanish Americas comes in this 1696 diary entry:

> Moreover, I find in myself, a strong Inclination to learn the *Spanish* Language, and in that Language transmitt Catechisms, and Confessions, and other vehicles of the Protestant-Religion, into the *Spanish* Indies. Who can tell whether the *Time* for our Lord's taking Possession of these Countreyes, even the *sett Time* for it, bee not *come?* This Matter I now solemnly pray'd over; beseeching the Lord, that Hee would accept of my Service in it; and I have, of late often done so! It may bee, I shall find, that this thing is of the Lord!

Mather's diaries mostly record his acts of prayer, devotion, and pious good works. *Bonifacius: Or, Essays to Do Good* (1710), his most widely reprinted and perhaps most influential work, is a digest and how-to manual that popularized a particularly Protestant form of "do-gooding." But the private writings also show him scrutinizing and testing some of his instincts about what God's direction might be. Aware of the temptation to glorify himself, his tentative convictions are often always laced with a little doubt: "It may bee, I shall find, that this thing is of the Lord!" As the following chapters explore, Mather had some reason to imagine Mexico among the places being readied for the "coming revolutions"—and that his prophesied importance as a writer might have to do with converting it to the Protestant way. Within two years, he had decided affirmatively on the question about whether this "strong Inclination" was indeed "of the Lord," and followed through this intention with action. During the same period, Mather recorded a Particular Faith that Abigail's new pregnancy would result in a son who would survive and carry on his legacy: no previous birth had been singled out in that way.[18]

Magnalia was an elaborate production, wrought with Augustan style and requiring the collation of many sources. It is perhaps not surprising that when Mather decided to make a spiritual autobiography out of the scraps of his diaries and their outtakes, he invented his own baroque structure for it. Puritan life writing was usually simple in form, but Mather divided *Paterna* into five-year units that he labeled "LUSTRES, of a Father's Life." "Lustres" was a neoclassical borrowing from Latin, meaning the five-year cycle of Roman census taking; it was not a common device in any genre. After the seventh lustre ends at age thirty-five, he starts on a new page: "Second Part, No Longer Divided into LUSTRES," because that would mark the birth of the son to whom the book was dedicated, "foretold unto me, in an Extraordinary Way, some years before" (by a Particular Faith). "For, *My Son,* it was not until after *Seven Lustres* of my Life were expired, that God bestow'd upon me, a Son that Lived unto an Age to Read what I write." Like other spiritual life writing, the explicit purpose of *Paterna* is to instruct through example, but the notebook's temporal structure offers a different lesson. The pivotal event was not conversion, but the moment when its author firmly entered the order of patriarchal succession.[19]

Mather had already begun learning Spanish when Creasy was born, and the process stretched over the entire year. Early in 1699, he writes:

> About this time, understanding that the way for our Communication with the *Spanish Indies,* opens more and more, I sett myself to learn the *Spanish Language.* The Lord wonderfully prospered mee in this Undertaking; a few liesure [*sic*] Minutes in the Evening of every Day, in about a Fortnight, or three weeks Time, so accomplished mee, I

could write very good Spanish. Accordingly, I composed a little Body of the *Protestant Religion*, in certain Articles, back'd with irresistible Sentences of Scripture. This I turn'd into the Spanish Tongue; and am now printing it, with a Design to send it by all the wayes that I can, into the several parts of the *Spanish America;* as not knowing, *how great a little Fire may kindle,* or, whether the Time for our Lord Jesus Christ to have glorious Churches in *America,* bee not at hand. The Title of my Composure is, *La Religion Pura, En Doze palabras Fieles, dignas de ser recebidas de Todos.*

Oh! how happy I shall bee, if the God of Heaven will prosper, this my poor Endeavor to glorify my Lord Jesus Christ.

"Design" here sounds an echo with the Western Design and the ill-fated fleet that Cromwell had sent to the West Indies a half-century earlier. How, though, did English settlers at this time imagine "the several parts of the *Spanish America*"? One part was the "Spanish Indies"—the islands of Cuba, Hispaniola, Puerto Rico, and the Tortugas—sources of extractive wealth that England sought to rival by setting up its own plantation system in Barbados and Jamaica. Another key part was New Spain, whose continental reach came closest to English settlements. The strategically vital Florida peninsula was connected through a ring of fortified cities around the Gulf of Mexico, especially Campeche and Veracruz, to the inland riches of mountainous mines and the baroque capital of Mexico City.[20]

The dual meanings of "Communication" convey the stakes of Mather writing to Spanish America. The word was used during this period both in the sense of an exchange of information or ideas and in its obsolete geographical sense: the routes of traffic between bounded spaces. Spain tried to maintain tight control over information as well as trade; the English colonies sought more of both, along with Spanish gold and silver that might alleviate its currency shortage. During this brief interval in the 1690s when the Europeans remained at peace, a significant opening did occur: colonials were allowed to trade locally made products between English and Spanish territories, as long as they did not sell manufactured goods. Mather expressed this in the phrase "the way for our Communication with the *Spanish Indies* opens more and more." It was a brief opening: the outbreak of Queen Anne's War, really a frontier war in the Americas, would change those terms after 1702, as Chapters IX and X explore. At the time of Creasy's birth and *La Fe del Christiano,* it made sense for Mather to imagine using the new currents of trade to carry a new wave of evangelization.

How Great a Little Fire

Mather had written *La Religion Pura* in late December or January, perhaps without a specific idea yet about how to print and distribute it. But he was not yet done. Sometime before March 4, he wrote *La Fe del Christiano* as well:

> About this Time, I sett myself to draw up, a compleat System of the *Christian Religion.* I comprized it in twenty four Articles; a *sacred Number* of Articles. And because much objection has been made against *Creeds* of an humane Composure, that this might bee liable to no Objection, I contrived every one of the Articles, to bee expressed in the express words of the *sacred Scripture.* When this was done, I turn'd it into the *Spanish Tongue,* and printed it, (along with my, *La Religion Pura*) under the Title of, LA FE DEL CHRISTIANO.
>
> My Design is, to attempt the Service of my Lord Jesus Christ, by casting this Treatise, into the midst of the *Spanish Indies.* And I employ constant Prayers upon this my Design, that it may bee favored by my Lord Jesus Christ, not knowing how great a Little Fire may kindle.

Mather figures the second tract as "a little Fire," just as he had called the first one "a little Body of the *Protestant Religion.*" In the spacious home he had bought with Abigail's dowry for two thousand pounds in gold, while Mather awaited the son prophesied through a Particular Faith, distressing things happened to the other "little bodies."[21]

The January 1699 diary entry that describes Mather's self-instruction in Spanish begins by relating "an uncomfortable Thing [which] happened in my Family." The youngest daughter, two-year-old Hannah (Nanny/Nancy), fell into the fire while playing in Mather's study and was badly burnt on her face and right arm. Tormented by the idea that Nanny's accident was punishment for his own sins, Mather closeted himself and fasted, drawing the inevitable spiritual analogy and praying for the "Salvation of the Children from the Fire of the Wrath of God." As sometimes happened—but sometimes did not—he was relieved by a divine reassurance: "I have this Day obtained *Mercy* for *all* my Children." He continues, "The *Fire,* that hath wounded the Child, hath added a strong *Fire* and *Force* to the Zeal of my *Prayer* for her." The extended metaphor of fire continues throughout this entry, which concludes with the report that Mather has undertaken to learn Spanish and wrote the first tract, "not knowing, *how great a little Fire may kindle*" from it. To salve the flame that wounded, he would make an analogue to conquer Spanish souls, reversing Catholic visual iconology with verbal ingenuity.[22]

Several weeks later, Nanny's accidental burn uncannily repeated itself, as the eldest child, eight-year-old Katharin (Katy) set her head-scarf aflame with a candle, burning her neck and hand. "This Disaster befalling my *eldest Daughter,* soon after that my *youngest* had suffered the like Disaster, it threw mee, into extreme Distress." The repetition might be a sign to attend even more closely to their spiritual welfare. He wrote another small book, *A Family Well Ordered* (1699), which proved to be one of the more enduring child-rearing manuals of the period, before returning to the Spanish project. In March, he composed *La Fe del Christiano,* and later in that year the two sister tracts would be bound together in print, in reverse order of their composition. Nanny's and Katy's burns also provoked a referred pain in their father as he labored to turn his mind in Spanish. The January entry about the composition of *La Religion Pura* continues: "But these my Studies, in Conjunction with some other Inconveniencies [*sic*], raised the Vapors of my *Spleen* into my *Head.* A grievous, painful, wasting *Head-Ache* seized mee." Again in March, as he was writing the second tract, he reports the recurrence of an "old Malady in my Jaw, and Head. But God sanctified it unto mee, to produce in mee those Thoughts and Frames, that were worth all my Pain." He theorizes that "these Buffetings from *Satan*" may be "permitted by Heaven, to annoy mee, because I am about a special Peece [*sic*] of work, whereby the Kingdome of *Satan* may receive a more than ordinary Blow": that is, the great accomplishment of stealing Spanish speakers away from the diabolical Catholic fold.[23]

Mather's worry that angelic visitations and prophecies could be easily mistaken for diabolical ones did not quite leave him. Perhaps the headaches and his daughters' burns were signs that God disapproved of Mather's dabbling in Spanish after all. He had wondered in 1696 whether "this thing bee of the Lord" or not. Elsewhere in *Paterna* he tried to answer the question of how to tell a true vision or Particular Faith from a false one.

How do I know this Operation from a counterfeit? My Answer is, that no words of mine can answer the Question; I *know* it, as I know the *Fire* to be the *Fire;* I *feel* it, but no words of mine can express, how it *feels.*

In the context of the children's trauma, "Fire" here is not just a well-worn metaphor for the Holy Spirit or for the gift of tongues, but for a kind of haptic knowledge: the body knows when touch burns. The moments when Mather is most present in his own body—in the monkish deprivation of his prayer closet, or fully feeling the bodily aches whose meaning he is trying to parse—are the moments when he is most able to identify with the pain of others, especially the women who surrounded him. Within the parameters of Christianity's immanent patriarchy, his views on female piety were progressive, if not completely consistent; in *Ornaments for the Daughters of Zion* (1692), Mather had defended women's rationality and capacity for spiritual insight and prophecy. He paid unusual attention to the education of his daughters: Katy had special gifts with languages and healing, one of Abigail's avocations as well. The referred bodily pain—or, perhaps, a diabolical cross-contamination—that flowed between Mather and his daughters during the weeks of his Spanish study and composition helped illuminate that epistemological question, of how to tell a true vision from a false.[24]

In the commentary on Genesis that he wrote for *Biblia Americana,* Mather rejects the common interpretation that Eve was more guilty than Adam. She had taken the forbidden fruit out of an excess of pious zeal, wanting to know more of God: as Helen Gelinas puts it, "Eve's fall was due to mistaking the devil for God's messenger . . . arrayed as he was in a disguise of shining light." If Mather's vision of an angel, prophesying that he would write words to stir the whole globe into salvation, turned out to be wrong, he had only made the same well-intentioned mistake as Eve. Mather identified with Abigail's pains in pregnancy and birth, too. Constant childbearing took a toll on her body; after giving birth to another male infant who did not survive, she developed painful tumors and suffered for several months. Mather prayed for her fervently, and was relieved to be given a Particular Faith that she would survive. So when she died in 1702, still in her early thirties, it was the first such divine reassurance to fail his test. After this we hear no more of angelic visitations or Particular Faiths. Chapter X returns to Mather's biological family, and to his nearly inevitable remarriage—but first let us turn to the Spanish tract itself, where the question of the body's health appears on the very first page.[25]

Sending Healthy Words to the Spanish

In early modern fashion, the lengthy title of the tract is a kind of manifesto in itself: "La Fe del Christiano: En Veyntequatro Articulos de la Institucion de *CHRISTO*. Embiada A LOS ESPANOLES, Paraque abran sus ojos, y paraque se Conviertan de las Tinieblas a la luz, y de la potestad de Satanas a Dios: Paraque reciban por la Fe que es en JESU CHRISTO, Remission de peccados, y Suerte Entre los *Sanctificados*" (The Faith of the Christian: In Twenty-four articles of *CHRIST'S* own institution / teaching. Sent out TO THE SPANISH, so they might open their eyes, and turn from the darkness to the light, and turn from Satan's power to God's: so they may receive through the faith that is in JESUS CHRIST, remission of sins, and be sorted among the Elect). The phrase "de la Institucion de Christo" makes sense on its own—it assigns foundational authorship to Christ, not to "C. Mathero"—and also recalls one of the pillars of Puritan theology, Jean Calvin's 1536 *Institutes of the Christian Religion,* which had been translated into Spanish by a Spanish Protestant convert at Oxford whose work Mather might have known (as I speculate in Chapter VII).

My transliteration fails to capture the visual prominence of "A LOS ESPANOLES." Both this and the author's line are set in the largest font size on this page, placing speaker and audience on an equal visual plane. The biblical epigraph below this, 2 Timothy 1:13, further suggests friendly, intimate address: "Reten la Forma de las Sanas palabras, que de mi oyste, en la Fe, y Charidad, que es en Christo Jesus" (Hold fast the form of sound words, which you have heard from me, in the faith and love which is in Christ Jesus). Teachings on the *corpus mysticum,* the mystical body of Christ that can represent both the practice of the Eucharist and the church itself, frequently reference this verse. The epigraph suggests that words, like bodies, can enjoy health (*sana,* which I have translated as "sound") or suffer disease: *sanar* is also the verb "to cure." In a theological context, it also signified salvation. Mather figured the Roman Catholic Church as the temporarily misshapen, diseased institutional body of Christianity—the faith they imagined themselves as curing. Reforming language, through rhetoric and biblical translations, was part of that cure.

The analogy extended further. The individual soul, like the body of Christ's church, was always prone to injury through contact with harmful influences (recall Mather's conclusion that Abigail's fright had resulted in his first son's misshapen body), but a godly doctor could (ad)minister a cure. Along with the whole of the tract's long title, this epigraph about holding fast to sound, healthy words reiterates the persuasive intent that Mather also expressed in his private writings about his new Western Design: in order to truly occupy *America,* the English would need to reclaim the word "Christian" from Catholicism. The tract thus entreats "LOS ESPANOLES," a term that carried overlapping senses as loquonym and ethnonym, to "turn from Satan's dominions to God's." His proposal follows the Puritan equation of the Pope with the Antichrist, with a demonic inversion or reversal of holy things. One might assume that Mather is demonizing by implication the non-English *spaces* of vast America, which were mostly still occupied by sovereign Indigenous peoples, but he is doing just the opposite. In *Magnalia Christi Americana* and carrying through to the encyclopedic *Biblia Americana,* Mather marshaled all his energies as a theologian, natural scientist, and historian to push the American hemisphere as a whole to the forefront of the world's intellectual stage. To understand how, the next chapter turns this page, reading the quotation from 2 Timothy alongside the other epigraphs on the title page verso.

Telling the Future of *America Mexicana*

The title page verso of *La Fe del Christiano* (Figure 3) contains two further epigraphs. The first is an abridged verse from "Apocalyp." (an abbreviation of the Spanish "Apocalipsis," the Apocalypse of John or Revelation), calling for the righteous to leave the wicked city governed by the Antichrist. In brackets, Mather glosses that city as "Roma" (Rome). The second epigraph is a more obscure Latin quotation: "Atqui jus divinum Ecclesia tollere, aut immutare non potest" (But the Church cannot modify or take away what is a divine right), attributed to "*A Costa* de procur. Indorum Salute, *p. 530.*" "*A Costa*" refers to the sixteenth-century Spanish Jesuit missionary, naturalist, historian and ethnographer José de Acosta, while "de procur." abbreviates his *De promulgatione Evangelii apud Barbaros, sive De Procuranda Indorum salute* (On the Propagation of the Gospel among the Barbarians; or On Procuring the salvation of the Indians), a seminal text of missiology first published in 1587 (hereafter abbreviated *Procuranda*). The unusual separation of the first letter of Acosta's name is not a typo on Mather's part: it reflects the printer's usage in one particular edition of the work, and the quote accurately correlates with a page number in that edition. This trail of Mather's reading shows him going beyond the better-known sources of English knowledge about Spanish America: Mather was more deeply engaged with Acosta than with any other Spanish writer, as this and the following chapter suggest. It was less a relationship of influence than of selective imitation and distortion, like Protestant evangelization in general. By setting these two epigraphs in apposition, Mather turns the words of Acosta, one of the master architects of Jesuit evangelization, against Acosta's own church.

The Compañia de Jésus or Society of Jesus, with its particular zeal for evangelization and education, was still in its early days when it trained Acosta and

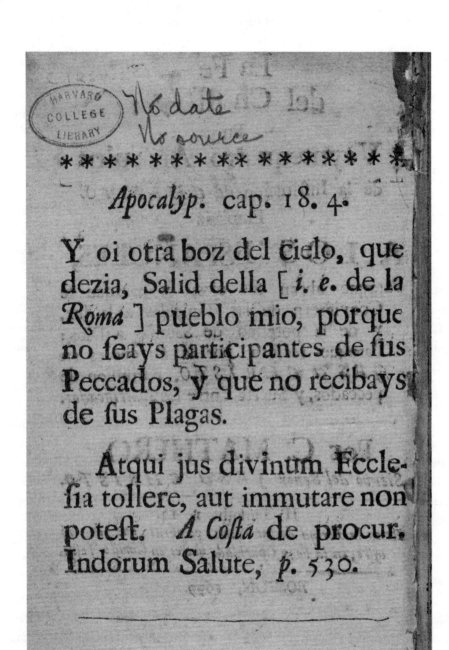

No date
No source

* * * * * * * * * * * * * * * *

Apocalyp. cap. 18. 4.

Y oi otra boz del cielo, que dezia, Salid della [*i. e.* de la *Roma*] pueblo mio, porque no feays participantes de fus Peccados, y que no recibays de fus Plagas.

Atqui jus divinum Eccle-fia tollere, aut immutare non poteft. *A Cófta* de procur. Indorum Salute, *p.* 530.

Figure 3: Cotton Mather, *La Fe del Christiano: En veyntequatro articulos de la institucion de Christo.* Title-page verso. *AC7.M4208.699f Lobby VI.3.33, Houghton Library, Harvard University.

dispatched him to Peru in 1570. He learned Quechua and established colleges and schools in the Andean region for training clerics and lay priests to become stronger footsoldiers in that mission. Building on his own experience, Acosta later composed *Procuranda* as a treatise on the proper method of evangelization. While it went to press separately, he continued writing *De Natura Novi Orbis libro duo* (On the Nature of the New World in Two Books), published in Salamanca in 1588 and then expanded for a 1590 version that would be widely translated and disseminated. Acosta's *Natural and Moral History* addressed geography, climate, botany, and biology (the "natural" aspects) as well as Amerindian ethnology, language, and history (the "moral" or human aspects). In the first two books of *De Natura Novi Orbis,* composed in Latin, Acosta examined the evidence to date for the theory of Amerindians as a lost tribe of Israel (such as purported similarities of Hebrew and Indigenous tongues), but found it unconvincing. In the five books added in 1590 (written in Spanish), Acosta defended the importance of understanding not only the hemisphere's potential natural resources to be exploited, but its Indigenous worldviews and histories.

The book contained a prodigious amount of information gathered both from personal observation and from legions of sources, including Indigenous and *mestizo* intellectuals. While in Mexico for two years, Acosta added to his research on Andean traditions the information gathered by a Nahuatl-speaking mestizo priest from Texcoco named Diego Durán and passed to his intellectual heir Juan de Tovar. Countering the triumphalist school of Spanish conquest historiography and building on the equally influential work of Bartolomé de las Casas, Acosta was both a curious observer and a defender, though a deeply paternalistic one, of the value of Indigenous lives. Along with the writings of Peter Martyr and Richard Hakluyt, Acosta's book quickly became one of Europe's principal sources of knowledge about the New World. English readers knew it through Edward Grimstone's 1604 translation from the Latin and Spanish as *The Natural and Moral History of the East and West Indies,* a translation that, importantly for this story, did not contain *Procuranda.* Chapter II described Mather's composition of *La Fe del Christiano* as an effect of a longstanding cause: the English desire to catch up to Spain's lead on the colonial project of transforming Indigenous America's demography through settlement and its cosmology through the spread of Christianity. This chapter takes up an intellectual problem introduced by that colonial project: how to understand America within sacred time and specifically within different visions of the world's end.[1]

Both Catholic and Protestant sects relied on the Bible as an outline of ancient history, and read its prophetic sections as a directional guide for acting in the present based on a promised future. For several years, Mather's companion in thinking about the Spanish language and Spanish America was his friend and onetime tutor at Harvard, Samuel Sewall. Their shared idea of evangelizing in Spanish augmented, and in some ways replaced, the "Design" of an earlier generation of Massachusetts settlers to help bring about Christ's return by converting Indigenous people: the work of the Society for the Propagation of the Gospel in New England. Contact with this nearby Indigenous world was an important pretext for Sewall's *Phaenomena quaedam Apocalyptica* (Some Phenomena of the Apocalypse, 1697), which argued for the special place of America in the millennial timeline of Christ's return, described so elliptically in Revelation. *Phaenomena,* too, draws on Acosta as it makes repeated references to Mexico: a fascination Sewall would not let go of. The geographical contours of that space were not precisely charted, but they touched on England's own territorial claims. The reference library that Sewall and Mather assembled to make their contemporaneous texts included a loaned copy of a "Spanish Bible" owned by two Sephardic Jewish residents of Boston. Puzzling through possible relationships between the ancient Hebrews of Scripture and the very present Jews and Indians around them, Sewall revived the "lost tribe" theory that identified Amerindians as Israelites, and that carried a particular interpretation of the millennial role of what he called "America Mexicana."

The Protestants' End Times and the
New England Company

No part of the Bible has inspired more fervid interpretation than the book with which it closes: John of Patmos's vision of the end of this world. Within the Roman Catholic Church a dominant interpretation emerged from Augustinian theology: the book did not describe or precisely outline future events; rather, it alluded allegorically to the struggles of the Church in the world. Yet across the centuries, splinter groups of Christians have persistently read it not just as allegory but as prophecy, developing an interpretive practice, eschatology, to decode its verses and plot them onto a timeline toward the apocalypse. Millennialism (also known as chiliasm) took its name from the part of Revelation that described the Second Coming of Christ and his thousand-year reign in the New Jerusalem. Crises and disasters within the interpreter's lifetime would spawn new keys to decoding the book's symbols (seven seals, trumpets, spiritual figures, and bowls) and disagreements about whether the peaceful millennium was already underway or not to occur until after his Second Coming. Many cosmologies incorporate a temporality of apocalypse: Mesoamerican calendrical systems, for instance, are predicated on an end to time. Christian millennialism, however, sets an urgent weight of the future upon one's present actions: it urges believers to do something right now to help bring about what has been prophesied.

Confronted after 1492 with a "fourth continent" not known to their authorities, Europeans had to fit the space of America—and its people—into biblical history. If all humans were descended from Noah, who had survived the great flood, this raised a question about where his genealogical line had splintered off to create Amerindians. The three known continents had traditionally been associated with the three sons of Noah. Were these previously unknown people Semites (from Noah's son Shem), whose line had branched off prior to the time the people of Israel formed? Or were they one of the fabled lost tribes of Israel, further down the Noahic line of descent yet still to be counted as Jews? This was an eschatological problem, too, for in some readings, the conversion of the Jews was a sign of Christ's imminent return. Columbus's own belief that America could be the site of the New Jerusalem was echoed in the writings of many missionaries involved in the initial sixteenth-century evangelization of New Spain and Peru, particularly the Franciscans. The Catholic Church did not encourage such applied eschatology. Reformation thinkers, however, took a vigorous interest in it. Identifying the pope as the Antichrist described in Revelation 14, and Rome as his seat, the New (or "Mystery") Babylon, made for a reading that it was Protestantism's messianic duty to defeat this false church with the restored and true one.[2]

On one aspect of the end times, many Catholic and Protestant thinkers agreed: the whole world must have the opportunity to hear the Gospel before Christ could return to defeat his enemies (the Beast, the Antichrist). The souls of 144,000 faithful "Saints" would be drawn from all ends of the earth. The New England Puritan settlers were well aware of how far behind they were in the labor of proselytizing. Even in the far northern reaches of New Spain, in present-day Florida and New Mexico, Franciscans, Dominicans, and others had begun missions in the sixteenth century, well before the English moved to settle Virginia and New England. They could not even claim to be the first Protestants to spread the Reformed gospel in North America: the French

Huguenots had already taken a turn at counterevangelizing the Catholics in Florida. Even as a second wave of settlers poured into Massachusetts in the 1630s (the "Great Migration"), the Jesuits were establishing a new string of missions in Quebec and across New France, setting the stage for a century of border conflicts to the north. This imperial and sectarian contest took on a specifically millennialist tone through the prolonged influence of an unexpected alliance between Puritans and Jews.

When Cromwell turned to his New England Puritan allies to construct the Western Design, Reformed theologians including John Cotton and Richard and Increase Mather were enthusiastically debating the eschatology of Joseph Mede, whose *Clavis Apocalyptica* (1627) was translated as *Key of the Revelation* in 1643. Mede's interpretation of prophetic scriptures argued that Catholic Rome was the New Babylon and sounded an alarm about the successes of Spanish evangelizing in the Americas. The first epigraph in *La Fe del Christiano* (Figure 3) is a restatement of Mede's interpretation of Revelation:

Apocalyp. cap. 18.4
Y oi otra boz del cielo, que dezia, Salid della [*i. e.* de la *Roma*] pueblo mio, porque no seays participantes de sus Peccados, y que no recibays de sus Plagas.

[And I heard another voice from heaven that was saying, Go out from her [i.e. *Rome*], my people, that you all may not be participants in her Sins, and that you do not receive her Plagues].

This gloss on "Rome"—taken directly from Mede—addressed *La Fe del Christiano* to Catholic readers: those who were, in his view, already under the thumb of the papal Antichrist. However, Mede's eschatology troubled New Englanders because of its conclusion that America was the "Gog and Magog" of the end times: the place from which the Antichrist's forces would assemble, led by those Spanish Catholics. As Reiner Smolinski writes, this interpretation of millennial events "consigned America to outer darkness. If Mede was right and the American hemisphere was not to share in the sacred geography of Christ's kingdom, then the Puritan Errand into the American wilderness was *nolens volens* an Errand in futility."[3]

Adding to Mede's urgency about converting Jews in order to hasten the coming of the Messiah, the learned Sephardic rabbi Menasseh ben Israel became convinced by the testimony of a traveler that Andeans observed Jewish

rites and spoke a degraded form of Hebrew. (This mis-identification of an indigenous tongue as Hebrew, which was often tried out as a potential lingua
franca during first encounters with people in the Americas, had a long lineage
dating back to Columbus and persisted despite contrary evidence, because it
so neatly addressed the problem of where "Indians" came from.) As part of
his campaign to have Jewish people readmitted to England, Menasseh en-
dorsed the Western Design. In the same year as Menasseh's text came another
polemic, Thomas Thorowgood's *Jews in America* (1650), with corroborating evidence from New England that came from the person most consequentially
committed to the theory of the Jewish origins of America: the Roxbury minister John Eliot.[4]

In the 1640s, the middle-aged Eliot shifted his personal sense of mission
from his settler congregation to the Wampanoag, learning the local Nipmuc
dialect of Eastern Algonquian from a trilingual child-captive known as Cockenoe. Over the next several decades, Eliot would become the figurehead of
the signature evangelizing project of Puritan New England: the establishment
of fourteen "praying towns" of Native proselytes that coexisted with the settler world, with their own churches and schools. The towns were supported
financially by the Society for the Propagation of the Gospel in New England
and the Parts Adjacent in America (called the New England Company to distinguish it from an Anglican Society for the Propagation of the Gospel that
was formed later). In the fundraising letters exchanged across the Atlantic,
Eliot and his collaborators reiterated the millennialist stakes of their mission:
evangelizing the world would hasten Christ's return. Although the Mather patriarchs would have sharp differences with Eliot over the years to come—
over, among other things, the lost tribes theory—they were among the bedrock supporters of the New England Company.[5]

Black Legend, White Legend, Algonquian Blood

The principals of the company had fully absorbed the Black Legend described
in Chapter II, rhetorically setting up their mission in virtuous contrast to
the Conquest (the so-called White Legend). They repeatedly cited Las Casas,
Acosta, and Thomas Gage (the Englishman-turned-Spanish priest-turned-
Puritan) as their authorities. In one of the letters exchanged across the Atlantic

between missionaries in New England and their backers, company officer Thomas Shepard wrote:

> The beginnings and foundations of the *Spaniard* in the Southerne parts of this vast continent, being laid in the blood of nineteene Millions of poor innocent Natives (as *Acosta* the Jesuite a bird of their own nest relates the story) shall certainly therefore bee utterly rooted up by some revenging hand; and when he [Spain] is once dispossest of his Golden Mansions and Silver Mines, it may be then the oppressed remnant in those coasts also may come in [to the Reformed church].[6]

Shepard's letter imagines an America not limited to its northern settlements but linked to the "Southerne parts." In addition to a prospect of vast American space, Shepard offers a providential sense of American time. Spain's missteps at the beginning could be corrected by the pious work of Englishmen in order to produce a future in which Amerindians would come together. The "oppressed remnant of those [Spanish] coasts," from the Taíno to the Maya to the Aymara, would also "come in" to the church that—in his vision—would already be full of Indigenous Protestant converts in Massachusetts. As viewed by biblical history, they shared a common ancestry as Americans; someday Native would witness to Native.

"Come in," "come over": Shepard's rhetoric of hospitality echoed the settler rationale that Native people had invited them to "Come over and save us," as the Massachusetts Bay Colony's seal said. Puritan evangelists spun the narrative that their response to this invitation would be a historical corrective to the slaughter and enslavement wrought by the *conquistadores,* distancing themselves from the all-out wars the English had already waged against the Pequot and the Powhatan Confederacy. The name of the company might echo that of the Company of Jesus (the "nest" that produced Acosta), but their turn at redoing the history of Euro-Indian contact would be different, because it brought the gift of individual Bible reading. Eliot's persuasive tracts raised the funds to "rearm" an old Daye printing press that had come over in 1638 with the goal of producing an "Indian Library" of Algonquian publications, to be crowned by a full translation of the Bible. The Cambridge Press, located in Harvard Yard, would produce some twenty Algonquian and bilingual titles including a translation of the Bible, *Mamusse Wunneetupanatamwe Up-Biblum God* (1663). In his English-language "Epistle Dedicatory" to that Bible's first edition, Eliot boasted that its existence was proof that the Puritans had by-passed the atrocities described by Las Casas. Chapter IV situates this Native print culture in hemispheric context; at this juncture, the fate of the first printing of the Algonquian Bible helps illustrate what had changed by the time of *La Fe del Christiano.*

The murder of one of the "praying Indians," John Sassamon, sparked King Philip's War, the organized campaign of Native resistance that stretched for more than three years beginning in 1675, decimated the region's population, touching nearly every English settlement but devastating the Indigenous world even more, and giving the lie to the New England Company's vision of peaceful coexistence. Cotton Mather was a teenager through the years of King Philip's War and, like Increase, penned a biased history of those events that cast the English as betrayed innocents, the sachem Metacom or King Philip as blood-thirsty, and the Native proselytes as unfortunates caught in the middle. Un-dermining centuries of historiography in that tradition, Lisa Brooks has re-told this shattering conflict from a Native point of view, re-creating the web of intertribal alliances among the Wampanoag, Narragansett, Nipmuc, and Po-casset who united in rebellion against English incursions upon Native lands. In Brooks's powerful retelling, the female sachem and war leader Wetamoo and the acculturated Christian Wowaus, known as James Printer, engaged in seemingly opposite ways with the English while sharing the same goal: the preservation of their people. She argues that Wowaus, educated at the Har-vard Indian School during its brief life and a skilled printer at the Cambridge Press before and after the war, lent an indigenous spiritual inflection to Chris-tian terms in the *Up-Biblum God.* The fact that angry English settlers de-stroyed most copies of the Massachusett Bible's first print run during the war made mockery of Eliot's contrast with the Spanish Conquest: the punishments wreaked on Native combatants—torture, rape, faraway enslavement, the public display of dismembered corpses—were as cruel as anything Las Casas had decried. When the New England Company reprinted the *Up-Biblum God* in a second edition in 1686, the "Epistle," and the reference to Las Casas, was absent.[7]

By the time of that second edition, the Protestant project of peaceful coex-istence through assimilation, represented by the praying towns, was in deep decline. Unable to reliably tell the difference between a Christian Indian and a potential enemy, many settlers called for an end to the accommodationist experiment. Sewall and Mather stepped in as commissioners of the New

England Company in 1698, amid their discussions about Spanish: their work at picking up the pieces of Eliot's local evangelical experiment was an important backdrop to their global design. When John Eliot died in 1690, Mather delivered his eulogy and published various versions of his life story, first in *The Triumphs of the Reformed Religion in America: The Life of the Renowned John Eliot* (1691). Here Mather pours Eliot into the mold of Moses, making him the apostle of the New World just as Old Testament events were thought to bear fruit typologically in the New Testament. Mather revives Shepard's strategy of invoking Las Casas to denounce a Spanish cruelty to the Indian that English behaviors could contrast. A chapter of this short book is devoted to Eliot's improvements upon the methods of Catholic missionaries, both to the south and to the north of New England: Acosta is not named here, but his work shadows Mather's rhetoric about Eliot, as well as Acosta's framing of his own writerly ambitions.[8]

Mather in Acosta's Aztlán

Although English versions of Las Casas's *Brief Relation* and Acosta's *Natural and Moral History* circulated widely, English readers in general had limited knowledge of the Luso-Iberian-Franco Americas, relying on Thomas Gage's account and on secondhand compilations of Spanish primary sources done by Peter Martyr and Samuel Purchas. Cotton Mather's curiosity took him further than the previous generation had gone: his unpublished commonplace books (*Quotidiana*) mention not only these sources but those that were available only in Latin, such as the works of historian Antonio de Herrera y Tordesillas and Jesuit theologian Francisco Suárez ("the learned Suarez"). The notebooks go well beyond the theological. They mention various kings of Spain and the "old kings of Peru," reflect on Arabic words in Spanish, and note travelers' observations about how "coffee and other fruits" grow in the tropics alongside "monkeys in the bay of Campechy." "The Spanish begets Big Sounding Names," Mather observes at one point. Some of this voracious information gathering simply reflects his curiosity; some was sifted into his writing intended for publication, especially as more sources were translated into English. *Magnalia Christi Americana* cites Garcilaso de la Vega El Inca, freshly translated in 1685; the *Biblia* also cites Agustín de Zárate, another early seventeenth-century source, new to English readers, who filled in blanks about Mexico. It is Acosta, however, to whom Mather turns repeatedly in the *Biblia Americana* as the main source for knowledge about the rest of America. There are thirteen references in the Genesis commentary alone; a final enumeration will have to wait until all the volumes of this commentary are published. Mather consults Acosta both on history (for example, discussing ancient customs of human sacrifice, "Acosta tells us, that the like, is in *Peru* very usual") and on theories such as the dispersion of the sons of Noah. To Acosta, the gathering of information on indigenous history and on American flora and fauna for the *Natural and Moral History* had been a secondary result of his life's primary work: to more effectively evangelize the world. Surely this resonated with Mather, who—as we will see—imagined his life as a reader and writer to be consecrated in the same way.[9]

Chapter II glanced over the Salem episode as a precursor to the Spanish project, but a section of *Wonders of the Invisible World* (1692) is worth revisiting, both because it mentions Acosta and because it indicates when Mather was able to augment his reading of the English translation of the *Natural and Moral History* with an original that also contained *Procuranda*. The reference occurs in a discussion of Satanic inversion: the way demonic forces could manifest as the evil opposite of a biblical event or Christian practice, such as the "black Mass." Inverting the pilgrimage of the ancient Hebrews through the wilderness to the promised land, the devil had led ancient Amerindian people to their own Jerusalem—Tenochtitlán, the place where the Mexica would overtake and develop into the capital of the Aztec Empire:

> That the Indians which came from far to settle about Mexico, were in their Progress to that Settlement, under a Conduct of the Devil, very strangely Emulating what the Blessed God gave to Israel in the Wilderness. Acosta, is our Author for it, That the Devil in their Idol Vitzlipultzli [*sic*], governed that mighty Nation. He commanded them to leave their Country, promising to make them Lords over all the Provinces possessed by Six other Nations of Indians, and give them a Land abounding with all precious things. They went forth, carrying their Idol with them, in a Coffer of Reeds, supported by Four of their Principal Priests; with whom he still Discoursed, in secret; Revealing to them the Successes, and Accidents of their way. He advised them, when to March, and where to Stay, and without his Commandment they moved not. The first thing they did, wherever they came, was to Erect a Tab-

ernacle, for their False God; which they set always in the midst of their Camp, and there placed the Ark upon an Altar.... And so they passed on, till they came to Mexico.[10]

Mather accurately paraphrases Book 7, chapter 4 of the *Natural and Moral History*. Grimstone's translation also writes "Vitziliputzli," nearly the same spelling as Mather, whereas the Spanish and Latin get closer to the Nahuatl version, "Huitzilopochtli," so this was almost certainly the text Mather had before him as he hurriedly wrote *Wonders*. Acosta had already done the work of drawing an analogy between the Mexica origin myth and that of the Christians (altars, priestly frocks, ritual prayers, the distribution to faithful worshippers of a dough symbolically made from the flesh of the deity). The arguments of Mede, Menasseh, and Thorowgood had likewise made reference to these Christian-seeming symbols. But Mather takes the analogy one step further. He extrapolates a lesson for New England out of Acosta's authoritative story of the pilgrimage from Aztlán: "The Devil which then thus imitated what was in the Church of the Old Testament, now among Us, would Imitate the Affayrs of the Church in the New." The same devil who had taken the form of Huitzilopochtli in the seventh century BCE somewhere in the west of the North American continent was now spectrally reappearing in Salem. Mather makes a point of including this particularly New World manifestation of witchcraft, assuming the ancient Mexica share some ancestry with the local Amerindians he also blames for these outbreaks of devilry in Massachusetts. He likens the sixteenth-century Spanish encounter with Native America to a kind of Old Testament that would be fulfilled by New England, as its figurative New Testament, in the seventeenth. *Magnalia Christi Americana,* a history of recent English attempts "made in the *American Hemisphere* to anticipate the State of the *New-Jerusalem,*" expresses this typology by arguing that Protestants had known about, and improved upon, the Spanish model. (Mather's reference to the Mexica origin story is unusual for its time, not seen among Anglo-American commentators again until William Prescott in the mid-nineteenth century. The story of the Mexica pilgrimage from Aztlán to Tenochtitlán is well known in the United States today thanks to the Chicano movement and its claims to ancestral land in the US southwest in the 1970s.)[11]

Magnalia makes another revisionist twist on Acosta's descriptions of Mexica altars, priestly vestments, and rituals of drinking from a chalice. Downplaying the importance of Columbus, Mather suggests that the "*New World was known, and partly Inhabited by* Britains, *or by* Saxons *from* England, *Three or Four Hundred Years before the* Spaniards *coming thither*": proof of which is "the Popish *Reliques,* as well as *British* Terms and Words, which the Spaniards then found among the *Mexicans.*" Mather then proposes that medieval Anglo-Saxon Catholics had traveled to Mexico by way of a land bridge through Greenland—a response, perhaps jesting, to Acosta's earlier theory of a land bridge over the Bering Strait. That would place New England's Indigenous inhabitants as earlier migrants than the medieval Mexicans, in addition to the Anglo-Saxons who came before the Genoese. Either way, in Mather's reckoning, New England shared a conceptual, historical, and prophetic space with New Spain across the vast landmass called "America."[12]

Sewall's Vision of Mexican Splendor

In his *Phaenomena quaedam apocalyptica* (1697), Samuel Sewall joined Mather in glorifying the work Eliot had done to ensure that all souls would have the opportunity to hear the gospel, a precondition of the Second Coming. Sewall is an important figure in New England history: fourteen years Mather's senior, he was one of the three judges who ordered executions at the Salem witch trials, but the only one to publicly apologize for his role. He was particularly close to Mather and, despite a divisive argument late in life, served as a pallbearer at Mather's funeral. He is also significant in the story of *La Fe del Christiano* at every turn: as a sharer of reference books and information, and as the apparent patron of its printing. Sewall did not see himself as a scholar: he was busily occupied as a magistrate, businessman, and landowner. But he remained deeply engaged with those theological questions that were also applied moral questions, of immediate relevance to New England's thriving. Slavery was one such question (as Chapter IX discusses); eschatology, as it addressed the intercultural conflicts of the day, was another. His two significant publications, *The Selling of Joseph* (1700) and *Phaenomena quaedam apocalyptica* (1697), address those two questions respectively. *Phaenomena* flips Mede's anti-American reading of the end-times drama and gives an affirmative answer to the question of whether "the Heart of America may not be the seat of the New-Jerusalem." Sewall uses a resonant metaphor:

> Mr. Eliot was want [*sic*] to say The New-English Churches are a preface to the New Heavens: and if so, I hope the preface and Book will be bound up together, and this Mexican Continent shall comprehend them both.

The "book" is both a temporal and a spatial figure here. As the "preface," New England comes before the millennial reign of Christ, but it also represents a small, initial Protestant outpost within a vast America, "this Mexican continent." The whole of the hemisphere had the potential to be the New Jerusalem.[13]

Sewall, too, suspected that events like the Lima earthquake of 1688 might be signs that the "sett Time" of the millennial clock was ticking. In 1686 he records notes on a sermon by a prominent Nonconformist minister newly arrived from England, the Reverend Samuel Lee. Lee "Said that all America should be converted, Mexico overcome, England sent over to convert the Natives, look you do it." Whereas Lee framed Mexico as a target to be "overcome" by English might in the struggle to win "all America" for Protestantism, Sewall's language in *Phaenomena* poses a surprising perspectival shift. Instead of New England expanding to conquer Mexico, "this Mexican Continent shall comprehend" (in the sense of include or encompass) both New England and New Spain. "Why may not *New-Spain* be the place of *New-Jerusalem?* It being part of the *New World*, one would think, carries with it no contradiction thereto."[14]

The capital of New Spain was, of course, Mexico-Tenochtitlán (historians use the conjoined term to reflect the persistence of Mesoamerican cultural and governance traditions through the early colonial period). Sewall plays out Mede's logic from an American center: the New World counterpart of Old World Rome, on the same latitude, would be Mexico City, which he calls "New Rome." He was wrong about the latitude—Rome is considerably farther north—but the climate and the city's setting in a valley surrounded by hills plausibly advance the comparison. The Franciscan architect Pedro de Gante had explicitly planned to remake the Aztec capital as a "new Rome," just as the pagan Rome had been transformed into a Christian city. The comparison was popularized by many Spanish writers in the sixteenth and seventeenth centuries, such as Bernardo de Balbuena's famous 1604 poem *La grandeza mexicana.* Reports of the city's baroque splendor, of its hundreds of thousands of inhabitants and imposing urban scheme, invited comparisons to classical empire: a seat of power, a hub of trade, a site of worldly glories. Intriguingly, Mather's *Quotidiana* contains a notation on "Seven hills of America," referencing a work by "a Spaniard" that lists cities claiming to be built, like Rome, on seven hills. The list includes Providence, Rhode Island; Asunción, Paraguay; and Chicontepec in Veracruz, whose name means "seven hills" in Nahuatl. Doctrinally and historically, it made sense to conceptualize America as a singular space.[15]

Although such a city as Mexico-Tenochtitlán may seem already as good as lost because it was under the sway of the Roman pope, *Phaenomena* proposes otherwise. Sewall asks, "Why may we not as well hope that God hath reserved Saints in *Mexico,* & other places of *America?*" The notion of "saints" who are "reserved" or set apart by God reflects the Calvinist notion of Election, or predestination. (As explained in the Transcription and Translation, Chapter XII, Mather would struggle to find a Spanish equivalent for the Elect before landing on "Suerte entre los Sanctificados": "to be sorted among the saved / sanctified.") While the conversion of Mexico to Protestantism must have seemed a far-off aspiration, Sewall raises it to amplify a very local point. In spite of John Eliot's recent death and the seeming eclipse of the New England Company's assimilationist vision after the bloodshed of King Philip's War, the Puritan community must not backslide on its duty to spread the gospel to "America," in the sense of Indigenous nations. *Phaenomena* is, among other things, a jeremiad, castigating New Englanders for failing to be as successful as Protestants (despite the cruelty of the "*Spanish-Iron* rod"). Rehearsing the history of the New World from Columbus through the Catholic missionaries, Sewall reminds them that they still must write that history's next chapter: "What is done or prepared by Papists among *Indians,* is not to be despised; but improved by Protestants." This introduces a section on Acosta.[16]

As Mather's retelling of the Aztlán story illustrates, Grimstone's rendition of the *Natural and Moral History* was available to him, and Sewall follows that translation in preferring the pre-Conquest name of Mexico over the more common secular term, New Spain. Near the beginning of *Phaenomena* he inserts seemingly extraneous details pulled from Book 7, such as a description of the Aztec calendar ("In the Computation of Time used by the *Mexican* Nation, their greatest period consisted of Fifty two Years, which they call'd a *Wheel*"). But it is likely that he had already made the lavish purchase of a rare original source: a copy of the 1596 Cologne edition of Acosta's *De Natura Novi*

Orbis, which contained only the first two books of the *Natural and Moral History* but the whole of *Procuranda. Procuranda* had quite a restricted circulation within the Catholic world, and it was not translated into English until the twentieth century. Sewall's purchase of the Cologne edition is a sign that his interest was piqued but unsatisfied by the Grimstone translation. Moreover, since there is no evidence of another copy in the inventories of Mather's library, it seems likely that he lent it to Mather—for the epigraph in Figure 3 gives a precise page reference to "A Costa de procur.," which aligns perfectly with this 1596 edition.[17]

In April 1699, a few years after *Procuranda,* Sewall inscribed on the flyleaf of this copy of *De Natura Novi Orbis* this notation: "Nunnacôquis signifies an Indian Earthen Pot as Hannah Hahatan's Squaw tells me." Historian Heather Kopelson, treating these marginalia as valuable archival shards of silenced Native voices, discovered that Hannah Hahatan was a Native Christian woman forced to give up her lands and relocate from Natick (Eliot's principal praying town) to Punkapoag after King Philip's War. Her presence in the Acosta book reinforces his vision of Indigenous America as a continuum: Sewall adds his bit of ethnolinguistic information to that gathered by Acosta, never forgetting that the primary purpose of such research was to gospelize those people. Although we do not know exactly when he bought this book and first read *Procuranda* in Latin, it would make sense of Sewall's preference for the Latin / Spanish term *America Mexicana* in place of the simpler *Mexico* that Grimstone uses. That preference bolsters Sewall's sense of a singular, continuous America.[18]

There are further signs in *Phaenomena* that Sewall absorbed information that was to be found in the Latin *Procuranda* but not in Grimstone's *Natural and Moral History.* The former focuses on the postcontact world, and the ways Europeans had more and less successfully proselytized; the "moral" or human books of the latter mainly stop at the moment of first encounter. One success Sewall attributes to the Spanish that is "not to be despised; but improved by Protestants" is the fostering of Native intellectuals to minister to their own people. He gives Acosta as the source for this claim:

> By means of the *Spaniard,* the *Indians* have a School in every Town
> for Reading and Writing: and Officers of their own to do Justice; except in matters of Life. I conceive Hope and Joy, when I read what
> catechetical Doctrine was by a Synod at *Lima* appointed to be taught

an *Indian* that would become a Christian. . . . If an *Indian* believe these Things, and Repent of his past life, and now will live according to the Command of God: he may be accepted for a Christian. Let Protestants now, for shame, arise, and shew that they have some breathings of a true Apostolical Spirit in them.

The "catechetical Doctrine" may well be one of the trilingual Latin-Spanish-Quechua *Catecismos* that Acosta worked on in Juli, Peru: he mentions them in *Procuranda* in his brief for the expansion of the printing press. The "Lima Synod" was a meeting to set policy on the status and use of Quechua and Aymara, as Chapter IV on missionary linguistics discusses. Other parts of the *Natural and Moral History* do describe the postcontact world—but on the question of language especially, Sewall appears to engage directly with *Procuranda:*

> And *Acosta* saith there are Men of God [among Catholic missionaries]; they are scarce indeed. But I may not pass by *Joseph Acosta* himself, whom I am inclined to judge a serious Man for the Conversion of the *Indians.* . . . I cannot but esteem him for his pressing and maintaining so heartily the Preaching of Christ to be the principal Thing. And he accounts it Ridiculous, for the *Indians* to say their Prayers they understand not a word of. He makes Explicit Faith necessary.

Here Sewall references the signature claim of *Procuranda:* the foundational Jesuit belief that evangelization must be done in the tongue of the people being preached to. Through a series of contrasts between the English and Spanish "plantations," Sewall goes on to suggest that the best impulses in Acosta, a "serious Man," had been reborn in Eliot and Thomas Mayhew, another Puritan who first learned the language of the people he hoped to convert. (Sewall does not mention another pioneering linguist, Roger Williams, on another side of a sectarian disagreement.)[19]

By returning to the old problem of Spain's historical head start and proposing that Mexico might share New England's destiny in the millennial future, *Phaenomena* yokes together local with global religious concerns and geopolitical designs, tantalizing listeners and readers with visions of the contemporary example of Mexico-Tenochtitlán. Although Sewall, the Mathers, and a handful of others continued to shore up the New England Company's mission of teaching literacy and the Gospel in Indigenous tongues, that project seemed, to most Bostonians in the 1690s, to have been a conspicuous failure. If Mexican missionaries had established in its Indigenous world "a School in every Town for Reading and Writing," as the New England Company had tried to do in Massachusetts, Sewall could infer that students were learning the imperial language, and perhaps Latin, as well as their own. That gave the Spanish language a new status: a transfer point by which Protestants might evangelize to all those other Americans.

The Sight of a Spanish (Jewish) Bible

Procuranda has much to say about language and evangelizing. Sewall manages to reference both topics in the epigraph on the title page:

> Act. 1.6–8. Lord, wilt thou at this time restore again the kingdom of Israel?—ye shall be witnesses unto me unto the uttermost parts of the earth; *hasta lo ultimo de la tierra.*
> —SPANISH BIBLE.

The attribution must have puzzled readers. As all Protestants knew, the Catholic Church forbade the Bible's translation into vernacular languages and actively discouraged lay folk from reading it. Spain was full of Catholics; how could there be a "Spanish Bible" and how had Sewall found a partial translation of the final phrase of those verses, so familiar to them? The epigraph excerpts a scene from the beginning of the book of Acts, when a risen Jesus gives his disciples their task: to spread the word to all corners of the world in order to restore Israel and claim God's kingdom for eternity. Sewall excises Jesus's rebuke to their question about the precise timing of his return (a verse that would have been well known to them: "It is not for you to know the times or the seasons, which the Father hath put in his own power"), but it is enough of a reminder that believers had work to do in order to put eschatology into practice. Acts 1:8 is a cornerstone of global evangelicalism. With the repetition of the final phrase in Spanish, Sewall performs a bit of pedagogy and teases the theme of Spanish, not as an Indigenous language, but as a legitimate means of reaching the unconverted across the globe.

71

Later in the treatise, as he explains the Mede-Thorowgood debate about the length of time Jewish people had been present in the Americas, Sewall writes:

> *New-England* is seldom wholly without them. Now there are two at *Boston;* viz. Mr. *Joseph Frazon,* and *Samuel Frazon,* his brother, to whom I am beholden for a sight of the *Spanish* Bible. *Joseph Frazon* was some-time Scholar to the learned *Yeosuah Da Sylva,* in *London.* They acquaint me, that the *Jews* were formerly very numerous in the *Dutch* Plantations in *Brasil:* their Father and Grandfather did dwell there. *Olinda* was taken by the *Dutch, Anno* 1629. How soon the *Jews* followed them thither, I am not certain. Yet at *Suranam,* and *Curasso,* there are plenty of them still.

Giving Joseph Frazon's intellectual pedigree, Sewall elevates him into the local expert on the Menasseh-Mede-Thorowgood debate about the lost tribe theory. The secondhand history is accurate: many Sephardim and *marranos* (nominal Christian converts who continued to practice Jewish traditions) fled to the New World in the sixteenth century. By the end of the seventeenth, they had established enclaves along the coast of Surinam and on islands like Curaçao, Barbados, and Jamaica. Rhode Island, with its chartered religious tolerance, was the largest Jewish community in New England, but the Frazon brothers braved the more hostile climate of Boston. Although New England Puritans had inherited the anti-Semitism embedded in the Western Christian world (Luther and Calvin included), as Michael Hoberman explains, these biases were overridden by sympathy toward the persecution of the Jews under the Roman Catholic Church. Cromwell's attention to Menasseh was mirrored in the later New England context by Mather and Sewall, both of whom tried repeatedly and unsuccessfully to convert them.[20]

Sewall is disingenuous about the "*Spanish* Bible," which can only have been a copy of the *Biblia en Lengua Española Traducida Palabra por Palabra de la Verdad Hebrayca* (Bible in the Spanish Language Translated Word for Word from the True Hebrew), known as the Ferrara Bible for the relatively tolerant Italian city in which it was first printed in 1553. After the expulsion of Jews and Muslims from Spain and Portugal in 1492, Sephardic exiles printed their long-circulated translation of the Hebrew *Tanach,* the scriptures that Christians would claim to be their "old" testament. "Española" here meant Ladino, the spoken dialect of central Spain during the centuries of *convivencia* (peaceful coexistence) between Muslim, Jewish, and Catholic Spain. That epigraph from Acts (originally written in Greek) was, of course, not taken from this Ferrara Bible, but Sewall could have found the identical phrase by turning to the book of Isaiah, where it appears three times as *hasta lo ultimo de la tierra*. In misrepresenting the nature of the "Spanish Bible," Sewall hijacks the religious convictions of the Frazon brothers: the slippage of the term makes them seem friendly co-religionists. In this respect, however, Sewall may have been be attempting to amplify the community's tolerance; earlier Jewish migrants who attempted to settle in Boston had been "warned out" by the selectmen. Revelation specifies that some of those 144,000 souls chosen to be saved will be found in New Babylon, and that the Saints and the unsaved would dwell together in the same place until that day. For some Christian interpreters, this is an argument against the making of enclaves, in favor of embracing outsiders in radically egalitarian social arrangements. In theory, the *ethnos* of New England's English people was never coextensive with the Elect. The Saints who would live eternally with Christ were typological replacements for the Chosen People of the Old Testament, not their genealogical descendants. In *Phaenomena*, Sewall hews to that inclusive vision.[21]

The "sight" of the Ladino Ferrara Bible excited Sewall because it was the mortar that filled in the gap between the historical Israelites, the precontact Amerindians (regardless of the answer to the lost tribe question), and the contemporary space of America. The Spanish American dominions that stretched outward from Boston were a vast hemisphere full of Indians and, as this news of the Sephardic diaspora proved, Jews. Hebrew was not their common language—although generations of hapless missionaries since Columbus's time had tried it out when meeting Indigenous people—Spanish often was. In 1704, Samuel was appointed court interpreter of Spanish and Portuguese in the trial of the pirate Quelch, suggesting he was known for his linguistic prowess. Joseph Frazon, whom Sewall portrays as the scholar of the two, died in Boston in that same year, but Samuel—a shipowner and captain—moved between Boston and the West Indies for decades, was presumed disappeared in a shipwreck off Barbados in 1705, and reappeared after epic tribulations to have his story published in Boston newspapers. Mather continued to contact him for decades, and he will return to this story in later chapters.

The Frazons were valuable to Mather and Sewall as native informants, and not only about Jewish scholarly traditions and the Ladino variety of the Spanish language that they apparently spoke as well as read. They were sources of information about two key locations in the Spanish-controlled Americas most proximate to Boston: the Caribbean and Mexico. English and Dutch Protestants carved what footholds they could in the Caribbean and along the coastal areas of Central America and the Yucatan. Just as Sewall was writing *Phaenomena,* the Company of Scotland launched a settlement in the straits of Darién, in present-day Panama. It appears that Sewall invested in this company, against the explicit directive of the English Crown, which did not want to risk another war. This colonization scheme, although sprung from Scotland's financial duress, epitomized the aims of the Protestant International: to encroach upon Catholic America with Reformed settlements. Although not located in Mexico proper, the Darién colony was located within the intendancy of New Spain. Had it been successful, it would have provided evidence to Sewall that in the future "this Mexican continent shall encompass" Protestants from its northern to its southern reaches.[22]

Goods and News from Mexico

Sewall's sources of information about Mexico, ancient and modern, were not limited to Acosta and whatever the cosmopolitan Frazons might have recounted. His attention to the place went well beyond the eschatological context of *Phaenomena* and spans decades. "I have long prayed for Mexico," Sewall would write a few years after the treatise was published. It was not only the rumored splendors of the greatest metropolis on the continent (a traveler told him of "the magnificence of the City . . . there were in it 1500 Coaches drawn with Mules"). It was also the particular set of trade goods, cacao and silver and cochineal, that Mexico exported indirectly and often covertly. In addition to his role as a superior court judge, Sewall was occupied daily with the management of family investments in trade. His wealthy father-in-law, John Hull, had been the first person in the colony to import chocolate (sold in balls, then mixed with other ingredients to form a beverage) and to popularize the luxury drink. Acosta had spurned it, Gage had loved it; Sewall sided with Gage. Diary entries record Sewall offering the drink to guests, or giving "2 Balls of Chockalett and a pound Figgs" to a friend who was ailing, perhaps for its rumored health benefits. In 1697 he breakfasted with the lieutenant governor "on Venison and Chockaltte: I said Massachuset and Mexico met at his Honour's Table."[23]

While it was far-fetched to imagine a military overthrow of Mexico by England, the presence of Creole commodity growers and potential direct trading partners in that country offered a source of hope that the powerful realm might decide of its own accord to cast off Spanish rule. The relative independence of the viceroys, and the relative weakness of the last Habsburg kings, was well known. In 1698, the same lieutenant governor "met us in his New Coach and read us out the Governour's Letter the News that New-Spain had revolted from the Crown of Spain and had crowned the Vice-Roy of Mexico their King." As English settlers awaited corroboration of this news, in December, learning with keen interest about "Fleet of the Scotland Company being at Jamaica," Sewall noted some (falsely optimistic) news about the settlement on the "American Isthmus" in Darién, and donated a dozen copies of his *Phaenomena* "to send them to welcome them into the New World." Sewall sent those copies by a man named John Bant, a sailor who had arrived in Boston that summer with stories about his shipwreck and peregrinations through the West Indies and the far northeastern reaches of New Spain: Florida, Texas, Tamaulipas. Bant's report crushed the rumor that a popular revolt had "crowned the Vice-Roy of Mexico their King." "Mexican Revolt is a sham," Bant reported, since he had traveled extensively through Cuba "And yet heard not a word of the Mexican Revolt. Which makes the Truth of it to be questioned here." Moreover, word eventually arrived that the hopeful Scots in Darién were driven out only a few months afterward by a Spanish fleet after being decimated by hunger and disease.[24]

Nonetheless, Sewall continued to look for signs of an impending revolt against Catholic Spain. In 1702, having heard Increase Mather preach that God was again sending America signs through the appearance of a comet, he wrote,

> Capt. Timo Clarkk tells me that a Line drawn to the Comet strikes just upon Mexico, spake of a Revolution there, how great a Thing it would be, Said one Whitehead told him of the magnificence of the City, that there were in it 1500 Coaches drawn with Mules. This Blaze had put me in mind of Mexico; because we must look toward Mexico to view it. Capt. Clark drew a Line on his Globe. Our Thoughts being thus confer'd, and found to jump, makes it to me remarkable. I have long pray'd for Mexico, and of late in those Words, that God would open the Mexican Fountain.

Reading the comet's appearance for signs of the continent's future, Sewall imagines Mexico as a deep aquifer of souls that, once tapped, would flow and flourish. For a city shaped by and on fresh water, it was not a bad metaphor. As late as 1708, Sewall continues to pray for a Mexican "Revolution," in both political and spiritual senses: "Reform all the European Plantations in America; Spanish, Portuguese, English, French, Dutch; Save this New World, that where Sin hath abounded, Grace may Superabound." But it is not clear whether Colonel Clark thought the impetus for change would come from above or below. The Glorious Revolution that brought Protestant rulers back to England's throne had been bloodless; the 1689 New England Revolt, in which Creoles rose against a governor who restricted their rights, was also bloodless. When it came to subordinated populations, however, what would constitute a righteous enough cause for a revolution that spilled blood? The dominant narrative about King Philip's War was not one of Native protest against their repeated injuries: it was one of unprovoked barbarism.[25]

The lieutenant governor's false news of an anticolonial uprising was probably a garbled report of the 1692 plebian riot in Mexico City, in which *castas*—mixed-race and assimilated Indigenous people—filled the streets in protest against the government's handling of food shortages. African descendant protestors in particular were indiscriminately punished by the viceroy, the Count of Galve, who restored "law and order" to the satisfaction of creole elites. Word of sporadic Indigenous revolts against the *encomienda* and other forced-labor systems of the Spanish Empire sometimes reached English ears, albeit in distorted and incomplete form. Primed by the Black Legend, Thomas Gage had once urged Cromwell to invade Santo Domingo, suggesting that the mixed African-Indian population there would welcome them as liberators; he was fatally wrong. English settlers had already seen organized revolts among forced laborers in their own "Plantations": colonial officials in Virginia were shocked during Bacon's Rebellion (1676–1677) to see white and Black servants rising against their British governor and allied Native tribes. It is a tantalizing possibility that word might have reached New England about the most stunning upset to Spanish rule in recent history: the brilliantly organized Pueblo Revolt in the northwest corner of New Spain. In 1680, under the leadership of Popé and his own millennialist promise of regeneration, thousands of Puebloans had allied in order to overthrow a century of Spanish colonial rule and to expel the priests who had claimed their lands for churches and missions. The pueblos remained free for twelve years until an expedition led by Diego de Vargas re-took them in 1692. One of the principal chroniclers of the 1692 plebian rebel-lion in Mexico-Tenochtitlán was Carlos Sigüenza de Góngora, who collated and published the first newspaper-like publication in North America, *El Mercurio Volante.* Its first issue contained reports of both events. It is not incon-ceivable that a ship passing through Boston on a West Indies route could have carried a copy of *El Mercurio Volante* from Havana. As the Bant anecdote sug-gests, information also circulated with travelers, fugitives, and refugees; it was one asset they could trade on. [26]

Such a migrant person brought news to Mather that prompted what might be the first mention of California in Anglo-American writing, in *Triumphs of the Reformed Religion:* "One escaped from Captivity among the Spaniards, told me, that the Spanish Friars had carried their Gospel into the Spacious Country of California. But they quickly gave over the Work, because Such a poor Na-tion was not worth Converting." Mather can only be referring to the first, failed efforts of the empire to establish military outposts in Loreto, Baja California, beginning in 1682 and following the shock of the Pueblo Revolt. When the Spanish were driven out of the Baja peninsula by an Indigenous alliance, the expedition's evangelical leader, the Jesuit Eusebio Kino, planned to return: along with spreading the gospel, he aimed to gather information about whether the "Spacious Country of California" was an island, or part of the continental land-mass. Kino only became well known after he established missions in the Pimería Alta (present-day Arizona and Sonora), after Mather wrote *Triumphs.* Like Sigüenza de Góngora, Sewall and Mather took an interest in the far reaches of the continent on which they had a foothold. They knew the contours of La Florida to the south, with its opening onto the Mississippi River: the *Natural and Moral History* had devoted several paragraphs to speculation on the shape of the North American interior. Having reinterpreted sacred time to cast the Americas in a starring role, the next logical step was to hasten the end times by bringing the Gospel not only to the native nations on New England's borders, but all the way to this *America Mexicana.*[27]

Moved by the same portents and rumors about past and present events in Mexico that inspired Sewall's *Phaenomena quaedem apocalyptica,* Mather wrote his own works on American eschatology, most significantly *Tripara-disus* (1724). Mather's pairing of *Procuranda* with a text from Revelation for the epigraphs of *La Fe del Christiano* trades upon Acosta's authority as a historian and evangelist of America while replacing the Jesuit's mission with a new Protestant one, embodied first by Eliot and then, prospectively, by the Spanish tracts themselves. If *La Fe del Christiano* was part of a millennialist impulse that assigned the whole hemisphere a shared destiny, however, it was also a pragmatic response to an evolving sense of the relative value of different missionary language practices, to which the next chapter now turns.[28]

· IV ·

From Language Encounters to Language Rights

By citing Acosta to open *La Fe del Christiano,* Mather honors Sewall's message in *Phaenomena* that "What has been done by the Spanish, is not to be despised but to be improved upon." Of course, Mather wanted to wrestle the Catholic Church for ownership of the term *Christian.* The title of *La Fe del Christiano* is most closely translated as "The Faith of the Christian [Man]," referring not to the Christian faith in general but to the individual (normatively marked with a masculine gender ending). Mather's title thus echoes that of the book credited with inspiring Henry VIII of England to abandon his Roman Catholic faith): William Tyndale's *The Obedience of a Christian Man* (1528). Tyndale had criticized the Church for not delivering the Word and the sacraments in a language that believers could understand. Like Tyndale, Mather uses these tracts to critique Catholic doctrine on several grounds, and he homes in on language practices in particular.

Article I of *La Religion Pura,* possibly the first complex sentence that Mather composed in Spanish, reads: "La Palabra de Cristo en sagrada Escritura, deve ser Gozada, Buscada, y Sabida par las Gentes de todas suertes: y es una grande Iniquitad, impedir el Vulgo de Leer de aquella preciosa palabra de la Vida" (The word of Christ in holy scripture should be enjoyed, sought out, and known by people of all sorts, and it is a great iniquity to keep the common person from reading out of that precious word of life). This article condemns the post-Tridentine Catholic practice of making devotional texts, but not the Bible itself, available to lay believers. Article II declares that the Scriptures are in themselves sufficient to show to way to eternal life, underscoring Protestantism's attention to individual Bible reading, which Puritans practiced with particular gusto. Several pointedly anti-Catholic theses follow: that only Christ, not the pope, should be considered the head of the church (Articles III, IV);

that prayers should not be directed at saints or other intercessors (V); that grace alone can bring one to salvation (VI); that the only true sacraments are baptism and the Lord's Supper, notably omitting confession, a mandatory and very important rite for Catholics (VII); that the Eucharistic bread and wine are only symbolic, not the transubstantiated body of Christ (VIII, IX); and that priests may marry (XI). Article X returns to the theme of language practices in the first and second articles, but this time in reference to oral rather than written contexts. Mather rejects the Latin liturgy: "Todos Exercisios de la Religion hechos en la Iglesia de Dios, deven ser hechos en Lengua sabida a Vulgo" (All religious activities done in God's Church should be done in a language known to the common person). *Vulgo* might also be translated as layperson—in theological contexts it referred to an unordained or lay priest—but the word "common" underscores the term's powerful association in early modern Castilian with the coarser manners and expressions of the masses. Whether Mather knew it or not, his usage here participated in the transformation of *vulgo* from a pejorative to a populist sense.[1]

As a late-arriving Creole, Mather's challenge in presenting the Word to Spanish-speaking "people of all sorts" was different from Tyndale's. At the same time Tyndale was in exile doing the forbidden work of translating the Bible into English, Franciscan missionaries in Mexico had already begun learning, preaching, and printing in Native languages to advance their objectives of evangelizing and assimilating the Indigenous world. The Protestant design upon America similarly navigated the language barrier through the methods of missionary linguistics. Although the tract reiterates the Christian's right to hear and to speak their vernacular tongue in church and other devotional contexts, Mather pays special attention to the lifting of prohibitions on the written word ("impedir el Vulgo de Leer"). As he saw it, opening access to literacy and to Bible reading distinguished the English "improvement" upon what the Spanish had done to Europeanize America. Protestant thinkers in subsequent generations would follow Mather's lead in elevating writing and literacy as their distinctive contribution to modernity and progress: intellectual history's version of the Black Legend. According to it, the Reformation brought about the elevation of "modern" languages over Latin, widespread literacy, and the triumph of the printed word as law. These combined factors were thought to produce liberal individualism and democratic governments—while in contrast Catholicism, as it regrouped into a Counter-Reformation, conservatively renewed its embrace of Latin, emphasized oral and iconographic worship, discouraged literacy, censored the press and kept books away from people, and through a combination of these factors produced social collectivism and populist-authoritarian governments. This narrative has generated persistent North-South oppositions that simply do not hold up under the scrutiny of historical scholarship.

The Catholic Counter-Reformation was not focused on keeping the Word away from the people, as antagonistic interpreters such as Mather insinuated. The Council of Trent reaffirmed the Latin Mass, but also recommended that the homily (the sermon and its explication) be delivered in the vernacular, the language of the *Vulgo*. The council reaffirmed St. Jerome's Latin Vulgate as the official translation of the Bible (while restricting its dissemination), but at the same time it encouraged the production of printed devotions and prayer books in every language spoken in the world, to be read by those with that skill and memorized by others. At stake not only in the conflict between Catholics and Protestants, but between the European Christian world and the Indigenous one, was how expansively to define the community of those who could read God's word, which rested on the definition of literacy itself. This chapter continues the discussion in the previous one, this time focusing not on Native origins as they influenced eschatological readings of America but on an expansively conceived notion of language practices that gets beyond the orality/literacy divide and asserts the coevalness of Indigenous languages as equally "modern."

The sixteenth-century Jesuit José de Acosta and the seventeenth-century Congregationalist John Eliot, introduced in Chapter III, reappear here as sedimentary layers upon which Mather's Spanish project was built. It is not that Acosta and Eliot were the only Europeans to engage substantially with Indigenous languages and their speakers; far from it. However, to both Sewall and Mather, the Acosta-Eliot pairing embodied the historical succession of one phase of missionary linguistics into a newly emerging one in which they aimed to evangelize Mexico in its *colonial* language, not its indigenous ones. The Jesuit order, founded in tandem with the Counter-Reformation, is especially known for its scholarly attention to language research, but Jesuits built on the learning practices of other mendicant orders, especially the Franciscans. Missionary linguistics had reshaped prior European language learning practices. In their experimental quest to attain bilingual proficiency, early missionaries moved back and forth between different modes of communication: heard and spoken, gestured and performed, and eventually written and read. Indigenous people participated in these encounters, not only as informants but as individual and collaborative makers of interlingual works that were variously written, printed, recorded, inscribed, and visually decorated. Mather's learning of French and especially of Spanish was rooted in an awareness that these Old World languages were already being worked into the American soil.

Language Encounters: Beyond an Oral-Written Binary

Colonial stories often begin with a scene of an unsuccessful language encounter that is eventually redeemed by finding, or training, an oral interpreter. Arriving in the Americas, Europeans were at first perplexed by their failure to find a common language: for centuries, they had been able to rely on bilingual intermediaries who could be found along trade routes to Asia and Africa. The famous translator figures of the early Americas, like Malintzín / La Malinche in Mexico, Tisquantum / Squanto in Massachusetts, and Don Luis de Velasco in Virginia and Florida were not European but Indigenous; their names may stand in for thousands of other interpreters fluent in many tongues that were useful along their own routes of trade or pilgrimage in the precontact world populated by tens of millions of people. Malintzín, Tisquantum, and Don Luis became multilingual through coercion, as captives or slaves. Frances Karttunen's classic study of Indigenous "interpreters, guides, and survivors" observes that their quick learning of the tongues of the Europeans was an adaptive strategy, and one with high stakes. Why do European feats of multilingualism seem to lend themselves less to such mythification; who among them is remembered as an important oral interpreter? As Karttunen warns, there is a persistent tendency to attribute superior oral skills to the "natural" facilities of supposedly primitive peoples and to posit that European traders, missionaries, and others were deficiently dependent on writing.[2]

The notion of a "language encounter," put forth by Edward G. Gray and Norman Fiering, adds language practices to the list of the so-called New World exchange. For linguists, cultural contact is the source of evolution: contact produces pidgins (the loading of vocabulary items from one language into the grammatical order of the other, intelligible at some basic level) and creoles (mixed languages that eventually become someone's mother tongue). These encounters were often performative and gestural, in addition to being spoken and sometimes recorded. American language encounters would powerfully shape the emergence of Western linguistics in the eighteenth century. These encounters were not neutral: they worked complexly within systems of dominance and control, particularly the ideological system that defined and classified the human. Important recent scholarship on the alignment of modernity and coloniality has highlighted and challenged the way valorizing alphabetic language cultures over nonalphabetic ones. The persistent, misleading idea that characterized civilizations on a progressive scale upward from orality to literacy has given way to a broader notion of linguistic communication.[3]

That it has taken centuries to appreciate the wealth of Indigenous American technologies of inscription and recording is a direct result of colonial language encounters and the way Europeans interpreted them. Early Spanish, French, and Portuguese observers prematurely determined that the people they met lacked writing systems, and for that reason were primitive. Confronted with glyphs on stelae in the *mundo Maya* and with *quipu* (a symbolic system using knotted cords) in the Andean region called Tawantinsuyu, they denied their status as texts. Confronted with objects vividly similar to European books, such as the Mesoamerican accordion-fold books made from *amotl* paper and symbolically red and black ink, they dismissed the texts as merely pictographic. In central and southern Mexico, most of the bark-paper codices that preserved ceremonial, administrative, and historical words and performance cues were destroyed; in the Mayan territories, which held out longer against Spanish armies, codices and other precious records were hidden and finally burned in an infamous auto-da-fé. As scholars like Walter Mignolo, Elizabeth Hill Boone, and Camilla Townsend have influentially observed, a powerful bias toward alphabetism born with colonial contact discredited Indigenous writing systems as such. The recent renaissance in the study of Nahuatl, Mixtec, and Zapotec codices has profoundly reshaped colonial Mexico history in particular. But it is not necessary to shoehorn all these recording methods into the category of "writing." Arguing that the rise of sound and visual media theory in the contemporary period can illuminate the colonial one, Matt Cohen and Jeffrey Glover have instead proposed the term "mediascapes," understanding "inscription as happening, and as being received, in relation to multiple, sometimes simultaneous, modes of communication": sound-making, speech, gesture, ritual exchange, the marking of things or landscapes.[4]

The evangelization of the Americas began in earnest in the middle of the sixteenth century with millennialist motives, as the founding "twelve apostles" of Franciscan evangelists streamed into Mexico and baptized a prodigious number of people. Motolinía (aka Toribio de Benavente) alone is said to have baptized 40,000 people in mass groups, defending that practice against the Dominican Bartolomé de Las Casas, who held to a stricter definition of conversion. A highly syncretized Catholicism emerged in Mexico, retaining strong aspects of Indigenous cosmology and ritual. Language encounters and the practices they involved were scaffolded into language policies, as church and state debated the proper place of Indigenous tongues.[5]

A Brief History of Language Practice and Policy in Colonial Spanish America

The Spanish arrived barely a century after the Aztecs had consolidated their hegemony over central Mexico, so they found elites, functionaries, and traders from several linguistically distinct groups: a ready reserve of translator-interpreters who helped the Spanish layer their institutions over preexisting economic and cultural orders. The Franciscans made ambitious plans to set up universal schools for teaching Spanish and training a cadre of Indigenous priests. This plan would also serve the state by reinforcing the authority and prestige of the elites from the former empire, now joined by a new caste of high-ranking mestizos of mixed Spanish-Mexica ancestry. In early colonial Spanish America, a small but potent group from Lima northward achieved what Enrique Florescano calls "critical assimilation," "maintaining their right to be different and assuming their human equality with the Spaniards." Literacy training—whether in the colonial language, the Indigenous language, or both—provided Amerindians and mestizos with additional tools of self-defense.[6]

The Colegio de Santa Cruz de Tlatelolco took this experiment in assimilation to a higher level: built over a preexisting Mexica school, it trained a Latin-literate elite to become priests. At the Colegio de Tlatelolco in particular, *talleres* (workshops) of Indigenous and mestizo intellectuals produced new versions of the *amotl* accordion books, recording in text and image Mesoamerican linguistic, cultural, and historical knowledge with the very same artisanal traditions that Spaniards outside the capital were busily erasing. Native and mestizo people in the *taller* of Bernardo de Sahagún collaboratively wrote and painted one of the jewels of American book history, the trilingual Florentine Codex in Nahuatl, Spanish, and Latin. Sahagún and a handful of other Spaniards immersed themselves deeply in the language and culture: Andrés de

Olmos created the first Nahuatl grammar at Tlatelolco before moving on to the Totonac and Huastec tongues. Most of the records of Mesoamerican cosmology, history, lineage, and maps were created during the first half-century after the Spanish takeover within a social context that gave those languages something close to coeval status. Nahuatl was identified as the *lengua mexicana,* and its use was promoted for general use by all Native peoples in 1578, making the administration of New Spain effectively bilingual, like Peru, for several decades. (Unlike Quechua, which was widely spoken across a long-standing empire, Mexico was an extraordinarily plurilingual country, so the imposition of Nahuatl was a colonialism within a colonialism.)[7]

The Crown soon concluded that the ambitious Franciscan plan to put schools everywhere in the República de Indios would be too expensive. Debates about education are inherently debates about the range of language practices to which some will be given access and others will not. Banning spoken language practices is notoriously difficult to enforce, but regulations could manage access to the new languages of power, Castilian and Latin. Despite the interest of many scholar-priests in preserving Indigenous knowledge through linguistic and religious assimilation, the first ecclesiastical councils of the Church in the colonies—held in Peru in 1551–1552 and in Mexico in 1555—made rulings that moved in the opposite direction. The utopian vision of many early Franciscans had been to put Native priests (trained in Spanish and Latin) in charge of their own people, but these councils distrustfully prohibited that. Frightened by the Reformation, the councils also restricted the circulation of devotional manuscripts in Indigenous languages as many priests cast doubt on the wisdom of literacy training: a 1588 letter worries that if *indios* could read, they might discover heretical "Lutheran" books.[8]

Instead, European and Creole parish priests were to learn the local languages and remain keepers of their flocks of converts. To train the needed numbers of priests, chairs devoted to Indigenous languages were established at the Jesuit Colegio de San Pedro y San Pablo in Mexico City in 1574 and at the University of San Marcos in Lima in 1579. The Indigenous and (increasingly) mestizo children of elites interacted with the República de Españoles in the cities, attending Spanish schools and sometimes these universities: there were seven in the Spanish colonies by 1600, nineteen by 1700. Belatedly, their multilingual and multimedial documents have been recuperated and republished as primary sources, reshaping a colonial Latin American history that for centuries was told almost exclusively through Spanish sources and perspectives. Prominent among these are the massive chronicles of Felipe Guamán Poma de Ayala in Peru and of Domingo de San Antón Muñon Chimalpahin Quauhtlehuanitzin (Chimalpahin) and Fernando de Alva Cortés Ixtlilxóchitl in Mexico, recorded alphabetically in Quechua, Nahuatl, Spanish, and Latin. During the seventeenth century, as Townsend documents, there was also an outpouring of collectively and anonymously authored pictographic books throughout Mesoamerica. In the universities, lesser-known names wrote and published works of theology and natural science and philosophy in Latin. Making an inventory of these creole and "Indian" Latinists, Jorge Cañizares-Esguerra argues that just as a binary conception of orality versus literacy binary flattens a more complex reality, so does the notion of a colonial Spanish America in which "what is indigenous is set against what is European." These artfully composed documents are only the tip of an iceberg of the recorded traces of Indigenous, African, and mixed-race subjects, whose voices and languages can also be found in legal pleadings and other records.[9]

Such piecemeal records offer clues into the way that prestige and influence were distributed in this multilingual world, particularly during the first century and a half of the Spanish empire. That world included several settler languages (for Iberians brought many regional languages with them in addition to Castilian); Nahuatl, Quechua, and the administrative languages of the stronger states of the former empires; and the thousands of regionally specific tongues of Indigenous and mestizo peoples, not to mention the languages of the initially small but growing number of Africans brought forcibly to the Americas. Language practices need not be regulated outright if they can be incentivized, and the ideological work of elevating a standard written variety of Castilian to the highest level of prestige was a powerful component of that work. It has struck many as a resonant coincidence that 1492, the year of Columbus's first voyage, also witnessed the completion of Antonio de Nebrija's Castilian grammar, the first ever created for a vernacular language. Nebrija's maxim, "Language is the handmaiden of empire," was a triumphant reference to the *Reconquista* that violently expelled Sephardic Jews and North African Muslims from Spain: purging Arabic influences and purifying usage along Latin models would reinforce that religious gain. To later observers, Nebrija seemed to prophecy Spain's coming global dominance and the application of this fetish of *pureza de sangre* to the languages and peoples of the Americas as a racial ideology of whitening, or *blanqueamiento*. It was during the first decades of this empire that the terms *castellano* and *español* became nearly synonymous as well.[10]

Nebrija articulated an argument for the complete Castilianization of the empire that always found proponents, no matter what the official policy. King Felipe IV issued a *cédula* (royal decree) in 1634 that ordered the replacement of Indigenous languages with Spanish, relegating Nahuatl to a subordinate position more like that of the other Mexican languages. Members of mendicant orders—those who had taken solemn vows to spread the Gospel—often dedicated themselves to Indigenous languages and could justify their continued study and use. Other members of the clergy were less enthusiastic than the missionaries, who were predominantly Jesuit in the southern part of Spanish America and Franciscan in the northern part (although exceptions abound). Horizontal and vertical conflicts between the different branches of the clergy, and with the church hierarchy, inflected local practices regarding Indigenous languages. The turning points would come after Mather's time, in the mid-eighteenth century, when Bourbon reforms enacted Castilianization policies and the Jesuits were expelled from the Americas. Even the once-prestigious Quechua professorship at the University of San Marcos was abolished after the Tupac Amaru II revolt in the 1780s, and the language was proscribed. The nation-building projects of the nineteenth century deployed a version of Nebrija's argument for a single, cohesive national identity to eradicate Indigenous languages through wholesale campaigns of education and assimilation.[11]

This brief sketch of Spanish American language practices and policies is necessarily reductive, but it introduces a timeline and some key concepts to the story of Mather's own encounter with Spanish two hundred years after Columbus: colonial language policies and practices that privilege certain uses, varieties, or language systems over others; prestige languages providing points of access for Indigenous and mestizo thinkers; grammaticalization and standardization as ways to sort people into categories of belonging. With those in mind, we return to José de Acosta's *De procuranda Indorum salute* as one among many features in that intricately embroidered design.

Acosta's *Procuranda* and Heart-Language

As regular clergy and missionary orders often divided over the question of how to communicate the Word of God to Indigenous America, Acosta epitomized the accommodationist approach of the Jesuits. Arriving in Lima in 1571, Acosta was dismayed at the local priests' minimal knowledge of Quechua, the governing language of the empire called Tawantinsuyu after its four regions. *De procuranda Indorum salute* was the result. Written in a neo-Aristotelian style that entertains both sides of an argument, pro and con, it is a deeply pragmatic book, offering both micro- and macro-level advice about how to gather and manage a flock of neophytes. It argues (following Las Casas) that the character of Amerindians is inherently good; it rails against the abuse of their labor; and it outlines a theory and practice of language learning. *Procuranda* was seen by more conservative forces within the Church as a radical work. While the *Historia natural y moral de las Indias* was licensed by the Inquisition and widely disseminated, *Procuranda* was abridged and censored in its Spanish versions. Its distribution in Latin was limited (although Jesuits worldwide came to know it well), and it was not available in English. When Sewall dispatched his overseas agent to find a copy of the rare 1592 Cologne edition that contained *Procuranda*, it offered him and Mather insight into the learning process of these earlier evangelists.[12]

Doctrinas, the small Indian-only settlements preferred by the Franciscans who had first begun this colonial work, were supposed to provide their parish priests with the opportunity to pick up the local tongue through immersion and constant practice. In return, they would teach the neophytes Spanish. But Acosta felt the results in Peru were very uneven. He intimates that these priests had only managed to do what a trader would, cobbling together a rudimentary pidgin or resorting to gesture and sign: time-honored contact language practices, but dangerously insufficient when it came to explaining doctrines like the Trinity. He argues that parish priests who don't know the local language are no better than "mercenaries" because they cannot protect their flock from corrupt translations. These might slip through by way of Indigenous translators, whom parish priests often used as simultaneous interpreters. Priests would deliver the liturgy in Latin, but Acosta wanted them fluent enough in the local tongue to deliver their own homilies.[13]

American languages, Acosta writes, are uniquely diverse, and learning them calls for brave new approaches and dedication. If Babel had split the ancient world into seventy mutually unintelligible tongues, as biblical history had it, "these Barbarians here have at least seven hundred!" ("Barbarians" is not an insult but a category indicating those who have not been exposed to Christianity.) *Procuranda* wrestles with the question of what counts as a dialect and what as a language. Acosta urges perseverance:

although it is a very hard and tiresome business to learn a foreign language, especially if it is a barbarous one, it is a great victory to do so
and the fruits of it all are exceedingly sweet, as well as being a great
testimony to the love of God.... Those that have a different language
must hear it in their heart-language and in their sentiments.

Acosta values affective attachment to one's "heart-language" in a way that goes
beyond pragmatics. "We ought not to give up acquiring the language, and to
teach it to the Indians, for the law of love dictates that it is better that we go
to them, rather than that they come to us." The phrase "It is better that we go
to them" makes a profound ethical stance: it values the difference and "tiresome" difficulty of the other's "heart-language" more than the surety of one's
own. Yet there is a price. Missionaries will get hold of the sweet fruit of other
people's language, then they will transform it into something that can be taught
back to the very people who owned it in the first place. Quechua speakers
should hear the Gospel in their own tongue, Acosta argued, but only after the
grammar and lexicon of that language had been studied sufficiently to prevent theological errors. Only then could Indigenous people be trusted to be
priests. Systemization, presented as the result of a two-way exchange motivated by the evangelist's love of the Indian, would enable surveillance.[14]

American Languages under Grammar's Orders

How does one explain the contradiction of Acosta's advice to "acquir[e] the
language, and then teach it to the Indians," the very people to whom it belonged? Alphabetization and grammaticalization are the answer. Missionary
priests, trained in the Scholastic tradition and deeply fluent in Latin, attempted
to order the speech they encountered within predominantly Latin alphabets
(although some innovated, or borrowed from Middle Eastern scripts, new
characters and diacritics to express phonetics, emphasis, and intonation). But
Greek and Latin, and the related languages later to be classified as Indo-
European, were sentence-based or fusional. Speaking very generally, most
Amerindian languages have a different morphological structure, or way of re-
arranging bits of language to make meaning: they are agglutinative, adding affixes
to the beginning, middle, or end of certain root words, usually verbs. Latin

grammatical texts, on which Nebrija's grammar was patterned (as were subsequent ones for European vernaculars), began with the alphabet and its pronunciation, and proceeded through the parts of speech from verbs and their conjugations to nouns, pronouns, and adjectives and their declensions. Syntax rules followed, explaining where to place these words.

The Latin-grammar model does not align well with agglutinative or compounding languages, in which affixes are added to the beginning, middle, or end of a morpheme and convey what would take a Latin or English sentence to express. A single complex word can convey meaning not only about an action and the time-frame in which it takes place but also about whether the subjects and objects are animate or inanimate, as well as many features of the environment. To reduce such expression to a single equivalent Spanish or Latin verb, as the grammaticalizers tried to do, was a recipe for failure to grasp key aspects of Indigenous epistemologies and cosmologies. Ushering these languages into Western grammaticality also forcibly standardized them, or rather designated one dialectal variety as the standard, much as the court variety of speech in Castile was to be the standard for all of Spain. Nonetheless, many missionary linguists editorialized admiringly on the expressive qualities of some feature of a language, and, like Nebrija, opined freely on where the purest and most refined varieties were to be found. With mostly uncredited Indigenous collaborators, these missionary linguists recorded and then tested each linguistic observation, moving back and forth between speech, gesture, and writing. Manuscript versions of their earliest vocabulary lists and grammatical schemes show the dynamic nature of this corrective and dialogic process. Print, however, lent them an aura of finality.[15]

The colonizing of the Americas had occurred, of course, alongside the technological refinement of movable type and printing, which exponentially increased the circulation of vernacular as well as Latin books. The idea persists that print was mainly a tool of the Reformation, but ample evidence demonstrates the contrary: not only did the Catholic Church directly introduce printing into many places, it embraced the possibilities of this form of dissemination with a motto of "control and exuberance," as one scholar put it. Despite the Inquisition and the elaborate licensing process it required (early books are prefaced with many pages of permissions to print from various officials), hundreds of thousands of books printed on the other side of the Atlantic poured into New Spain in the sixteenth and seventeenth centuries. Most of these were printed in Spain, but some twenty thousand items are thought to have been printed by the several presses in Mexico City (and later, in Guadalajara and Antigua, Guatemala) prior to 1800. The printing of grammars and vocabularies of Indigenous languages was, Marina Garone Gravier argues, a primary rationale of the establishment of the first American printing press in Mexico-Tenochtitlán in 1537 in order to accommodate the bilingual order described earlier in this chapter. Language learning, scholarly ordering and standardizing, and Christian indoctrination were all loosely conjoined in the work of the sixteenth-century press in Mexico-Tenochtitlán.[16]

Alonso de Molina's *Vocabulario en lengua mexicana* (1555), the first bilingual Indigenous-language work to be issued from the press following the work of other writers in manuscript, ushered in other printed works in Nahuatl, Otomí, Purépecha, Huastec, Mixtec, Zapotec, Tepehua, and several Mayan languages, some accompanied by Spanish and a few not. According to Garone Gravier's count, 287 works in twenty different Mesoamerican languages were published in Mexico City before 1600. Together, these represented 17 percent of early Mexican imprints, a significant number given that most other productions of the press were shorter governmental and ecclesiastical decrees; as language policies shifted in the following century, that number markedly decreased. Generally, for each language an *Arte* (grammar) and *Vocabulario* (lexicon) would be produced. Also fundamental was the *Doctrina Breve*, as the shorter Tridentine catechism was called; in some languages there was also a *Catecismo Mayor* (Greater Catechism), a longer version that included Bible stories. In a few languages, a *Confesionario* (Confessional) offered scripts to help priests understand all manner of potential sins so they could administer the sacrament of confession. Long books of prefabricated sermons (*Sermonarios* or *Pláticas*) were produced in Nahuatl. Contemporaries sometimes referred to all these publications, where doctrine and linguistic information were comingled, by the general term *catecismos*. Together with the marked-up manuscript records of missionary language encounters, these printed works—arranged along a scale from simpler to more complex—make up what Ralph Bauer calls "one of the main and earliest genres of colonial American literature—the 'art' of reducing non-Western languages to the rules of writing grammars and dictionaries." (Ways of reading these genres literarily are further explored in Chapter VI.)[17]

This print project was well underway by the time Acosta reached Lima, where press production lagged noticeably behind that of Mexico-Tenochtitlán. At the request of the third Provincial Council meeting in Lima, which was still roiled in debate about restrictions on Indigenous language use, Acosta followed up *Procuranda* in 1583 with a trilingual catechism in Spanish, Quechua, and Aymara, the first book to be published in Peru: *Doctrina christiana, y catecismo para instrvccion de los Indios.* In *Procuranda,* Acosta outlines three pillars by which the massive challenge of evangelizing the Americas may be met: the university, the printing press, and what he calls "genuine love of the Indians," which will be expressed person-to-person:

> now many elegant and copious writings, whose lessons may be of use to the serious student, have been published so that every day, better and more prepared people are being turned out [to the missionary field]. Through reading these works, learning them off by heart and through frequent written exercises of imitation, our knowledge of the language will rapidly increase, so that the chairs of native languages that are publicly established are very useful indeed. But all these are just theory and a shadow of what the real struggle is all about. We have to enter the real world and study seriously with the Indians themselves through frequent conversation and through hearing and speaking with them, the language will then become familiar to us. Then we have to move on to sermons, leaving behind shame and fear. In fact we have to make many mistakes to learn not to make any mistakes! At first we will have to carry the grammar in our head and the words, but later on the words themselves will follow the grammar automatically.

Language learners who are introduced to these "elegant and copious" printed works in educational institutions will be cycled into oral immersion ("enter the real world and study seriously with the Indians themselves"). Acosta's attention to the affective dimension of this process ("leaving behind shame and fear," being accepting of mistakes, iterative learning, using *realia* and immersion) resonates with contemporary best practices for second-language acquisition. Reading and writing, listening and speaking are set into reciprocal and reiterative process. Although *elocutio,* eloquent and correct style, would seem like the most difficult skill for a non-native speaker to master, Acosta had insisted on it: only by approaching the local linguistic culture on its own terms could a priest be truly effective. He states that wherever a parish priest is fluent in the local tongue, the *Indios* are reverent and faithful Christians. When addressed in their own language, the people "follow him with the greatest attention and are delighted by his eloquence, becoming carried away with emotion.

There they are, open-mouthed with their eyes riveted on him, hanging on his every word." *Procuranda*, then, did not so much invent as systemize an ac-commodationist practice of evangelizing by "going to them," in contrast to the assimilative process of imposing a colonial language upon proselytes.[18]

Print and School in New England
Missionary Linguistics

Christian missionary linguistics, sparked by the vast field of potential converts appearing in America and expanding to the rest of the globe, profoundly in-formed modern Western linguistic theory, even as the figure of the pioneer European in a language encounter morphed from a missionary into an eth-nographer intent on discovering racial difference during the eighteenth and nineteenth centuries, as Sean Harvey's history of the American roots of the field shows. For that intellectual history, the sectarian difference between Cath-olic and Protestant would seem meaningful: Edward Gray argues that they shared a concept of language as a "gift from God," but the stress on verbal elo-quence among Catholics (Jesuits in particular) and on training for individual Bible reading among Protestants led their theories of language in ultimately different directions. Given the evidence for New Spain and Peru as hubs of textual production and dissemination, as well as an amplified notion of com-munications and "mediascapes" that includes Native inscription in all its forms, a simple oral / written distinction seems unhelpful. The task is to decide how much relative significance to assign to the Bible itself in the plurilingual spaces that missionaries cultivated. En route to Mather's transmission of what he would call the "express words" of that Bible in *La Fe del Christiano*, then, we need to assess how the first Protestant evangelists approached the task of learning and using Indigenous languages in light of their belatedness relative to the Catholics. Keeping the focus on the New England Company as the di-rect through-line to Mather, as outlined in Chapter III, the locus of sectarian comparison will be the work of John Eliot, Thomas Mayhew, and the Wam-panoag people who aided each of them in learning their Eastern Algonquian tongues.[19]

Whether or not the founders of the New England Company had direct ac-cess to Acosta's *Procuranda*, their shared training in humanistic traditions, and their shared investment in the printing press, resulted in language learning practices similar to those of the Catholics who had preceded them. Thomas Gage, that influential double agent, shared information about these practices in *The English-American*. When Gage arrived in northeastern Guatemala in the 1620s, the Dominicans there had already "composed grammars and dictionaries" in Pokom'chi, a Mayan tongue. One "gave me therefore a short abstract of all the rudiments, which consisted chiefly of declining nouns and conjugating verbs, which I easily learned in the first fortnight, and then [memorized] a dictionary of Indian words." Then, he writes, "I practiced what I had learned by talking with the Indians, until I was able myself to preach to them." Gage uses Acosta's paternalistic language of Christian love to describe the work of the evangelist and his *elocutio*, as does Eliot. Unlike Gage, however, Eliot remains humble about his fumbling mistakes with Wampanoag, which he finds very difficult, and like Acosta he is overwhelmed by a profusion of usages that he is unsure whether to call different dialects or different languages. Eliot, too, began with an affective connection: he claims to have learned the language from a Wampanoag child translator who had learned English after being taken captive in the First Pequot War. Recording notes from these encounters, testing and correcting his hypotheses, Eliot eventually published *Indian Grammar Begun* (London, 1666), a century after similar pedagogical texts had begun appearing in Mexico City/Tenochtitlán.[20]

"Legendo, Scribendo, Loquendo, are the three means to learn a language," Eliot wrote at the start of the *Indian Grammar Begun*, emphasizing the classical pedagogy in which he had been trained with this Latin formula: reading-writing-speaking. The idea of four interconnected proficiencies—reading/writing, listening/speaking—naturalized itself in the era of print, and endures as a basic tenet of language teaching today. Eliot leaves out the role of active listening, the *audiendo* that pairs with speech, erasing his initial acquisition stage and emphasizing the end goal: to achieve the eloquence of legendary evangelist-preachers. The *Indian Grammar Begun* was meant, like the productions of the Mexican and Peruvian presses, to train other preachers and teachers through his grammaticalization, both European and Indigenous (Acosta's "teaching the language back to them"). The way Eliot frames this phrase with reading and writing at the forefront reflects his Cambridge-trained orientation to look to the universities, with their apparatuses of libraries and associated scholarly publishing arms, as authoritative sources of knowledge. Training ministers was the central objective of Harvard, founded in a second Cambridge in 1636. It did not establish a chair or professorship in Indigenous tongues, as the

University of San Marcos had, but it did establish, at the New England Company's behest, a program to train converted Massachusett, Narragansett, Wampanoag, Pequot, Mohegan, and Delaware youth and send them to minister to their people. These scholar-ministers were taught in English, Latin, Greek, and Hebrew, but forbidden to speak the languages in which they were supposed to preach to their people. Segregated into their own cramped quarters, the Indian College was a far cry from the Colegio de Tlatelolco. Only a handful attended (among them Caleb Cheeshahteaumuck, whose Latin address gives powerful evidence that these students were intellectual equals), and most died at tragically young ages.[21]

The longer-term strategy of the New England Company imagined print as more long-lived than persons. The Cambridge Press replaced the Indian College in its building in Harvard Yard. As mentioned in Chapter III, it took in substantial donations of equipment to make available Algonquian-language works that would be useful both for incoming English missionaries and for literate Wampanoag. As in Mexico and Peru, the Cambridge Press produced works of doctrinal-linguistic instruction of ascending size and difficulty, beginning with a catechism (1653), a brief outline of doctrine with the Ten Commandments and the Lord's Prayer, Genesis (1655), Matthew (1655), the New Testament (1658), and finally the entire Bible (1663). Later, this library in Algonquian would be augmented by the *Indian Primer* (1669), Eliot's *Indian Dialogues* (1671), a few translations of tracts and sermons originally written in English (including one of Mather's), and the later contribution of Experience Mayhew, the *Massachusett Psalter* (1709). Because Eliot's inner circle of linguistic experts was drawn from the praying town of Natick, its Nipmuc dialect was the basis for the standardized written form, and Native converts like James Printer/Wawaus, Job Nesuton, and Cockenoe appear to have done much or most of the translation, composing, and skilled printing, as recent scholars have persuasively shown. These productions, like the Florentine Codex, might be better thought of not as products of Eliot's consistent authorial hand, but as the work of a *taller* like Sahagún's in Mexico.[22]

By the time Cotton Mather got to Harvard in 1675, however, this gestating experiment in the coexistence of Indigenous language with English and Latin in the devotional-intellectual realm was already fading. The battles of King Philip's War came within a few miles of the college, and Increase Mather was reported to have sent Cotton, as a young man, to hold up Metacom's skull as a sign of English victory. Cotton Mather witnessed not the apogee but the decline of missionary linguistics in New England. As he lionized Eliot later in *Triumphs of the Reformed Religion* (1691) and *Magnalia Christi Americana* (1701), Mather surely had a hand in the erasure of Indigenous collaborators who had been vital to the very accomplishment for which he most praises Eliot: the "Indian Bible." In the passage on "Criolian degeneracy" in the 1689 Election Sermon that had brought him to public prominence (discussed in Chapter II), Mather warned that the "the seminaries of Canada or Mexico" were producing priests rapidly. Gage had described the colleges in Chiapas and Guatemala City derisively, but if he had already read the chapters on the universities in Lima and Mexico City/Tenochtitlán in Grimstone's translation of Acosta's *Natural and Moral History*, he would have had a good grasp on the Catholic educational infrastructure elsewhere in America. In *Triumphs*, he presents Eliot as an improved version of his Spanish predecessors but he imaginatively deprives those Mexican seminaries of books. Linking Eliot's sacred task to Harvard's, he writes,

> One of his Remarkable Cares for these illiterate Indians, was to bring them into the use of Schools and Books. He quickly procured the benefit of Schools for them; wherein they profited so much; that not only very many of them quickly came to Read and Write, but also several arrived unto a Liberal Education in our Colledge, and one or two of them took their degree with the rest of our Graduates. And for Books, t'was his chief desire that the sacred Scriptures might not in an unknown Tongue be Locked or Hidden from them; very hateful and hellish did the policy of Popery appear to him on this Account; Our Eliot was very unlike to that Franciscan, who writing into Europe gloried much how many thousands of Indians he had Converted, but added, That he desired his Friend would send him the Book called the Bible; for he had heard of there being such a Book in Europe, which might be of some use to him.

Mather is evasive about how, exactly, the "sacred Scriptures" are "Locked" away from Native people: were they hidden until proselytes learn to read in English ("many of them quickly came to Read and Write"), or hidden because until their own tongue had been raised to coeval status as a printed language? It is not clear which "Franciscan," supposedly ignorant of the very existence of the Bible, Mather means, but the Black Legend origins of this jab are unmistakable. Soon after *Triumphs* was published, and as Mather recast and repurposed his life of Eliot, the Indian College / Cambridge Press building was destroyed in 1693.[23]

It was also in these earlier works that Mather made often-quoted derisive comments about the nature of Indigenous languages, mocking the word length produced by agglutination in *Magnalia*. In *Triumphs,* he posited that the absence of the [r] sound in Algonquian was a mark of barbaric status. There is no real evidence that he knew so much as a greeting phrase in any Native language (he claims to have addressed a demon once in Algonquian), although his beloved uncle John Cotton had been a missionary among them and Cotton's son Josiah far surpassed him in linguistic skill, writing out a vocabulary. The sincerity of such statements is difficult to judge, but it is unfortunately common to find similarly disparaging references about the "barbarous" nature of Indigenous languages in the commentaries of avowedly sympathetic Europeans like Acosta. Mather's pride in having sermons of his translated into Algonquian and Iroquois will be discussed in Chapter IX, but for the moment we can observe how his identification with Eliot's heroism in ensuring that "the sacred Scriptures might not in an unknown Tongue be Locked or Hidden" transfers onto his Spanish project.[24]

The phrase recalls Article I of *La Religion Pura:* "La Palabra de Cristo en sagrada Escritura, deve ser Gozada, Buscada, y Sabida par las Gentes de todas suertes: y es una grande Iniquitad, impedir el Vulgo de Leer de aquella preciosa palabra de la Vida" (the Word of Christ in holy Scripture should be enjoyed, sought out, and known by people of all sorts, and it is a great iniquity to keep the common person from reading out of that precious word of life). Just as the Cambridge Press's Indian Library had begun with catechisms and proceeded gradually toward a translation of the entire Christian Bible, *La Fe del Christiano* may have been conceived as a forerunner of a library of devotional works in Spanish. The tracts formed a selective Bible in miniature, a tiny seed of what might have come: Sewall continued to imagine "the bombing of Santo Domingo, the Havana, Porto Rico, and Mexico itself" with "Spanish Bibles" in a letter sent a few years after Mather's work was published. The Chapter VIII will return in detail to the production of *La Fe* and its afterlife. The point here is that with such defenses of preaching, printing, and reading in the vernacular, Mather casts himself as an American evangelist in the heroic shoes of John Eliot: both of them following in the footsteps of Tyndale and Luther. Accusing the Catholic world of a "great Iniquity" in suppressing the word of God, he makes Protestants appear to be the only Christians who embraced the printed book as a devotional technology in the Americas. It is a painful irony that Mather makes this claim in the twilight of those brief decades when Algonquian-language texts were issuing from the Boston press, and as the number of printed works in several Indigenous languages of Mexico and Peru were also declining. Setting aside the genre of Bibles for personal use, the differences between print cultures in the early colonial North and South are principally a matter of scale, not of kind.[25]

Jus Divinum: The Question of Language Rights

To close this overview of missionary linguistic and language practices in the Americas, let us return to Mather's carefully cited reference to *De Procuranda Indorum salute* on the title-page verso: "But the Church cannot modify or take away what is a divine right." Placed next to the injunction to come away from Babylon, glossed as Rome, it suggests that a Christian has a *divine right* to break away completely from the Catholic Church. Acosta's original phrase, however, referred to a different aspect of the question about when there might be a higher authority than that of the Church. "But as the Church cannot modify or take away what is a divine right, so from that it has been deduced that it is not a divine right for people to receive the Eucharist, even at the hour of death." The line appears in the final section of the book, in which Acosta protests the practice of not allowing Indian converts in Peru to partake of the Eucharist, or Lord's Supper. That effectively rendered them second-class Catholics. Mather has taken Acosta's sentence completely out of its radically egalitarian context.[26]

Like Mexico's 1550 ban on ordaining Indigenous priests, the ban on taking Communion was an anxious, racialized response to the theoretical equality of converts who had demonstrated sincere piety. In Mexico, some Indian converts did take the Eucharist, but there was fear that their own notions of transubstantiation and ritual eating would get in the way of approaching this with proper holiness. Maintaining a bright line between the Eucharist and existing rites that seemed cannibalistic was of paramount importance for evangelists of both sects. The New England Congregationalists also regulated access to the Eucharist, limiting the sacrament to those who had been admitted to full church membership after affirming a conversion experience. Instead of reinforcing the caution of Mather's own church, however, Article IX of *La Fe del Christiano* supports Acosta's tendency to view Holy Communion as a divine right for all Christians. Mather composed, on his own, this sentence: "El Detenimiento del Vaso de los Legos en Eucharistia, es Praesuncion y Sacrilegio Vedado par nuestro Señor Jesu Christo" (Holding back the cup from laypersons at Eucharist is a presumption and a sacrilege, prohibited by our Lord Jesus Christ). The thrust of it is to undermine priestly authority altogether, rather than to uphold the Congregationalist view that gave church leadership authority to decide who could take Communion.[27]

La Fe del Christiano begins, then, with an intertext from the most famous missionary linguist about the rights that God gives to believers directly. But it extends Acosta's *jus divinum* into a more generalized right to hear the Gospel in a language the common person can understand. Mather may have struggled to find equivalent Spanish terms for the common person and lay person, and his reading of *Procuranda* may have influenced his linguistic decisions. This passage contains a Castilian term already antiquated in his day: *lego,* rather than *laico,* to mean the laity (laypersons, not priests who had taken sacred vows). *Lego* did not appear in any of the early modern English-Spanish or polyglot dictionaries that are described in the imaginative reconstruction of his library in Chapter VI, although *Vulgo* does. Acosta frequently uses the Late Latin *laicus* and its classical predecessor, *vulgus.* Historical morphology later became one of Mather's intellectual hobbies: there are extensive notes in his *Quotidiana* in the early 1700s about the derivations that Spanish and other Romance languages took from Latin. By following Acosta carefully here, he could have inferred Spanish *lego* based on the progression of *vulgus* → *vulgo.* In a consonantal shift, the Latin *c* became the Spanish *g:* for instance, *lacum* → *lago* and *sacrātum* → *sagrado. Laicus* → *lego* would have made sense. Both *vulgo* (in "Todos Exercisios de la Religion hechos en la Iglesia de Dios, deven ser hechos en Lengua sabida a Vulgo") and *lego* are categories that democratically include all nonordained Christians—that is, all who are not priests or ministers—regardless of their ethnic origin, regardless of the language they speak.[28]

Within the contemporary logic of human rights, a twentieth-century postwar rhetoric, there is still no consensus that language is a fundamental human right. The United Nations, which has issued statements about linguistic discrimination, does not possess any means to enforce such a right: to the contrary, national, colonial, religious, and market institutions conspire at many levels to render the speakers of some languages less powerful than others. Mather's idea of *jus divinum* was not the same as the modern notion of human rights, but his repurposing of Acosta's radical position on individual rights outside the purview of the Church suggestively moves from participating in a single sacrament, Communion, into something larger: using one's own native tongue. Mather peppers the first thing he composed in Spanish with three variations on the theme of language rights. He is not simply echoing Luther's old complaint against the Latin Mass but thinking through the terms of a dilemma that the English empire inherited as soon as it tried to imitate its Catholic predecessors: how to assimilate an Indigenous America whose continued sovereignty it could or would not allow. As with the use of the Aztlán myth to understand diabolical events in Salem, Mather in *La Fe del Christiano* adapts Acosta to his own purpose, triangulating Eliot's missionary work into a new historical stage that would be his own.

· V ·

Becoming a Spanish Indian

———————

Mather left only two thin accounts of his process of learning Spanish. One, in the *Diary*, reported that he was able to write in the language after only "a Fortnight's study": Thomas Gage claimed to have learned Pokom'chi in the same amount of time, so perhaps he had that earlier missionary linguist in mind. The description in *Paterna* offers a bit more detail:

> I will on this Occasion mention to You, My Son, One pretty Strange Experiment. I have rarely had upon my Mind any Strong *Impulse* to address *another Nation* in their *own Language*, but I have had a Scarce accountable Assistance, in a *few Dayes* to come at that *Language*. So far, that I have with my own Hand, and Skill, Written Books in it, which have been printed for the Intended Services. I have Books Extant in more than Two or Three of the *Living Languages;* the Good Effects whereof I am Waiting for. But then, by Disuse, and for want of Conversation, I have Soon Lost some of these Languages.

The "Two or Three" living languages included French and Spanish; the "or" perhaps reflects uncertainty about how to classify the Algonquian and Iroquois works that were translated for him. The passage suggests both independence and collaboration: "my own Hand, and Skill" wrote the tracts, but only through "Scarce accountable Assistance." What kind of help could not be rationally accounted for; what was "Strange" to the sensations (the eighteenth-century sense of "experiment") about this process? Mather follows Acosta and Eliot in assuming that writing and speaking reinforce each other ("by Disuse, and for want of Conversation, I have Soon Lost some of these Languages"). The "Scarce accountable Assistance," then, suggests the unexpected help of one or more persons whose dialogue helped him learn. Who could have offered Spanish conversation?[1]

Joseph and Samuel Frazon, the Sephardic Jews who claimed Ladino Spanish as a heritage and perhaps a private home language, are candidates. At some undetermined date, however, Mather deeply damaged his relationship with one or both brothers by manufacturing what Sewall called a "Pretended Vision," a "Forgery." Moreover, Samuel was frequently at sea on trading voyages. Another source of assistance, however, may have been as near as Mather's own household, in the form of a servant referred to as a "Spanish Indian." Just as omnibus terms like *African* and *Negro* erased distinctions between Mande, Ibo, or Kongolese, the category of *Indian* forcibly melded together a multitude of peoples with intricately developed cultures, languages, and histories of interethnic relations, whose difference from one another was sometimes acknowledged and sometimes caustically ignored. "Spanish Indian" may have been used as an ethnonym, to set apart Indigenous people from far away whose tribal affiliations were not among those known to the English, or it may have been what I am calling a loquonym, to indicate that this person spoke Spanish either as a first or second language. An Englishman in Carolina in 1657 gives a report that one of "our Indians" (an ally from the Sewee people) had spotted an opposing party of "Spanishe Indians." Mather's repeated used of *Spanish Indian* is another early use of a term with a violent history, one that would be used increasingly over the course of the eighteenth century.[2]

La Fe del Christiano, Mather wrote, was destined for "the several parts of the *Spanish* America." Habsburg Spain divided the governance of America to four *virreinatos* or viceroyalties, leaving the Council of the Indies to administer an overlapping structure of *real audiencias,* or royal courts. Mather may have been intrigued by Acosta's account of Peru, but the *Virreinato* closest to him was Nueva España (New Spain). New Spain was further divided into "several parts": five *audiencias* whose capitals were Manila (protecting Pacific and Indian Ocean trade routes), Guadalajara (northern Mexico, including what are now the western and southern parts of the United States, a region dominated by sovereign Indigenous people), Antigua (present-day Central America and southern Mexico), Mexico City (which governed the valleys, mine-rich mountains, and the port cities around it), and Santo Domingo (seat of governance for the Caribbean islands and the northern coast of South America). Mexico-Tenochtitlán, which Sewall understood to be the most splendid and populous city in the hemisphere, seemed far distant. But the vast lands claimed by Spain and England increasingly touched at their North American fringes. Their border was Carolina, a tenuous English claim that, in this period, was finally consolidating as a colony with a feasible master plan of settlement. The plan required beating back the military might of the Spanish and their Indigenous allies in La Florida. Where there is a borderland, there are border dwellers, refugees, travelers, and transients: the very people whose contact-language practices became the basis for the evangelizing described in Chapter IV. To consider the possibility of Spanish speakers closer to hand, this chapter returns to Mather's household: this time with a view toward the other nongenealogically related persons who went in and out of that household in the capacity of laborers.

A Special and Signal Return

The first reference to such a person in Mather's writing appears in 1681. At eighteen years old, having just completed his master's degree at Harvard and not having yet begun his steady stream of published sermons, he somehow found the means to present his father Increase with an extravagant gift:

> I bought a *Spanish Indian,* and bestowed him for a *Servant,* on my Father. This Thing, I would not remember in this Place [i.e., the diary], but only because I would observe whether I do not hereafter see some special and signal Return of this Action, in the Course of my Life. I am secretly perswaded [*sic*], *that I shall do so!*"

Assuming that this "Spanish Indian" did not self-liberate from Increase's household or get sold, Cotton would have continued to see him daily for at least the next few years. Recalling that Mather recopied and redacted his diaries in later years, destroying the originals, the anecdote stuck because his own prediction did come true, proving the larger pattern of divine significance that Mather habitually sought in everyday life.[3]

The "special and signal Return of this Action" is recorded as happening in the late summer of 1696, during the period when Mather and Sewall were discussing Mede's millennial theories in the context of New Spain. It may have been around this time, too, that he experienced the angelic vision (described in Chapter II) assuring him that he would write important works in many tongues and thus evangelize to the whole world. Mather writes, at first, recursively, recalling his long-ago gift:

> About fifteen years ago, I bought a *Spanish Indian,* and bestowed him for a *Servant,* on my Father. About three Years ago, *Sir William Phips,* our Governour, bestowed a *Spanish Indian* for a *Servant* on myself. My *Servant* affecting the Sea, I permitted him, to go to Sea; and **being an ingenuous Fellow,** I gave him an Instrument for his Freedom, if hee serv'd mee till the End of the year 1697. Two years ago, the *French* took him, and I lost him. The Loss occasion'd mee to make a cheerful Resignation, unto the Will of God. But I was hereupon perswaded and often expressed my Perswasion, that my Servant would be **return'd** unto mee. In the beginning of the year, an English *Man of War,* by taking the vessel, wherein my Servant was, retook him. Nevertheless, the *Captain* of the Man of War, being a Fellow, that had no Principles of Honour or Honesty in him, I could, by no means recover my servant out of his hands, **who intended to make a perpetual *Slave* of him.** So, I gave over my Endeavors to recover him; chiefly troubled for the Condition of the *poor Servant.* But then, a strange Conjunction of Circumstances fell out, that the churlish Captain was compelled without any Consideration, but what I should please, to *restore* Him. And my Servant being **so strangely returned,** I sett myself to make him a Servant of the Lord. (Bold emphases mine.)

There is much to take in here: Mather's symbiotic relationship with governor William Phips; the apparent emotional attachment to "his" Spanish Indian (whom he sees as a deserved reward for his prior generosity); the man's tantalizingly untold story of Caribbean piracy; his deliverance into the hands of a villainous Englishman who means to enslave this redeemed captive; finally the mysterious change of the bad captain's heart, followed by a homecoming: a happy ending for Mather at least, who triumphantly claims another soul to evangelize.[4]

Mather offers little detail in the *Diary* or *Paterna* about his servants, except when noting as godly his efforts to instill piety and obedience in them. But if this bondsman spoke some Spanish, in addition to being geographically identified by his origins in Spanish territory, he could have been an agent in the "conversation" of the winter of 1699, perhaps even part of the intended audience of *La Fe del Christiano*. As previous chapters established, during the few years the man was absent at sea until the time he reappeared in 1696, Mather was engaging in discussions with Sewall about Spanish America. The anecdote ends with Mather pledging to "make him a Servant of the Lord." Eliot had done this with the Indigenous people who taught him to speak the Massachusett dialect, exchanging language skills and then proselytizing to them. Why, Mather may have thought, could he not follow Eliot's paternal lead, and do the same with "his" Spanish Indian?

Following the lead of historians of slavery who have challenged the traditional evidentiary norms of history for failing to convey either the subjectivities of the enslaved or the violence that attended their lives, this chapter speculates on the presence of this "Spanish Indian" in Mather's Spanish project. As with many such figures in the American past, the sole record of this man's existence is mediated by the words of people who enslaved him: what Saidiya Hartman names as "the scandal of the archive." I want first to flag the nonchalance with which Mather writes "I bought a *Spanish Indian*," and to reject the option of referring to him with a possessive, as "Mather's Spanish Indian." Instead, I will refer to him by the invented name of Tuqui. Modern reconstructions of the Timucua tongue once common across northern Florida have variously identified the word's meaning with the nouns "return" and "resurrection" or the verbs "arise," "grieve," "oppress": the proliferation of senses of the word seems appropriate to the impossibility of narrating his life, since there is no trace of it beyond this single mention in Mather's diary. Mather's use of "Return" here serves his own personal typology, allowing him to interpret Phips's gift of chattel as a "special and signal Return" of his oppressive gift to Increase Mather years earlier. My gesture of naming Tuqui, on the other hand, registers a grievance with that instrumental treatment, moving beyond the limits of the written evidence into what Hartman calls "critical fabulation": a recuperative strategy as impossible as it is necessary. It responds to the frustration of the archival dead end by acknowledging the desire for a new story—a story in which Tuqui might have *returned* to the place and people of his birth, or at least to sovereignty over his own person, outside the bounds of Mather's household.[5]

Although the passage offers no physical description of this man, it is clear that his features suggested enslavability to the "churlish Captain." Mather does not specify Tuqui's place of origin (about which he was surely curious, given his demonstrated interest in things "Spanish"), but he does find him, upon investigation, to be an "ingenuous Fellow." "Ingenuous" was a Latinism that entered learned English in the sixteenth century to indicate that one's innate character was noble and trustworthy (*In + genuus*, from *gignere*, to beget, thus "inborn"). Mather uses the term several times in *Magnalia* to indicate a gentlemanly character, but this is the only instance in which he applies it to a non-English person. It was also used by English writers to describe freeborn Romans, as opposed to freed former slaves: Mather knew this classical history well. In which sense, then, did Mather mean it? After Phips (a governor who had made his fortune in the Caribbean) transferred him as property, Tuqui must have engaged Mather in dialogue. In this unrecorded exchange, Tuqui communicated something to the minister whom he was now supposed to call Master: either that he was of noble birth, character, or education, or that he was legally freeborn and had been unjustly enslaved. Whether they spoke in English or some other idiom, Tuqui effectively expressed something about his life experiences, skills, and preferences, culminating in his "Affecting," or desiring, to be allowed to work at sea.[6]

Contractual servitude for both white and Indigenous people had been an important component of labor practices in the New England colonies from their inception. But the insurgency of King Philip's War further entrenched settlers' suspicion of Indians and expanded the numbers of chattel slaves in perpetual descent under the law. Slave status was becoming not a changeable result of warfare or unlucky circumstance, but a part of one's ontological being. It seems that Phips thought he was "bestowing" on Mather Tuqui's body in toto—but if the passage is indeed using "ingenuous" in its neoclassical sense, then Mather changed his mind about the legal status Phips had assumed about the man. As a result, Mather decided to commute his enslaved status to that of an indentured servant, writing a promise of manumission ("I gave him an Instrument for his Freedom") predicated on a four-year contract.[7]

There may have been a financial incentive for Mather to follow Tuqui's wishes and sign him to a ship's crew: perhaps he received an advance on the man's wages or was promised a share of profits upon the ship's return. Years later, Mather objected to the prospect of the "churlish Captain" putting an "ingenuous Fellow" in chains for life: "I could, by no means recover my servant out of his hands, who intended to make a perpetual *Slave* of him." Mather's claim is not without self-interest: the captain's found-property claim opposed Mather's, as the holder of his bond. But beyond the legal question of property, there was the legal question of personhood. The two appear to disagree on where Tuqui lands in the nascent order of chattelized race: the commodification and dominion, not just of a body's labor, but of its "perpetual" life and through one's descendants. Perhaps Mather's "Endeavors to recover him" involved going to a magistrate. Something or someone changed the captain's mind, however, and he was returned "without any Consideration [i.e., payment], but what I should please."

The diary's mediated account is silent as to Tuqui's features, origin, and speech communities or proficiencies. If his "Spanish" looks signaled a connection to New Spain, where would he have been classified within the system of *castas,* the intricate set of protoracial terms that sought to make sense of admixture, of colonial ethnogenesis? Or should "Spanish Indian" be read as an adjectival phrase here—a demonym for someone who came *from* the Spanish Indies, specifically meaning the Caribbean? In that case, was Tuqui Black? The term "Spanish Indies" was sometimes used in English, but much less commonly during this period than either "West Indies" or "Spanish America"; as an adjectival usage, it is rare. If any legal authority considered Tuqui a Spanish subject of African descent, this might make him enslaved or free, though the latter status would require a paper trail to prove his freedom. But within the Spanish empire, *Indios* were vassals who could not be legally enslaved. Mather's own confusion suggests that Tuqui's Spanishness have inhered in some other feature than his appearance: his language, or his affiliation with some other Indigenous nation in the Spanish Empire. It is not my intention to bring a final judgment to this productively unsettled question. Some other appearances of the noun phrase "Spanish Indian" in contemporaneous English texts, however offer material for our critical fabulation.[8]

A Spaniard in the Vineyard and a Florida Masquerade

In the 1660s, Eliot's contemporary Thomas Mayhew began to evangelize among the Gay-Head Wampanoag of Martha's Vineyard, where he had been granted land. Mayhew and his family learned the Wampanoag language themselves, helped shield the town from English wrath during King Philip's War, and made an ultimately doomed experiment at bilingual coexistence, propped up by the Society for the Propagation of the Gospel in later years. Mather had deep ties to this community, including family ties through his cousin, the linguist Josiah Cotton. In Experience Mayhew's *Indian Converts* (1727), a text from the last phase of that experiment meant to persuade the colonial government to leave the community alone, one of the exemplary subjects is a Christian named James Spaniard. Mayhew explains that "This Man was sir-named [*sic*] *Spaniard*, because **he was a Spanish *Indian*,** being, as I have heard, brought from some part of the *Spanish Indies* when he was a Boy, and sold in *New-England*" (bold emphasis mine). Tangled in a tautology whereby the Spanish Indies produce Spanish Indian-Indians, Mayhew makes it clear that New Englanders had always treated James Spaniard as both an Indigenous person and a foreigner. It seems to be taken for granted that after being freed by his white mistress he would live with other "Indians," even though the Gay-Head Wampanoag were not of his *ethnos* and he did not speak their language. Among them, the surname Spaniard reminds others of his incommensurable difference. Mayhew recounts that he was at first reluctant to join the Wampanoag church, but eventually did so despite his melancholy about not being able to return to his own country or speak again his native language. Mayhew offers James Spaniard's story as proof of what piety and grace can overcome. When the man came to speak to Mayhew about "the Concerns of his own Soul,"

> not being a Compleat *Master* of either the *English* or the *Indian* tongue, he could not express himself very aptly in either the one or the other of them; but the *English* he seemed to understand best.

James Spaniard married a woman who spoke the local Wampanoag dialect (said to be mutually unintelligible to the one spoken in Eliot's praying towns, although they shared printed texts). He could not speak it well, though, and prayed with her in English. Experience Mayhew, raised to be bilingual through immersion, would have been in a good position to judge Algonquian dialects, but he does not even hazard a guess at the language of which James Spaniard *was* the "Compleat Master." Was it Spanish, an Indigenous language from elsewhere in the hemisphere, or both?[9]

Another text from the period tracks the term Spanish Indian to the zone called La Florida: present-day Florida, Alabama, Georgia, and South Carolina. Jonathan Dickinson's extraordinarily popular true-adventure narrative *God's Protecting Providence* was published in 1699, the same year as *La Fe del*

Christiano. Shipwrecked en route from Jamaica, Dickinson's party of twenty-four men, women, and children, including ten slaves, passed themselves off as Spaniards to avoid being killed as they walked the "Wild Coast" of central Florida, then inhabited by the Jaega (or Jobe), Santaluz, and Ais people. Even a Quaker planter like Dickinson knew that Florida was Spanish territory where the English were hated: upon their first encounter with the locals, one mariner prostrated himself on his knees and gave a passing imitation of Catholic piety. Luckily for them, among the party was one Solomon Cresson, who possessed a valuable survival skill: "speaking the *Spanish* language well, it was hop't this might be a means for our delivery." Cresson coached the other men about how to perform their role as Spaniards by teaching them a few words, but they constantly feared their ruse would be found out. As the survivors made their slow way northward, they sought directions in Spanish from Indigenous people they met: not everyone understood, but several, from various tribes, did. As they drew nearer to the Spanish fort at St. Augustine, the number of Indians familiar with the Spanish language increased. One chief, who could "speak *Spanish* better than any we had met with yet," was unconvinced by their story, and pronounced Cresson to be "Nickaleer [Englishman], no Comerradoe," using the common term for a Spaniard (*camarado*). Escaping these threats, they were tested by a returned former slave in Cuba, who had learned English there. To judge the suspicious story the castaways were telling, he asked the group what some berries were called: "but perceiving his drift, and having learned the name of them, as the *Spaniard* calls them [*uvaes*], then he would tell us that the *English* called them *Plumbs* . . . for he would be striving to trapp us, viz, Joseph [Kirke], Solomon, and me, in words." Finally meeting a Spanish military patrol, they dropped the pretense altogether; the nineteen survivors eventually reached St. Augustine, where they were fed, clothed, and allowed by the Spanish authorities to pass on to English Carolina.[10]

Dickinson recounts their encounters, as they neared St. Augustine, with Christian, Spanish-speaking Amerindians living in towns: it was in one such place that the inhabitants "made a discovery of him [Cresson] to be no *Spaniard*," though these people did not harm him. Further north they spoke at greater length, presumably in Spanish, with "two or more *Indians* that were converted to the *Romish Faith.*" Dickinson is impressed by the relative prosperity and order of this mission town, where a resident friar gives them food. *God's Protecting Providence* offers firsthand testimony about the final decades of what had been a long coexistence between the people of the eleven Timucua chiefdoms and Spanish missionaries, soldiers, and a few ranchers in north-central Florida. Dickinson describes here what was a vital, transcultured region in which Spanish had long become entrenched among Indigenous people as a rudimentary form of communication with Europeans—a lingua franca for trade networks that extended outward in several directions from La Florida. Dickinson does not use the phrase "Spanish Indian," but his story is full of Spanish-*speaking* Indians who have made alliances but retain some autonomy over their own lives.[11]

Indigenous Adaptations in La Florida

La Florida had been one of the original Euro-American contact zones. Favorable winds and currents made it a relatively easy sail from Havana, and sixteenth-century history is punctuated by a long list of European expeditions: those of Pánfilo Narváez, Hernando de Soto, Tristán de Luna, as well as the Frenchmen Jean Ribault and Réné de Laudonnière. Anna Brickhouse, retracing the different tribal and imperial intersections in colonial Florida, identifies it as a premier zone for "unsettlement": the active choice-making of Indigenous persons when confronted with European desires. Using translational knowledge of European languages for their own ends was such a tactic, as the Dickinson narrative illustrates. The Calusa, Ais, and Tequesta in south Florida who toyed with the Dickinson group by testing their Spanish skills had thwarted many early efforts at settlement and missionization. The Timucua to the north, on the other hand, made a tentative alliance with early Huguenot settlers like Laudonnière, who established Fort Caroline in 1564, only to see French imperial prospects wither against Pedro Menéndez de Avilés's new stronghold in St. Augustine. (This early loss of a Protestant settlement in North America to the Catholic empire was known to Mather.)[12]

La Florida was centered on the town and fort of St. Augustine, established to protect the shipping zones around Havana and Veracruz yet dependent on the interior. Early governors tried to establish provisioning networks and military allies among Amerindians rather than subjugate them. Following the model of early New Spain, the Franciscans were called in to develop a network of doctrinas, or parish churches, with towns built around them. The network eventually extended to forty-four Christian towns among the Timucua-speaking chiefdoms and those of nearby language groups: the Guale of the present-day Georgia coast and the Appalachee of the northwestern Florida plateau. As in Mesoamerica, many Indigenous people found this social model adaptable to their needs after enduring several generations of new biological disease agent and ecological changes postcontact. The Timucua had lived in loosely confederated villages prior to contact, under a strong *cacique* structure based on matrilineal status and sometimes headed by female chiefs. These Timucua chiefdoms retained a fair amount of sovereignty for decades, many allying with the Spanish but living outside the mission towns; moreover, there is strong archaeological evidence that their religious practice was syncretic, strongly inflected by their own cosmology.[13]

At the height of their influence around 1630, the Franciscans claimed to have catechized 50,000 Indigenous souls in Florida; of those, 20,000 were baptized, leaving a sizable number who did not integrate into these church-centered spaces. Sixteenth- and seventeenth-century La Florida, like other provinces, was bifurcated into a República de Españoles (Republic of Spaniards) and a República de Indias (Republic of Indians), nominally segregating each group and assigning labor demands along with legal protections to *Indios* who were to be administered by the assigned religious order. State and church overlapped, and usually complemented, each other's control. Because St. Augustine was so wholly dependent on this mission interior for its food supply, Spanish governors mostly did not exercise the degree of brutal dominance over the local population that was typical in, for instance, the Andean mining region. Instead, in Florida between the mid-sixteenth and the mid-seventeenth centuries, Spanish Catholicism was modified and adapted into existing Indigenous social arrangements rather than replacing them. The social organization of La Florida, while far from a utopia, offered a different model than the hostile peace in New England during Mather's time. It was less harshly administered than the contemporaneous missions among the Pueblo peoples of the Southwest, who adopted Christianity in much lower numbers and overthrew their would-be conquerors for twenty years; it was also less zealously bent on eradicating all former lifeways than the Franciscan missionaries in late eighteenth-century California would be.[14]

This is not to suggest that relations in Timucua country were always peaceful. The Guale formed an organized uprising known as Juanillo's Revolt against the missionaries in 1597; the Appalachee, too, resisted the Spanish forcibly. The Timucua Rebellion of 1656 was a well-organized campaign spurred by the governor's thoughtless draft of additional warriors of the highest social rank, in violation of previous agreements; he further required they bring their own provisions during a time of food shortage. Most importantly for this story, the mission towns were the site of a new linguistic world, much evolved from the contact-zone practices of pidgin speech and trade jargons that characterized first encounter. The coexistence of Timucua proselytes and Spanish religious and military administrators was recorded in print, and it introduces an important point of comparison to the missionary linguistics described in previous chapters, from the Mexican Franciscans and Acosta through to Roger Williams, John Eliot, and Thomas Mayhew. This bilingual exchange persisted not just for one, but for three to four generations.

Pareja and the "Floridian Language"

The Franciscan priest Francisco de Pareja (1570–1628) arrived in Florida in 1595. Assigned to the doctrina of San Juan del Puerto, near present-day Jacksonville, Pareja claimed that he learned the Mocama dialect of Timucua in six months, and set out to streamline that process for his successors, as Acosta was doing in Peru. Pareja took note of the ten or more different varieties of this language spoken across the region, even as he standardized it into a written Timucuan. He quickly rose within the Franciscan organizational structure to become head of the province, and prepared several bilingual texts including three catechisms, a grammar, a vocabulary, a confessional, and a tract on Heaven and Hell that also contained the rosary and various devotions—all licensed by the Inquisition and published in Mexico City between 1612 and 1627. After Pareja's death, Gregorio de Movilla, another Franciscan, added two more short titles in 1635. Tellingly, by that time, Mocama had come to be called *la lengua floridiana* (the language of Florida), just as the Tenochtitlán dialect of Nahuatl became known as *la lengua mexicana*. All that is known of the Timucua language today comes from the sum of these written texts, which historian Alejandra Dubcovsky and linguist George Aaron Broadwell have extensively reconstructed.[15]

Pareja enthusiastically promoted Indigenous-language training among the Floridian parish priests. Although not a Jesuit, and he was not likely to have read Acosta's *Procuranda* before coming to Florida, there are instructive similarities. Pareja's "Prólogo al lector" to the 1614 *Arte* argues that not having a deep knowledge of the language of "los naturales" is dangerous both to the potential converts and to the priests, who imperil their own souls if they fail to ensure their flock's understanding. Previous missionary efforts in La Florida had failed, Pareja says, because "muy mucho nos impide la ignorancia de su lengua" (ignorance of their language impedes us very much). Missionaries, he says, would succeed "quando entienden lo que se les dize" (when [the priests] understand what [the Indians] are saying). He argues for extensive two-way language training: "it is insufficient to understand their language *more or less*, but rather one must learn, with much care, to understand well the words and manner of speaking that they have, because lacking this, it may happen that rather than preaching the truth, one preaches errors and falsehood" (emphasis in original). He rests his case on Romans 10:17 (faith is by hearing, and hearing by the word of God): "Y esta palabra de Christo se [h]a de predicar en lengua inteligible a los oyentes, para convertirlos y traerlos a la Fé, y confirmarlos en ella, por la inteligible predicacion" (And this word of Christ must be preached in a language understandable to the listeners, in order to convert them and bring them to the Faith, and affirm them in it, through preaching that can be understood.) Mather's words about reaching listeners "en lengua sabida a Vulgo" in *La Fe del Christiano* echo this doctrine as well.[16]

Pareja, not Williams or Eliot, is the nominal author of the first printed text in a language indigenous to the area that would become the United States. But he lacked one advantage that Eliot and his team of translators and skilled artisans at the Cambridge Press did have: immediate access to expensive printing equipment, which had been provided (as Chapter IV showed) by pious underwriters after a fundraising campaign in England. By Spanish law, only the capital of each *audiencia* was allowed to have a printing press. Thus, while it may not be surprising that the backwater military town of St. Augustine lacked one, so did the well-established city of Havana. The press in Santo Domingo, the administrative center of the Caribbean and Florida, was hamstrung by lack of materials and printed mostly broadsides. To make his books, Pareja had to travel to Mexico City, petition superiors in multiple offices to sign off on his materials, contract with the printers, supervise the reading of proofs, and carry the bound books back to Florida. This was a five-hundred-mile sail to Havana; another of twice again that length to Veracruz; and an overland journey of a month or more to the capital, for the Camino Real was as yet incomplete. It may be that he made the voyage only twice: four of the extant works bear copyright dates of successive years, followed by a long gap until the revised catechism in 1627. Pareja died in Mexico City in 1628, not yet fifty years old.[17]

Also like Eliot, Pareja clearly enlisted native speakers as collaborators: his *Catecismos* are lengthy, and the *Confesionario* alone contains hundreds of pages of material. These collaborators would have been brought up in the mission schools to be literate in their own language, and it would have been logical for one or more of them to accompany him to Mexico City to help with the process of correcting proofs; the many pages of errata suggest that this was done methodically. Several visitors to the Timucua missions mention converts who knew how to read and write their language, and Pareja boasted of the missions' success with literacy training. Pareja's fellow evangelists working in Central Mexico, such as the Franciscan Bernardino de Sahagún and the Dominican Diego Durán, provide a suggestive model of such collaboration, actively cultivating a class of multilingual, multiliterate Native intellectuals. The social arrangement of the Timucua, like that of the Nahua, rested on a matrilineal hereditary elite, and thus New Spain's model of colonial governance through a cooptation and cultural assimilation of the Native elite might have seemed a resonant model for Pareja's own: more like the Nahua, in any case, than the fearsome barbarians and cannibals depicted in other missionary accounts about the fringes of that realm. There is no Florida equivalent to the Florentine Codex produced by Sahagún's workshop, but the fact that the Timucua Rebellion in 1656 was plotted, in part, by means of letters sent among Timucua suggests that the people found no small utility in the *technē* of writing. A letter written in 1688 in Timucua by several chiefs to the Spanish king also survives, suggesting that even as the mission system was collapsing, some Indigenous people held onto literacy in their native language.[18]

Like the Cambridge Press in Massachusetts that published Eliot's Indian Library, Mexico City's Spanish-Indigenous printers operated under license from the colonial authorities. They struggled to adjust to conditions of an unreliable supply chain for materials like paper, ink, and type. The major difference between them was not that the Inquisition added an additional filter of bureaucracy and censorship, it was that each outreach project had a different vision of its ultimate goal—of the pinnacle in this ascending structure of producing increasingly complex and diversified texts in local languages. From the beginning, Eliot's aim had been to produce a Natick Bible. His team labored over the project for years, publishing some parts separately as they were completed. In the Catholic Americas, where the Bible was forbidden to lay readers, other advanced texts were translated once the basic works were completed:

theological tracts, dialogues, saint's lives, and devotional prayers. Among Pareja's lost Timucua works, according to his permission letters, were tracts describing Heaven, Hell, and Purgatory, and extolling the mysteries of the rosary: advanced reading, perhaps, for some of his Florida students. Chapter VI will explore some of these works in the context of the entangled genres of grammatical and doctrinal pedagogy.

As Dubcovsky and Broadwell point out, this considerable body of Timucua-language writing is little known despite the wealth of historical writing about Spanish Florida and, more recently, the literary-historical scholarship on New England print culture that centers the Algonquian work produced by James Printer (Nipmuc) and other Christian Wampanoag. Complemented by the output of Nahuatl-language works in particular in Mexico City, the literate Timucua stand as further evidence that Indigenous people were not the passive subjects of evangelization and imposed alphabetization, but rather active agents in knowledge production that has borne fruit for decolonization projects today. Yet this Floridian body of print is doubly peripheral, for it falls to the margins of two nation-based historiographic traditions that were imposed later. Mexican scholarship on Indigenous-language print does not include Pareja's and Movilla's texts—presumably because Florida was never part of the nineteenth-century national boundaries of the Estados Unidos de México, even though it had been part of colonial New Spain. Attention to the Algonquian Indian Library, on the other hand, reinforces rather than challenges the long historiographical tradition of making New England the metonymic place in which US culture supposedly originated. This is particularly true, as Chapter IV suggests, for print culture, which has been seen as the technological handmaiden to democracy because of the location of the first printing press and first newspapers in Boston. Both prior to and during the heyday of the Cambridge Press, the Timucua texts that circulated through Florida launched important transformations in language exchange, through both print and translation.[19]

Spanish Speakers in the Indigenous Southeast

Let us now return to Tuqui, and to the question of what "Spanish Indian" meant to Mather. What was the knowledge of Spanish among the Timucua, both those who joined the mission towns and those who did not? A 1630 visitor to Santa Elena observed children learning Spanish in the mission school. Whether one's initial exposure to the concept of the alphabet took place in Timucua or Spanish—or both at once—Pareja's *Vocabulario* and perhaps passages from the *Catecismo* might have been used as teaching texts in either direction. (The *Confesionario* was strictly for use by priests, and the *Arte* was geared toward Spanish learners of the language; the book of prayers and devotions does not survive, but such a text could have been allowable for a layperson to read.) Given the small number of missionaries and the many thousands of square miles of La Florida, Pareja's support for basic literacy instruction may have been a preliminary step toward cultivating a native class of lay priests. By 1606, there was a seminary at St. Augustine, presumably for male children in the República de Españoles, but if patterns from elsewhere in the *Reino* applied, there must have been mestizo children in the city as well. Pareja sent his brightest Timucua students to St. Augustine. In contrast to later practices in colonies like the Philippines—where priests and governors took pains to prohibit Indigenous people, even converts, from learning Spanish—the colonial language was heard and taught side by side with the native one in Florida's República de Indias. When the Timucua population plummeted in the later seventeenth century, privately owned haciendas were established and "Mexican Indians" were brought to labor there along with Africans, adding new linguistic inflections to this site of ethnogenesis.[20]

Given the many decades of prior contact with European voyagers, traders, and missionaries, some Floridian people would have already taken in some Spanish words and phrases orally. The cosmology of Genesis that is rehearsed at great length in the *Catecismo* instructs the Timucua that they are peers to those strangers: "De Adan y Eva descendemos todos, españoles, franceses, ingleses, moros, indios, y negros, y todo genero de gentes y los buenos Christianos yran al Cielo, y los malos al Infierno" (From Adam and Eve we are all descended, Spanish, French, English, Moors, Indians, and Blacks, and all manner of people; and good Christians will go to Heaven, and bad ones to Hell). In the Timucua version below this sentence, the words for "French," "English," and "Moors" are loan words from Latinate roots—*francesisco, inglesico, turcoco*—while "Spanish," "Indian," and "Black" all borrow in the other direction. That is, they add a descriptor to the Timucua noun *ano,* meaning "male person," and the intensifying suffix *-co: anonaioco,* combining *people + letter,* for "Spanish"; *anopiraco,* or *people + unbeliever,* for "Indian"; and *anochucuco,* or *people + black.* Such terms create new identities for these groups in the Florida context: they Timucuanize a new American social context. The loan words may attach to less essential concepts or less used terms: the French had already abandoned Florida, and Turks and Englishmen were so rarely seen in Pareja's time that the language did not require a neologism for them. All that would change, however, in the latter half of the seventeenth century.[21]

Beginning in the 1660s but accelerating sharply in the 1680s, slave raiders began to decimate the Timucua, Guale, and Appalachee towns: those with resident priests, and many others in the network without. Their numbers had already been dwindling due to disease and the disruptions to family life that occurred when St. Augustine ramped up its demands for labor tribute and food production. But as first the Westo—and later an assortment of other displaced peoples like the Yamasee, Apalachicola, and Creek—entered the lucrative trade of slaves for guns, their fragile population collapsed. (The Westo themselves were Iroquoian and had been pushed out of the Lake Erie region, and then out of Virginia, by an increasing English population.) While taking war captives as slaves had long been a practice among Mississippian peoples in this region, this moment applied a new and brutal commodity logic that yanked the practice outside of traditional models of alliance and rivalry, adoption and kinship. When Jonathan Dickinson describes the Spanish language-ruse in *God's Protecting Providence,* he fails to mention why the Amerindians they met had been so wary of Englishmen in the first place. The English had encouraged these slave raids (by proxy, so that they could not be accused of overt acts of war). The chaos induced by the intra-Indian slave trade was but one tactic in a complex struggle between England, seeking to expand its domain in the Southeast, and Spain, seeking to keep its toehold on the continent. It culminated in outright war in 1702. By that point, between 24,000 and 50,000 souls had been exiled from La Florida, transformed into commodities known as Carolina Indians and Spanish Indians.[22]

Unarmed, the Timucua in the doctrinas were easy prey. The towns were raided and abandoned one by one; by 1682 only ten mission towns remained, sheltering a thousand inhabitants. Raiders plunged further, targeting refugees and peoples who had never been missionized, and the tables turned on the Westos as the English came to fear the prospect of Indians with guns. Indigenous life across present-day South Carolina, Georgia, and northern Florida was transformed utterly, with the remnants of peoples coming together into new polities like the Yamasee. The fort at St. Augustine held a remaining Spanish military position, and the Amerindians who congregated there (among them, ironically, some Westos) intensified their identification with the Spanish colonial world as a way of defending themselves. After years of local Spanish officials pleading for help from *audiencia* officials, the last few Christian Timucua were sent to Havana in 1706 before the advancing British, refugees on their final exodus. Many of the Timucua fleeing slave raiders exhibited both traits: they were Spanish-speaking refugees who made the sign of the cross. Some holed up in St. Augustine and were sent by Spanish authorities to Cuba for protection. Others ran and hid and assimilated into the Creek and other newly forming communities.[23]

These refugees forged their survival through ethnogenesis. As La Florida and Louisiana were gradually incorporated into English territory, the Seminoles would form by absorbing the Yamasee and remnants of other Mississippian peoples and runaway African-descendant peoples: some repopulated abandoned mission towns in Florida. As Chapter IX elaborates, Indigenous and Black people came together more and more over the course of the eighteenth century, and even after the term "Spanish Indian" had all but disappeared in the nineteenth, traces of a Spanish-speaking Native world were noted in isolated places from the Florida panhandle to Arkansas.[24]

Spanish Indian Refugees in New England

The trade in Amerindian peoples of the Southeast was so lucrative because of the severe labor crisis that had gripped all the English colonies after white immigration dropped off at the end of the English Civil War. As previously mentioned, the presence of one or more Indian servants was common in seventeenth-century settler households. Some were seasonal wage-laborers who cooked and wove alongside English folk; sowed crops for and with them; traded and tanned leather and helped build ships and houses for them. Rarely, however, were they bound for life. Christianization, assimilation, and provisions against chattel slavery in English custom and law were marshaled to manage the terms of this coexistence, which—like the Timucua missions—was structurally unequal and not always peaceful, but was a coexistence all the same. It is well known that King Philip's wife and children were sold away to Bermuda as punishment for his revolt, but hundreds of other Wampanoag and their allies went with them, both as punishment and as a tactic to prevent further sedition. The atmosphere of paranoia and retribution that followed this outbreak of violence only magnified the abrupt drop-off in new immigrants from England and Scotland. To satisfy the labor shortage, new persons—pillaged from Spanish Florida and the Carolina border zone, as well as Caribbean-trafficked Africans—were forcibly brought there to fill the gap.[25]

Speculatively, Tuqui and James Spaniard might well have been culled from among those thirty or fifty thousand souls taken forcibly out of this region. They might have been descendants of Francisco Pareja's informants, mission-born neophytes who could speak some Castilian, or Spanish-allied Indigenous groups who necessarily cultivated some interpreters who could communicate with the Spanish, as Dickinson's party discovered. A year before the eighteen-year-old Cotton Mather "bought a Spanish Indian for my father," a party of Westos, Uchise, and Chiluque had raided Santa Carolina de Guale, one of the oldest missions. Two years before Governor Phips "gifted" Tuqui to him, the mission at San Juan de Guacara, along the Suwanee River, had been torched, and its people led off in chains. These were only two of the dozens, perhaps hundreds, of acts of organized human pillaging that swept through the region. If Tuqui was a second-, third-, or fourth-generation missionized man with some exposure to writing and textuality, he might have recognized himself as an addressee of Mather's tract for converting Spanish Catholics, for the Timucua word for "Christian" was also a loan word, the same one that appeared in the tract's title: *Christiano*.[26]

Even if he was not Catholicized, if he was simply someone born in the region during the fearful years of violence and chaos, forced to move from place to place in advance of slavers, a knowledge of how to communicate with Spanish soldiers and settlers would have been a great advantage to Tuqui. Jerald Milanich argues that as the dwindling mission towns became "refugee villages" clustered near the protection of St. Augustine, "it is probable that Spanish was heard as frequently as Timucua." During this forty-year Carolina-Florida border crisis, in which Native peoples were caught between the ever-diminishing choices offered by competing agents of colonialism, they often ended up working against each other. Some of the same Westo who had carried out Indian slave raids became part of this captive labor force of "Carolina Indians," and their antagonists the Yamasee too. Multilingual spies were highly prized, and even those who had not been part of the mission system tried to pass as Spanish.[27]

In theory, the two terms that Englishmen used in lieu of tribal belonging markers—"Spanish Indian" and "Carolina Indian"—could have been used to distinguish between captives originating in Spanish Florida (the Timucua,

Guale, Mocama, Appalachee) and those from the Carolinas, mostly their enemies (the Edisto, Catawba, Cusabo, Tuscarora). In practice, though, once these
people were treated as slaves, it is not clear how many people in Massachusetts could make a distinction between *Spanish* and *Carolina*. Ships from
Charleston brought both to Boston, and African-descended persons from the
Caribbean too. Sharp-eyed labor contractors were familiar enough by this point
with the appearance, dress, and self-presentation of a variety of Northeastern
Native peoples; the difference between a local and a "Carolina man" just in
from Charleston would have been palpable. And not only to the English.
The Gay-Head Wampanoag understood James Spaniard to be a different
sort of "Indian" from them. The additional gradation of "Spanish Indian"
arises from particular cultural or linguistic traits that marked them as *not from
here*. It could have been a few words or a fluent stream of the rival empire's
language spoken aloud. It could have been an unexpected knowledge of Christian practice in its "Romish" (in Dickinson's phrase), that is Catholic, form:
uttered Latin phrases, self-decorations with a cross, a gesture at prayer. As
was the case with Cotton Mather's retelling of the life of Tuqui, such terms
tell us little of what we really want to know about these outsiders. How did
they speak, eat, dress, love, survive? What alliances did they forge among other
dispersed peoples? How did "Spanish Indian" work in the assignment of degrees of freedom by the arbitrary measure of race, and how did it overlap with
"Spanish Negro"? These racial categories multiply in the period after *La Fe
del Christiano*, during the first quarter of the eighteenth century, to which
Chapter IX will return.

Most importantly for Tuqui's story, under Spanish law after 1679, *Indios*
could not be enslaved, although as vassals their labor could be conscripted. If
Tuqui had lived through the violence of the Carolina-Florida contact zone, it's
conceivable that he was a subject with certain legal protections, an "Ingenuous"
man in the Roman sense of the word: freeborn, in some way that he managed
to communicate to Mather. They could have struck a bargain. In their unequal
parley, Tuqui might have held the bargaining chip of something Mather
wanted at the time: skill in Spanish "Conversation," the lack of which, Mather
says, made him eventually lose his skills. The next chapter examines the formal
relationship between learning a language and learning doctrine through the
written genre that imitated two-way conversation—catechisms and dialogues—
and returns from there to Pareja's *Confessionario*.

· VI ·

Teaching by Catechism and Conversation

The speculative scene conjured in the previous chapter imagines Tuqui, the "Spanish Indian," being summoned to Cotton Mather's study to offer up the sounds of Spanish. Since teachers were referred to as "Masters," such a scene would ironically invert Tuqui's status as servant. Mather indicated that "Conversation" was an essential part of his language learning process, but this speculation may seem too far-fetched: Mather's study was lined with books; why would he seek out a native (or, in this speculative case, Native) speaker of it? Given the historical descent of Castilian from Latin, a language Mather knew well, could he not have crutched his way to a passable written proficiency in a modern Romance language? Having situated Mather within a tradition of missionary linguistics that moved dialectically between the spoken and written word in Chapter IV, this chapter retraces the speech-intensive methods he had followed for learning Latin as a child, and considers how they shaped later learning experiences. Early modern Latin acquisition involved successive building of the four proficiencies: listening/speaking and reading/writing. Mather's speech impediment as a youth may have made him especially attuned to the role of the body's speech organs in such processes. The timing of his Latin learning in early childhood is meaningful not only for what it tells us about the physiological and affective aspects of his multilingual skills, but for the way it connects the didactic genre of the catechism to the genre of *La Fe del Christiano*. Small Books like this taught the beginner basic articles of the faith: a kind of first grammar of Christianity.

Here, too, European contact with the Indigenous world through missionary linguistics prefigures Mather's attention to Spanish and, as Chapter IX shows, to French—the other rival Catholic tongue in the hemisphere. The catechism, a brief condensation of knowledge often but not always shaped as a script of questions and answers, was commonly used to instill not only religious doctrine but other forms of knowledge as well. Textbooks for literacy training in New England conjoined religion and the ABCs, working up an ascending ladder of size and complexity akin to the clusters of religious-linguistic texts produced by the missionaries and their Indigenous collaborators introduced in Chapter IV. With Tuqui's potential Florida origins in mind, this chapter returns to the Franciscan missions on the far northern reaches of New Spain, triangulating Mexico-Tenochtitlán and Boston/Cambridge with the Timucua-Spanish texts produced by Francisco de Pareja and Gregorio de Movilla. From vocabularies and pronunciation guides to grammar outlines to short and long catechisms, Catholic Indigenous libraries were produced gradually, beginning with shorter texts and scaling out to more complex ones, as the Algonquian Indian Library was. The sects divided, however, over the text at the pinnacle of that scale: the *confesionario* (Confessional) in the Catholic tradition, the Bible in the Protestant. Eliot's corps of Wampanoag translators had followed the custom of the Reformation's first Bible translators in releasing first one of the Gospels, then the New Testament, and then the entire Christian Bible; the works on language learning were issued later.

The genre of catechism, in its small form, cast the learner in the role of child. As employed by both Christian sects, it established a paternalistic relationship between the master (or answerer) and the student of doctrine or a second language. It was a conversation in which the questioner remained forever subordinate. In the language-learning context, listening with understanding and repeating back with one's own embodied speech were intended to be precursors to the production of original speech. In the humanistic dialogue, a didactic genre similar to the catechism, questions and responses were meant to serve as examples on which to model one's own arguments, rather than scripts that must be repeated by rote. Thinking about the scale of these Indian Libraries generates a question common to all pedagogical scenes: At what point is an initiate in a new form of knowledge, whether religion or a second language, encouraged to organize individual thought into original speech? To what degree is a proselyte encouraged or allowed to depart from the script, to move from catechism to dialogue, to talk back? Theories of Protestant individualism figure the apex of their model of missionary linguistics, individual Bible reading, as the sign of having achieved such competency. The *confesionario*, in contrast, retained the signal feature of the catechism: its arrangement into a fictive script of question and answer, which would seem to inhibit the learner's growth into individual initiative. But so did Mather's own leviathan of a text, the *Biblia Americana*. Thinking about the genres of religious-linguistic instruction along a progressive scale raises questions about questions.

Living Latin as a Child

Contemporary neurolinguistics tells us that infants are hard-wired to acquire their first language (abbreviated as L1 in the field). They hunger for it like food and absorb it indiscriminately from all around them. But for every human excepting a few bilinguals-from-birth, adding a second or third language (L2) taxes certain brain functions in a different way than in acquisition of their first language. The key functions are those that govern, first, how speech organs shape themselves to utter sounds (phonology), and second, the neural processing of syntactic and morphological rules, which allow us to produce meaningful language spontaneously. In early childhood, language is acquired through reinforcement of syntax patterns the child hears: the brain lays down grooves in procedural memory that then guide the child, when she begins to speak, to guess the right order of words in an utterance and to form new words based on those patterns. Beyond this early developmental window of neural plasticity, however, the brain will take different, more laborious routes to process the mental guesswork that precedes original speech. An adult who attempts to learn an L2 cannot just reproduce toddler sounds and rewire her brain. This is why the contemporary research field of Second Language Acquisition (SLA) emphasizes in its very title that acquisition does not follow predictably from, or even necessarily require, instruction. SLA proposes and tests theories about how best to enhance the process by studying the corpus of linguistic input in the L2 an individual is exposed to and that they themselves produce, as well as the social and affective environments in which they acquire it. While there is much debate about neuroplasticity, and how long the window of ideal L2 acquisition extends, there is general consensus around the benefits of beginning in early childhood, especially for phonology, which involves training the speech organs. The contact-zone practice of training captive children from conquered groups to serve as translators, mentioned in Chapter III, indicates that this observation about the plasticity of child learners is an ancient one.[1]

If immersion from childhood, with ample input in the L2 as well as L1, was and is a gold standard for producing bilinguals, Experience Mayhew offers a striking example of a European who grew up with that proficiency in a local language. Grandson of the missionary linguist Thomas Mayhew, who brought up his family within a community of Wampanoag on Martha's Vineyard, he learned their language "as I did my Mother Tongue." He contrasts this pedagogical experience negatively to his later one with Latin and its "strong rules." Yet this schoolboy experience with Latin texts was not everyone's. Latin, or more accurately Neo-Latin, was Cotton Mather's first L2, and he began it very young. To prepare him for Ezekiel Cheever's grammar school, Increase Mather began speaking to and showing him words in Latin even as he learned his ABCs. When the boy was judged too weak to walk to school, his father took over the instruction. He later had "daily Discourses" in Latin with his own sons, sending Creasy down the street to study with Increase as well. Mather's Neo-Latin training would have seemed necessary for his patriarchal succession into the ministry, it is true, but, to use a contemporary insight from SLA theory, his biggest advantage to becoming an English-Latin bilingual may have been affective. As a child, he realized that this skill was assigned high value by a person whose emotional rewards were meaningful to him. Further, he—like Experience Mayhew—was situated in a high-input environment so that his brain could learn habits of dual-language memory processing. This influenced third, fourth, and subsequent languages that he learned.[2]

In theory if not always in practice, one was to learn Neo-Latin by incorporating all the four proficiencies now presumed necessary in modern languages, and in the classroom or in the rarified privileged home setting of the Mathers it had the same basis: high aural input and high oral output, reinforced with sight reading. In the sixteenth century, Renaissance humanism had revived Latin and convinced European elites to transform and "purify" their own vernaculars with Latin-derived words. Desiderius Erasmus and his acolyte the Spanish-born Juan Luis Vives promoted literacy education in Neo-Latin alongside the vernacular for elites: the missionary linguistic practices described in Chapter III put Erasmus and Vives into practice. Mather's lifespan tracks the gradual decline of Latin in the West: young Benjamin Franklin's "Silence Dogood" satires made Mather's habit of inserting Latin phrases sound like an ancient and pompous vestige of a former age. But during his early childhood, it was still the lingua franca of European learning, especially in theology. Nor was it a dead language for seventeenth-century political elites: treaties were still written in it, which ensured that Neo-Latin had to retain at least some component of speakability for pan-European gatherings.

As Jürgen Leonhardt puts it, "as long as it was in active use, this Latin 'second language' remained a living language. Learning it was more like learning any 'modern' foreign language ... no other way of teaching it would have made sense." In Spanish America, as outlined in Chapter IV, Indigenous and mestizo children were trained in Spanish and Latin; the rector of the first university in Mexico published a Latin instructional text in 1554 that sang the glories of Mexico-Tenochtitlán as the new Rome, just to make the comparison fully explicit.[3]

As with missionaries in the Americas, the use of Latin textbooks for Europeans reinforced rather than replaced oral acquisition. The durable *Latin Grammar in English* of William Lily, which (with its English explanations) had remained essentially unchanged since its royal adoption in the mid-sixteenth century, began with pronunciation exercises. Each day in the grammar school classroom started off in a cloud of sound as sections were recited back to the master; examinations involved oral declamation as well as written tests. While contemporary language classrooms tend to pair up the passive and active aspects of each of the four proficiencies—for example, listen to a question and speak a response to it, or read a passage and then write a response to it—earlier pedagogues might mix the oral and written, or crisscross between the L1 and L2. For instance, the master might read aloud a Latin passage that the students would have to hear correctly (active listening), then translate into written English. Such oral "spot translations" were carried forward into more challenging texts like Vives's *Exercitatio linguae latinae,* also a Renaissance invention. By the time of Mather's adolescence, he was taking notes in Neo-Latin on sermons that he heard delivered in English to hone his skills at this kind of cross-proficiency translation under time pressure.[4]

Mather entered Harvard at the prodigious age of eleven, having passed the entrance qualification to "readily make and speake or write true Latin in prose." (Note the ambiguity of "speake *or* write": a compromise by which the admissions committee might allow in weaker but well-connected students.) He wrote in *Paterna* that he impressed the college examiners with the fact that he "could Speak *Latin* so readily." To promote overall fluency in Latin, Harvard undergraduates were supposed to speak it exclusively while they were on college grounds, as Scholastic educational institutions continued to do in Europe and the Americas and as language-immersion schools attempt to do today. This sonic atmosphere of spoken Neo-Latin was intended to set the bodies of Harvard undergraduates apart from the rest of the Cambridge community, like the long black robes they wore and their regulation short haircuts. As Harvard's president, Increase Mather had tried to impose strict linguistic discipline (the practice was already dying out at Oxford and Cambridge), but the total-immersion ideal was difficult to enforce. Nonetheless, Latin phrases including jokes and insults were still exchanged over the weak beer the students drank at table. Greek, too, left the classroom and brought its sounds to the student's daily recitations. Oral spot translations were required at communal prayer times: one boy would be called up to read and then translate an Old Testament portion from Hebrew to Greek in the morning, or a New Testament portion from English to Greek in the evening. Some ingenious Harvard students inserted cheat sheets into the large Bible used for those spot-translations at prayers—a practice known as "hogueing." Perhaps Mather ratted out some of the cheaters, for he became the "Object of *Inhumane Derision*" at college. By then his stammer, apparently mild in childhood, had become crippling. He was hazed so frequently by the older boys at Harvard that Increase had to file a complaint to get it to stop. Here Mather encountered an obstacle even beyond being the youngest, smallest student at the college: his recalcitrant body.[5]

"Physick" for the Disabled Tongue

One can imagine the humiliation of the stammer. If he could not deliver public addresses like his famous father and grandfathers, how would he achieve prominence as a member of the governing elite? He later described the fear of stuttering in wrenching terms: "You *Sitt Alone and keep silence, because you have born* what you have *upon you; yea, you put your Mouth in the Dust* and speak little more than the Dead." In the shadow of this disability he chose to study in medicine ("Physick") at Harvard as an alternative career, and that decision would propel him beyond even his father's considerable understanding of natural philosophy. Some biographers have psychologized Mather's youthful stammer as a manifestation of his anxiety about meeting his family's high expectations. The stammer has also been used to explain his astonishing output as a writer.[6]

The record does not specify whether Mather's speech misfired only in English-language social situations that stressed him: it would be illuminating to know whether it affected his oral recitations in Latin, Greek, or Hebrew.

But since phonology is important in learning a spoken language, its relevance here is that it drew Mather to careful observations of the physiology of the vocal organs. On the advice of a grammar school teacher, he undertook prescribed speech therapy for his stammer after Harvard. He was instructed to "prolongue [*sic*] your Pronunciation," drawing out phonemes and syllables—and also to sing. Puritans are not known for church singing, but Mather found success in attaching tone and melody to the *Psalms.* In 1718, he would put out *Psalterium Americana* (discussed in Chapter VIII), an edition of that Hebrew book that appealed both to the learned—it was annotated with multiple translated versions, including from the Spanish—and to the lay singer who loved music. He became known as an eager conversationalist, and in one diary entry repenting of a hurtful thing he had said to someone, he writes, "I give up all my *Speaking* Powers and organs unto the Holy Spirit. . . . May I not affect *Loquacitie*." He deadpanned about himself, "there is nothing more frequent, than for *Stammerers* to speak Ten times more than they need to."[7]

Mather advocated that others proliferate their spoken as well as written language proficiencies in a short advice book titled *Manuductio ad Ministerium* (1726), intended to be distributed to all Harvard graduates. In it he continued to insist on the importance of honing all four proficiencies in Latin: future ministers must be "Able not only to *Write,* but also to *Speak* in it, with *Fluency* as well as *Purity;* and confute the common Observation, that tho' *Englishmen* do often *Write* . . . the best *Latin* in the World, yet **they often *Speak* it but indifferently.** For this Purpose you will do well frequently, both to employ your Pen, for composing *Discourses* or *Epistles* in it; and likewise to maintain frequent *Conferences* in it" (bold emphases mine). He knew that fluency could be maintained only by conversation ("Conferences"). For Mather, linguistic encounters were not only intellectual but embodied: pronounced, taken to the tongue, felt on the palate. Speech troubles—whether a stammer or a tongue that produced only "indifferent" fluency despite training—were problems of bodily conformation, and thus both a spiritual problem to be treated with prayer and a problem of "Physick." Mather did, eventually, become a "doctor" in the sense that he received an honorary degree when he was made a Fellow of the Royal Society of London the emergent scientific community of England. In his campaign for this coveted honor he corresponded with the society and responded to the research of others published in its *Philosophical Transactions,* making annotations on an article about the famous case of the deaf-mute Alexander Popham, whom two English doctors claimed to have trained to speak. In the absence of someone to converse with and listen to, Mather would have had to do, like Popham, with other scientific methods for reconstructing sounds out of visual traces and bodily cues.[8]

Mather's Latin laid the groundwork for his Spanish, and not only in the etymological and historical senses. The significance of spoken Neo-Latin as a living language to him makes it unlikely that he would have tried to bypass the oral proficiencies, listening and speaking, when learning French and Spanish. Samuel Frazon, Indigenous people from Spanish-speaking places like Florida, ships' captains and former pirates all represented more than potential converts: they were potential research partners who provided the "Conversation" without which, by his testimony, he would later lose some of his proficiency in those languages. *Imagined* conversations were also fundamental to the way Latin, and the Christian faith, were taught on the page.

Questions of Language, Alphabetization, and Indoctrination

The first Latin textbook encountered by boys of sufficient means to be sent to a grammar school like Ezekiel Cheever's was known as an Accidence. John Brinsley's *The Posing of the Parts of the Latine Tongue* (1612) was a widely used example that Mather may have used. It begins:

> Q: What booke do you learn?
> A: The Accidence.
> Q: What booke is that?
> A: A book which teacheth al the first grounds of the Latine tongue.

Those "first grounds," or "accidents," are simplified grammar points. The students reciting back the answer in this exchange are being taught to consider language not as a natural reflex, but as an order of knowledge to be analyzed. In their parallel education as Christians, they would also be asked, from a young age, to analyze the sinful state of their own souls and learn to reach a state of repentance. The close relationship between religious and second-language instruction for European elites can be guessed by the fact that the term *catechism* described both. While other educational aids could be called catechisms at an advanced level (as in the Ramist tradition where scholars produced detailed outlines of a field of knowledge, as Mather did at Harvard), the condensation of complex knowledge into a few points was particularly associated with training beginners. The printed genre of the Q&A format in which many catechisms circulated binds Mather's childhood experience with the paternalistic treatment of Indigenous converts in the Americas.[9]

For the first few hundred years of the Common Era under the early Church, "catechizing" referred to the instruction of believers by word of mouth. Literacy was uncommon and unnecessary: a catechized Christian would know by heart the basic principles of the faith, summarized in the Apostle's Creed and its lengthier elaboration the Nicene Creed. Reciting these creeds was a way to "confess," or proclaim in public, that the Christian would live or die by them. Catholic practice ritualized the confession of faith into the Latin mass, as the *Credo* ("Credo in unum Deum, Patrem omnipotentem"); voices spoke this in unison, joining the individual believer to the community. The manuscript catechisms that circulated in the Middle Ages (luxury goods that they were) committed these creeds to the page, but they also served as handbooks for proper Christian conduct in the social world. Protestant Reformers complained that such catechisms overcomplicated the Gospel in its original, or "primitive," tenets; to return to an unsullied Christian faith, they set out to reenact this word-of-mouth instruction by making the written genre of the catechism resemble the oral indoctrination practiced by the Apostles.

To do this, Protestants would unpack the familiar language of these collectively recited creeds to read as individual declarations of faith. Martin Luther kept whittling down these declarations until he arrived at the *Small Catechism* (1529), which punctuated doctrinal statements with questions like "What does this mean?" Jean Calvin prepared his *Geneva Catechism* (1537–1538) in the now-familiar Q&A format, distilling the principles in his *Institutes of the Christian Religion* into a form that even children could understand. Whatever its content, the catechistic genre born in the sixteenth century can be summarized as a mimicked dialogue between a master and student (or minister and spiritual beginner), aimed at a wide readership, scaled intellectually so as to begin from first and simplest principles and lead up to complex ones. The authority of the truths expressed by the questioner is never in doubt.[10]

Calvin's template is visible in the steady seller penned by Mather's grandfather John Cotton, *Spiritual Milk for Boston Babes* (London 1646; Boston 1684). At just sixteen pages (thirteen of them containing questions and answers), it is the same length as *La Fe del Christiano*. The conceit of a spoken encounter between two voices brought the oral dimension of acquisition into the very heart of its written one. *Spiritual Milk* proceeds deductively, with each question back-stitching into the previous answer, as the opening lines illustrate:

> Q: What hath GOD done for you?
> A: God hath made me, He keepeth me, and He can save me.
> Q: Who is God?
> A: God is a Spirit of himself and for himself.

Through such connecting stitches, Calvinist catechisms like *Spiritual Milk* were augmented and stepped up toward increasingly complex forms. So too with Brinsley's Latin *Accidence:*

> Q: What mean you by the Construction of the eight parts of speech?
> A: The construing, or framing, and setting together of the eight parts of speech.
> Q: Where begins the eight parts of speech?
> A: In speech.

Here the abstraction "parts of speech" is brought down to earth by comparing a sentence to an act of building ("framing, and setting together"). The second question/answer may seem tautological, but it is not: building one's own meaningful sentence in Latin must begin "in speech," that is, with the practice of speech acts. The *Accidence,* like other textbooks, was a script for performance, recitation, and memorization in a group, so that all students could hear. Speaking and actively listening to Latin as a second language did not replace reading and writing in it, but they were mutually reinforcing proficiencies that accompanied growing English-language literacy. The size and scale of the book grew along with the spiritual "child."[11]

The questions and answers that outlined rules and definitions in an elementary catechism—whether it taught religious doctrine or the rules of Latin—shared many formal traits with the way English children were alphabetized in their first language and trained to read. As Jennifer Monaghan, Patricia Crain, and others have shown, Cotton's *Spiritual Milk* was adapted into Algonquian as the *Indian Primer* (1669), which became the *New-England Primer* (1687–1690): a near contemporary of *La Fe del Christiano.* The *New-England Primer,* in turn, has a claim to be one of the most influential colonial books ever published because it was later integrated into Noah Webster's "Blue-Backed Speller," used across the United States well into the nineteenth century. Using illustrations of the letters of the alphabet and syllabaries, the *New-England Primer* took students progressively through stepped-up concepts to a higher level of literacy as well as a more likely salvation. The *Primer* started with an iconic illustrated "A," for "In Adam's fall we sinned all," a first stage to opening one's own Bible and reading "In the beginning was the Word," when the student was ready for that advanced textbook. New Englanders legislated universal literacy education, though it was distributed differently among poorer and richer towns, boys' schools and dame schools, settler elites and bondservants. Across that range of colonial classrooms, rare was the school equipped with individual copies for every student, so serial reading aloud was a way to stretch the capacities of those copies. Crain stresses the oral and aural quality of the primer, even when read silently: "the additions and repetitions . . . lend to print the copiousness of oral performance. Through repetition print replicated recitation, imitating aural echoes."[12]

Literacy training in the colonial period did not offer systems of English grammar: the "grammar" in grammar school meant Latin until later in the eighteenth century. But Mather's poetic tribute to his schoolmaster Cheever expresses the same interlacing of language and doctrine as does the *New-England Primer:*

> *Grammar* he taught, which 't'was his work to do:
> But he would *Hagar* have her place to know.
> > The *Bible* is the Sacred *Grammar,* where
> > The *Rules* of speaking well, contained are.
> He taught us *Lilly,* and he *Gospel* taught;
> And us poor Children to our *Saviour* brought.

Lily's Latin grammar contains "rules" that must be memorized, just as the Bible contains its Old Testament "rule of law" (the Ten Commandments), and the New, its "rule of prayer" (the Lord's Prayer). Both of these are set forth in *La Fe del Christiano* in Mather's Spanish. The other analogy in the poem is even more suggestive: Lily's book is to the "Gospel" as Hagar is to Sarah; the secular is subordinate to the sacred. But in addition, it suggests that the rote memorization of grammar rules or biblical commandments is only the first steppingstone toward spiritual self-mastery and righteous living. In the poem's analogy, grammar-rule memorization is an elementary stage one must pass through in order to "speak well": to do as Mather did before the Harvard examiners, and produce *original* speech on demand. The next lines of the poem state the parallel goal for the student of doctrine:

We Constru'd *Ovid's Metamorphosis*
But on our selves charg'd, not a *Change* to miss.

The italicized terms underscore the wordplay between the Latin "metamorphosis" and its English translation, "Change." In a pious life, the "Change" would be an individual conversion experience, the moment in which a believer experiences a transformative feeling or vision of their salvation through Christ. This is a moment that cannot be taught or bought, though it must be trained for through repentance, prayer, and Bible study. (A verified conversion experience, we may remember, was necessary to become a full member of Mather's church, endowed with the right to take Communion and share in church governance.) The testimony of one's conversion had to be "confessed" before others in one's own original words. Just as knowing how to construe a line in Ovid was the precursor to speaking fluent Neo-Latin, knowing Gospel and doctrine by heart readied you for the gift of the Spirit ("us poor Children to our Saviour brought"). The road to mastering a second language invoked for Mather and his English contemporaries the model of devotional submission. A teacher or master took on the role of the answerer in a catechism: offering grammar rules, like the laws and rules of pious Christian conduct, to be memorized and absorbed into the heart and graven through repetition into the body's muscle memory.[13]

A wealth of scholarship has shown how such early modern pedagogies, applied to European and Indigenous people and emblematized by the catechism, gave way historically to Enlightenment philosophies of language. In the English context, John Locke separated theories of mind and language from Christian traditions, with powerful implications for educational practice. For second-language teachers, the empirical turn exemplified by Locke would spark the idea of more "natural" methods: imitations of the way children were thought to learn their first language, including the picture-books of Comenius. Proponents of the Natural Method in its various guises claimed that bypassing written explanations and logic would trigger language production instinctually. It seemed the opposite tack than these catechisms took. But this rejection of the catechistic structure was not necessarily more effective, either in producing bilinguals or in producing converts.[14]

American Catechisms, Catholic and Protestant

After Luther and Calvin made use of print technology to spread the Reform widely through inexpensive catechisms, the Council of Trent, the decade-long gathering at which the Roman Catholic Church regrouped to shape its response as the Counter-Reformation, adopted a catechism as well. The approved Tridentine catechism had four parts: the Apostles' Creed, the Sacraments, the Decalogue, and the Lord's Prayer and other prayers. As outlined in Chapter IV, Catholic missionary linguists had already brought to print numerous doctrinal and linguistic works in the sixteenth and early seventeenth centuries. These textual representations of a print-enabled language encounter were arrayed on a scale from small to large, simple to complex. Often an Indigenous-language learning library would begin with a brief *cartilla* or *plática* giving the essentials of pronunciation and basic words (*silabeo*), then move on to works on vocabulary and grammar. The more explicitly doctrinal works might be produced afterward or simultaneously. Standardizing a practice at which the Mexico-Tenochtitlán press was already adept, Acosta proposed to the Council of Lima in 1590 that each language of evangelization must have a *catecismo breve* and a longer one. The Jesuits in New France, though deprived of a printing press of their own, wrote several. By the time Francisco de Pareja and his Timucua collaborators reached Mexico to shepherd the manuscripts for the first bilingual works in the *lengua floridiana* past the Inquisition's tiers of authority and to the print-shop, such clusters of texts comingling doctrinal and language training were routine.[15]

Pareja's first work was a *Vocabulario*, which has not survived—but two complementary catechisms have, both appearing in 1612. The *Cathecismo en lengua castellana, y Timuquana: En el qual se contiene lo que se les puede enseñar a los adultos que an de ser baptizados* (Catechism in the Spanish and Timucuan languages: In which is contained everything needed to teach to adults who are to be baptized) (Mexico, 1612) was shorter and directed at priests in the first stage of evangelization; *Catechismo y breve exposición de la doctrina christiana* (Catechism and Brief Outline of Christian Doctrine) (Mexico, 1612) was more detailed, perhaps made to double as a teaching text for Timucua proselytes learning to read their language along with Spanish. The texts that followed are longer and more ambitious: *Confessionario en lengua castellana y timuquana con unos consejos para animar al penitente* (Confessional in the Spanish and Timucuan Languages, with Some Advice for Encouraging the Penitent) (Mexico, 1613) and the grammar text or *arte* discussed in Chapter V, *Gramatica de la lengua timuquana de Florida o Arte y Pronunciacion de la Lengua Timucuana y Castellana* (Grammar of the Timucuan language of Florida, or Grammar and Pronunciation Manual of the Timucuan and Spanish languages) (Mexico, 1614). After the long gap during which Pareja returned to Florida, the final text he supervised, *Catecismo y examen para los que comulgan, en lengua castellana y timuquana* (Catechism and examination for those who take Communion, in the Spanish and Timucuan languages) (Mexico, 1627), indicates that the question of administering Eucharist had been solved in favor of the converts. These five extant works were issued decades prior to John Eliot's first Massachusett Algonquian composition: a catechism, of which no copies survive.

There were of course differences between Catholic and Protestant catechisms, but both evangelical sects were careful to prepare a variety of them—as the different Timucua catechisms, attending to slightly different needs, suggests. Not all used the format of scripted questions and answers. Mather's Spanish works are written as a list of articles of faith, but that was a similarly catechistic format, and they contain the essential *reglas de la vida*, rules of life: the Ten Commandments and Lord's Prayer. Mather wrote more catechistic works than any other colonial New Englander: at least twelve, including the new Boston edition of his grandfather's *Spiritual Milk for Boston Babes*, originally published in London. In 1702 alone, Mather published three Small Books with this structure, including *Cares about the Nurseries*, which becomes a kind of meta-commentary on the scene of the questioner and answerer.[16]

Cares about the Nurseries turns a perennial parenting issue—children asking many questions—into an opportunity for inculcating Christian principles. When this happens, Mather advises parents to devise in response their own leading questions that have an answer of "YES, or NO, or one word or two." The authoritative parent thus becomes fully in charge of the truth: the fewer possibilities for genuine critical exchange, the better. But at the same time, Mather stresses that parents should not let "the *Children* patter out by Rote the words of the *Catechism*, like *Parrots;* but [parents should] be Inquisitive how far their *Understandings* do take in the Things of God." The concern that children would mindlessly "patter out by Rote" these lessons—which they had in fact been *taught* by rote—extended to other budding Christians, especially, in his paternalistic view, Indigenous ones. Over all Christian missiology in the Americas hung a cloud of anxiety about insincere conversions.[17]

Mather's choice of a symbol for mindless speech was not casual. Parrots had become associated with Catholic cardinals during the Reformation due to their red color and the wealth associated with keeping them as pets, metaphorically condemning the wealth of the Church. "Parroting" as a term for mindless repetition was enabled by the spread of travelers' tales from the Americas about the bird's uncanny, unreasoning imitation of speech. This readily became, for Protestants, further evidence of the bad faith of missionary priests who baptized in mass numbers: their sect-switching informant Thomas Gage had accused priests of extorting superficial affirmations of faith from neophytes who would parrot the words their interrogators wanted to hear. Living in Guatemala among the Pokom'chi Maya, he noted their devotion to the quetzal, whose feathers were made into ritual garments, and drew parallels between those allegedly primitive rituals and the rhetorical culture of the rote recitation of the *Credo*. Gage indicted his fellow Dominicans for not being "Inquisitive how far their *Understandings* do take," as Mather put it. A selective English reading of Las Casas, too, fed this English generalization that Indigenous Catholics had been too insincerely converted. Part of the problem, as Ralph Bauer brilliantly outlines, is that conversion signified philosophically different things: an alchemical rather than fundamental change in the Scholastic tradition, a rebirth in the Calvinist. But they continued to use the same didactic genres to reach that end, including the dialogue or *coloquio,* a looser and more advanced form of the catechistic script.[18]

Scripting Dialogues and Confessionals

In Latin instruction, the humanistic dialogue was the learner's next step along the road to mastery. Desiderius Erasmus's *Colloquia Familiaria* (1518, 1526) helped bring the Neo-Latin pedagogy of Mather's childhood into being. This colorful—and borderline heretical—textbook, featuring characters such as greedy monks, lazy schoolboys, and virtuous role models, advanced a student's knowledge of Latin vocabulary and grammar while captivating him with dangerously up-to-the-moment arguments against the excesses of princes and bishops. Its content was often politically coded. Reading the complex arguments aloud, and translating them, was a set of training wheels that would help the Latin student produce complex, original language of his own. In Europe, the genre of the dialogue then evolved into much more than a language-teaching tool: it served pliably as the structural conceit for hundreds of published works on astronomy, mathematics, political theory, and even the news of the day during its lifespan, from roughly the mid-sixteenth to the late eighteenth centuries. John Eliot's final work, *Indian Dialogues* (1671), chose the genre for just the reason of its ubiquity: "what way more familiar, then by way of *Dialogues?*" he asks in the Preface.[19]

Eliot ingeniously casts both of the two speakers as Indigenous: one a convert, the other a skeptic. He uses the dialogue form didactically to address points of intercultural disagreement. The dialogues draw readers into the orbit of European thought and social practice by disavowing, for example, the deity of the sun and moon, which the convert in the dialogue had dismissed with biblical logic. Backhandedly, the dialogues thus preserved information about the very beliefs Christianity sought to stamp out. But Eliot's was an English version, although he wrote that "If the Lord give life, and length of dayes, I may hereafter put forth these or the like Dialogues in the *Indian Tongue.*" This Algonquian-language dialogic text never materialized. Among the Indigenous-language imprints produced in colonial Mexico City, however, were *Coloquios* (Dialogues) in Nahuatl, from which scholars are only beginning to mine insights. Transferring the second-language medium from Latin to an Indigenous tongue, Allison Bigelow argues, made for "a hybrid space of historical actors and literary imagination in which different ways of knowing . . . are evaluated with serious play."[20]

What distinctions of structure and scale might be made among texts structured in Q&A format; what kind and degree of dialectical reasoning did they foster? It may be tempting to contrast the Spanish *coloquios* with the English Dialogues, for there is an unresolved sectarian struggle over the legacy of Erasmus and the Renaissance humanism with which he is associated. His *Colloquia* reinvented the medieval Scholastic tradition of the didactic (in which each question and answer reiterates and repurposes the features of the prior answer) into a more mimetic style, imitating real-life speech and persuasive tactics. The first mode reinforces a set of truths that learners are not encouraged to doubt; the second trains learners to make their own arguments. One works deductively, asking students to restate knowledge; the other works inductively, encouraging them to produce it. One seems more closed, the other more open. For generations of intellectual historians narrating the rise of Western modernity from within a Protestant frame, the Erasmian dialogue has been read as an opening toward the currents of invidualism, secularism, and eventually scientific empiricism. In this progressive model of history, textual forms of questioning shape a subject's ability to question authority and received wisdom; the allegedly closed Scholastic mindset was superceded by a more open one. Thus, one could infer different intellectual, cultural, and political paths for the Catholic and Protestant worlds, especially for South and North America. The Coda will address the lingering harm of this version of Protestant history, but literary critics of the Erasmian dialogue have in any case read it quite differently. The *Colloquia* and dialogues inspired by it may seem to invite opposing views to be voiced, only to cunningly argue them away and disavow them. Some commentators, indeed, find Scholastic rhetorical forms more conducive to genuine dissent.[21]

The Catholic / Protestant binary dividing forms of, and relationships to, textuality culminates in the status of Bible reading: the ultimate aim of the progressed set of printed works in the Cambridge Indian Library. For Catholics, the desired end of learning about the faith through the basic process of catechizing was to live piously within the Church's fraternity; its rituals and sacraments were thought enough to feed the believer a steady diet of biblical examples and stories. In the context of the linked instructional-doctrinal works that missionary linguists and their collaborators produced in the Americas, the Catholic collection of texts included a further genre beyond the *coloquio:* the *confesionario.* When Acosta, in the passage that Mather took out of context for his epigraph to *La Fe del Christiano,* argued for the rights of Indian Christians to take Communion, this decision put even more pressure on the linguistic capacities of European priests. A confirmed believer deemed ready to participate in that sacrament would need to make confession to a priest beforehand. The *confesionario* became the most advanced "textbook" for European bilinguals, serving both as ethnographic introduction and interrogation manual.

Priestly confession, or reconciliation, was one of the seven traditional Catholic sacraments that Reformers reduced to just two (baptism and the Eucharist). Protestants rejected the notion that telling one's sins to a priest—and performing the formulaic kinds of penitence required, which could seem like the rattling off a few memorized prayers—had anything to do with receiving God's grace.

Sacraments by definition are ritual acts that call for scripted speech performances, and this explains why in the Spanish Americas the scramble to produce priests bilingual in the Indigenous languages built up a library appropriate to those sacramental occasions. Latin was the language in which the sacraments were administered, but the Indigenous grammar books helped Spanish speakers explain the significance of those sacred words of the anointment of the sick and dying. Confession, too, began and ended ritually with Latin set prayers, but the exchange itself was too complex to be contained in a catechism; it involved branching trees of possible questions and answers. In order to understand confessions by Indigenous congregants, the priest would need a high level of *listening* proficiency in the language, including the ability to understand differences among spoken dialects.

Pareja's 1613 *Confessionario* was the lengthiest Timucua text, running to over two hundred pages of close-set type. Because of the unpredictable nature of what a neophyte might tell a priest, this *Confessionario* anticipates in detail the distinctive sins that might be committed by chieftains, midwives, ballplayers, single women, or *sodomitas* (a general term for those engaging in homosexual acts). The genre of *confesionarios* in general was designed to shepherd those neophytes through a multitude of their traditional practices and help them determine whether or not they were sinful under the new religious regime. For this reason, the two Timucua *Confessionarios* are invaluable ethnographic documents, despite their clear bias: Pareja, according to one scholar, "ends up recording the very practices he would like the Timucua to give up." Figure 4 illustrates a few pages describing one such traditional practice, abortion.[22]

A complex question such as this one: "Did you order that the bones of the game [animal] must not be thrown away, unless the game would no longer enter into the snare or trap, but that they must be hung up and placed upon the roof of the house?" gives a window into spiritual practices in which hanging the animal's bones on the roof pays homage to the spirit of that animal, protecting future hunts. It also captures some of the cultural distance that the Franciscans traversed as they strove to translate spiritual concepts: the way grace is conjured by the phrase "The love of God makes you vomit up sin" suggests a nuanced layering of one cosmological view of body and spirit over another. This detailed naming and description of the very heretical beliefs and "barbaric" practices the priests were trying to stamp out are also visible in the other Spanish-Indigenous *confesionarios* and *coloquios* published in Mexico City. Moreover, in their extraordinary reconstructive work with this language, Ale-

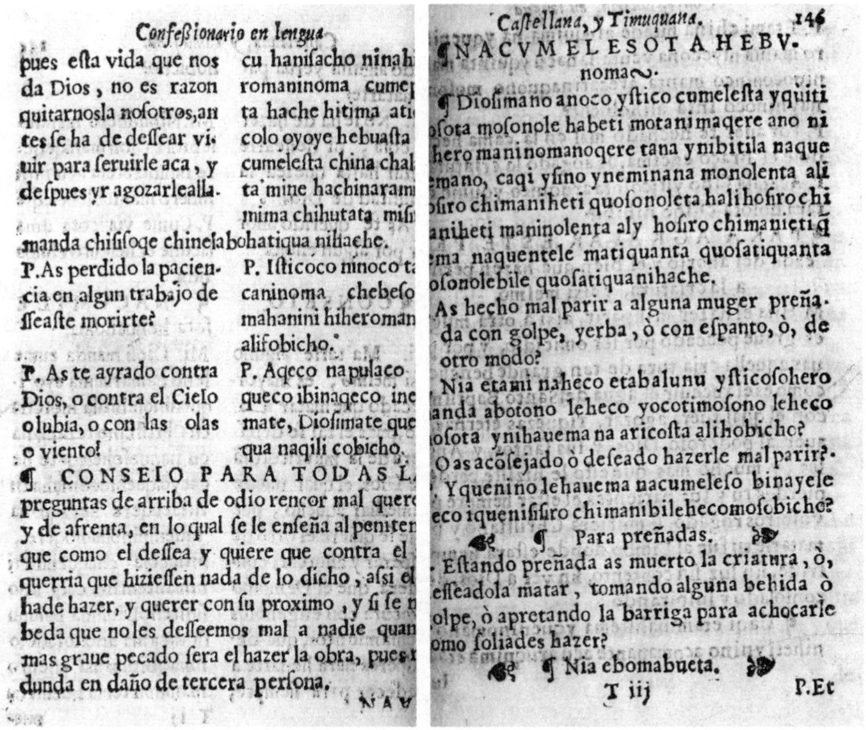

Confeßionario en lengua

pues esta vida que nos / cu hanisacho ninah
da Dios, no es razon / romaninoma cumec
quitarnosla nosotros, an / ta hache hitima ati
tes se ha de dessear vi- / colo oyoye hebuasta
uir para seruirle aca, y / cumelesta china chal
despues yr agozarlealla. / ta mine hachinaram
   / mima chihutata misi

manda chisisoqe chinelabohatiqua nihache

P. As perdido la pacien- / P. Isticoco ninoco ta
cia en algun trabajo de / caninoma chebeso
seaste morirte? / mahanini hiheroman
   / alifobicho.

P. As te ayrado contra / P. Aqeco napulaco
Dios, o contra el Cielo / queco ibinaqeco ine
olubia, o con las olas / mate, Diosimate que
o viento! / qua naqili cobicho.

¶ CONSEIO PARA TODAS L.
preguntas de arriba de odio rencor mal quere
y de afrenta, en lo qual se le ensena al peniten
que como el dessea y quiere que contra el
querria que hiziessen nada de lo dicho, asi el
hade hazer, y querer con su proximo, y si se n
beda que no les desseemos mal a nadie quan
mas graue pecado sera el hazer la obra, pues t
dunda en daño de tercera persona.
   NAV

Castellana, y Timuquana. 146

NACVMELESOTAHEBV.
   noma~.

¶ Diosimano anoco ystico cumelesta yquiti
osota mosonole habeti motanimaqere ano ni
hero maninomanoqere tana ynibitila naque
mano, caqi ysino yneminana monolenta ali
osiro chimaniheti quosonoleta hali hosirochi
aniheti maninolenta aly hosiro chimanietiq
ma naquentele matiquanta quosatiquanta
osonolebile quosatiquanihache.

As hecho mal parir a alguna muger preñada con golpe, yerba, o con espanto, o, de
otro modo?

Nia etami naheco etabalunu ysticosohero
anda abotono leheco yocotimosono leheco
osota ynihauema na aricosta alihobicho?

O as acosejado o deseado hazerle mal parir?-
Y que nino lehauema nacumeleso binayele
eco iquenisisiro chimanibilehecomoscbicho?

¶ Para preñadas.
Estando preñada as muerto la criatura, o,
esseadola matar, tomando alguna behida o
olpe, o apretando la barriga para achocarle
omo soliades hazer?

¶ Nia ebomabueta.
   T iij   P.Et

Figure 4: Pages from Francisco Pareja, *Confessionario en lengua castellana, y timuquana con algunos consejos para animar al penitente* (1613). The Spanish and Timucua facing pages discuss prohibited practices, including abortion. Reproduction courtesy of the John Carter Brown Library, Brown University.

jandra Dubcovsky and George Aaron Broadwell demonstrate that the Indigenous collaborators subverted the Spanish doctrines: "failing to note the subtleties of the language under translation, Pareja compiled texts that contained significantly different Timucua and Spanish versions." This translation gap in even the seemingly "closed" genre of Pareja's *Confessionario* suggests the possibility that we may hear these Timucua through what James C. Scott's refers to as "hidden transcripts"—the openings in seemingly unequal conversations between dominant and subordinate interlocutors by which the subordinate can secretly exercise their own agency—may have offered some space to maneuver.[23]

Perhaps, in spite of its seemingly closed genre, this particular *Confessionario* was much more like a humanistic dialogue than it seems on the surface, especially given the possibilities for its use. A visitor to Pareja's mission in 1614 reported that the priest had assembled a cadre of Timucua women, as well as men, whom he considered devout and well prepared enough to catechize others of their gender because, "with regard to the mysteries of the faith, many of them answer better than the Spaniards." In Florida, some Timucua lay priests were empowered to perform the rite of reconciliation: that is, they confessed other Timucua. This could have meant that they asked *each other* the questions in the *Confessionario*, perhaps taking over the book some of their people had helped make. The Office of the Inquisition did not reach as far as Florida, but if it had, a tribunal might well have condemned this practice: one of the first questions in an interrogation for heresy was who had taught the defendant their articles of faith. Without romanticizing these openings for "hidden transcripts" or forgetting the mass destruction wrought by colonization and evangelization, one might conclude from the Timucua *Confessionario* that a given text's classification as catechism or dialogue may have been less important than the relative grip of Christian paternalism in determining how far the proselyte's original thought might go. It should go without saying that from the perspective of Indigenous people, these purportedly Catholic and Protestant modes of instruction would have been more alike than different.[24]

On Mastery and Scale

The image on the cover, taken from the record of a visitor to the Timucua missions, depicts Pareja's *taller* or writing workshop—but it is not meant to reinforce the notion of the Franciscan's mastery over his student-collaborators. Dubcovsky and Broadwell's analysis effectively disproves the idea that he was their sole or even primary author. My interest in the image centers on the individual proselytes who are each writing on their own. One approaches Pareja's desk: ready to answer, perhaps, or instead to question. The logical end of my critical fabulation about Tuqui is to imagine him into the scene portrayed here—and, further, to install him as the Catholic-associated authority on the Spanish language to whom Mather himself had to turn with his questions. If their relationship involved the exchange of valuable information, who was ultimately the master, and who the student?

In the shorter catechisms of Latin, literacy, and Christian doctrine that this chapter has surveyed, authority clearly goes to the master/answerer, not the scholar/questioner. Edmund Morgan comments of Mather's *Cares about the*

Nurseries, with its suggestion that parents respond to annoying questions by limiting the children's responses to a simple yes or no: "This method of instruction was not designed to give play to the development of individual initiative." That is surely an understatement. At the same time, Mather's parental teaching tactics could be much more open-ended: some years later, he writes that he instructed "My four Children (who can use their pen), to retire, and write each of them an Answer" to the question of how best to spend their lives. When Mather decided to structure *Biblia Americana* as a series of longer questions and answers, it represented a departure from the conventions of traditional Bible commentaries. One of the modern editors of the ten-volume *Biblia,* Kenneth P. Minkema, describes this structure not as a throwback, but as an innovation. Traditionally, to use Bible commentaries, readers were expected to look up verses on their own. Departing from this convention to use "a dialogic format of questions-and-answers, reflecting both a Socratic as well as a catechistical method," was a sign of "Mather's inventiveness, his liveliness, and his acquaintance with current trends."[25]

Scale, of course, makes a difference in the questioning text's openness to question. Whether one figures instruction as steps along a road or levels on an ascending ladder, it is clear that Mather relished the challenge of moving up and down the scales available for him as a writer. The *Biblia Americana,* with its virtually unpublishable million words of multicolumned commentary, represents one extreme of length, while his Small Books that attempt to distill the faith into its barest essentials represent the other. Perhaps the better figure for Mather's corpus of didactic work is not that of a progressive road or a ladder, (as the grammars and catechisms were imagined), but of a bellows: the accordion-pleated leather and wood device that sent a concentrated blast of oxygen toward a flame. Whether his writing expanded to its fullest length (as in the *Biblia Americana*) or contracted to its smallest (as in the twelve articles of faith in *La Fe del Christiano*), it sought to target the oxygen of Scripture-revealed truth toward the space where the apostolic fire was languishing. Schooled by these pedagogical forms, he became a brilliant player with textual scales. *La Fe del Christiano,* as one of Mather's many "Small Books," is both product and example of a way of thinking about how to condense and distill knowledge into portable forms that a reader could later expand on their own. Later in life, as Mather came to identify more strongly with the ecumenical turn of the global Pietist movement, he produced a fully bilingual Latin-English book titled *The Stone Cut out of the Mountain / Lapis e Monte excisus* (1716), which allowed him both to keep polishing his Latin style and to keep winnowing Christianity down to its basics: in one, he got it down to just three maxims. Ever optimistic, he thought *Lapis* might help convert a nearby French Jesuit.[26]

Mather's awareness of Catholic missionary linguistics, with which he shared a second-language immersion experience in Latin and essential ways of understanding didactics arising from it, led him to assign a paradoxical status to the Spanish language. In one sense, I suggest, he treated Spanish as if it were *an American spoken language,* akin to the hundreds of Indigenous tongues on its vast landscape. In another sense, its study did not require the privations of living as a missionary himself, as his uncle and cousin had done. It took him instead back across the Atlantic, to the Renaissance courts of Europe, through the imagined dialogues of early Spanish-English instructional manuals—to which the next chapter turns.

· VII ·

Books as Keys to the Spanish Tongue

By holistically cultivating all four proficiencies of listening and speaking, reading and writing in Indigenous American languages, European missionary linguists of the sixteenth and seventeenth centuries followed a path familiar to them from learning Latin. For most, Latin was their first second language, learned through oral as well as text-based input and output and relying on both inductive and deductive reasoning: techniques that are not so distant from the best practices promoted by SLA theory today. Cotton Mather's proficiency in spoken Neo-Latin, reinforced through intimate exchanges with his father at home, reflected a privilege unusual among his childhood classmates at Cheever's grammar school. The modern European languages would not be taught in classrooms until the late eighteenth century, but in Mather's time a conceptual divide between "classical" and "modern" languages was already widening. Different pedagogical philosophies would perform that divide in the way they approached the four proficiencies. The "grammar-translation" method became the norm for learning Greek and Latin through reading and writing exercises alone, while a new cadre of modern language teachers experimented with "natural" methods claiming to be imitate the acquisition patterns of the L1, foregrounding aural input, visual aids, and behavioralist drills of tedious repetition. By the late nineteenth century, this pedagogical division of the four proficiencies reinforced a vitalist metaphor for classifying languages as either dead or living, classical or modern. The marginalization of the study of Indigenous languages in academic settings today is a consequence of that divide: where does a course in Nahuatl fit within a university structured to separate classics from modern language departments?

Mather did not make such sharp distinctions between classical and modern. However, the persona he cultivated as a missionary of the printed word in languages other than English led to an inconsistency in the way he assigned value to Indigenous languages. The enumeration he gives in *Paterna* indicates how he shuffled the deck of his language-learning experience in order to claim a lineage both as a learned theologian and as a missionary to the Indigenous world in the mold of Acosta and Eliot: "I am not unable, With a Little Study to Write in *Seven Languages;* I have written and printed in them." The number seven was repeated in *Manuductio ad Ministerum* and in his son Samuel's posthumous biography, which lists the titles of his "Indian sermons" as proof of these prodigious feats. At Harvard, Mather had studied Latin, Greek, and the three Semitic languages crucial for biblical scholars (Hebrew, Aramaic, and Syriac / Chaldean); he added French around 1690 (by unrecorded means) and Spanish, as we have seen, in 1699: that totals seven. Generously counting the Greek and Hebrew words, lines, and passages he inserted into various texts as "writing and printing" in those languages, this math only adds up if we substitute the two ancient scriptural languages he could *read* for the two Indigenous languages—both ancient and alive—in which his works were *published.* Mather never directly claimed to have mastered Algonquian or Iroquois—his publications in both were prepared by translators, as Chapter IX explains—but the enumeration seems deliberately misleading about his skills as a linguist. Looked at from another angle, however, it shows an acknowledgment of Indigenous languages as coeval living human tongues: all fallen since Babel, and all necessary for the evangelist to consider.[1]

As Chapter VI shows, the cluster of didactic-linguistic works that European missionaries created for Amerindian languages included word lists, a grammar, and sometimes more complex works that could be used by advanced students of the language. But comprehensive printed manuals for learning the modern European languages were a relatively recent innovation, and Mather incorporated them into his learning process somewhat differently than he did with texts in Latin. Linguist Paul Kroskrity distinguishes between language ideologies (social norms, values, and affective attachments about language systems and varieties) and language attitudes (individual applications of those values). Language learning textbooks, as this chapter explores, offer a time-stamped portrait of those ideologies. Given that Mather traveled so little and that his sense of the world was mediated by books and informants, the manuals that were available to English learners of Spanish would have influenced the way he imagined the relationship between the language and the culture as a whole. The way such bilingual brokers portrayed the genealogical relationship of Castilian to Latin, its later reshaping through contact with Arabic, and its relative value as a courtly, trade, or scholarly language reflected English linguistic ideologies. Mather's individual attitudes toward Spanish were complicated by his sense of its urgent American context: its imbrication in both sectarian and geopolitical struggles to master an Indigenous space. His worries that the "wasting Head-Aches" he suffered during the winter of his intensive language study might be related to the association between Spanish and papism are reflected in a puzzling entry in *Paterna*. Briefly noting that in early adulthood he had learned French, he writes,

> I afterwards mastered another Living Tongue of a Nation considerable both in *Europe* and *America,* so far that I composed and published a Book in it, for the prosecution of some great Evangelical Designs. But what it was, I will not mention, Lest I be discovered.

The reference to *La Fe del Christiano* is unmistakable, but why the secrecy around naming Spanish as this "Living Tongue"? In *Paterna,* Mather does consign some material he considers very private to his son's eyes alone, such as his borderline-heretical vision of a comely angel prophesying a great authorial career for him: that episode is rendered even more private by being in Latin. What social assumptions or ideologies attached to Spanish, but not to French, that might justify this apparent fear of being "discovered" as the true author of a Spanish book?[2]

The title page of *La Fe del Christiano* (Figure 1) does not cloak his identity very well, if at all:

Por C. MATHERO,

Siervo del Señor JESU CHRISTO

(By C. Mathero, Servant of the Lord JESUS CHRIST)

The author figure is hardly hiding here: while it's not unusual for a minister to refer to himself as a "servant of the Lord Jesus Christ," the word "CHRISTO" and the byline "MATHERO" are set in equally large type and aligned visually on the page. Mather signed his name in Latin as "Cottonus Matherus," inscribing that on the flyleaf of a book when he was only eight years old; he usually added titles, such as "The Reverend and Learned" or, once he was admitted to the Royal Society, "F.R.S." Perhaps he did not know that the Spanish equivalent of his first name was an Arabic borrowing, *algodón,* but the first name was less important in any case. If he were trying to pass as a native speaker, a more convincing alias would have been *Madero:* in fact, the seventeenth-century pronunciation of his surname was more likely *MaDDer,* not *MaTHer,* and that name's significance in Spanish (to indicate something made of wood) held potential for pious wordplay: the fuel for the apostolic fire. However, "Mathero" could have been a logical translation guess if he had learned, from one of the textbooks this chapter will describe, that the Latin nominative masculine singular "-us" (as in *Matherus*) shifted over the centuries into the Castilian oblique noun ending "-o." Or it could be a guess based not in such scholarly attention to historical morphology but in a simplistic and lazy hearing of the language: in the United States today, for instance, English speakers often add a terminal -*o* onto an English word to form "mock Spanish," a tribalist hostility masquerading as humor (as in "Cinco de Drinko").[3]

Whatever his reasoning, the self-translation of *Mather* to *Mathero* is a reminder that the affective motivation of learning another language is heightened by the excitement of creating a new persona. Transforming himself into "C. Mathero," Cotton was no different than the thousands of Kaitlyns who become Catarinas in Spanish-language classrooms all over the United States today. Continuing with this classroom analogy, this chapter tries to reconstruct the parts of his Spanish study that were mediated by the invisible teachers in books by measuring his level of proficiency, using *La Fe del Christiano* as a kind of final exam. Correlations between his idiosyncratic usages and those of the available early modern texts for English speakers wanting to learn Spanish help illuminate the points at which his motivations and language attitudes intersected with broader language ideologies.

Grading Mather's Spanish Homework

How good *was* Mather's Spanish? The answer is somewhat complicated by the fact that significant portions of the two tracts are formed out of citations from a Protestant Bible, whose travels to New England are explored in Chapter VIII. Those citations do help indicate the strong and weak points of Mather's grammar and usage, in that he frequently decides to abridge the biblical text or substitute a word, and sometimes this called for a different verb conjugation. (The abridgments and replacements are all noted in the Transcription and Translation.) Mather composed from scratch twelve complete declarative sentences (the twelve articles of *La Religion Pura*) and the twenty-four topic headings of *La Fe del Christiano*. His original language forms a corpus of about four hundred words. One-fifth of these are inflections of the same morpheme, meaning that he uses both the masculine and feminine forms, the singular and plural forms, or different conjugations of the same verb. Morphology is difficult to acquire efficiently from an unguided aural / oral learning process in which the learner tries to "pick up" scattered bits of overheard input and piece them together in the right ways. Learning a few rules for word formation speeds the process along and reduces errors. Perhaps he was talking in Spanish with Tuqui or Samuel Frazon, but it seems certain that Mather consulted at least one Spanish textbook during his "few hours of evening study." Some textbooks, as we shall see, included only grammar points while others contained a lexicon; Mather might have also had either a Spanish-English dictionary or one of the Renaissance polyglot dictionaries that organized words alphabetically according to their Latin equivalent (often referred to as a *calepin*, in the same generic way that *Webster's* is used today).

What Mather left on paper from his Spanish study not only helps us assess his proficiency, it also provides a guide to his possible instructional texts. Learner language (or "interlanguage") is used in SLA theory to refer to the halting, often unidiomatic speech or writing that a beginning learner makes actively. It is unlike "baby talk" in one's native language because, as Chapter VI outlined, the neural pathways for syntax are laid down early. Interlanguage is characterized by interference from the native language: that is, when assumptions about morphology and syntax get in the way of supple, idiomatic language production in a second language. For example, an English-speaking beginner in Spanish might want to follow their intuitive sense of word order and, to express the thought *I like the blue sky,* come up with *Gusto el azul cielo* ("I am pleasing the ceiling blue") instead of *El cielo azul me gusta.* Not only is the latter syntactically normal in Spanish, but the conventionality of *el cielo azul* rules out the alternative semantic possibility of "ceiling" for *cielo.* Rather than simply dismissing such bits of learner interlanguage as erroneous or bad, applied linguists use them to predict points of interference and try to work around them. Like accented speech, interlanguage can betray the user's native tongue.[4]

Applying this nonjudgmental assessment to the parts of *La Fe del Christiano* that were originally composed in Spanish, we can see Mather's sentences are syntactically well constructed. He correctly uses pronouns and direct and indirect objects. All his verbs are conjugated properly across regular and irregular forms, both in the indicative mood (present, preterite, imperfect, and future are all represented here) and in the subjunctive ("al fin que consigamos Salvacion eternal" [so that we might gain eternal salvation] (*Fe* 11). He correctly inflects, or matches the gender and number of nouns, with adjectives and articles. There is something odd about the subtitle, "En Veyntequatro Articulos de la Institucion de *CHRISTO*. Embiada A LOS ESPANOLES." What is the referent to "Embiada"? What is being sent to the Spanish? According to the rules of agreement, it can't be the "veyntequatro artículos" (twenty-four articles), and the likely terms for book or tract (*libro, folleto, folletín*) are all masculine, so "embiada" can only refer to the singular feminine noun "Fe." This is not quite logical, since it's the articles that are being sent out, not "faith" in the abstract.

Mather's interlanguage "accent" as an Englishman can be perceived as well in subtler questions of usage. For instance, he is sometimes uncertain about when to add a definite article (*el/la*, "the") to a noun: his Latin could not help him here, since it has no articles. Romance languages, however, use articles even more frequently than English does. This is a common area of interference for native English speakers. Mather usually fails to supply the definite article necessary before an abstract or general noun: in the phrase "al fin que consigamos Salvacion eternal," for example, "la" should precede "Salvación." He makes similar mistakes with "baptismo" in Article VII, "Eucharistia" in Article VIII, and "purgatorio" in Article XII. He also stumbles on the convention known as the personal "a": when a personal noun or pronoun is in the position of a direct object, the preposition "a" should precede that word. Thus his phrase "impedir el Vulgo de leer" (to prevent the common person from reading) in Article X should read "impedir *al* Vulgo de leer." Other interlanguage slips from his failure to recognize the many exceptions to the general rule that descriptive adjectives should follow the noun in Spanish. Mather grasps that *grande* means "great" rather than "large" when placed before a noun, but he does not know to abbreviate it to *gran*, writing "Es una Grande Iniquidad" (it is a great iniquity) instead of *una gran iniquidad* in Article I.[5]

These are relatively minor mistakes that would not prevent a Spanish speaker from understanding the gist of the sentence, which is why SLA practitioners tend not to overcorrect interlanguage so as not to discourage students' efforts to keep producing more speech (especially if the instructor is trying to encourage inductive processing). These intermediate-level nuances are rarely covered in the early modern English-Spanish manuals I discuss in the next section. And none even attempts to explain when Spanish speakers might instinctively place an adjective before, rather than after, the noun it modifies (i.e., nonrestrictive adjectives), for these are questions of style and convention. Poor Mather blunders into translating "the Second Coming" as "la Venida Segunda," following what he thinks is the proper noun-adjective order, but it has always been *La Segunda Venida* in idiomatic usage: the inversion sets this instance—this "coming"—apart from all others, in the same way that the convention of capitalizing the "S" and "C" does in English today.

Also difficult to codify for second-language learners are the uses of prepositions. How to translate the prepositional "for," as *por* or *para,* poses a notorious problem for English speakers even when they are proficient in Latin (*per* and *pro* are the Latin antecedents, but the usage changed so much that they are highly unreliable as translation guides). While some of the early manuals try to shoehorn Castilian grammar into the long-disappeared Latin case system as a way to offer at least a rough guide to certain prepositions (like *de* and *a*), only one textbook offers any rule about the various uses of *por* and *para.* Mather correctly uses "por" twice in Article VI of *La Religion Pura,* but the non-Spanish word "par" appears in two other places. It's difficult to grade this part of the exam: did he mean to write *para* (in which case his guess was wrong in both instances), was this an interference from the French preposition *par,* or was it simply a transcription error introduced in the printing-room? Other errors seem to have crept in that way: Mather surely meant to write *comieras* (that you should eat) when discussing the Last Supper of Christ, not the *comierdas* of the text, which appears to be a portmanteau of "eat" and "crap" or "shit."

The endnotes to the Transcription and Translation explore in more detail Mather's linguistic as well as theological choices. My translation preserves this rather mortifying typo not to embarrass Mather, but as part of its larger effort to see *La Fe del Christiano* as his Spanish contemporaries might have done. Good teachers encourage original speech production by removing the shame of the mistake, and generous interlocutors overlook the nonstandard usages that pepper a learner's interlanguage with the written equivalent of a thick accent. Translating across time introduces a further estrangement to the contemporary reader because of the odd or inconsistent spelling and capitalization practices in early modern texts. A key word in the title, *Christiano,* does not conform to contemporary spelling rules. Academies of language and prescriptive institutions were established in Europe a few decades after Mather published this tract: later reforms by the Real Academia de la Lengua Española (Royal Academy of the Spanish Language) simplified many Spanish orthographic conventions for classically derived words, such as using the digraph *ch* for derivations from the Greek *chi* (X): Mather's *Christiano* was not a misspelling. The Real Academia also simplified to *c* certain Latin-derived words containing *ct* and *pt* (whose earlier forms appear in Mather's *sancto* versus today's *santo,* holy), acknowledging centuries of phonemic change that had made the spoken [c] disappear. It tried to fix the idiosyncracies of orthographic practices that oscillated between *x* and *j* (as we see in Mather's *dixo* for the modern *dijo,* "he said"); *v* and *b* (as in *biviente* for *viviente,* "living"); and between the cedilla (ç), *z,* and *c* for sibilants whose pronunciation was widely varied among Castilian speakers.

The fact that English did not follow the same path in regularizing spelling means that it is more difficult for us to perceive how, in Mather's time, English and Spanish resembled each other on the page more closely than they now do. *Christiano* became *Cristiano* in Castilian, whereas *Christian* stubbornly remains in English despite the silencing of the [h] in both languages. In both early modern tongues, the spelling of certain Latinate words wavered: between *i* or *j* (as in *Iesu/Jesu, Iesus/Jesus*), between *u* and *v* (each of which could be a consonant or a vowel), between *n* and *m.* And the *virgulilla* (˜), commonly known as a tilde in English, was not, at that time, a defining quirk of Spanish alone. A leftover from manuscript abbreviation practices, it was used by printers in many languages, including English, in the early book era to shorten a word with a nasalized ending; it could appear over *m, n,* or over vowels. In both languages, consonants on some words could be single or doubled, as in the *Sabbado* (for *Sábado,* Sunday) we find in Mather's tract. Diacritical marks were used sparingly, and inconsistently, to show syllabic emphasis in the printing traditions of both countries; in Spanish the *grave* accent (`) was still used along with the acute accent (´) over vowels; now only the acute is used. But one notable difference between the two is that hypercapitalization was quite common in early modern English, as Mather's writing displays, but considerably less so in the Romance languages. My translation reproduces this practice: his Spanish-literate contemporaries would have been as struck as we are by the text's apparently random capitalization of words that had no apparent connection to sacred concepts—words like those for "condition," "kill," and "with." Noting the idiosyncrasies of spelling and usage between early modern versions of English and Spanish is helpful in another way. Individual printers were fairly consistent in their stylistic choices. Thus, comparing the orthography of different seventeenth-century textbooks offers valuable clues about which works Mather most likely consulted in his learning and composition process.

Unpacking the Spanish-English Textbook Library

The printing and dissemination of instructional, scientific, and technical manuals was foundational to the spread of ideas in early modern Europe. The category capaciously absorbs everything from Erasmus's Latin dialogues to treatises on mining methods to how-to lessons on falconry. As Anthony Grafton notes, almost everything published in the period might have been used as a textbook, citing a reader's notes on the *Odyssey* that branch out from etymology to geography to ethics; the *Biblia Americana* uses the Bible as its master text in just this way. Chapter VI sketched the role of elementary-level texts designed to induct children—and Indigenous proselytes—into Protestant Christianity and literacy at the same time. Early schools that taught Latin grammar, such as Ezekiel Cheever's, became "grammar schools" that taught prescriptive *English* usage in the eighteenth century, and historians of the book have reaped abundant examples of the ways that textbooks shaped individuals within particular ideological formations. Although the introduction of print did not completely transform practices of second-language learning, it did accelerate the transformation of language proficiency into a kind of commodifiable knowledge that was now sharable among invisible strangers. Rather than threatening the livelihood of the vernacular-language tutors who had been a feature in European elite life since medieval times, the first bilingual manuals of the mid-sixteenth century actually increased demand for them outside the court context, as language schools opened in cities. Manuals for learning a second language have received somewhat less attention from historians of the book, perhaps because they exceed the boundaries of specific national contexts. But these texts, which could be used with a tutor or as guides to self-study, did their own kind of cultural work, testing theories of the origin of language and speech, and reproducing biases about the foreign culture within which that language was embedded.[6]

Samuel Sewall wrote a memorandum in 1691 requesting that his London agent purchase "Some Spanish Books; Barthol. de las Casas in Spanish, and in English too; Grammar and Dictionary, if to be had; and what else you shall see Convenient for my purpose of getting a Smattering of the Spanish Tongue; provide you exceed not forty shillings, and come below it as you will." It would have taken a while to fulfill such a request, as the voyage took five to seven months in each direction, but the timing allows for Sewall to have made sense of the epigraph he plants in *Phaenomena:* "hasta lo último de la tierra." At least one of these books, as we shall see, was still in his library when it was inventoried after his death; he may well have shared them with Mather. Mather's own library was legendary, as he writes in *Paterna:* "I had a Secret, & a wondrous Blessing of God upon my *Library. A Good Library* was a thing, I much desired & Valued; and by the Surprising Providence of God, it Came to pass, That my *Library,* without my pillaging of your Grandfathers, did by cheap, and Strange Accessions, grow to have I know not how many more than *Thirty Hundred* Books in it; and I Lived so near your Grand-fathers, that *his,* which was not much Less than Mine, was also in a manner *Mine.*" There are no Spanish books in the reconstructed inventories made by twentieth-century scholars of the Mather libraries, which were split and partially sold off after Cotton Mather's death, but those inventories are admittedly fragmentary. There was the Harvard College library too, and although Increase Mather was president during the time of the Spanish project, he was rarely in residence, and even as a Fellow, Cotton was not allowed to take books off campus; it is also not clear whether this library owned many Spanish books yet. Sewall's phrase "if to be had" suggests he was not quite sure whether language-learning manuals for English speakers wanting to learn Spanish were readily available (at least, within his budget). There were in fact nine English-Spanish manuals in existence at the time, each a plausible candidate for the two to have used. Each offered a different vision of the cultural capital that attached to an Englishman's knowledge of the Spanish language; they also told different stories about its relationship to classical Latin.[7]

The paradox of the Protestant hostility and suspicion toward the Spanish Empire that Mather inherited was that Castilian language and literature continued to enjoy an elevated status across Europe, despite the Reformation's disavowal of all states loyal to Rome. Dutch-Spanish and Flemish-Spanish manuals emerged at the very start of the age of print in the Low Countries, then under Spain's control. Spanish was the second language of the Holy Roman Empire: the first address to a papal assembly in a language other than Latin was in Castilian, and an Italian-Spanish manual appeared even before French-Spanish or Portuguese-Spanish instructional texts. There were no English-Spanish manuals in print at the time of Henry VIII's divorce from his Spanish wife and from Catholicism. The first two appeared in 1554, when his daughter Mary Tudor wedded the young Felipe II of Spain, and England briefly returned to Catholicism as the state religion. These manuals were translations of polyglot dialogues produced by a Dutch teacher, Noël van Barlaimont, widely copied all over Europe for generations; I have excluded these exceptionally rare texts as possibilities for Sewall and Mather's libraries. England and Spain were at war for the next twenty years and the teaching of Spanish as a courtly language stalled, though there appear to have been many bilingual spies moving across the Bay of Biscay.[8]

It was the literary cosmopolitanism of the Renaissance, not statecraft, that brought the first three widely circulated English-Spanish textbooks into being in quick succession in 1590–1591. The Italian and French literary forms of lyric poetry, proverbs, and dramatic genres that spread through translation to England were supremely generative; figures like John Florio taught eager clients (perhaps including Shakespeare) and authored textbooks for the hordes of courtiers, scholars, and writers who felt compelled to brandish some French and Italian. Spanish literature of this period, dubbed *el Siglo de Oro* (The Golden Century) to convey the figurative wealth of its Baroque poetry, drama, and picaresque narratives, as well as *Don Quixote,* was influential as well, in spite of the ongoing undeclared war at sea between Elizabethan England and Spain. A dedicatory poem in Richard Perceval's *Bibliotheca Hispanica, Spanish and English Grammar and Dictionary* (London, 1591) acknowledges that "Though Spanish speech lay long aside within our British isle" compared to the popularity of French and Tuscan (Italian), "Yet now at length (I know not how) steps Castile language in." Castilian, claims the poem, is "more stately" than its rivals, "as full of pretty proverbs, and most dainty privy quips,/ Of grave advices, bitter taunts, and passing galling nips."[9]

Perceval's own "Ad Lectorum" acknowledged that there might be others besides courtiers and writers who might need the textbook, calling Spanish "the tongue which by reason of the troublesome times, thou are like to have most acquaintance." Though mostly a dictionary, the *Bibliotheca* contains a concise grammar outlined in the same sequence as a Latin one. A few years later, Perceval's work was incorporated into John Minsheu's *Dictionarie in Spanish and English* (London, 1599). Minsheu, an experienced traveler and perhaps former prisoner in Spain, styled himself a "Professor of Languages in London," and he democratized Perceval's dictionary by making it easier for a nonscholar to look up words: instead of using a Latin headword to locate an entry, he introduced the now-familiar two-part lexicon, with one section moving from English to Spanish and the other going in reverse. Minsheu's preface fends off criticism of the book's imperfections by resolving "to put on merchants eares, to heare with patience everie mans speech and dispraisings of his wares." Perceval signed himself "Gent.," emphasizing the cultural capital to be gotten from modern language learning; but for Minsheu the manual is a product in a marketplace, a "ware." Merchants would have had occasion to bargain with Spanish intermediaries and to value Castilian as a lingua franca for the transoceanic trader: despite Spain's official protectionism of its American and Asian trade routes, the sale of wines from the Balearic and Canary Islands remained legal and profitable; smuggling and three-way evasive trade abounded throughout the seventeenth century. This Minsheu / Perceval teaching text evolved through several further editions.[10]

Having "Englished" the alphabetical order of the Perceval dictionary, as he wrote, so that it no longer forced users to search by Latin headwords, Minsheu would go on to do the same to Calepino's polyglot dictionary. *Ductor in Linguas, The Guide into Tongues* (1617), a gigantic folio-sized overview of eleven languages, was the first book sold by subscription. These were the only non-monolingual Spanish dictionaries produced in England until later in the eighteenth century, and either could plausibly have been purchased by Sewall's agent. Whether Mather used them when writing *La Fe del Christiano* is a different question: there are many deviations between Mather's spellings of common Spanish words and those used in the Perceval / Minsheu volumes. The Perceval / Minsheu cluster of books uses "i" for Spanish spellings in words like *veintiquatro, instruir, ir,* and *iglesia,* where Mather uses "y"; they also choose the now-modern orthographies for the Greek- and Latin-derived words *santo, bautizar,* and *caridad,* and a single-consonant version of *deseo.* It is clear that Mather was at least consulting other sources that followed different conventions, so this detective story moves on to the remaining seventeenth-century language manuals.[11]

Another adapted text published in this period was John Thorie's *The Spanish Grammer [sic]* (London, 1590), a translation of *Reglas Gramáticas* (Oxford, 1586), a Spanish-language treatise on the differences between French and Spanish grammar as they derived from Latin. It had been composed for academic purposes by Antonio del Corro, a Spanish convert to Protestantism and a professor of theology at Oxford. Thorie, his former pupil, added a fourteen-page lexicon to del Corro's manual and took it to a London publisher with both names on the title page. Thorie omitted del Corro's prefatory argument for learning languages: to keep the peace by becoming "vezinos de una misma ciudad" (neighbors of the same city; i.e., citizens of the world). Instead, he told Englishmen that studying the language would "doo you good and redowne to your profit." Although the connection to an exiled Spanish Protestant is suggestive, it is unlikely that Mather used either version, as very little of the vocabulary of *Le Fe del Christiano* appears in Thorie's brief lexicon, and del Corro includes very few irregular verbs.[12]

The third of these Elizabethan-era textbooks, William Stepney's *The Spanish Schoole-Master* (1591; reprinted 1619 and 1620), appears on a 1730 list that Samuel Sewall's son made of the books he inherited from his father—so it presumably guided Sewall's journey, at least. The title was published by Richard Field, a master printer known for his likely friendship with Shakespeare and who also disseminated (under the pseudonym "Ricardo Campo") the work of Spanish Protestants, such as Cipriano de Valera's Spanish translation of Calvin's *Institutes,* as shown in Chapter VIII. Stepney's title echoes Roger Ascham's treatise on teaching Latin, *The Scholemaster* (1570), as well as Claudius Holyband's language-teaching manual *The French Schoolemaister* (1573), and prefigured Edmund Coote's democratizing pedagogy in *The English School-Master* (1596). Like John Minsheu, William Stepney was neither a scholar nor a gentleman, but someone who had traveled in Spain and parlayed that experience into a marketable skill. His schoolmaster persona, speaking in the "Epistle to the Reader," welcomes varied readerly motives for learning the language: "I doubt not but that in the future age the Spanish tongue will be as well esteemed as the French or the Italian tongues, and in my simple judgment it is farre more **necessary** for our countrey-men than the Italian tongue is" (emphasis mine).[13]

In keeping with this embrace of all manner of readers, from the university to the court to the shops and docks, *The Spanish Schoole-Master* contained a much broader range of materials than its competitors, the Thorie / del Corro and Perceval / Minsheu texts. It featured seven new dialogues for learning everyday speech, one for each day of the week: Monday for travel; Tuesday, buying and selling; Wednesday, judging character; Thursday, eating and drinking; Friday, conventional speech with servants; Saturday, conventional speech with equals; Sunday, churchgoing. It's amusing to imagine Sewall and Mather reading aloud such lines from the dialogues as "Wherefore dost thou laugh, hedgehogge?" ("De que os reys puerco espin?") (64–65), or the earthy exchange in an inn, where the traveler attempts repeatedly to get the chambermaid to kiss him—and in response to her protests of virginity, insists that this makes her extra dainty: "soys tan mezquina, besad me os supplico" (you're so stingy! kiss me, I beg you) (112–113). In addition to dialogues, it contained daily prayers; thematically grouped word lists useful in everyday life; and *refranes* (translated by Stepney as "sentences," but the meaning is more like "sayings") which translated cultural values and supplied writers and wits with new material. Suggestively for the way English-Spanish manuals might index the tensions of the Reformation / Counter-Reformation, the sections in parallel-text format—the preface, lexicon, and dialogues—sometimes show disjunctive translations that create a space for religious indeterminacy. The Spanish version of the *Credo*, the Apostle's Creed, uses the phase "la sancta yglesia catolica" ("the holy catholic church") (159) although the Anglican version at the time had already replaced *catholic* with *Christian*. While the English-language "Epistle to the Reader" urges the pupil to "go forward in the learning of the tongue, that he studie above all things to be a good Christian, a loyall subject to his Prince, and a profitable member in his countrey," the Spanish-language "Dedicatoria" to Sir Robert Cecil preceding it commends him to be "buen subjeto a su Reyna, provechoso Patron a su Patria, y que goza con los Sanctos perpetua felicidad" (a good subject of his Queen, and a profitable patron to his country, so that he may enjoy eternal happiness with the saints).[14]

The presence of Stepney's *Spanish Schoole-Master* among Sewall's books makes it a leading candidate for Mather's use—but if it were his sole source, it was sadly inadequate to his task. Stepney's grasp of usage norms was imperfect (he shows confusion over the use of the informal *tu* versus the formal *vuestra*, for instance), and his grammar section is extremely abbreviated, giving only regular verb forms plus the auxiliary verb *hacer* (with different spellings than those used in *La Fe*) and nothing on other elements of syntax. Stepney impatiently refers the reader wanting more detail to find a different grammar "very exactly shewing all the parts of speech" (29). Stepney's brief, nonalphabetic word lists are inadequate to the vocabulary of *La Fe del Christiano,* and as with Perceval / Minsheu, his spelling conventions do not align with Mather's in several instances. No Elizabethan guide explained the rules of gender agreement or discussed prepositions; these usages were left to the reader to learn inductively.

Three additional English-Spanish textbooks were published during the Jacobean period, and would have been fresher finds for Sewall's book buyer. As with Thorie's appropriation of del Corro, many of these titles simply repackaged the work of others. For instance, an anonymous *A Grammar Spanish and English* published in London in 1622 was a translation of a Parisian French-Spanish book by César Oudin from 1619, and the translator also pirated the dialogues that went along with it, originally published in Paris by Juan de Luna. De Luna (translator of the picaresque novel *Lazarillo de Tormes* and one of the only native Spaniards to be involved with these seventeenth-century manuals) retaliated with his own parallel-text work, *A Short and Compendious Art for the Learner to Reade, Write, Pronounce and Speake the Spanish Tongue,* in 1623, excoriating Oudin's detailed grammar as being too Gallicized. He may have been undermining the Englishmen Minsheu and Stepney as well when he argued, "three or four yeares in a countrey, is not sufficient to know it." De Luna's twelve dialogues were thought to be so amusing and illustrative that they were copied by English and American textbook writers well into the nineteenth century. Then, John Sanford's brief *Propylaion; or an Entrance to the Spanish Tongue* (1611, 1633), only sixty-four pages long, offered an innovative fold-out table of irregular verbs printed in a small typeface. A scholarly work, comparing various Spanish authorities on pronunciation and accentuation rules, it recalled the Ramist "catechisms" of condensed knowledge that Mather had used and written in his Harvard years, and is a plausible reference source.[15]

There was a decades-long gap until two more new manuals appeared toward the end of the seventeenth century. James Howell wrote an English grammar for foreigners and attached a brief grammar of Spanish in 1662; and J. Smith's *Grammatica Quadrilinguis* (1674) served as an omnibus speed-introduction to the three major Romance tongues for the English student. Smith's text draws from and popularizes the polyglot grammar tradition (he admits to borrowing from Oudin), but it makes questionable inferences about Romance philology— calling Spanish a compound of Latin and French, for instance. The introduction to the *Grammatica* offers fascinating material for the history of language ideologies, for example: "The Spanish is like the People, grave and stately, and constant to one Garb." These Restoration-era texts, however, devote relatively few pages to Spanish, copied from other sources; neither contains a lexicon, and the orthographic conventions don't consistently match Mather's.[16]

The Key of the Spanish Tongue

There was another seventeenth-century book, however, that would have offered nearly all the linguistic tools necessary to build Mather's Spanish book: Lewis Owen's *The Key of the Spanish Tongue,* published in 1605 and reprinted in 1606. At roughly four inches by two inches, this modest duodecimo edition was meant to be slipped into a traveler's cloak or valise—the forerunner of the ubiquitous vest-pocket phrasebooks and dictionaries published during the century preceding the Internet. As with "schoolmaster," the word "key" appears in the titles of a number of early modern English books that promise a concise introduction to, or outline of, a skill: a "help," as in *A Key to Knowledge, A Key to the Gospel, A Key to Gauging* (accounting), or, and most famously in the North American world, Roger Williams's *Key into the Language of America, or, An help to the language of the natives in that part of America, called New-England* (1643), which grapples so fascinatingly with Narragansett. Although there was no documented copy of it in Boston at the time, Owen's title stands out among the candidates for being both practical and capacious.

To begin with, Owen's pronunciation guide is the most detailed of any among the early modern textbooks. About half of the *Key* is devoted to a detailed list of verb conjugations, grammar rules, and a paragraph on tendencies of Latin to derive to Spanish: all bits of knowledge that Mather displayed. It contains four new dialogues and a short dictionary section which contains every noun, verb, and pronoun in the sections that Mather composed himself, with the exception of a few abstract words to translate theological concepts like "transubstantiation" and "redemption": these, as detailed in Chapters VIII and XII, usually appeared in the Bible translation he consulted. Owen's market-conscious subtitle, *A plaine and easie introduction whereby a man may in a very short time attaine to the knowledge and perfection of that language,* is echoed in Mather's word choice in his diary entry about learning Spanish "in a very short Time." Owen's *Key* uses a diacritical mark above the letter to indicate nasalization ("gramar" for "grammar," "lõger" for "longer"), a scribal abbreviation used by Sewall and sometimes Mather, but rarely uses accent marks on

Spanish verbs. This might help explain the lack of diacritics in Mather's text: if one of your few printed models for a strange language rarely used accented vowels, they would not have seemed obligatory. The *Key* explains exceptions to the gendering of certain articles (switching to the masculine article before feminine words beginning with a vowel, as in *el agua*), but it does not have a separate section on prepositions, so Mather would have been thrown upon the sample dialogues to figure out the difference between *por* and *para*, one of the areas in which he slipped. The sample conjugations given in Owen's manual, moreover, are among the most commonly used in *La Fe: enseñar* (to show / teach); *oyr* (to hear); the auxiliary verb *aver* (now *haber*), spelled twice in Mather as *avia* in imperfect and *aya* in imperative; and *hazer* (to do / make). Despite Owen's claim to be no scholar, the *Key* does contain a few pages "shewing the conservation or mutation, of Spanish letters, in such words as are descended or borrowed of the Latine": a mini-lesson in historical morphology that surely would have been of interest to Mather.[17]

But the most suggestive correlation comes from comparing the idiosyncrasies of orthography, in this period prior to standardization, among the candidate manuals and *La Fe del Christiano*. Using the same corpus of about four hundred words that represents his original composition in Spanish, I compared over a dozen terms whose spelling varies among del Corro / Thorie, Perceval / Minsheu, Stepney, Owen, Oudin / de Luna, Sanford, and Smith. Mather's orthographic choices align most closely to Owen's, matching in nearly every case. (The test words were *agora, ansi, baptismo, biviente, boz, cabeça, annunciada, charidad, creyere, dever, dexo, dezia / dixo, embiar / ada, ensalçar, enseñar / ava, escriptura / escripto, escuridad, exercicio, governarse, passar, quando, sancto, yglesia, yra*, and the number-forms *doze, veynte y quatro.*) The notable difference between Owen's orthography and Mather's is that Owen, like every other English textbook author, uses the modern spelling of *pecar / pecado*, which Mather consistently spells with a double *c* (*peccado*): this, as I will suggest in Chapter VIII, comes directly from the Bible translation he used.

If Mather relied for his sense of standard Castilian upon Lewis Owen—and perhaps upon Bartolomé de las Casas, if Sewall's book buyer had indeed been able to procure a Spanish copy for him—then it belonged to a world of a hundred years prior. The Frazon brothers' Ladino, both spoken and written, would have introduced another somewhat antique register to the varieties of sailor's Spanish heard in the port at the turn of the eighteenth century. Owen's dialogues were workaday, and his vocabulary list, like Stepney's, was stuffed with terms for food, animals, tools, the spaces of cities and villages—along with the Spanish equivalents to "a man's yard" (*pixa*) and a woman's "dugges" (*tetas*). The English side of the parallel-text dialogues would have seemed quaint to Mather too, but perhaps no more so than the English into which Thomas Shelton translated Cervantes's *Don Quixote* in 1612. (In one of Mather's surviving commonplace-books, titled *Quotidiana*, he mocks a writer he does not respect as a "Don Quixot of the Quill," but it is not clear whether he actually read the novel in either language.) The point is that even in 1699, Owen's *Key* would have remained a supremely useful book commodity, despite its age and modest cut size. These attributes, in fact, would likely have made it an inexpensive secondhand purchase for a book buyer. Alternately, perhaps there had been no need for Mather to rely on Sewall's generosity or send to London on his own for Spanish books: the crews and officers of the ships plying the Wine Islands and the West Indies trade routes routinely bought and sold useful things to local traders. Mather could have picked up a *Key*, battered by maritime use, from one of those traders, like an enterprising college student scanning for secondhand textbooks.[18]

Mather's desire to learn Spanish in order to evangelize in America made him a different sort of textbook user than those anticipated by these London-based authors. With the exception of the exiled Protestant Antonio del Corro and the probably Catholic Juan de Luna, the authors of the late sixteenth- and seventeenth-century textbooks were all Englishmen who had traveled within the Spanish Empire and "translated" what the English perceived as Spain's jealously guarded institutions. Like Thomas Gage, Lewis Owen was a figure of ambiguous religious loyalties who spent his early childhood in England until his Catholic family sought refuge in Spain. He joined the Jesuit order as a young man, but returned to England disillusioned and became an Anglican. In the "Epistle Dedicatorie" to the *Key of the Spanish Tongue*, he cites his experience of living among Spaniards as the source of his authority. He states that he wrote the book reluctantly, at the behest of "diverse worshipfull Gentlemen and Marchants" who found the existing choices wanting. Owen assumes these readers need no further convincing that Spanish has a clear use-value: "To comend the subject I neede not, for the use, which is great & ample, will [prove the] necesitie & profit thereof." Owen insinuates his sectarian leanings by including something that no previous English-Spanish teaching text contained: an entire book of the Bible, 1 John, in Spanish. The first epistle of John seems an unusual choice. The Cambridge Press Indian Library, for instance, began its Bible translation project with one of the Gospels. However, Owen's innovation would have provided rather perfect inspiration for Mather's outreach to Spanish-speaking Catholics: 1 John is directed not at unbelievers but at those who have already accepted Christ, directing them away from false prophets, alerting them to the end times, and reminding them of key tenets of the Christian community based on love. Mather includes two citations from this book in *La Fe del Christiano*.[19]

Unlike the Natick linguist-artisans who produced the *Mamusse Wunneet-upanatamwe Up-Biblum God,* there was no need for Mather to translate the remainder of the New Testament. Either he or Sewall knew of the existence of Spanish Protestant translations made in defiance of the Inquisition, for in April 1698—several years after requesting his first Spanish textbooks with a budget not to exceed forty shillings—Sewall sent by way of a ship's captain heading to Amsterdam more than forty pounds in gold to augment his collection with the ultimate prize. Along with some linen for his wife and some marbled paper, this amount was to purchase a "Spanish Bible of Cypriano Valero" and an Italian Bible as well. Mather could see that Owen's section containing 1 John used the Geneva Bible translation for the English, but if he did not know that the Spanish section was taken from the 1602 Cipriano de Valera translation, the *Biblia del Cántaro,* the arrival of Sewall's package of luxury goods would have made it abundantly clear. The following chapter begins with Mather's measured and sometimes dissident use of that expensive and rare book.[20]

· VIII ·

Impressing the Word in Exotic Types

From the start, Mather's "Design" "to draw up, a compleat System of the *Christian Religion*" and "to attempt the Service of my Lord Jesus Christ, by casting this Treatise, into the midst of the *Spanish Indies*" included Bible verses as evidence for each of his arguments against Catholic doctrine: "because much objection has been made against *Creeds* of an humane [human] Composure, that this might bee liable to no Objection, I contrived every one of the Articles, to bee expressed in the express words of the *sacred Scripture*." The verb *contrive* suggests that ingenuity was required to get those "express words." The diary also suggests a concern with creating a printed object that would appear legitimate in the eyes of readers in "the Spanish parts of America": it should "bee liable to no Objection." While previous chapters explored the human and textual resources that were available to Mather as he composed original Spanish sentences and phrases, this chapter shows how he borrowed, abridged, and quarreled with the "express words of the *sacred Scripture*" in a particular Spanish translation of the Bible: the expensive and rare folio text Sewall had ordered from Amsterdam. His decomposition and recomposition of those verses would be mimicked materially in the work of the printshop.[1]

Cotton Mather, who ordered and supervised hundreds of print jobs in his lifetime, knew the capacities of the press as intimately as anyone who was not himself an artisan, and his composition strategy in this and other works involved an intricate process of selection. Coming up with original Spanish sentences and phrases represented one kind of "human composure," but the term also conjures up the scene of the printing room, where "composition" meant the skilled and tedious practice of selecting and arranging individual bits of type onto a composing stick and setting those lines of type into a frame for impression. The scholar composed a manuscript text; the laborers in the printshop composed its multiples. The making of *La Fe del Christiano* posed a challenge to the printer's ingenuity, as well as to Mather's. In addition to adding glosses with chapter and verse references in the margins, a passably Spanish-looking text would require what were known as "exotics": special types, here the enye [ñ] and cedilla [ç], not normally found in the English type cases of the time. Clues in the printed copies suggest relations between the unidentified printer and the earlier press artisans of Boston who had worked with languages other than English: foremost among them Algonquian, for which exotic types had been cast in England to supply the Cambridge Press. *La Fe del Christiano* thus shares a material as well as intellectual genealogy with missionary linguistics in the Americas.

Translating the Bible into Spanish

Given that a primary Reformation complaint against the Catholic Church centered on direct access to the Bible, the making of vernacular translations was of fundamental importance. Pious Congregationalists freely toggled between the Geneva and King James translations; comparing translations was not only a devotional exercise for Mather but a frequent starting place for the learned commentary he offered in sermons. At Harvard, Mather had studied the classical languages of the source texts that were known at the time—Hebrew, Greek, Syriac, Aramaic—and he taught his daughter Katy to read Hebrew so that she could (as he saw it) come closer to God's original language, of which all human tongues were a fallen representation. He owned more than one polyglot Bible, a virtuosic example of print technology that allowed the user to compare the source texts together on a single page next to the two Latin versions: St. Jerome's Vulgate (approved by the Catholic Church, but regarded as flawed by Protestants) and Erasmus's *Textus Receptus*. At the same time, translation was not a free-for-all; the fear of inaccurate translations informed arguments against the use of Indigenous languages in evangelization projects across the Americas, as suggested in Chapter IV. Although it is possible to imagine Mather setting his polyglot Bible next to his Spanish grammar and dictionary and setting out to translate all the "express words of the *sacred Scripture*" that appear in *La Fe del Christiano,* this would have been both theologically risky and unnecessarily laborious. Catalogs of Mather's library do not include any Spanish Bibles, but again the specificity of Sewall's carefully preserved notebooks and payment memoranda are helpful. The Spanish Bible that Sewall had requested from Amsterdam in the spring of 1698 was just what Mather needed to complete his task, and apparently it arrived within a year.[2]

The fact that Sewall knew to request the "Spanish Bible of Cypriano de Valero" suggests that some amount of information on the history of biblical translation among the Spanish had spread across the Atlantic. He and Mather may have known of King Alfonso el Sabio, who in the thirteenth century had rendered the Bible into Castilian: known as the Alfonsine Bible, it was never circulated. Defying the Catholic Church's ban on translation, early Spanish Lutheran and Calvinist translators began this work again, printing and covertly distributing their work from Protestant enclaves such as Basel, Amsterdam, and London. Among them was the Oxford-based exile Antonio del Corro, whose Spanish-French grammar is described in Chapter VII; his translation of sections of the Bible was synthesized with the work of Francisco de Enzinas by Juan Pérez de Piñeda, who published the first complete Spanish New Testament in Venice in 1556, and a version of the Psalms in 1557. Casiodoro de Reina made a separate translation of the whole Bible, using the Ladino Ferrara Bible as the basis of his New Testament; this became known as the *Biblia del Oso* (The Bear Bible; Basel, 1569) for its title-page engraving of a bear pawing at a beehive (a visual pun on the name of the printer, Mattias Apiarius). Reina was a late convert to the Lutheran wing of reformism. His translation was soon adapted by the Calvinist convert Cipriano de Valera, who called his version (New Testament, Amsterdam, 1596; complete, Amsterdam, 1602) a second edition of Reina's. It became known as the *Biblia del Cántaro* (Pitcher Bible), for the title-page engraving of a water pitcher figuratively pouring out God's word. Reina's version was reprinted in 1622 without Valera's changes; Valera then issued a "corrected" version in 1625 that became the definitive source for multiple reprintings and is now called the "Reina-Valera Antigua." This version history is important because it pinpoints the precise edition that Mather used.[3]

Between the time he published the *Nuevo Testamento* in London in 1596 (with Richard Field, who also printed Spenser and Shakespeare, here disguised as "Ricardo Campo") and the time he finalized the translation with the "corrected" edition in 1625, Cipriano de Valera experimented with several decisions about translation and orthography for the first Amsterdam *Biblia del Cántaro* that he later reversed. *La Fe del Christiano* contains several of these idiosyncrasies, which appear in the 1602 edition and nowhere else. In the Lord's Prayer, for instance, Valera wrote "Sea sanctificado tu nombre" in place of Reina's "Sanctificado sea," though he later changed it back; Mather uses the former, and also follows the 1602 "suéltanos" (forgive us) instead of "perdónanos" in that familiar passage. In the 1602 edition, Valera chooses "gentes" (peoples) instead of "Gentiles"; Mather does the same. Many other apparent deviations from the Reina-Valera Antigua also show that Mather was simply following the earlier Valera: for instance, "Id y doctrinad" rather than "enseñad" (for the command to evangelize in Matthew 28:18), and "vaso" rather than "copa" for the cup of the Eucharist. Most striking is the spelling of *pecado* (sin), a word Mather predictably uses several times, with two "c"s instead of one. This spelling of *peccado* was not given in Perceval's dictionary or in any of the early modern English-Spanish textbooks. Valera regularized it to *pecado* in the 1625 edition, so Mather must have standardized his own usage according to the 1602 edition. (The endnotes to the Transcription and Translation distinguish between places where Mather has actively changed Valera's version, and where he might only seem to do so if a reader compares his text to a later Reina-Valera Antigua.)

Access to this Spanish Protestant Bible provided something the secular English-Spanish textbooks could not: renditions Mather could consider reliable of theological concepts that were not found in the basic vocabulary of the English-Spanish learning manuals, such as the best word for "the common person." Recall the significance of language rights in Chapter IV, where Mather turned Acosta's words in the epigraph into a different meaning to emphasize the importance of hearing God's word *en Lengua sabida a Vulgo*, a language known to the common person. "Vulgo" is not in any of the textbook lexicons or in Richard Perceval's dictionary (though it does appear in some "Calepinos"). It is, however, the very term preferred in the Reina-Valera; contemporary Spanish translations substitute *multitud*. Proscribed by the Inquisition, none of these early Protestant translations was able to root itself into Spanish-language literary culture in the same way that the King James Bible, its near-contemporary, did in English. However, that historical comparison would prompt nineteenth-century missionary societies in the United States to revive the Reina-Valera as the basis for many later Protestant translations. Similar to the King James, the "original" sixteenth-century language of the

Reina-Valera Antigua has a foundational status today among certain Spanish-speaking evangelicals. A Roman Catholic Spanish Bible was not authorized until 1773.[4]

As indicated by Sewall's forty-pound budget for his order to Amsterdam (including the bolt of household linen and Italian-language Bible he requested as well), the 1602 Valera was a large, expensive folio volume. And it was rare: the number of copies printed in 1602 is not known, but less than one hundred are catalogued in libraries worldwide today. One can imagine both the owner and Mather admiring and lingering over this *Biblia del Cántaro* simply on the level of its existence as a book object. This copy did not remain in the possession of Sewall's heirs, but it is likely that one of surviving copies in the special collections of US libraries has its provenance from this first known import of a complete Spanish Bible to the hemisphere. That does not mean Mather's Spanish rendition of the "express words" was also the first: in seventeenth-century New Spain the censorship apparatus was a leaky valve, as Carlos González Sánchez has shown. Despite the Inquisition's listing of religious materials, a range of Latin and Spanish devotional texts circulated among but also outside of religious orders. Spanish-language versions of the Psalms and the Gospels of Matthew and John—not coincidentally, verses prominent in *La Fe del Christiano*—were found in early book inventories in Mexico too.[5]

Mather as Composer: From Psalms to Sorts

Beyond its practical function, the 1602 *Biblia del Cántaro* would have been a useful literary supplement to Mather's and Sewall's Spanish learning. Although it would take centuries for most Spanish readers to encounter it as a source of Siglo de Oro poetic language, Mather integrated the Reina-Valera translation into his commentary on the Book of Psalms in *Biblia Americana:* the only part published during his lifetime. *Psalterium Americanum: The Book of Psalms in a Translation Exactly Conformed to the Original* (1718) is perhaps the best source from which to extrapolate Mather's sense of poetry, as well as his theory of translation. The title of *Psalterium* carried the same message as that of *Magnalia Christi Americana* in terms of highlighting an American contribution to global knowledge. The "original" to which the English translation "exactly conformed" is of course David's biblical Hebrew. But because the devout reader was encouraged to look at more than one English translation of the Scriptures, the *Biblia* section on Psalms supplements Mather's English versions with those in every other language he could find. Without categorizing languages into living and dead or classical and modern, Mather finds divinity in the plenitude of language. He does not, however, include the Algonquian translation in the *Massachuset Psalter,* a 1709 adaptation of the earlier work of Job Nesuton and John Eliot. Despite the devastation wrought by King Philip's War upon the Algonquian print project, Experience Mayhew pressured the SPG into funding new devotional texts; this is the only imprint that explicitly credits the Nipmuc artisan-intellectual James Printer on its title page.

Mather's *Psalterium* cites Spanish translations four times, more than Italian, German, or French versions. Sometimes the comparison seems unnecessary: "Methinks the Spanish Version well expresses it; *Tomare possession,* or, *I will Take Possession of Edom,*" referring to Psalm 60, adds nothing. But sometimes Mather offers insight to puzzling renditions in the English: explaining the puzzling "all my Springs are in thee" in Psalm 87, he inserts "the Spanish translation, *Mis Oios,* meaning the *Eyes* of a watchful Providence." About Psalm 126 he writes: "And now, lett the *Spanish* Gloss yett more particularly and emphatically tel you, who those *Weeping Husbandmen* are. *Los Trabajos & Los Pios, Ministros del Evangelio, no serrán sin Fruto.* The Labours of the Godly Ministers of the Gospel, shall not bee without Fruit." Finally, about Psalm 27:4 he writes, "The Spanish in my Opinion hath a good Hint upon it: *Buscar en mis Dubdas* [dudas]. To *Enquire,* for Direction in the *Doubtful Affayrs* of his Kingdome." The six compact syllables of the Spanish resonate as a poetic kernel of truth that the long-winded English explication cannot replicate. Given that he wanted *Psalterium* to be used in churches as well as in homes, this is a surprising welcome for a language otherwise he had associated with diabolism and the Black Legend in the early 1690s, as we saw in Chapters II and III. It appears that reading the Reina-Valera Bible and writing *La Fe del Christiano* changed Mather's perception of the language itself.[6]

Psalterium was not only a scholarly work but a sort of hymnal, with Mather's own blank verse translations offered as the text for singing. New England Puritans are not known for integrating collective singing into their worship: it smacked of the ecstatic tendencies of Mass, or of the many "enthusiastic" sects who had been denounced for tipping too far into the realm of feeling the Spirit move the body (one such sect was called the "Sweet Singers"). The great age of hymnody and church songs was yet to come, through the successive Great Awakenings or evangelical revivals that would begin in the 1730s.

The adaptation of hymn singing by the Native and African American congregations who took hold of that salvific tradition and made it their own is the foundation of "American" music—a story outside the historical bounds of this one. Yet the Congregational churches did encourage chanting or singing of the Psalms as a devotional exercise. That the *Bay Psalm Book* was the first book published in the colony is proof of this, as is Mather's authorship of a tract titled *The Accomplished Singer* and his friendship with Isaac Watts. As a young adult, Mather had been instructed to cure his stutter by singing the Psalms aloud, because one could not stammer and sing at the same time. It is hard to imagine that, as he collated both the Spanish versions of Psalms and the verses of the Reina-Valera Bible, he would *not* also practice saying them aloud. As with second-language learning itself, listening and speaking, reading and writing were cultivated successively, not in isolation.[7]

The commentary on Psalms in the *Biblia Americana* is representative of his writing process in the entire work. As Reiner Smolinski explains in his general introduction to the ten-volume edition whose publication was finally undertaken in 2010, Mather composed it by sorting through "literally hundreds of tomes" for insights, sorting them into the place best suited for each gleaming bit. This million-word magnum opus may be seen as an early version of Vladimir Nabokov's twentieth-century fantasy of the perfect translation as one "with copious footnotes, footnotes reaching up like skyscrapers to the top of this or that page so as to leave only the gleam of one textual line between commentary and eternity." For the first Spanish tract Mather wrote, *La Religion Pura,* in particular, he used a similar process with Sewall's copy of the 1602 *Biblia del Cántaro* as the single source text. Mather pieced together the citations directly from Valera; however, he frequently condensed verses to make them fit into the available space. On a few occasions he changed Valera's translation into one that he, seated before his polyglot Bible, found more appropriate—or that better fit the limited space available in the four-sheet, sixteen-page work he had planned. These deviations from Valera are noted in the Transcription and Translation.[8]

The diary's mention of ingeniously finding the "express words of the *sacred Scripture*" turns authorship into an act of the compositor in the spiritual printing room, piecing together bits and pieces cast in the sturdy lead of God's word. Mather called this tract "a little Body of the Protestant religion": a body that was not solely mortal (i.e., not of "an humane Composure"), but fused to the backbone of the sacred Scripture. The term "composure" aligns the work he was doing in his study with the work he knew someone else would soon be doing in the printshop. It was the compositor's job to align the hundreds of metal sorts, or types, onto a composing stick. Just as a printer chose type from the case and lined them up in their proper order, Mather plucked verses from the Valera translation and positioned them artfully to buttress the point he was making. In this analogy, the Spanish Bible verses were like "sorts": precious materials imported, like the heavy cases of printer's type that arrived in the colonies from across the Atlantic. The plural noun *los suertes* in Spanish was used by printers to refer to the set of all individual types of one character (a letter or symbol). But it also meant much more than its modern sense as "fortune" or "luck." A now-obscure meaning of *suerte* indicates a sort, character, or kind of person. The term is used twice in prominent places in *La Fe*, once in the title, wishing that the Spanish reader would be "Suerte entre los Sanctificados": one with a place among those redeemed and saved by God, which I have rendered "be sorted among the Elect" in order to keep its multiple meanings alive. A phrase at the beginning stresses that the Bible should be read by people "de todas suertes," of all sorts or kinds. Again, the Perceval dictionary and the textbook lexicons contained only the definition of *suerte* as "fortune," but the Reina-Valera does use it in this context.[9]

Was the analogy of setting types and "sorts" already in Mather's mind when he recorded phrases in his diary like "I sett myself to learn the *Spanish Language*" and "I sett myself to draw up" the articles of faith? Writing of the headaches he suffered, Mather says: "God sanctified it unto mee, to produce in mee those Thoughts and Frames, that were worth all my Pain." When an entire page of type-form was complete, the compositor would lock it into a rectangular "form," or chase, for printing. Mather saw himself—perhaps self-aggrandizingly but in line with his conviction about his life's mission—as the weak bodily "Frame" into which God would impress the right "Thought" in Spanish.

The Case of the Missing Printer; or,
the Printer's Missing Case

The *Psalterium* was one of a small group of Mather's publications that fits our contemporary idea of a book: a substantial object bound in stiff boards covered in leather, cloth, or paper. (His other steady seller, *Bonifacius: Or, Essays to*

Do Good, was more popular posthumously.) Most of the 300-plus titles that Mather authored, in contrast, were not intended to be bound separately. Lacking boards as coverings and simply stab-sewn together, these Small Books were mobile and lendable. Their lack of covering was not a liability but an avenue for personalized usage: Matthew Brown has demonstrated that a pious reader might choose a selection of texts by size and theme and pay a binder to make a personalized "book" out of them. Not only was Mather invested in collecting printed works; he kept the local economy of publishing afloat. He gathered patrons to front the printing costs and provided a means for them to be repaid through subscription for the *Psalterium,* but that was an exception: usually he convinced patrons to sponsor the costs of printing some of his other sermons as pious donations. Some he paid for himself. Whenever more than one printer was active in Boston, he spread work among them, either to encourage competition or to make them all beholden to the family in some way. Book historian Hugh Amory notes that Boston printers carefully maintained their tribalistic ties: one publicly declared that they would not dare to print anything not approved by their "particular Friends and Imployers," Increase and Cotton Mather. So what did the printer think when Mather brought in this manuscript—in a foreign language never before submitted to the local press, and with a few demanding features like the margin glosses—to be reckoned for size and estimated cost?[10]

From the look of the finished product, it is evident that whoever composed and set *La Fe del Christiano* used a motley assortment of types, making them less than uniform and misaligned. This is particularly visible in the medium sizes of type employed on the title page and reused elsewhere for headings: one letter is noticeably larger or smaller than others in the same word and line, and some "o" sorts are rounder than others (see Figure 1). This suggests a motley case, put together from sets that had been sold at different times by type foundries. Other imperfections such as faintly inked type may suggest worn-out types or hasty work during the impression stage. The falling-off of the "O" at the end of "MATHERO" and the misalignment of "Ch" on "CHRISTIANO" on the title page could be the result of type that was composed correctly, but poorly locked into its frame. Are these signs of a journeyman's work? Finally, contrary to the English statute that printers must identify themselves, there is no printer listed beneath the title—only the designation "BOSTON, 1699." As David D. Hall has established, Mather experimented with many versions of his authorial byline, including anonymity, his first initials, the terminal initials of his two names, and finally the honorific initials "F.R.S.," for "Fellow of the Royal Society," in his final years. Yet only about a dozen among Mather's four hundred or so works lacked an attribution for the printer in this way.[11]

Surely Mather's conversation with the printer touched on the problem of how the Spanish language was to be represented in English type. The answer to that problem would depend on the printer's inventory of type sorts, and these all had a lineage going back to the Society for the Propagation of the Gospel in New England. The materials may show the hidden hand of the persons who worked them, so it bears retracing this lineage briefly. As described in Chapter IV, the press equipment that arrived in the colony in 1641 at the behest of the Society for the Propagation of the Gospel in New England was moved to the grounds of Harvard College as the Cambridge Press, by Sargeant Day Green and briefly Marmaduke Johnson. This press and its equipment were well used and ultimately "rearmed" by a new infusion of thousands of pounds of newly cast type in 1655 to meet the technical demands of the *Mamusse Wunneetupanatamwe Up-Biblum God.* This second shipment of type included extra K and Q sorts, a few "exotics" (such as Hebrew and Greek letters, and vowels with accents and circumflexes), and a special sort cast just for Algonquian languages: the double oo. The direction of the Cambridge Press passed to Green's son Samuel. During the 1680s, the Green family monopoly was periodically challenged by other printers who set up across the river in Boston: first Richard Pierce and then Benjamin Harris, each of whom brought new cases of type with them from England. In 1692, the Cambridge Press issued its final publication (a sermon by Cotton Mather), and the remnants of its equipment, including the type cases, were taken across the river to Boston, where Samuel Green's son Bartholomew carried on the family trade in partnership with John Allen, as "B. Green & J. Allen."[12]

The twentieth-century bibliographer who did the monumental work of cataloguing the work of all the Mathers, Thomas Holmes, assumed that the Green & Allen shop produced *La Fe del Christiano.* It's a logical inference, since there are no surviving imprints from any other Boston printers in that year. Green and Allen had at their disposal cases of several sizes of Dutch-forged types in the Janson/Elsevier style that were used for roman and italic letters; they also had a few cases of the Gothic/Black Letter typeface used for contrast and emphasis. Some of the stylings of *La Fe del Christiano* depart from Green and Allen's usual design work for Mather and others: none of their extensive range of type ornaments is used in the Spanish work (only a row of asterisks), nor is there Gothic contrast type. Perhaps the shop's supplies were so tied up in larger, more important projects that they could not spare the right sizes of type for this one. But that does not explain why a well-established printer would not list his name on the title page. A Spanish imprint would not be sold in Boston, so the attribution wouldn't help with local advertising for the shop (whose address was often included too), but the potential to have one's name spread to Mexico City and beyond was surely appealing. There is, however, another possibility.

At some point in 1699 or 1700, Bartholomew Green's much younger brother and apprentice, Timothy, left to open his own printshop. There is no record to tell whether Timothy had his brother's blessing, and with it a starter-kit of some of the press equipment that they had inherited from their deceased father, Samuel. Timothy Green was then only about twenty years old, and his name does not appear on an imprint as the printer until 1700. But that first job was indeed a work of Cotton Mather's. Timothy was one of Mather's congregants and would thrive on his patronage; Mather performed his marriage, but not Bartholomew's. If Mather gave *La Fe del Christiano* to Timothy as his first independent job, it could explain the anonymity: the young printer wasn't fully set up in business yet, or didn't want to go public. It would also explain the motley type in the heading and title-page lines. Other substitutions suggest necessity as the mother of invention: the uppercase Greek *upsilon* (*Y*) is used for an italic Y, and the lowercase *upsilon* (υ) steps in for an italic U (Figure 5). In contemporaneous publications from Green and Allen, the proper letter-forms for Y and U are used; the type designers tried to ensure the *upsilon* would be distinguishable from Roman letters. This is further evidence of make-shift cases of type that had been cobbled together from leftovers.[13]

An ideal type case inventory for *La Fe del Christiano* would have included special characters to represent the accents on verbs like *señaló, crió, entró,* and *amó:* the diacritics make a crucial distinction between *he showed* in the past tense and *I show* in the present tense, and between noun *amo* (master) and verb (s/he loved). Mather was punctilious in making sure that diacritics appeared in Latin, Greek, and Hebrew passages in his other works; the Cambridge Press equipment had included Greek and Hebrew cases as well as the commonly occurring diacritics in Algonquian: ò, ó, è, é, â, ê, and ô. There are none in the Spanish tracts, even though the Green and Allen shop possessed them. The printer did, however, find a way to represent two other "exotic types," as they were called. To represent five instances of the Spanish cedilla (ç) (the voiceless

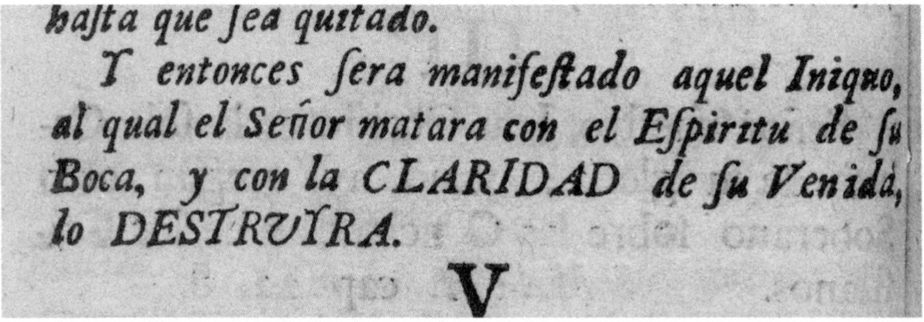

ḫaſta que ſea quitado.
*   T entonces ſera manifeſtado aquel Iniquo,*
al qual el Señor matara con el Eſpiritu de ſu
Boca, y con la CLARIDAD de ſu Venida,
lo DESTRUIRA.
V

Figure 5: Detail from Cotton Mather, *La Fe del Christiano: En veyntequatro articulos de la institucion de Christo,* showing the uppercase Greek *upsilon* (*Υ*) used for an italic Y, and the lowercase *upsilon* (υ) for an italic U. *AC7.M4208.699f Lobby VI.3.33, Houghton Library, Harvard University.

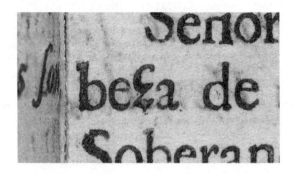

Figure 6: Detail from Cotton Mather, *La Fe del Christiano: En veyntequatro articulos de la institucion de Christo,* showing further typographical innovations to make Spanish letters, here the cedilla (ç) apparently formed with an upside-down [z] in Black Letter type. *AC7.M4208.699f Lobby VI.3.33, Houghton Library, Harvard University.

alveolar affricate later represented, in most words, with *z*), the compositor borrowed a lowercase *z* from a case of Black Letter type and turned it upside down, so that the round bowl of the descender would resemble the *c* shape sitting atop a tail that passably resembles a circumflex (Figure 6). Either way, it represents the kind of "ingenuity" that Mather described himself exercising by getting his hands on a Spanish Bible.[14]

The single typographic gesture that most dramatically sets off today's Spanish alphabet as "foreign" to readers of English is the wavy line that turns an *n* into an *ñ* (enye). Referred to in English as a tilde, the superscript eyebrow has the more specific name of *virgulilla* in Spanish, where visually, it performs no other function than to affirm the absolute distinction between the two letters *n* and *ñ:* a vowel written without an accent mark will probably be understood anyway, but *cono* (cone) should not be confused with *coño,* a vulgar expletive. Mather would have recognized it as a more universal symbol not particular to Spanish: as a suspension mark, used first by medieval copyists of Latin manuscripts and then carried forward into print technology as a way to conserve precious paper and ink. Early English printers used it to squeeze a line by rendering—for example—*longer* as *lōger,* found in Owen's *Key to the Spanish Tongue* and surely in hundreds of the older books in Mather's library. But Owen, and all the reference sources for the Spanish language, did not treat the *ñ* character as optional, nor did printers in Spain or Mexico-Tenochtitlán; it was included in every typecase.[15]

The enye posed more than a design challenge, for it was required in one of the most important words in the text, the title of Jesus as Lord (*Señor*). With movable type, it is important that an entire line of types be of uniform height so as to fit the horizontal spacers that would be added to separate lines of type—one could not easily add a swung dash above a regular "n." The *ñ* appears eighteen times in the main text, so the printer lacking a case of the right exotics resorted to a different strategy: improvisation. The standard English printer's case did, however, contain the English alphabetic ligatures that were then in common usage: æ, œ, st, long s-plus-t (ft) and double f (ff) were cast separately as individual sorts. Here the compositor, or perhaps the shopowner or perhaps even Mather himself, had the inspired idea to craft his own enyes out of existing ff types.

Someone used a tool, perhaps a metal file, to break the ascending lines on the left and right sides right above the point where the bar of the first f met the second, leaving a curved bow shape on the top that looked something like a tilde. For the italic font, the descender would have to be filed away as well. Figure 7 compares close-ups from the text that illustrate the similarities between this hacked *ñ* and the ft, in both roman and italic fonts. There are no instances of the ff digraph in this text to compare it to because that combination is rarely used in Spanish, but the long-s was designed with the same internal spacing as the f. A close examination shows that the internal space between the two vertical ends is too cramped; the top of the n is flat rather than rounded; and the eyebrow lacks the proper low-high-low-high undulation of a virgulilla. (Although there are no ff digraphs in *La Fe del Christiano,* the long-s plus t ft was exactly the same but with only a partial crossbar; Figure 7 shows a comparison between ft and *ñ*.) This hacked character does, however,

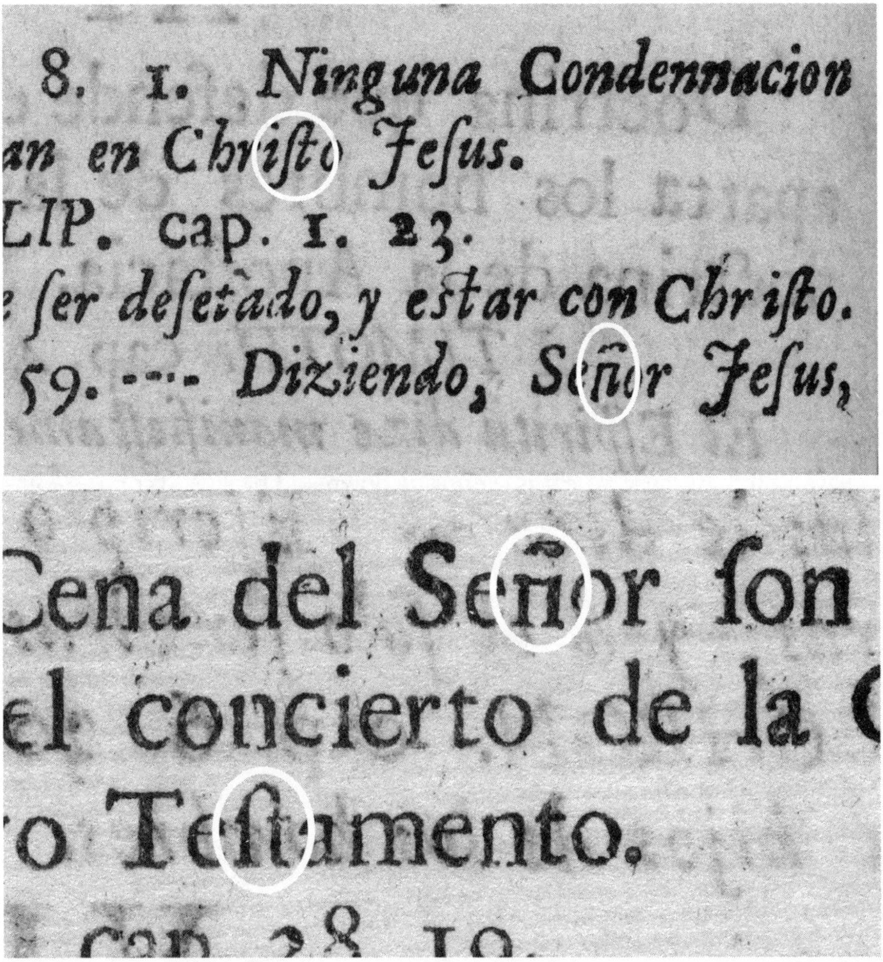

Figure 7: Detail from Cotton Mather, *La Fe del Christiano: En veyntequatro articulos de la institucion de Christo,* showing the making of *ñ* types by filing ff sorts. Since no ff characters appear in the text, a long-s plus t digraph is shown for comparison. *AC7.M4208.699f Lobby VI.3.33, Houghton Library, Harvard University.

approximate fidelity to the Spanish, and thus to the linguistic particularity of the key word *Señor.*

There was no type foundry nor paper factory in New England, so printing materials were carefully hoarded and repaired whenever possible. Once the metal was filed away, the individual types could not be restored to their original shape or reused. Based on the layout of four pages to a printed sheet, ten individual ff types had to be sacrificed to make these more authentic-looking characters. The printer was willing to destroy his own equipment in order to meet Mather's exacting standards: perhaps Sewall, who paid for the job, might have dangled the possibility of printing more Spanish-language work in the future. He used a good, strong coarse white rag paper: the best extant copy, held at the New York Public Library, is apparently pristine. If Mather did give this challenging assignment to Timothy Green as a trial first commission, the young upstart passed his test. Timothy Green's first acknowledged imprint, dated 1700, was Cotton Mather's *The Great Physician,* and Mather placed twelve major print jobs with him in the three years after that.[16]

Composing movable type is an intricate skill, perfected by repetition and muscle memory of the sections of the wooden case where each letter was always stored. Because type was set upside down and backwards on the composing stick, a lore has arisen that these hand-press era craftsmen were like automatons and did not read the manuscript before them for its sense. Yet there is ample evidence that this is not true. Very frequently, works appearing in another language included an apologetic paratext explaining that any errors were due to the printer's lack of understanding of the *sense* of the material. Owen's *Key to the Spanish Tongue* contained one: "what faults soever have escaped the print, impute them not unto mee, for that the Printer is neither acquainted with the language, nor yet well provided with such letters and other things, as the Spanish tongue doth require." The first French pamphlet that Mather had ordered from a printer, Ezechiel Carré's *Echantillon de la Doctrine que les Jésuites enségnent aus Sauvages du Nouveau Monde* (1690; printed by Green & Allen and discussed in Chapter IX) likewise came with an "Avèrtissement" [*sic*] begging the reader's pardon for any errors that had crept in because "L'imprimeur nèntend [*sic*] ni nôtre Langue ni l'Ortografe" (the printer does not understand either our language or its spelling), and directs any readers who wish to see the original Jesuit texts Carré quoted to consult with the "fidele et irreprochable Ministre Monsieur Mather" (pious and irreproachable Mister Mather). By comparison, *La Fe del Christiano* contains few obvious typos: "Gradu" for "Grado," for instance. Either Mather read the proofs very carefully, or the compositor knew something of these languages.

That microscopically small enye was, to invoke Mexican American slang, *rasquache:* improvised out of humble, rustic materials to provide its own form of cobbled-together aesthetic pleasure. Someone went to considerable trouble to honor the difference a diacritical makes. That they did so in Boston, in the traditional headwaters of US America's literary culture and the source of its Americana, reminds us how entangled that space was with the rest of the Americas. Since Mather was apparently the first English settler to discuss California in a public speech, it seems fitting to mention that when Agustín V. Zamorano set up the first printing press in California in 1834, purchasing equipment from Boston that was shipped around Cape Horn, he too had to disfigure the ff sorts to make his own enyes in order to publish in Spanish. Zamorano made peace with the lack of diacritics in the English typecase (and apologizes to the reader for them), but he was not willing to forego this alphabetic sign. Into our own time, the letter *ñ* has continued to represent an unassimilable cultural distinctiveness of the Spanish language. Within the United States, the enye has a particular association with Latina/o/x populations, a connection that the Coda takes up in closing. First, echoing Sewall's epigraph to *Phaenomena*, let us follow these copies of *La Fe del Christiano hasta lo último de la tierra.*[17]

Sending by All Ways to the Spanish Americas

Folded, cut, assembled, and stab-sewn together down the middle, the two large double-sided sheets that stacked up next to the printing press were transformed into Little Books. Bundled in string, they were brought by an apprentice or servant to Mather's two-story brick house on Hanover Street, near Prince. What was his plan for getting this strange package of conviction and ambition to "all the parts of the *Spanish* America"? He does not specify, but we can infer from the way he treated his hundreds of other titles. Boston's booksellers offered his histories for sale, and Amory identifies some of Mather's works being printed in editions of one to two thousand. Hall, however, estimates that in most cases only two to three hundred were printed, usually through subventions from patrons or from Mather himself. They mostly belonged to the gift economy: offerings to the Lord. As Mather wrote in *Paterna*, "While I was giving away *Good Books* Written by *other men*, I had all along a Secret Perswasion, That a Time would Come, when I should have as many *Books* written by *myself* Like-wise to give away. And I have Lived Since to see this Perswasion most Remarkably Accomplished." Mather is affirming his own sense of having been ordained with a divine mission to write, certainly, but he is also making an important distinction between printed works as pious gifts and printed works as property, as a later passage in *Paterna* makes clear: "While I gave away *Small Books* unto others, God gave *Great Books* unto me." The precious bound volumes in his own and his father's libraries were his most valuable possession and ultimately the only asset he was able to leave his heirs.[18]

Mather often left single copies with parishioners on pastoral visits, and mailed others to acquaintances abroad. But he also blanketed Massachusetts with them, inventing a pyramid-style distribution system for the region. Katherine Grandjean documents how, in 1704 (when he supplied most of Timothy Green's business), he ordered a thousand copies of a treatise on family prayer and divided them into "Bundles," each with a separately printed letter with a blank for the address. Filling in that blank by hand, he directed each bundle to a pious acquaintance in other towns with the request that they distribute them. In addition, he records many times in his diary that he has "scattered *Books of Piety,* about the *Countrey;* yea, in all the Towns." However, one copy immediately went to a Boston neighbor, none other than the Frazon brothers, either Joseph or Samuel:

> whereas, I have now for diverse Years, employ'd much Prayer for, and some Discourse with, an infidel *Jew* in this Town; thro' a Desire to glorify my Lord Jesus Christ in the Conversion of that Infidel, if Hee please to accept mee in that Service ... writing a short Letter to the Jew, wherein I enclosed my, *Faith of the Fathers,* and, *La Fe del Christiano,* I sent it to him.[19]

The Frazons' conversations with Sewall and Mather, and their loaning of the Ferrara *Tanach* to Sewall to give him "a sight of the Spanish Bible," had this presumably unwelcome payoff. The opening they had generously offered the two Puritan intellectuals into the linguistic and religious pluralism of the "American Hemisphere" turned the brothers into targets of Mather's evangelism. A quarter-century later, he would still be trying to convert Samuel, as Chapter IX details. In *Faith of the Fathers,* written just after *Fe,* Mather had shown off his knowledge of Biblical Hebrew and of medieval rabbinical traditions with the aim of convincing Jews that Christ was their promised Messiah. Pairing this tract with the anti-Catholic message of *La Fe del Christiano* would seem to be barking up the wrong tree: Jewish readers did not need to be told that Purgatory was a fiction. Yet the gesture builds solidarity with the Sephardim on the basis of their persecution by the Inquisition. It also follows logically from the Acostian principle of language rights: preach to the people in their own language, so that the words will reach their hearts. Showing off his Spanish skills was not out of the question as a motive, either.[20]

To extend Mather's usual distribution reach for the Small Books even farther—closer to larger clusters of Spanish speakers—would require more ingenuity. At the time of *La Fe del Christiano,* the postal system in the English colonies had just reached a crucial stage in its evolution: only in the 1690s was communication between settler outposts like Connecticut, New York, and Virginia regularly in the hands of English letter-carriers from point to point. Previously, long-distance communication had relied on multiple negotiations with Native intermediaries for permission or assistance in moving packages through their sovereign realms. We can better understand now Mather's 1696 diary entry, when he mused over the spiritual advantage of spreading the Gospel in Spanish now that "the ways of Communication" were opening "Every Day more" to the lands in Spain's dominion. A mail packet could be sent overland to Charleston, that frontier to the south where the English sought to advance into Spanish and Indigenous Florida.[21]

One tract did apparently reach the Netherlands: Mather received a second-hand report from an acquaintance in London in 1701 saying that "Your *Spanish Faith,* is gone further than it may be, you thought," to Protestants there who were referred to interchangeably as "Spanish" and "Portuguese." Ship traffic did not go directly from Charleston or Boston to Veracruz and Havana, and Mather's hopes about that opening within the Americas would soon be dashed. Nonetheless, it is likely that he followed what he described as "a Method, of lodging *Books,* which may be Instruments of Piety, in all the Vessels of any Burden, that may sail out of these Colonies." One such was titled *The Mariners Companion* (1709). If these Small Books were refused by the hands of sailors or less pious mates and captains on the docks, they could also be left discreetly on top of their trunks during his many ship's visits. He could imagine how boredom at sea might change a reluctant reader to an eager one. If the New England–based sailors passed the tracts on to someone else in Bermuda, Barbados, or Jamaica, so much the better: more readers, more potential sinners turned to the true God. Printed materials were not yet seen as disposable, so he could optimistically imagine each tract passing through multiple hands by way of this redistribution by strangers in those distant islands, where so many cultures, bodies, and languages comingled. It would have been a gamble, but not an outrageous one, to include tracts in the other common Caribbean languages, Spanish and French, among the English ones he left on ships outbound from Boston.[22]

Samuel Sewall, a former printer himself, likely paid for the printing of *La Fe del Christiano;* he records an expense for a "Spanish sheet." It was another of his pious redistributions of his father-in-law's trade-derived wealth: the same wealth that allowed him to treat Mather to a morning drink of chocolate, that exotic commodity cultivated by Indigenous laborers in southern Mexico and exchanged through growing hemispheric trade routes. Geopolitical developments in the years immediately following 1699 negatively affected that trade, as Chapter IX shows, but Sewall never entirely let go of the notion that the Spanish tracts Mather had written could be the first, modest building blocks in what would become a cluster of doctrinal texts that scaled up from small to large, as described in Chapter VI. In the spring of 1704 he writes to one of the overseers of the Society for the Propagation of the Gospel that the society might do well to branch out from evangelizing to local Native people: "It would be well if you could set on foot the printing of a Spanish Bible in a fair Octavo, Ten Thousand copies; and then you might attempt the Bombing of Santa [*sic*] Domingo, the Havana, Porto Rico, and Mexico it self. I would willingly give five pounds toward the charge of it, if it shall be agreed to be convenient to be done. Mr. Leigh commends the Translation of Cipriano Valera, which I am the owner of, in folio." It is unclear how serious Sewall is being here—his single folio copy had cost at least four times what he proposes contributing toward the making of ten thousand—but he does recognize that such a Spanish Bible would need to be smaller and more compact than his prized 1602 *Biblia del Cántaro.* In 1709, when the governor of Cartagena visited Boston, Sewall suggests, "If you should have a mind to look upon a Spanish Bible, I can lend you one of good Translation."[23]

If sending *La Fe del Christiano* on board vessels was indeed part of Mather's and Sewall's distribution strategy, their "operation" was already covert, eluding the Inquisition's censors by traveling separately from shipments of larger books, which were routinely examined and licensed in viceregal capitals. The tract's small size would have made it easy to slip into a folder or interleave with another text. Mexican historian Alicia Mayer has searched for traces of *La Fe del Christiano* in Mexican Inquisition records. While she found no items specifically naming Mather (or "MATHERO"), one 1709 letter from a functionary in Manila (which was then part of the intendancy of New Spain, which controlled the Pacific route through Acapulco) refers to "el libro cathezismo [sic] de los ingleses enemigos de Nuestra Santa Fe Catholica impresa en lengua castellana" (the catechistic book printed in the Spanish language by the English enemies of our Holy Catholic Faith). This catechistic book had been suppressed before it could reach readers in the Philippines. As Carlos González Sánchez notes, much of our knowledge of reading practices in colonial Spanish America comes not only from such Inquisition lists and bookseller's advertisements, but from inventories that were prepared for dividing the valuable property of the dead. The "cheap printed matter that we know was extensively used, published, purchased, and possessed" in the bustling capital cities is precisely what was *not* inventoried and preserved. So the possibility remains of another copy turning up someday, in the vast Archivo de Indias in Seville or in a private library, perhaps with its title page torn off or reused for some other purpose. Not one of the three extant copies in the United States has a provenance record. At least one of them was likely a copy Mather had saved for himself. Not long after the printing was completed, he practices his Spanish by reading back his own composition: "I went over the several Articles, in my La Fe del Christiano, in my meditations; and examined my want of Conformity to it, in *Godliness* both of Heart and Life." As with the *Psalterium,* Mather allows himself to revel in the divine plenitude of human language. It is a striking moment in which the student attempts to internalize the second language by reading *as if* it were one's own. This copy probably passed, like his other printed belongings, to his heirs through the legal work of patriarchal succession. The final chapters now return to this household and family context, first by way of an unexpected French connection.[24]

· IX ·

Racial Fears on Eighteenth-Century Frontiers

The rumors Sewall had heard in the 1690s about popular unrest in Mexico City, although not completely false, failed to materialize in a "revolution" in either the political or religious senses. Mather had made a hopeful reference to an "opening of the Ways of Communication," a relaxation of trade restrictions with the Spanish-controlled West Indies, but it turned out to be brief. Europe's War of the Spanish Succession spilled over into the Americas when England declared war on both Spain and France in mid-1702. Already existing border tensions at the edges of the continental colonies periodically broke out into violence that drew each empire's Native allies into the fray during the decade-long Queen Anne's War, as the sporadic American conflicts were called. Mather registers his disappointment about this blow to his plan to distribute *La Fe del Christiano* through commercial networks on the dedication page of *Theopolis Americana* (The American City of God), a paean to the worldly and heavenly glory of Boston that he published in 1710:

> Tho' our, Fe del Christiano, and our Religion Pura, cannot **yet** have its operation in the Spanish Indies, nor our Vrai Patron des Saines Paroles, in the French; **yet** let us Bait and Wait. (Bold emphasis mine.)

The first "yet" is temporal, suggesting a plan interrupted by an unexpected turn of events. The second reasserts hope that the plan may still work in the future. The "Bait" was laid for the "operation" of bringing the whole hemisphere over to Protestantism: for the moment, that would have to suffice.[1]

In the French text that Mather refers to here, *La Vrai Patron des Saines Paroles* (1704), Mather reworked the anti-Catholic precepts he had composed in Spanish for *La Fe del Christiano*. This chapter opens by situating *La Vrai Pa-*

tron as a companion text to the Spanish, briefly sketching Mather's distinctive sense of the French language. It was a language of both Catholic enemies and Huguenot friends; of Europeans, Creoles, and some Indigenous nations along the northern border with Canada who, like the "Spanish Indians" of Florida, could manage the lingua franca of the empire with which they sometimes chose to ally themselves. During the first decade and a half of the eighteenth century, Mather continued to wage his evangelical war against Jesuit missionaries by having a sermon destined for the western frontier translated into Iroquois and Dutch. Closer to home, he first attended to and then neglected the Wampanoag-language ministry whose care he had inherited—figuratively but also literally, in that he was one of a small group of local commissioners for the Society for the Propagation of the Gospel—from John Eliot. In keeping with the paternalistic attitudes of colonial missiologists across the Americas, he founded and donated funds to schools that would teach literacy skills to "Indians" and "Negroes," but in the language of assimilation, English.

The reference to a "French Indies" in *Theopolis Americana* returns us to the space into which Tuqui had disappeared in captivity to "French pirates." Queen Anne's War pinched Boston's sea trade and rerouted ships; privateering and privacy ran rampant. At the same time, New England became more dependent on, and entangled with, the inter-American slave trade. The categorization of personhood according to racialized physical features was well underway, as Boston's laws increasingly restricted the rights of those who were labeled "Indians," "Spanish Indians" and "Negroes." Mather's ties to Boston's new merchant elites, who dominated his congregation, led him to write an infamous tract on slavery, *The Negro Christianized* (1706), which tried to split the difference on the grave moral questions raised by the colony's increasing dependence on chattelized, rather than bonded, laborers. If Queen Anne's War was the defining macro-scale event of the early eighteenth century in the story of Mather's multilingual hemispheric evangelism, the corresponding crisis at the micro level of his household was the excruciating illness and death of its matriarch, Abigail, also in 1702. This and Chapter X thus continue the narrative line opened at the beginning of this book: an account of Mather's own household, anchored in structures of patriarchy and paternalism. Here the focus lands on the African-born man named Onesimus, who lived in Mather's house for over a decade at the start of the eighteenth century before insisting on his freedom.

A French Work Patterned on the Spanish

Mather's relationship to the French language provides a vital point of comparison to his Spanish work. If he imagined, through his reading, what the sixteenth- and early seventeenth-century Spaniards Antonio del Corro, Casiodoro de Reina, and Cipriano de Valera had risked by turning Protestant, he was more immediately moved by the persecution of the Huguenots. Refugees from Catholic France after the 1685 Edict of Fontainebleau deprived them of civil and religious liberties, the Huguenots scattered across the Atlantic were generally allies of the English. Mather noted the presence of "French refugees" in Boston as early as 1687, where the foreign Protestants formed their own church, which met in the Boston Latin School until they built their own structure in 1715. He befriended one of its longtime ministers, Ezechiel Carré, to whom he referred as "mon Reverend Ami." They shared a concern about the deep incursion of French Jesuits across the hemisphere, but particularly in Canada: a concern that only deepened as generations of Huron and Haudenosaunee peoples made alliances with the French, some even converting to the religion of the Cross. Jesuit evangelists, who were devoted language learners, had built missions and *réductions* not only to the immediate north of New England, in present-day Canada, but to the west, fanning out from present-day Wisconsin through the Ohio and Mississippi river valleys.[2]

Although Mather intimated in *Paterna* that he had learned French around 1690, he left no further details about the process. It likely involved Carré, for in the same year Mather shepherded to print an exposé of alleged Jesuit lies, which Carré had written in French, with an endorsing preface, also from Mather: *Echantillon de la Doctrine que les Jésuites enségnent aus Sauvages du Nouveau Monde* (Sampling of the Doctrine that the Jesuits Teach the Savages of the New World) (1690). Published in the same year as John Eliot's death, this preface shows Mather burnishing his hagiography of the "Indian Apostle" and reiterating the anti-Catholic motifs of *Triumphs of the Reformed Religion*. Into the benightedness of the pre-Columbian world, he argues, Eliot had heroically beaten back *Les Diables* by printing a Bible "et plusiers autres bons Livres en leur langue Barbare" (and many other good books in their barbarous language). The "Missionaires de Pape" (pope's missionaries), on the other hand, have only pretended to bring souls to God, instead availing themselves of the Indians' wealth and labor power and replacing their Indigenous religion with a cultic Catholicism that is a "copie fidele du Paganisme" (exact imitation of paganism).

Mather's endorsement suggests he was also responsible for getting the work to Samuel Green and John Allen's shop for printing, and likely for rounding up the funding to print it. As Chapter VIII notes, *Echantillon* is riddled with errors that are excused in the preface by the explanation that the printer did not know French, though the mistakes could equally well have been Mather's. The authorial voice in Mather's preface states "Jesuis un Americain," the missing space awkwardly making *je suis* (I am) look like *Jesuit*. What was intended as a contrast ends up underscoring a proximity: both sects were out to claim Indigenous souls and bodies, fighting over sectarian understandings of diabolism and the work of invisible spirits in the world, as discussed in Chapters II, III, and IV.[3]

Mather let his French go unused while he was preoccupied with Spanish, but the two were, logically, paired in his conception of the hemisphere's future. In May 1699, he prays for the Spanish and French parts of America and is rewarded with a vision "that the Light of the Gospel of my Lord Jesus Christ, shall bee carried into the *Spanish Indies;* and that *my* Composures, *my* Endeavours [*sic*], will be used, in irradiating the Dark Recesses of *America*." *Patron* was just the right word to include in the French composition that followed in 1704, for *La Vrai Patron des Saines Paroles* (The True Example of Healthy/ Salvific Words) looks very much like *La Fe del Christiano*. Because the sole surviving copy has no title page, we can only speculate on whether he turned to the same printer as for the Spanish tract, but *La Vrai Patron* resembles *La Fe del Christiano* in size, typeface, and style of the page numbers (centered at the top in brackets). The resemblance goes beyond the text's physical appearance. The content of the French tract was modeled closely on the Spanish one: although not an exact translation, a side-by-side reading gives the strong impression that Mather placed the earlier Romance-language text in front of him as he composed. *La Vrai Patron* is also a sixteen-page outline of the basic tenets of the Protestant faith, divided into two sections. Mather titled them "Le Premier Essai" and "Le Second Essai" (as if addressing the ghost of Montaigne). The second part, which begins on page 7, is heralded by the phrase, "Voila la Religion Pure!" in a strong echo of the Spanish *La Religion Pura*. The first essay enumerates fourteen articles of faith; the second lists them—but, as in the Spanish tracts, each article is backed with a chapter and verse citation from the Bible. Most of the biblical citations are the same, including the citation from 2 Timothy that serves as one of the epigraphs for *La Fe del Christiano* ("Reten las Sanas Palabras") and as the title of the entire French tract (*Saines*

Paroles). As with *La Fe*, it foregrounds the idea that healthy, sound words (using *sain,* a term associated with "salvation") will purify the corruptions of Roman Catholicism.[4]

Both Romance-language tracts attack the stress points of the doctrinal argument between the Reformation and Counter-Reformation. Mather defends the sacraments of baptism and the Eucharist as the only biblically sanctioned ones, rejecting the other five Catholic sacraments (11). As with *La Fe del Christiano,* an entire article in "Le Premiere Essai" is devoted to the work of the angels as working on behalf of the Elect (the French goes into more detail about fallen angels). "Le Second Essai" restates another epigraph from the Spanish tracts: "Assurement, l'Eglise Romaine est la Babylone à l'égard de laquelle la voix du ciel nous dit dans l'Apocalypse" (Surely, the Roman Church is that Babylon concerning which the voice out of Heaven spoke to us in the Book of Revelation). Readers are urged to direct prayers directly at God rather than to "les Anges ni les Saints" (the angels or the saints) (9); to read the scriptures directly (9); to reject pardon or forgiveness of sins from any human as opposed to seeking it from God (10); to understand transubstantiation as metaphorical rather than literal (10); and to reject the idea of Purgatory (11). Most importantly for this story, the tract repeats his earlier Spanish assertion that the faith cannot be spread without recognizing the language rights of others: "Il faut que les Services de la Religion dans l'eglise soient faits en un Langage connu" (10) (Religious services in the church must be done in a language that is known / recognized). The phrase "un Langage connu" doesn't go as far as specifying *whose* language this is: the Spanish has it more specifically as "lengua sabida a Vulgo," a language known to the common people.

"Le Second Essai" within the tract roughly parallels *La Religion Pura,* although the French version adds separate prose paragraphs, using the same or similar epigraphs as the Spanish model after which it was patterned. The French, too, ends with French versions of the Lord's Prayer and Ten Commandments. There are a few other differences. The word *échantillon,* which had been featured in the title of Carré's 1690 tract, appears in the final paragraph of *La Vrai Patron:* "Cet Echantillon Suffit, pour faire voir quelques sons les Raisons qui vous doivent obliger a vous separer d'avec *Rome*" (This sampling is enough to show the reasons that you must separate yourself from Rome) (11). In content as well as in their status as non-English printed objects, *La Vrai Patron* and *La Fe del Christiano* were themselves *échantillons,* samples that gave a taste of non-English American tongues. Just as he had adapted his

Spanish "Composure" into French, he would reuse *La Vrai Patron* as part of a longer French work published near the end of his life, *Une Grande Voix du Ciel à la France* (Boston, 1725). That tract was intended, as the title suggests, to be smuggled into France itself. But in the early years of Queen Anne's War, the more immediate threat was on New England's own borders.

Captive and/or Catholic

Although Mather had written that *La Fe del Christiano* and *La Vrai Patron* were destined for the Spanish and French Indies, respectively, his son and first biographer Samuel Mather wrote that the latter was "design'd for the Instruction of our French *Captives*." Read as "French Protestants held captive," this referenced those Huguenots who were imprisoned for their religion throughout the Old and New Worlds. But the phrase also means "our English compatriots held captive by Frenchmen," including Mather's own cousin John Williams, taken as a prisoner of war to Montreal after the Deerfield raid of early 1704 and whose story Mather would later shoehorn into a very popular captivity narrative. Before and after the Deerfield raid, the colony's northern border with French Canada—including the nominally English, but strongly Indigenous colony of Maine—were considered danger zones for the souls of settlers, as well as for their bodies. Teresa Toulouse has powerfully argued that these popular narratives of captivity and redemption often welded together fears of Catholics, Indians, and the Devil with male anxieties about women's bodies. As she observes, some of the women Mather had written about in the early 1690s as cases of demonic possession or witchcraft were stamped by a prior experience of captivity in the French-Indian world that exposed them to cultural and linguistic otherness. For instance, Hannah Duston's Abenaki captors had been French Catholic proselytes. Mercy Short, who had similarly been redeemed from successive Abenaki-Sokoki and French captors, was later tormented by a malicious spirit. Mather recounts that during his treatment of Short, this demon taunted her by pulling a French Catholic devotional book titled *Les saints devoirs de l'âme dévoté* (The Holy Duties of the Devoted Soul) from Mather's library shelves while he was out of the room. Mather does not explain to readers why he possessed a copy of this diabolical book in the first place. But it may be that he was inspired to craft Protestant replacements for such Catholic devotionals earlier in the decade, as a result of these interviews with Short and Dunstan. If his Jesuit opponents were circulating works like these in the two major imperial languages of North America—along with, perhaps, the manuscripts revealing how they had learned to speak to Indigenous people in their own tongues—then *La Fe del Christiano, La Vrai Patron,* and *Another Tongue* would go out to do battle with them in print.[5]

Mather's French and Spanish tracts could stand on their own as salvos in the long doctrinal quarrel between Catholics and Protestants in Europe, of course. However, *La Fe del Christiano* and *La Vrai Patron* were forged in the motivating circumstance of this long sectarian and imperial rivalry to control Amerindian souls and bodies. For the late-arriving English, multilingual evangelism might mean ministering to "Pagans" who had never heard the word of their God (as the SPG's mission would have it), or it could mean "curing" them of a diseased form of Christianity to which they had already been exposed by Jesuits. The threat of Protestants being taken captive and held for ransom among Catholicized Indians, as Duston and Short had been, intensified after 1702 as the Americas became a theater of Queen Anne's War, which cemented the Spanish-French alliance. But the settlers did not need Indigenous people to infect them with Catholic heresy at second hand. A three-part catechism Mather published in English in 1708 was designed to combat "the Apostasy of some few of our People to *Popery* in Canada": Even "our People" were susceptible. A 1717 diary entry records his fervent prayers for cousins being held in "Captivity among the Spaniards." The persons to whom Mather was refers here is unclear, but one can imagine him fearing their faith might wobble under such stress.[6]

From a Native perspective, of course, it was the Europeans who subjected them to forms of cruel captivity from which—as with the combatants in King Philip's War punished by Caribbean slavery—there was rarely any "redemption" or return to their own lands and people. As Chapters IV and V detail, an enormous range of linguistically adept, partially assimilated Native, African, and ethnogenetically mixed people moved through North America on the cusp of the eighteenth century, unsettling religious and cultural boundaries in ways that often confounded categories of identity. The man I have called Tuqui, standing in speculatively for those Timucua refugees later enslaved as "Spanish Indians," would be one example; Mercy Short's Sokoki captors—practicing Catholics who were conversant and perhaps literate in French—could be another. Posthumously, Samuel Mather opined that *La Vrai Patron* was "design'd for the Instruction of our French *Captives*," imagining its readers either as Huguenots or as New Englanders. Yet his father's own lines in *Theopolis Americana* imaginatively cast the Spanish and French tracts into the Catholic "Indies," where they might reach other audiences who were literate but not European. Whether Mather himself was able to imagine this non-white readership is open to question. Yet such a realization would have been consistent with his other concessions to what was coming to seem the natural course of empire: if more and more Indigenous people were assimilating to settler ways, writing in Spanish and French would be a shortcut to reach them. For he came to believe that the practice of learning and fostering Indigenous languages defended by Acosta and Eliot, the conviction that "it is better that we come to them" in their own rich and dizzying range of God-given languages, was no longer viable. To measure the interconnectedness of his Spanish and French work with the theological and social questions posed by Indigenous linguistic pluralism, it is helpful to see where he began to deviate from their example.

Indianisms, Past and Present

Mather's *Another Tongue Brought in to Confess the Great Saviour of the World* (Boston, 1707) represented a further salvo in the religious dimension of the multiple and complex conflicts associated with Queen Anne's War. Translated by Edward Bromfield and sponsored by the Society for the Propagation of the Gospel, this publication outlined the maxims of Protestantism in English, Dutch, and Iroquois to aid lay Protestants in "correcting" the work of French Jesuit missionaries among the widespread peoples of the Haudenosaunee Confederacy, especially advanced in the Mohawk Valley of present-day New York state. Mather's anti-Catholic outreach work in the French of *La Vrai Patron* and the trilingual pages of *Another Tongue* was pragmatic: the Mohawk were powerful trading partners of the Dutch Protestants in Nieuw Amsterdam. *Another Tongue* was not his first encounter with the language of the Mohawk. As far back as his 1691 encomium to John Eliot, *Triumphs of the Reformed Religion,* Mather had agitated about the relative success of Franco-Indigenous evangelizing when he saw one of their bilingual catechisms for himself. "The Catechism which is in the Iroquoise Language (a Language remarkable for this, that there is not so much as one Labial in it) with a Translation annexed, has one Chapter, about Heaven, and another about Hell, wherein are such

Thick-hull'd passages as these . . ." He goes on to ridicule the way Catholics explained Christian doctrine, using back-translation from the French to make the catechism sound unhinged. To pen this ravishing book review, however, Mather would have had had to spend time studying this catechism's French facing pages, just as he had presumably done with the Catholic devotional *Les saints devoirs de l'âme dévoté* that the Mercy Short account reveals as being in his personal library. Given the aura of danger that Mather had summoned around these Catholic books in the context of witchcraft, he seems to practice a kind of exposure therapy upon himself, risking the contamination of "Apostasy to *Popery*" that accompanied them for some English captives.[7]

Mather's derisive remarks about the Mohawk language lacking /l/ sounds in *Triumphs of the Reformed Religion* recall his complaints against the Algonquian language elsewhere in that earlier text: that the lack of the /r/ sound in this local tongue, along with the agglutinative properties of its syntax to make long words, was a sign of the people's barbarous nature.[8] But *Another Tongue* is a handsomely produced volume. If Mather's push to get *Another Tongue* into print had much to do with an intensification of anxiety about Franco-Indigenous alliances during Queen Anne's War, it also represented a return to the original Catholic plan to catechize Indigenous Americans in their own language, and with the aid of print. If he had mocked that effort among the Jesuits in *Triumphs*, he re-committed to it after *La Fe del Christiano*. It was this project that led Samuel Mather, in his biography, to claim that his father had "mastered" the Iroquois language in his forty-fifth year (aligning with the 1707 publication date), distorting a reference in *Paterna* to the seven languages in which Mather had *published* to insinuate that he deserved credit for composing it in Iroquois as well. Suggestively, however, Samuel mentions Iroquois in the same sentence as Spanish and French as languages in which his father sought to "better extend his usefulness beyond the limits of his own country": the distortion vindicates Iroquois as a living modern language of sovereign peoples of other "countries," coeval with the European languages of empire.[9]

With his ill-informed characterization of Algonquian speech in *Triumphs of the Reformed Religion*, Mather does not position himself as Eliot's language student. His later work does, however, claim the paternalistic, protective aspect of Eliot's mission. By the end of the 1690s, it was no longer the past Indigenous world described in Acosta's *Natural and Moral History of the Indies* but the *contemporary* condition of Indigenous linguistic plurality described in Acosta's *Procuranda* that was on Mather's mind. Perhaps prompted by Tuqui and his "Strange Return," or by his conferences with Sewall about Mexico's present state and future destiny, Mather went back to his Acosta volumes to pull the epigraph for a printed sermon that admonished Englishmen for inciting drunkenness in Native people so that they could take advantage of them. *A Monitory, and Hortatory Letter to those ENGLISH, Who Debauch the Indians, by Selling Drink Among Them* (1700) used a line from Acosta aimed at sixteenth-century liquor distributors in Peru as evidence that "Indians" in general are particularly vulnerable to alcohol. Having assumed common ancestry between local and distant Amerindians since his earliest writings about America, Mather traces that commonality to the present day, positioning himself as a defender of Native peoples in the manner of Las Casas: a would-be Indianist.[10]

Epistle to the Christian Indians (1700), written around the same time as *La Fe del Christiano*, likewise illustrates how Mather took on the Eliot mantle of the benevolent father. It begins by telling Native listeners and readers to give thanks for the language rights they enjoy, thanks to Eliot and his spiritual heirs. They were to be grateful that the Bible has now been "translated into your Language. Among all the thousands of Nations of *Indians*, on this mighty half of the World, there is not one besides you, so *Lifted up to Heaven*. And you have *Catechisms*, and other Treatises, in your own Language, to help you in understanding of the Bible." *Mamusse Wunneetupanatamwe Up-Biblum God* was indeed the first Indigenous Bible in the hemisphere, but Mather neglects to mention the hundreds of "catechisms and other treatises" in several Indigenous tongues that he clearly knew were already in circulation, in print and manuscript, in areas reached by Catholics: the Mohawk catechism was only one. The presence of at least three "Spanish Indians," with whom he conversed at the very least about God, in his household gave him further reminders of the vastness and diversity of Indigenous life. His audience, of course, already knew—from centuries of well-established communications routes across the continent—that there were faraway peoples speaking different languages, who were not like the Europeans but who were also called "Indians" by them. Migrant strangers like James Spaniard, who found a place among the Wampanoag, were a reminder of those extratribal contacts and exchanges—to which the English were not privy.[11]

While Mather frequently identified the American hemisphere, this "half of the World," as the locus of God's providential future, the vision of a singular America resonates differently in these paternalistic treatises than it does in *Magnalia Christi Americana*. There, he had insisted on the glory of the "Whole

Hemisphere" in order to lionize pious English Creoles as the better heirs of Britain's ancient glory than the Spaniards. That was a contest among European tribes. Mather's two Indigenous-language translations also show an effort to consider the local context together with a larger continental and hemispheric one: linking the local bands and coalitions in the Algonquian-speaking Northeast not only to the Haudenosaunee, but to the "Spanish Indians" he had read about in Acosta and whose continuing existence he was aware of, although he likely could name not so much as one of their languages or nations. *Epistle to the Christian Indians* encourages his Native audience to imagine that they belong not only to their own band of people, but to the "thousands of Nations of *Indians,* on this mighty half of the World," to the Americas writ large. More than a callback to Columbus's original misnomer, this is an early instance of Creole *indigenismo* or Indianism: the effort among pan-Americanist liberal elites in the nineteenth and twentieth centuries to apply a single cure, assimilative "modernization," to a multitude of peoples across the continent by emphasizing their common ancestry and condition. Its counterweight— pan- and intertribal organization by Indigenous people themselves—would, on the other hand, become one enduring route to anticolonial resistance.[12]

Moving Away from Indigenous Tongues

The timing of *Another Tongue* and *Epistle to the Christian Indians* correlates with Mather's investment in French and Spanish printed works: the latter became, among other things, potential tools to combat the Catholicization of Indigenous people. But these different language projects also coalesce with his assumption of duties as a commissioner of the Society for the Propagation of the Gospel, the New England Company, in 1698, and the beginning of an overseas correspondence with German Pietists through which he could glimpse the global influence promised to him as a young man in that vision brought by an angel. Mather's reports as an SPG commissioner (if not a fluent missionary on the ground) were now of great interest not only to the Society's English benefactors, but to a much wider Protestant audience. As Jan Stievermann summarizes, Mather "increasingly came under the influence of the Pietist ideal of a world mission and began to view the work amongst the Native Americans within the framework of a global evangelical effort that reached from Halle, Saxony, to the East Indian mission at Malabar." In *India Christiana* (1721), Mather takes as his theme the meeting of the "two Indies," West and East: it contains letters Mather exchanged in Latin with Lutheran missionaries in India who worked in the Tamil language.[13]

In 1707, Mather arranged for a Nipmuc translator to render his *Epistle to the Christian Indians* into the written Algonquian that had been standardized in the Cambridge Press Indian Library. This completed the inventory of the seven languages that Samuel Mather claimed he had mastered—though as with Iroquois, the count misleads by conflating publication with composition. It was, however, one of the last Algonquian imprints. With the exemplary praying town of Natick nearly deserted, and no bilingual schools remaining to teach literacy in the written Algonquian that could be understood by speakers of several dialects, the New England Company's support of Native Christians turned to schools and churches that gave instruction only in English. The community of literate Wampanoag in Noepe/Martha's Vineyard, with Experience Mayhew as their vocal advocate, continued to request replenishment of their disintegrating stock of pious works. Mayhew's *Massachusett Psalter,* as Chapter VIII described, adapted the Eliot-era translations to better suit their local language. But the community's plea for a new edition of the Bible—the very text that had been presented to them as the core of devotional practice, the apex of literacy instruction—failed. After some forty years of use, their copies of *Mamusse Wunneetupanatamwe Up-Biblum God* were scarce and worn. In 1721, Mather went to visit Noepe and to issue a recommendation for the English backers on this ongoing question. His answer was not what they wanted to hear:

> most of your commissioners are averse to doing it [reprinting the *Up-Biblum*] at all, and rather hope to bring the rising generation by schools and other ways, to a full acquaintance with the English tongue, in which they will have a key to all the treasures of knowledge which we ourselves are owners of. My own poor opinion is that the projection of anglicizing our Indians is much more easy to be talked of than to be accomplished. It will take more time than the commissioners who talk of it can imagine. 'Tis more than you have done to this day for your Welsh neighbors and captives. However, I will humbly show you my further opinion: that the reprinting of the Bible will be much

sooner and cheaper done at London, than at Boston. The experiment we made in printing the Psalter not long ago [a reference to Experience Mayhew's 1707 work], convinced us what a tedious and expensive undertaking that of the Bible must be, if in this place it be gone upon. Seven years would not be enough to finish the work at our presses, whereas little more than a seventh part of the time would perhaps dispatch it with you, if such a person as Mr. Grindal Rawson or Mr. Experience Mayhew (both of whom are most expert masters of the Indian language, and preachers to the Indians in it) might pass over the Atlantic and keep close to the supervisal [*sic*] of the press-work.

In this letter, Mather does not impose monolingual English as the only route to evangelizing: his analogy of the way the British kept the Welsh in a kind of internal colonialism seems a defensive move against the metropole's haughty judgment of the colony. His acquiescence to an assimilative plan in which Native people would be instructed in English, handing them "a key to all the treasures of knowledge which we ourselves are owners of," is accompanied by a pragmatic observation about the extraordinary time such assimilation might take. Perhaps he grasped at some deep level the simple truth that many, likely most, Indigenous people did not desire those "treasures" at the expense of their well-being and sovereignty.[14]

Rather than rejecting altogether the Acostian project of linguistic coevalness—"it is better that we come to them"—Mather recommends against the local reprinting of the *Up-Biblum God* on pragmatic grounds. He was not mistaken about the high cost of imported supplies in Boston or its rudimentariness for book production relative to London. His suggestion of sending Rawson (who had translated John Cotton's catechisms) or Mayhew to London in order to supervise the printing and proofs recalls Pareja's repeated travels to his own center of print culture, Mexico City, with bilingual Indigenous collaborators to oversee the printing of the Timucua library. This is a case, however, where Mather tries to split the difference on a moral commitment and ends up on the wrong side of history, as I will argue he does with *The Negro Christianized*. He fails to defend vigorously the very thing he was simultaneously celebrating in *India Christiana*: missionizing in the language of a people despite its seeming difficulty to outsiders. Mather's letter goes on to resign his post as commissioner after more than twenty years of service, citing a long list of other responsibilities weighing him down. (There were reasons for the tone of exhaustion and demoralization, as Chapter X describes.) After this decisive stroke on Mather's part, the active cultivation of a culture of reading and printing in Indigenous languages was thus suspended in New England for some decades. Later in the eighteenth century, Moravians in New York and Pennsylvania would revive this vision of a bilingual community of Indigenous Christians, and Eleazar Wheelock's school in Connecticut would produce the linguistically gifted Mohegan evangelist Samson Occom. But with this withdrawal of support from New England's most prominent intellectual went whatever was left of the tenuous legitimacy of New England's Indigenous languages in settler eyes.[15]

The Sea of Stolen Spanish Indians

Although Mather mentions in diary entries and letters that he has made efforts to establish schools for the acculturated Native population living in Boston, there is no corroborating evidence about these schools—no details about instructors, spaces, or resources. In a sign of the rapid expansion of the African-descended portion of the city's labor force compared to the Indigenous one, he more and more frequently links "Indians and Negroes" as the eighteenth century goes on. In 1717, for instance, after repeated mentions over several months in the diary of his desire to raise funds to "produce and support a *Charity-Schole*, for Negro's in Evenings, to learn to read, and be instructed in the Catechism," he writes, "I have now a *Charity-Schole* erected for the instruction of Negros and Indians, whereof I am at the sole Expence." If Mather ended up funding the school himself, this suggests that he failed to persuade his congregants of its necessity. Although the copula linking "Indians and Negroes" implies a firm boundary, it cannot describe the many people of mixed ancestry who destabilized that boundary, as the ambiguous status of "Spanish Indian" in V suggested. That discussion of Tuqui's possible origins moved between the continent—the shattering Timucua homeland in Florida—and the oceanic spaces of the West Indies, where he was taken captive by French pirates. It was a different thing to traverse that sea as a racialized subject in the early eighteenth century than it had been in the 1690s.[16]

In addition to the influx of Spanish and Carolina Indians brought to New England as slaves through the 1720s, the early eighteenth century saw the African diaspora swell into New England. Boston's economy had always been dependent on the sea, but increasingly it was local capital that funded trading voyages. The routes of seaborne commodities also shifted, from the North Atlantic destinations of the first colonists toward a preference for southern routes making for the outer Antilles: to the Tortugas for salt and then on to Barbados, exchanging sugar or molasses for rum. Boston took its place in an ascendant global economic system based on the wealth and specie of the extractive plantation economies of the Caribbean. Barbados was the main English hub of the African slave trade, which included enslaved people already "seasoned" to labor in the French, Spanish, Dutch, or English islands. As historian Gregory O'Malley has demonstrated, Creole traders began to bring these kidnapped Africans to North America at the end of the seventeenth century. Ships would carry a few enslaved people at a time alongside legitimate cargo from Barbados and sell them in entrepots like Charleston, New York, Philadelphia, and Boston. This intercolonial traffic within the Western hemisphere—not the ships bound for the Gold Coast with slaves as the sole cargo—"entangling the profits of many traditional trades with the buying and selling of people," was the principal route of the African diaspora to colonial North America.[17]

While Queen Anne's War put a damper on direct New England trade with Spanish and French colonies, smuggling and privateering flourished. Although by Spanish statute *Indios* were considered vassals who could not be enslaved or sold, Afro-descendant people were assigned to a range of legal categories. While an exponentially growing number of them were enslaved, there were ample populations of free people of color—variously called Afric, African, Ethiopian, mulatto, and other terms indicating mixed heritage. Under the privateering laws of the 1670 Treaty of Madrid, Englishmen were bound to free any "Spanish Negroes" who could show proof of their free status, and those whose masters came forward to redeem them could be ransomed; any seized captive not able to produce such evidence became human booty. However, an ample historical literature testifies not only to the inconsistent application of *castas* within the Spanish Americas, but to the lack of attention or will on the part of the English to observe Spanish codes. Sewall's diary recounts such a case in January 1709, of a "Spaniard" who disembarked in Boston saying that he was a free Black man who had been wrongly enslaved by an English captain named Teat. He pleaded with the Council of Selectmen to shelter him and support his petition for freedom. Teat, however, "alleg'd that all of that Color were Slaves," demanding that the court look at him to see that it was so. Against Sewall's protest, Teat won. Just a few years later in 1712, New York newspapers identified the instigators of an organized rebellion against slave-holder property interchangeably as "Spanish Negroes" or "Spanish Indians," setting off mass interrogations and arrests and resulting in the execution of twenty-one people of color. When the state's governor later investigated the case, those men pleaded the same: that they were free Spanish subjects taken and sold as slaves because of their skin color.[18]

As its population incorporated more Africans and nonlocal Native people, New England legislatively "delimited a race frontier that separated whites from Africans *and* Indians," as historian Margaret Newell demonstrates. She shows how Native people were held in involuntary servitude, in spite of laws purportedly forbidding their enslavement during peacetime, through forms of "judicial enslavement" such as the sentencing and sale of people as restitution for debt, the illegal extension of bond agreements, and the capture of child apprentices. Tracing the presence of Spanish and Carolina Indians among this group of the enslaved, scholars like Newell and Brett Rushforth have underscored the fact that the nascent racial logic of the colonial period was quite far from a Black/white binary, and that Blackness and slave status did not conjoin until long after Mather's time. Still unanswered, however, is the question of how visual regimes of racialization by appearance (skin color, physiognomy, hair) coalesced around "Spanishness," and how and when the sounds of linguistic otherness played a part in such identifications.[19]

The lives of "Spanish Indians" and "Spanish Negroes" are mostly visible through the mediation of archival records, such as Sewall's court petition, and evidence of criminalized behavior, such as running away. As newspapers began to be published in the eighteenth century, runaway ads offering a wealth of detail about apprentices, indentured servants, and the enslaved "Spanish Indian" appeared regularly throughout New England and the South, and the collective portrait these ads paint is racially indeterminate. In 1706, a Rhode Island newspaper advertised a runaway "Spanish Indian Man-Slave" with a "broad face, a broad flat nose." Safidillah, a "Spanish Indian Man-Servant" sought in 1723, had "hair pretty long and somewhat oiled" and "speaks good English" (implying it was not his first language). The Boston *Gazette* in 1764 described "a Spanish Indian servant, named Charles," with "long straight black Hair, small Eyes, high Cheek Bones" who "speaks *French* well, also a little *Indian* and broken *English*," who escaped along with his girlfriend (described as a "mestiza," in what must be one of the first appearances of that term in

English), taking with them weapons and a forged pass: "He is more than common white." Two runaway ads mentioned group escapes of Spanish Indians in collaboration with Black people, as in this 1712 description: "Ranaway from their Masters in Connecticut Colony the following Negro's and a Spanish Indian . . . [who] speaks very good English." Again in Rhode Island in 1730, two men escaped together: "a Spanish Indian Man named Warmick, about 24 years of Age, of a middle Stature, and Slim, Short Hair . . . And a Mallagasco Negro Man, Named Cato, about 21 Years of Age, a Thick Short Fellow of a Tawney Complection [*sic*]. . . . They both Speak good English." In both cases, their linguistic abilities were meaningful clues to Englishmen, suggesting that accents might be responsible for someone being designated a Spanish Indian. Black and Indigenous populations were conjoined by association in a caste of servitude, their physical differences less consequential than their status as outsiders.[20]

As outlined in Chapter III, colonial Creoles in Mexico had designed a spectrum matrix to classify all possible intermingling of populations originating in the continents of Europe, Africa, and America. But the effect of trying to distinguish between the many *castas* was to birth the generic category of *las castas:* people of color classed as lifelong laborers. Early eighteenth-century Boston may not have had *castas* paintings or observed genealogical mixing in the same way, but through the first half of the eighteenth century, it shunted "Indian" and "Negro" into parallel spaces of servitude, applying the same constraints on their behavior. A 9 p.m. curfew was instituted for both groups, and Sewall's diary registers their systematic mistreatment. His 1716 remark is often quoted as evidence that the chattelization of bodies was well underway: "I essay'd June, 22, to prevent Indians and Negors [*sic*] being Rated with Horses and Hogs; but could not prevail." His diary also records chilling instances of the everyday violence of slavery: in 1712, "This day Mr. Wm Pain's Negro Woman cast her self from the Top of the house above, 40 foot high"; in 1717, "Zeb. Thorp was accused by this Negro [Mrs. Hedge's Ethiopian woman] of Ravishing her."[21]

Despite miscegenation laws designed to keep the (clearly ineffective) legal boundaries restricting Indian slavery clear, they had children together as well. By 1723, the town Selectmen had made further regulations: no weapons, no stopping to fraternize while on errands. The church bell could toll only once for the funeral of "any Indian, Negro, or Mulatto," and it was mandated "that they be carried the nearest way to their graves." The Selectmen wanted to give these groups, now increasingly converging, no occasion to gather or (with the example of the 1712 Manhattan rebellion perhaps in mind) to organize an armed resistance. When a "Spanish Indian damsel" who had served his family ("a very useful servant") died of bleeding in the lungs in 1718, Mather wrote in his diary the only scrap of information we have about her: when he preached at her burial, "Many Indians and Negroes came to hear it." More and more, he lapsed into that additive phrase as a way to imagine the *convergence* of two subgroups of his "flock." It is no wonder that Mather found it impossible to raise funds for his school to teach "Indians and Negroes" to read, even if the text was an English Bible.[22]

Reckoning with *The Negro Christianized*

There is no question that Mather thought of this interspersed group of servants in a paternalistic way. (Never one to resist wordplay, he wincingly refers to them once as the "black sheep" of his flock.) The "*Charity-Schole*" he mentioned in the 1717 diary was a reanimation of a project going back as far as 1693:

> a company of poor Negroes, of their own Accord, addressed mee, for my Countenance to a Design to which they had, or erecting such a Meeting for the welfare of their miserable Nation, that were Servants among us. I allowed their design and went one evening & prayed & preached with them, and gave them [the] following orders, which I insert duly . . .

It is worth noting that these Black men themselves began the group: they sought his "Countenance to a Design which they had." The gathering was held between seven and nine on Sunday evenings, and Mather paid for Benjamin Harris to print a broadside with its rules. Those members who were not free must get permission from their masters to attend, and should police each other's moral behavior. It was a reprinted copy of these "Rules for the Society of Negroes" that "Spaniard Dr Mather's Negro" brought to Samuel Sewall in 1714 on the way from Increase Mather's house. This broadside, held at the Library of Congress and enshrined in its "American Memory" digital exhibit, is the sole remaining trace of this society, and it is not clear whether it met consistently for all the years in the interim, or whether it was restarting after a pause, as seems more likely from Mather's sudden concern with it in 1716–1717. Regardless of Mather's own motivations, by offering literacy—however constrained by the limits of Bible reading and the requirement to attend church—the society provided an imaginable pathway for Black men toward participation in colonial citizenship. As burdened as the organization surely was by its accountability to powerful Creoles like Mather, this fraternal society may have done more than read the Bible together. The historian Lorenzo Greene identifies it as a forerunner of the Prince Hall Masons and Black Methodists who, later in the eighteenth century, became liberationists.[23]

Was Spaniard (whose "Spanishness," like that of other figures mentioned here, could have inhered in his place of origin or in some linguistic trait) a member of this society? Had he been commanded by Increase to bring the rules sheet over to Sewall or did he do so of his own accord? Famously engaging slavery proponent Joseph Saffin in a debate, Sewall published a tract arguing for the abolition of the slave trade, *The Selling of Joseph,* in 1700, defending his servant Adam's inability to legally marry a Black woman kept in a neighboring household. He freed—but kept in his employ—other servants. Mather had invoked Christian hierarchies of master and servant to describe the duties of the latter in *A Good Master Well-Serv'd* (1696), but (as Elizabeth Ceppi observes) there he managed to keep the questions of the servant's origin and appearance apart from the question of their prescribed behavior. This would change by the time of *The Negro Christianized.* Departing from Sewall's abolitionist position, Mather cites ancient history as precedent for the practice while staunchly upholding monogenesis: the idea that all humans were descended from the same parentage and thus equal in the eyes of God, although their environmental surroundings may make them inferior in other ways. Slavery could, however, be justified as a rationale for bringing souls to the light of Christianity, though it required a solemn commitment to the paternal work of catechizing and literacy training on the master's part.[24]

Providing scriptural arguments both for the intellectual and spiritual equality of Africans and for their enslavement, *The Negro Christianized* is a confounding work. Mather expected that the tract would "Enrage the Divel" because it condemned swaths of white slaveowners for not attending to the spiritual welfare of their servants by teaching them to read the Bible: owning slaves without doing those things, or treating them inhumanely, was a grave sin. "Thou shalt

love thy Neighbor as thy self. Man, thy *Negro* is thy *Neighbor.* 'Twere an Ignorance, unworthy of a *Man,* to imagine otherwise." In his reading of biblical
history, expanded at greater length in the *Biblia Americana* commentary on
Genesis, the original Adam had been of "Tawny" color (a word most often
associated with indigeneity), and differences in skin pigment were the minor
result of different climatic influences as humans spread across the globe. Later
Black Christian thinkers would likewise defend monogenesis; Mather follows
the longstanding association of Noah's son Ham as the founding populator of
Africa, but rejects any curse or foreordained inequality upon them. Noting that
"a majority of Humankind on the *Globe* are copper-colored, a sort of *Tawnies,*" he ridicules the assumption that "none but the *Whites* might hope to be
Favoured and Accepted with God!" In its published version, the sermon also
includes a catechism that may be not only read *to* enslaved Africans, but *by*
them, as literacy training is one of the obligations of the Christian master. "If
you withhold *Knowledge* from your *Black People,* they will be *Destroy'd. . . . You*
must answer for it." The deep reading of *Biblia Americana* with which Jan Stievermann surrounds the pamphlet shows Mather consistently holding to his
conviction that all human souls were equally likely to be among those that God
had foreordained to be saved, as well as his Calvinist belief in the necessity of
Bible reading, which demanded that everyone be given access to the tools of
literacy.[25]

The Negro Christianized is a key, and contested, document in the history of
racial ideas in English America. On the one hand, Ibram X. Kendi puts Mather
at the head of his history of racist thought in America, calling him "America's
first great assimilationist": "By the [eighteenth] century's end, African slavery
sounded as natural to the colonists as the name 'Cotton Mather,' and hardly
any intellectual was more responsible for this binding than Cotton Mather
himself." On the other, Stievermann's extensive and learned analysis of this
tract as an extension of *Biblia Americana* decries the way "his texts have too
often been read through modern assumptions about racism and its sinister alliance with religion," and concludes that "his attitudes are not expressions of
racism in the modern sense." If Kendi's conclusion lacks distribution evidence
from a book-history perspective—the tract was not reprinted until the twentieth century, and it is not clear how widely known or available it was in the
years after Mather's death—Stievermann's insists on a kind of *sola scriptura* accounting of the formal writing alone, setting aside what evidence there is of
Mather's own life.[26]

As generations of Black intellectuals have documented, however, racism is best understood as irrational at its core. The publications demonstrate Mather's theological *reasoning;* the private writings—acknowledging the limitations through which we must read them—suggest that he struggled to reconcile that rational view with a negative affective response to both Black and Indigenous people. He had been deeply socialized into a tribalism that privileged emotional connections to his own *ethnos* and genealogical relations, regardless of what his own theology might instruct. Both Mather and Sewall were susceptible to the settler consensus that responded emotionally to persons of color as unassimilable strangers among the colony's white Christians. Sewall, the abolitionist, wrote with outrage in his diary that someone had "used him worse than a *Nigro.*" Mather seemed apoplectic when a Bostonian mocked him by giving his "Negro-man" the name of "Cotton-Mather," as Chapter X details. As with Mather's frequent and casual comments on Indian "barbarity," in these emotional slippages one can sense an effort on the part of these Creole elites to yoke themselves back from an instinctive predisposition toward fear and bias. The need for a sense of the past that goes beyond the documentary evidence a dominant group saved about their own doings, that brings the people rendered anonymous because of their status as racialized outsiders back into the picture, is precisely the aim of speculative and counterfactual history.

Mather may have feared that *The Negro Christianized* would anger slaveowners, and it probably did, but the response of his own congregants showed approval—and posed a test of the convictions expressed in it. They gifted him human property to call his own.[27]

The Self-Liberation of Onesimus

Mather attached to this man, born perhaps in Ghana, the unwieldy but significant name of Onesimus. In New Testament history Onesimus was an enslaved man—no racial character was ascribed to him—who escaped and converted to Christianity after hearing the Gospel from the Apostle Paul. Paul wrote a letter to Onesimus's master, Philemon, sending him back "that you might receive him forever, no longer as a slave but more than a slave—a beloved brother." In some traditions of this history, Philemon converts and voluntarily frees Onesimus as Paul wished, while Onesimus becomes a bishop. Like Paul's first epistle to Timothy, which condemns "man-stealers" (sometimes translated as "slavers"), the book of Philemon is one of the key texts for the Bible arguments against and for slavery. It is not clear whether Onesimus came to him with any shred of Christian faith that would have allowed him to join the Society of Negroes, but Mather stood by his determination to "make him a Servant of the Lord," as he had promised to do with Tuqui.[28]

Onesimus appears sporadically in Mather's diaries, often as resistant to the patriarch's orders. The catechizing probably began right away. If the Society of Negroes was still regularly meeting, the prospect of joining this small place of Black fellowship might have been an incentive for Onesimus to come to a confession of faith. Article IX of the "Rules for the Society of Negroes" states that the group should require that new members "learn the *Catechism;* And therefore, it shall be one of our usual Exercises, for one of us, to ask the *Questions,* and for all the rest in their Order, to say the *Answers* in the *Catechism;* Either, the *New-English* Catechism, or the *Assemblies* Catechism, or the Catechism in *The Negro Christianized."* Some years after Onesimus joined the household, in 1712, Mather—who called his children into his study to question them on spiritual matters, as outlined in *The Family Well Ordered*—flipped the hierachy of age and made one of his children "hear the Negro-Servant say his Catechism." The subjection of a grown man to the rhetorical position of the questioner, with a white child in the position of answerer, sets the Black servant under the child in a disturbingly prescient way that calls to mind the ritual humiliations of nineteenth-century slaveholders. As with the language textbooks and doctrinal manuals examined in Chapter V, rote repetition was an act of obedience to and internalization of the "master." For Protestants, however, such catechistic learning was meant to lead to independent thinking, and Onesimus showed that spirit.[29]

Onesimus lived in the household for ten years, marrying and fathering a child, although it is not clear whether they too lived with the Mathers. Mather acknowledged him as the source for his knowledge of inoculation, which was tried out during the smallpox epidemic of 1721, as Chapter X details. He earned money of his own by working outside the Mather house, and asked to purchase his freedom several times, finally receiving it in 1716. The draft of his manumission document is preserved among Mather's papers, and it reveals that Mather had originally proposed that, in addition to his purchase price, Onesimus was to continue chopping and bringing wood for the family every week for a year and donate a percentage of his monthly income to them. These lines were crossed out, however, and the final agreement does not include them. Although Onesimus's pre- and postslavery names are not recorded, his voice can be perceived in the dialogue of these crossed-out lines of the draft, rejecting the master's terms and proposing others. In leaving the household, he resisted Mather's biblical analogy. In the story of Philemon, Onesimus willingly subjects himself to enslavement again out of love for Paul, the man who had converted him. This love story, the fiction upon which Mather named Onesimus, would become the source of some of the most twisted collateral damage in the story of slavery in the Americas: the notion of the slave's affectionate attachment to the master, which persists to this day as the "magical negro" trope.[30]

Hemispheric Frontiers

Mather's copula of "Indian and Negro," and the ethnically and linguistically varied population that the English referred to as "Spanish Indians," are further reminders that the idea of race as a Black / white binary is a later imposition upon the complicated reality of colonial times—and our own. The Indian element in the ascendant order of racialized chattel slavery is gestured at in Mather's own description of *The Negro Christianized*, which addressed "the Christianity of our *Negro* **and other** *Slaves*" (bold emphasis mine). He further writes, "the late Calamities on the American Islands, I thought, had a Word in them, to quicken my doing of this Work." These "Calamities" referenced the periodic acts of resistance among enslaved populations: the kind of resistance that Sewall and Mather, in their different ways, were desperately trying to prevent. Mather proposed to send a copy to "every *Family* of *New England*, which has a *Negro* in it . . . but also to send Numbers of them into the *Indies* and Write such Letters to the principal Inhabitants of the Islands, as may be proper to accompany them." Over the decade when Onesimus lived with him, Mather could not ignore the increasingly brutal conditions in the British Caribbean plantation system, a system that could not possibly accommodate his model of the small scale of household slavery. They bore an overpowering resemblance to the conditions Las Casas had condemned in the Black Legend view of hemispheric history he and Sewall had absorbed years earlier.[31]

In the same year of Onesimus's manumission, 1716, Mather wrote: "Our Islands are indeed inhabited by such as are called Christians. But, alas, how dissolute are their Manners! And how inhumane the way of their Subsistence, on the sweat and Blood of Slaves treated with infinite Barbarities!"The islands of Barbados and Jamaica were "inhumane," and that spread northward into the other English plantation zones, especially to Carolina. When England's initial farming economy was transformed into large, slave-dependent plantations beginning in roughly 1710, English slave ships began making direct trips from the Gold Coast to Charles Town. Cato's Rebellion, the first of many slave revolts to upend Carolina, would follow in 1739. Perhaps from his conversations with Tuqui or other "Spanish Indians," Mather grasped the long-term implications of the Florida-Carolina border's transformation into a slave-trading zone. The Chickasaw uprising of 1715, he opined, was the result of the "iniquity" of this trade:

> The Colony of *Carolina*, to the Southward of us, is newly destroy'd by the dreadful Judgments of God, for which an uncommon measure of Iniquities had ripened it. The unhappy people, in carrying on their Trade with the Indians, had greatly Injured them and provoked them: And the scandalized salvages [*sic*] at Last, conspired, and broke in upon them, and with a massacre of the people, whom their first Fury fell upon, among which were fourscore of the Traders, they laid the Countrey waste.

He notes in gruesome detail the "barbarities," and reports it is now feared that the Indians are forming alliances not just to destroy Carolina, but the rest of the colonies, "under a French and Spanish Instigation." Depraved English slavers (included among the "Traders") were responsible for the "injuries" and provocations Mather references.[32]

Returning to a theme from Chapter III: in his later years Mather integrated these fears about the English sins of man-stealing into a second phase of millennialist writing. Stievermann writes that "In his final years, Mather became ever more certain that the West Indian and Southern colonies would be consumed in the flames," citing the millennialist text *Triparadisus* (1725): "Amongst the Instances, wherein Iniquity does abound amongst the Nations of the Earth, most certainly the Slave-Trade, and the Usage of Slaves, almost every where, but very conspicuously in You, o Carribee-Islands, it calls for a Judgment without Mercy, on Men becoming worse than Wolves to one another."

That men should become wolves—or worse—was a sign of the breakdown of what Mather viewed as the fundamental, benevolent hierarchies of God and man, pastor and flock, master and servant, father and child, man and woman. The binary of white and Black, or white and "Tawny," was not among those Christian hierarchies in theory, but social and economic forces aligned them in practice. If those practices distressed Mather, he decided they were beyond his capacity to vigorously resist. And in the decade-long span that stretched from his eldest son's adolescence until Mather died in 1728, the order of "a family well governed," as the title of his tract put it, would fail spectacularly at a personal level.[33]

· X ·

The Shipwreck of the Family Design

What became of the near-parallel births of the Spanish tracts and of Increase Mather Jr., the intended reader of *Paterna* who was to continue the line of patriarchal succession? Just as the missionary-language experiment of *La Fe del Christiano* did not launch a series of more elaborate books leading up to the "bombing" of Mexico and the Caribbean with Spanish-language Bibles, as Sewall hoped, Mather's conviction about his newborn son Creasy did not work out as his "Particular Faith" had promised. Moving forward from the geopolitical developments in the first decade of the eighteenth century, this chapter circles back to Mather's household to highlight his genealogical family, without letting go of the larger household's mirroring of emergent hemispheric structures of race. Mather was not the first Christian to struggle to close the gap between the faith's theoretical commitment to a universal love for all humans regardless of descent and the ineluctable pull of tribalism, with its magical feeling of blood kinship. As Chapter IX suggests, he went so far as to support (both in words and in financial deeds) training in literacy and piety for his "Indians and Negroes"—but was unable to produce from that doctrine of the equality of souls either an abolitionist position or a final defense of Indigenous language rights, resigning his position as commissioner of the New England Company rather than support the Wampanoag of Martha's Vineyard in their efforts to keep their language alive.

The non-European people he knew best came into his view as members of a servant class, and a biblically based paternalism about the master-servant hierarchy compounded their seeming difference. Borrowing an analogy from the two-way form of the catechisms used to teach doctrine and second languages, he may have held them back at the stage of listening and rote repetition that he associated with young children (as suggested by the scene in which he forced his "model slave," Onesimus, to recite the catechism before the Mather children). However, the gaps of information about the household in Mather's private writings give room to imagine the servants upsetting this hierarchy, engaging in dialogue, talking back. Before Onesimus walked away from the household, the African's own original speech in English (a tongue that he himself had learned once), offered Mather invaluable medical information. Onesimus's talking back also earned him the adjective "Froward," or insolent, and led him to negotiate successfully his own terms of freedom. In their differences, in their desires, bodies got in the way of the ideal workings of family government as an earthly model of the divine order. Those desires would separate Mather from Creasy as well. Ironically for this tale of patriarchy, the genealogical descendant who did the most to preserve his work was a woman who also chose, to an unusual degree, her own direction.

Mather as *Paterfamilias*

The composition of *La Fe del Christiano* was offset, as described in Chapter II, by other household dramas: the daughters of his first family, Katy and Nanny, were frighteningly burned by fire, with Mather suffering other pains alongside theirs. If the act most often recorded in Mather's diary is prayer, the second most common is injury and illness. One of the epigraphs to *La Fe del Christiano* made an important parallel between salvific words and healthy bodies: *sanas* in the *sanas palabras* referred to in 2 Timothy signified health and healing, as well as salvation. As a minister with interests in medicine, Mather saw himself as a physician for the soul. Soon after the Spanish tracts were dispatched to the Indies, as we saw, Abigail slowly and painfully died; her death ended his belief in the "Particular Faith" as a sign of reassurance from God about the future. His second family with Elizabeth Hubbard, however, restarted the project of patriarchal succession, as it brought him a second son, Samuel, and then a third. But the winter of 1713–1714 brought the worst outbreak of measles yet to strike Boston.

Cotton Mather—no stranger to mortality, having already buried brothers, sisters, a wife, and six babies or young children—experienced it as the worst single holocaust of his life. November was "A month which *Devoured* my Family." To the grave went, one after the other, a toddler named Jerusha, of whom he was especially fond, an unnamed female servant he had just succeeded in converting, and twin babies—a boy and a girl. Worst of all was the loss of Elizabeth, the only mother that Creasy, Abigail's youngest child, could remember. Also among the dead in that epidemic was a baby son of Onesimus, unnamed in the record, like his mother. Mather stood in his pulpit the Sunday afterward, called himself "One who *lives* in the midst of *Deaths*," and tried to console the flock with that old homily: live as if you will die today, conducting yourself with the humility and piety that follows from the acceptance of mortality. He tried to preach strength but broke down bereft, asking his congregation to pray for him who had no strength left. "The Cross is a dry sort of Wood; but yet it proves a fruitful *Tree*," he wrote in his diary and in Elizabeth's funeral sermon.[1]

Mather was fifty when the measles epidemic struck and left him as the principal guide through daily life for his six surviving children. The older Mather girls—Katharin / Katy, Abigail / Nibby, and Hannah / Nanny—were adolescents and young adults, all unmarried, at the time of the "devouring" epidemic. They were of an age to take charge of Elizabeth's surviving children: Elizabeth / Liza (also Lizzy), age nine, and Samuel / Sammy, age seven. But it was his older son Creasy who, at age thirteen, came to occupy the center of Mather's attention as he began to pick up the pieces of this familial devastation. Mather's approach to raising children belies the attempts of later ages to depict the Puritans as coldly detached, punitive, even abusive parents. Stern as the Calvinist concept of original and escapeless human sin was, it did not translate into corporal punishment, which Mather opposed. Instead, as he wrote in *Paterna*, it was better to cultivate such love of child for parent that the withdrawal of their good graces would suffice as a form of discipline. This meant barring the child from their turn at reading the Bible or studying with their father in his library. His son Samuel's posthumous biography of Mather mostly cuts and pastes from *Paterna* (and thus often reads as hyperbolic), so what he adds to his father's selective self-assessments seems more reliable:

> He would not, as I more especially knew in his latter Days, keep a morose Carriage towards his Children, nor at an haughty Distance from them; but forever when they came into his Presence he would condescend to the Familiarity of an Acquaintance; and thus he would instruct and edify, thus allure and charm us, thus make us love his Society, ever come into it with Delight and never leave it but with Sorrow:—Which Method, I believe, will work more forcibly upon any

Children of common Sense and more engage them to love their Parent
and encline them to be good and vertuous, than any crabbed Looks,
austere Orders or surly Demands whatever.

"Especially as I knew him in his later days" suggests that Samuel, as one of the
second wave of younger children, may have compared notes with his older sib-
lings and discovered the benefits of a parent mellowing in middle age. ("Con-
descend" here has the contemporary meaning of "descend": not "talking down
to" in an abrasive way, but coming down a level, as the children's friend.) Even
taking into account the hagiographic nature of a son's biography, terms like "al-
lure" and "charm" and "love" suggest feelings that went beyond mere duty.[2]

Because Mather's sect of Christianity viewed the family as a mirror of God's
paternal hierarchy, "Rebellion against Family Government" was a sin against
God, as he wrote in the 1707 sermon *The Best Ornaments of Youth*. His own
children broke rules: Creasy and Liza set off fireworks; Sammy stole a sweet.
His writings also hammer home the lesson that children are not their parents'
possessions to dispose of, or to take personal pride in: "The Good Thing that
is in any Young People, 'tis the Workmanship of God." Bragging on one's
children is like calling "The Geese all Swans! And the Crow telling, what a
Fine, white Bird she has!": the parent here is the sin-blackened crow trying to
take credit for the piety-whitened child. At the same time, birds were his fa-
vorite metaphor for talking about his children. "I would grow yett more fruitful
in my Conversation, with my little *Birds*, and feed them more frequent and
charming Lessons, of Religion," he resolves in one of many diary entries about
playing teacher to his children. For example, he might make the children read
aloud from "A Book of Piety" and then "*apply* it" to something in their own
lives. Learning and piety were "ornaments" that went together.[3]

As Chapter VI elaborates, Mather gave the children speech to repeat, or
texts to copy out, on the pedagogical theory that such scripted repetition
would eventually build up to the production of original speech. This extended
to the girls: Mather's insistence on the education of daughters, while not coeval, was ahead of most. Given a manuscript written by a pious woman to
read, Katy, the eldest, copied out the entire thing. She kept commonplace
books, like her father, and later wrote her own musings on piety. "Such were
her Accuracy at her *Needle*, her Dexterity at her *Pen*," he noted later, using the
metonymy made famous in Anne Bradstreet's poems. He made sure Katy became "Mistress of the Hebrew Tongue," later ribbing Harvard graduates who

might complain about the difficulty of that language, "Even our little Damsels ... make nothing of coming at this Uncommon Ornament." The description of learning a biblical language echoes the title of his well-circulated tract about women's proper conduct, *Ornaments for the Daughters of Zion*, in which he advocates for the advanced and practical education of women. Katy also studied medicine; in *The Angel of Bethesda*, he suggests that the interest came from her deceased mother, Abigail, whom he credits for her healing skills.[4]

The children's education extended to languages. If Mather taught Katy Hebrew, he might have also given her some Greek and Latin, but there was of course no grammar school that girls might prepare for. He mentions speaking Latin with both Creasy and Sammy; he does not explicitly mention that they attended Boston Latin School, but they must have. (Samuel's biography does state that Creasy "passed thro' the learned and polite education of our schools.") Although he had expressed hesitation in *Paterna* about dabbling in the Romance tongues, in 1717, when Sammy and Liza, both in the second set of children, "of their own Accord, incline to learning the French tongue," he paid for a master. It was likely a member of Ezechiel Carré's Huguenot church who ran a French school: Mather sent a bundle of copies of *La Vrai Patron* to that master in 1711, "to be studied by the Scholars, that they may at once learn the Language, and Improve in Knowledge and Goodness."[5]

If reading *La Vrai Patron* was an act of piety, both speaking and reading French could increasingly be seen as an accomplishment in polite society. As with the foolish "Geese" showing off their children, displays of genteel accomplishments and good taste could be done either flagrantly (which would be a sin) or moderately (as an ornament). Beyond trying to ensure the safety—in the sense both of salvation and of bodily wellness—of his children, Mather also tried to direct how their "Good Things," their talents, would be employed purposefully. To witness in the world would require recognition by it. As Mather took over the ministry of his father's church, more of its parishioners were entering its mercantile elite, and accordingly many of his later sermons address the question of how to be a businessman and still be a man of God.

Both *Bonifacius, An Essay Upon the Good* (1710) and *Theopolis Americana: An Essay on the Golden Street of the Holy City* (1709), spoken before the General Assembly, attempt to balance the ideal of a Puritan community with the reality of Boston's commercially oriented, increasingly diverse population. As Jennifer Jordan Baker puts it, "the New England economy, increasingly based on intangible and abstract forms of wealth during Mather's lifetime, only made more indecipherable the workings of providential dispensation." To what degree Mather compromised himself in adapting to this ascendant order of mercantile capitalism, which made New England society increasingly resemble the class structure of the old country, has been a topic of considerable debate; Perry Miller, for example, indicts Mather for what he sees as the hypocrisy of this self-adaptation. His congregation was full of West Indies merchants, and in earlier days, perhaps with Abigail's dowry, he apparently did some speculative investing on the cargos carried by Boston ships. Mather wrote of *Theopolis,* "I bore due Testimonies against the Corruptions of the *Market-Place,*" yet he was also clearly part of it, as Creasy's experience with entering that marketplace would show.[6]

The Career Path for a Creole Gentleman

Starting in the boy's adolescence, Cotton Mather introduced Creasy to their own private teaching text: *Paterna,* the notebook dedicated "To My Son" and intended to instruct him in pious manhood through his father's example. These one-on-one sessions likely focused on the passages in the first, second, and third "Lustres" that recall Cotton's teenage awkwardness, uncertainty about his faith, and "sinful thoughts," presumably about the management of wayward sexual desires. They also conversed about his profession. When Elizabeth died it was drawing close to the time when Creasy would have been sent to Harvard to train for the ministry. But despite the Particular Faith Mather had experienced in 1699 promising that this son would become a great servant of God—and despite having been sent down the street to his grandfather Increase's house for regular tutoring—Creasy either did not sit, or did not pass, the College's entrance exam, effectively closing that career to him. Mather then focused on determining where "the Genius of the Child lay." Creasy was interested in mathematics more than in natural philosophy and theology. Mather wrote at the time, "I would still ply him with all possible Methods for a most liberal Education in other Points; that he may be a man very useful in the World." Mather's *Bonifacius: An Essay to Do Good* (1710), one of his most popular works, had underscored this very theme of the exemplary, pious man of business.[7]

Just prior to the measles epidemic, in August 1713, Mather had sought guidance through "intimate conversation with Heaven" with regard to the "Disposal of my son *Increase*": "disposal" meaning the finding of a place for him, as well as answering to his character's "disposition." Mather apprenticed Creasy to a "religious Family, of a Merchant in good Business." After that merchant died (perhaps also in the epidemic), in early 1715 Mather drafted a letter in Creasy's voice to John Frizzel, a wealthy parishioner of whom Mather had requested financial favors over the years. (Mather kept a copy-book of his own letter drafts; presumably Creasy copied this out in his own handwriting before it was sent.) Ventriloquizing the young boy, the letter reminds Frizzel of his bonds with the family and begs "that you will also be my father" by taking him into his shipping business:

> 'Tis too well known that my inclination is more for business than for learning. And being inclined unto the business of the sea, my friends have a prospect of my arriving sooner to some figure on that element than on the long wharf or the dock.
>
> I have pretty well perfected myself in the theory of navigation. And it is now necessary that I take a few voyages for the practick part. I must go aboard some ship as a school for my education. . . . I confess my desire that the ship whereof your son is the commander may be my school.
>
> Here I would most heartily submit to my father's expectation that I apply my hand unto every action aboard, whereof the master and mate shall judge me capable, and yield an exact obedience to all their orders.

Frizzel agreed to this internship, and Creasy shipped "in the quality of a passenger, but with a design to accomplish himself in the practick part of shortly commanding a good ship, whereof he has already got much of the theory." Mather steered Creasy toward a way "of arriving more speedily to significant business by the sea": not to begin as a clerk in a trade house (i.e., working "the long wharf or the dock," which was perhaps his first job with the merchant), but to climb the ranks from officer to ship's captain.[8]

While the college path would have sent Creasy to the ministry, the law, or medicine, this other route could indeed yield a formidable social position. Creasy's internship took him on a sea voyage to England, where he was to stay with Cotton's brother Samuel, a well-off minister. But Creasy somehow arrived there without the funds he had been given to pay his uncle for his upkeep. It's not hard to imagine how a sheltered fifteen-year-old, traveling alone, could have been stripped of his purse by all manner of officers' and sailors' cunning, especially if he was trying to learn their ways. It is a sign of the chill between the one son of Increase Mather's who resettled in the old country, and the other who embraced his American Creole identity, that Samuel demanded reimbursement of his nephew's lost expense money.[9]

Mather pushed his family's ties with the merchant gentility further. After the measles epidemic swept away much of his family, he swore he would not remarry. However, he became enamored of Lydia Lee George, the stylish widow of a merchant—and also the daughter of a prominent Anglican minister with whom Mather, in his younger days, had had many public disagreements. They married on July 5, 1715, while Creasy was away in England. Mather's letters to Lydia are much more intimate than most of his correspondence (no letters to his other wives have survived). When she went away on a brief trip, he lamented that it seemed ten years: "ever since you left us, a palpable darkness is come upon our whole family.... We enjoy nothing as we used to. We are not sensible that the sun shines into any room in the house, nor that our chocolate has any sugar in it." Between the 1690s, when he sipped the expensive drink in Sewall's parlor while talking of events in Mexico City, and this moment, Mather's household economy had come to take for granted the luxury goods of chocolate and sugar, both associated with the new gentility and the West Indian sources of their wealth. Intriguingly, this was also the season in which he consented to Onesimus's terms of manumission.[10]

Marriage as Strategic Alliance

Creasy returned from his year in England in May 1716, and Mather described him as "much polished, much improved." Given that Puritan ministers often spoke out from the pulpit against dancing, it may seem shocking that he paid for both a fencing master and for dancing lessons for Creasy, to "render him a more finished Gentleman." Gentlemanly status, signaled by such accomplishments, was useful to ship's officers and especially for entrepreneurial captains: interpersonal connections were everything in securing investors who could lend credit with which to undertake speculative trade. Creasy entered a "lucriferous, agreeable, and honorable" business, moving from one place to another over the next five years: a "Store-house" is mentioned in the diary, and one letter connects Creasy to a customs collector. Extant documents indicate that Creasy had mastered the neat roundhand that had come in vogue for business: very different from his father's handwriting. When Mather became exasperated once by some behavior of Creasy's that seemed impious—it could have been an actual misdeed, or simply independent-mindedness on the young man's part—he appealed to the "Secretary" in his place of business. Mather loaned him "Proper Books, to employ him in the Intervals of Business . . . and furnish his mind with valuable Treasures": surely books of piety were among these, but Mather's library had many other manuals for developing worldly skills. His younger brother Samuel would describe him this way:

> INCREASE; a young Man well beloved by all who knew him, for his Superiour good Nature and Manners, his elegant Wit and ready Expressions.

Again accounting for the hyperbolic nature of the posthumous tribute, terms like "elegant Wit" and "Manners" underscore Creasy's accomplishments as an eighteenth-century gentleman with a good education, the gift of gab, and the personal charm implied by "Good Nature."[11]

As Creasy was getting his cosmopolitan polish in England and finding his way in an occupation compatible with the family's claim to gentility, Katy became ill with tuberculosis, suffering for months before her death in December 1716 at the age of twenty-six. Mather had delivered funeral sermons for his wives, but this was the first he had to write for an adult child: "The *Death* of such an One, and Especially if there has been in such an One a *Constellation* of every thing that could Endear a Daughter, cannot but be a *Killing* Thing unto a Parent." That sermon was published alongside a number of Katy's own pious writings, including a poem that urges young women to read "*Books of Truth*" and to "*Write & Work* as for high purpose born." A generational divide lurks in the divisions of *Victorina:* Mather's sermon emphasizes her love of God, while her friends underscore her accomplishments as a "Gentlewoman," and a poetic elegy by "J.P." praises above all her intellectual abilities ("A *Mind* that with its early Vigour shone"). The poem describes her "skill in *Languages*" and "Her *Quill* that wrote rare things, now pluck'd by *Death*." Although her soul "ran the round of *Female Sciences* / But not please so, her Greater Genius bent / On *Higher Points,* in them her Hours she spent. / With *Liberal Arts* and *Various Skill* adorn'd, / Her Soul a trifling Conversation scorn'd." She, too, had shared with her father a love of the library.[12]

In addition to Katy's death, there were other signs of crisis. The integration of Mather's children and their new stepmother, who brought her own dependents into the household, did not go easily. Mather's initially fond relationship with Lydia also went awry. By 1717, he describes the "distresses which a furious and froward Stepmother brings upon my Family," resulting in "several abused Children." ("Froward" was a term he had used about an insubordinate Onesimus as well.) He was concerned enough about the children's welfare that he moved Nanny out of the house. Lydia herself would take her leave of it more than once. He several times describes her as "mad"; he began writing in his diary in Latin or Greek or with coded symbols because she did not like the way she was described in it, and he had to hide the volumes from her. Lydia's perspective on their relationship is missing from the record, along with two crucial years of the diaries.

Mather's biographers portray him as deeply disappointed in his firstborn son for not following him into the ministry, and for not leaving their regular prayer sessions together with a conviction of faith that reassured his father that he possessed "serious piety." No doubt he wanted him to make the public confession of faith that would make him a full member of the church (and thus a Boston freeman, with a vote and influence in secular matters). In fact all of Abigail's children were slow to do so: Katy was in her twenties when she attained membership, and Nanny did not join the church until her father's final illness, when she was around thirty. (Sammy and Liza, in contrast, made the confession while in their teens.) After all their father's lessons, they surely felt the weight of needing to do this with complete sincerity, not just mouthing the words like parrots. Yet, having observed his children's "Genius" carefully, Mather also had every incentive to launch Creasy into the "lucriferous" business world of Boston. He had close-up views of both the gritty action of the wharf—he was fond of ministering to ship's crews and pirates—and the parlors of the merchant gentry in his congregation who pulled the strings of that lucrative world. Creasy's turn to business could also be an avenue to secure the future of the extended family's dependents, who now included Mather's widowed sisters and their children as well as Lydia's niece.[13]

A year and a half after he returned home from England, after the crises of his sister's death and the household's stepmother, Creasy's name was read out in public in a very different space than the congregation. In November 1717, "an Harlot big with a Bastard" (Mather's ugly words) "laid her Belly" to his "poor Son Cresy." Three magistrates dismissed the paternity suit as without merit, but given the family's influence and the challenge for many women in proving accusations against male judges, this means little. If Creasy had been repentant, Mather probably would have said so in his diary: it seems they were not in accord about what this episode meant. Perhaps Creasy and the woman Mather called a "Harlot" had had consensual sex but for whatever reason could not marry; perhaps she was a sex worker; perhaps he had raped her. Whatever the judges said, Mather seemed certain that "my Miserable Son" was guilty of a sin, if not also a crime. After a few days of recording his distress and anger in his diary, Mather changed his tune: "I considered the Sins of my Son, as being my own," and renewed his efforts to converse and pray with him and advance his career, as before.[14]

The sections of *Paterna* about Mather's own young manhood obliquely referred to his "lusts." Marriage was a way to redirect wayward sexual energies. It was also—in the genteel business world that kept revolving alongside the spiritual and intellectual life Mather inhabited in his study and pulpit—an excellent way to secure bonds of credit that were needed for entrepreneurial trading. The term "disposal" that he used when ruminating over thirteen-year-old Creasy's career path did not mean discarding, but placing advantageously. In a letter from 1717, Mather writes that he had arranged a match between Creasy and the daughter of a merchant family, but the incident with the "Harlot" apparently quashed that match. With that betrothal, Mather was in some sense treating Creasy like a daughter, to be strategically and successfully allied with a pious but well-placed family. Conjecturally, Mather would likely have encouraged, and perhaps exerted a good deal of control over, his children's choice of marriage partners. However these matches came about, Nibby was married to a merchant; she died in childbirth in 1721. Liza was married to a shipmaster at nineteen years old, and died following a miscarriage a few years afterward. Nanny/Nancy, who never married, was one of only two of Mather's twelve children who would outlive him.[15]

A Time of Debt and Derision

In the family government model, Mather understood his duty as patriarch to involve not only educating his children in matters spiritual and practical but providing for their temporal survival. And yet in the years following the measles epidemic, he slid into serious financial trouble himself. In July 1717, months before the crisis of Creasy's paternity suit, Mather sold the Hanover Street house that he had bought so triumphantly with two thousand pounds in gold shortly after his marriage to Abigail, likely with her dowry. The purchaser was—who else?—a ship's captain. They moved into a house closer to the wharf, which his congregation rented for him. The sale of the house may have been motivated by an escalating financial crisis within the household. When they married, Lydia had protected her own inheritance with a prenuptial agreement preventing Mather from accessing it. She also brought Mather into a financial entanglement apparently beyond his capacity to manage: her daughter's husband died and Mather was named administrator of the estate, which was complicated by multiple debt claims. Between muddling this executorship and poor financial planning of his own—some biographers speculate that he did too much charitable giving (including to the "school for Negroes and Indians"), some suggest he pilfered from the estate, but this is all speculation—Mather found himself in such a state of indebtedness that creditors of the estate publicly, and humiliatingly, threatened him with jail. Among them was Samuel Sewall's son. The debt crisis went on for some years. At one point in 1719, Mather noted that the family would no longer run up bills on credit, but "pay as we fetch," noting they needed "Frugality for our Expences."[16]

Another exposure to public scrutiny occurred in May 1721, when smallpox arrived in Boston by way of a ship from Barbados. It set off a raging epidemic among a population that had grown up without much exposure to the pathogen. As Cristobal Silva observes, epidemics, like comets and earthquakes, were understood by Puritans as prompts to scrutinize what they had done to provoke God's disfavor. If the 1713 measles epidemic had made him more conscious of his duties as a parent, this one sent him back to knowledge he had gained when Onesimus still lived with him. Mather had already corresponded with the Royal Society about the potential of a treatment then under discussion in Europe, inoculation. Five years after Onesimus had successfully demanded his freedom, Mather credited "An African in my service," a "pretty intelligent fellow," who "had undergone an operation, which had given him something of the smallpox and would forever preserve him from it . . . and whoever had the courage to use it was forever free of the fear of contagion." Together with the physician Zabdiel Boylston, Mather embarked on a campaign to inoculate the younger generation, beginning with Sammy, to demonstrate the efficacy of the procedure to others.[17]

Silva has provocatively linked this religious interpretive practice with the origins of English settler racism: at first the bodies of Indigenous people seemed more prone to epidemic diseases than the settlers, while later they seemed less so. The cyclical collapse and recovery of communities who endured epidemics became, for the English, a kind of "grammar through which they understood the world." Rumors of the African source of Mather's and Boylston's inoculation campaign spread, and anti-inoculation crowds (egged on by James Franklin's *Courant,* in which young Benjamin Franklin published a satirical series mocking Mather as "Silence Dogood") decried the procedure in racist terms. One threw a primitive Molotov cocktail through Mather's window. Even Sewall, whose friendship with the family appears to have been stressed by this point, reported on his concern with Mather's well-being. That December, a "Lieutenant on a Man-o-War" picked up the gossip that Mather was a friend of "Negroes," named his enslaved man "Cotton-Mather," and bragged it about town. Mather notes this in his diary, but does not say whether he was more offended by the implication that he was a friend to Black people or by the visiting officer's mockery of the family name. Then Creasy, apparently seeking to defend his father's honor, "exposed himself to much Danger" by challenging the lieutenant in some way. He laments Creasy's "Abandonment" to "foolish Courses" that will bring him misery—and he also laments that so many people despised him. "O dismal Case! O doleful Case! I am a Man of Sorrows and acquainted with Griefs. But I am now afraid of my Sorrows!"[18]

The relationship between father and son had been up and down. Creasy was sent out to live with a bachelor minister, a not uncommon practice. A month before the epidemic, Mather wrote angrily that Creasy was involved in a "Night-Riot with some detestable rakes"—although, in the posttheocratic order of the new Boston, the difference between a gentleman and a rake may have been a matter of perspective. The term "riot" was used to describe rowdy, drunken crowds, but also referred to political gatherings and protests. At the same time as his personal finances plunged him deeper into debt, he seems to have relied on Creasy for financial advice, suggesting that father-son advice was now being exchanged in the other direction:

> Child,
> What in the world shall I do!
> But having such a son in my quiver I shall not be afraid of my adversary at the gate . . .

[Mather lists the people who are dunning him.]

> . . . if once I get out of debt, I promise myself never to get in it again.
> In the view of that, you have already delivered me from one much greater encumbrance. If you can in the same view deliver me from this lesser one, I think I have no more to afflict and humble me.

However, you have a mind as ingenious and projecting on such occasions as mine is beyond all expression awkward, as being wholly swallowed up in what is for the good of others, to which I have been all my days entirely devoted.

I request your advice to me, and if it may be without any disadvantage to you, your interposition in the present difficulties, which, I hope, are the last in which you will find involved,

One who loves you as well as yours,

Mather presents himself here as "awkward" with money, too busy doing good to pay attention to financial details. He admires Creasy's cleverness at managing business affairs, and indicates that Creasy has previously "delivered" him from one "much greater encumbrance," perhaps through investment tips gained on the front line of his business (the South Sea financial bubble burst in 1720, destroying many fortunes) or perhaps through discreet connections to moneylenders whom this prominent minister could not risk approaching directly.[19]

With Creasy pointed on a path toward being the family breadwinner, this left Sammy, who was seven years younger, as the designated heir to the Mather line of ministers. In 1721 Sammy was sent to Harvard at the patronage of a friend, since Mather could no longer afford the tuition. A short letter in Latin left among Mather's papers, addressed to "Mi Fili" (My son) and dating from this late period, could have been directed at either of them, since although Creasy did not attend college he had been trained in Latin since childhood. Mather encrypted his most unorthodox confessions and most personal thoughts in Latin: both in *Paterna*, as the vision of the angel described in Chapter II, and in the diary of these later years, presumably to keep Lydia from reading them. The situation the letter is addressing is clouded, but the affectionate tone is clear: "To me you were always beloved, and (perhaps because you yourself desire more) not merely a duty to me."[20]

We do not know exactly what kind of business Creasy worked at to gain "a mind as ingenious and projecting" about finances as his father's was about religion. "Increase Mather, Jr." signs with a beautiful flourish a check to a banker in the spring of 1721, in payment to an artisan, North Ingham, who sold compasses, navigational, and surveying instruments. The handwriting matches a letter in Mather's draft correspondence about the colony's larger debt crisis, caused by a currency devaluation: perhaps Mather had asked Creasy to be his amanuensis for that letter or (given his son's experience in the business world) to help him compose it. Perhaps the purchase was a clue that Creasy continued to harbor designs of being a ship's navigator, or perhaps he used the gentlemanly accomplishment of his eighteenth-century roundhand as a clerk for one of the many merchants, brokers, and insurance agents related to the shipping industry in Boston. There would be much instructive correspondence to write: letters requesting or extending credit; informing people about a commodity they were speculating in and expected to have in on such a date; setting prices; making out bills and insurance bonds. The key to success in the shipping industry was keeping the hold filled with a variety of commodities on each leg of the voyage and plotting strategically about where and when to offload each so that they would fetch the highest price. Bostonians with a bit of spare capital regularly speculated on the voyages of others. To have "delivered" his father from some of the debt, he may have been in a position to watch carefully what other merchants were trading most profitably or have been privy to secondary speculation markets. What is clear is that this business eventually took him to the Caribbean.[21]

Cast Away

John Frizzel, the parishioner to whom Mather had appealed for help in placing Creasy on a voyage to England to learn the art of navigation, was a model of how to amass wealth in early eighteenth-century Boston. After a few successful trading voyages, he stepped back from the dangers of seafaring to invest the profits into a shipyard, which led him to open his own mercantile house and use his capital in other profitable ways, such as purchasing real estate along "Frizzel's Lane" near the Mathers' North or Second Church. Frizzel owned ships with partners in Boston and Barbados that plied the West Indies trade routes. Mather had other powerful connections with merchants, including Samuel Frazon, the Sephardic Jew whose interactions with Sewall and Mather are described in Chapters III and VIII. Over the years, Mather frequently mentions in his diary praying for the conversion of "that poor Jew." Frazon occasionally returned to New England from what was apparently a permanent home in the West Indies, including once in 1713 at the same time that Mather was helping steer Creasy toward the sea. In a letter from 1724, he addresses Frazon as "My never-forgotten friend" and flatters him: "Your gentlemanly temper and carriage, as well as your descent, has always given you a singular share in my love...."

If you should see New England again, while I am yet living upon earth, you will not want friends from whom you will find many civilities." He may have thought of Frazon as not only a potential convert, but another potential contact who could help with the family's foundering investments, both literal and in the metaphorical sense of his son's social and career trajectory as an eighteenth-century Creole gentleman.[22]

Because Mather's diaries from 1722 and 1723 are missing, we can only infer that Creasy's actions "settled down" after the smallpox crisis and the public furor directed against the whole family. One way or another, by 1724 Creasy was on board a trading vessel to Barbados, the sugar boomtown of England's southern colonies and the most common destination for Boston ships from 1700 forward. It would have made perfect sense for Mather to have given Creasy some of his Spanish and French tracts to distribute on that voyage—or voyages, as it is conceivable that he also went to sea in those intervening years. The busy port of Bridgetown was a point of contact with the mostly Catholic Caribbean. If Barbados was the ship's main destination, that did not mean it was the only port of call: interisland trade might have been on the agenda, if necessarily off the books. An English Creole might meet others with both sanctioned and unsanctioned business in nearby Spanish-controlled islands and territories: Puerto Rico, the Venezuelan coast, Santo Domingo, Cuba. Perhaps the father also packed in Creasy's trunk a handy copy of Lewis Owen's *A Key to the Spanish Tongue*. If Creasy was working as a factor, that is, a commercial agent buying and selling on commission while moving from port to port, it would have been prudent to speak a little Spanish to handle customs, read official communication from Spanish governors, or negotiate the purchase of salt on the tiny, Spanish-controlled Tortugas islands, a frequent port of call for New England ships.[23]

On August 20, 1724, word arrived that Creasy's ship had left Barbados but not reached its destination, and was presumed lost at sea. Mather was plunged into mourning, though he doubtless hoped against hope that Creasy was but a castaway who might be rescued, like Jonathan Dickinson and his party in Florida. Then he heard on September 5 that the ship had landed safely in Newfoundland. Two days later, however, the news came that the Newfoundland rescue was of a different ship, and he gave Creasy up for truly dead. He wrote four funeral sermons for Creasy, announced as tribute to the son who perished "On the Sea, where he was doing Business." Three were compiled to publish under the general title of *The Words of Understanding;* another, *Tela*

Praevisa, was published separately. They movingly recount the "Fountain of Tears" that this loss provoked in "his Afflicted FATHER, upon his Extinction in the Atlantic Ocean." *Tela Praevisa* comes to peace with the loss by presenting the written profession of faith that was left behind on the father's desk by the departing son. This article of repentance, Mather claims, proves that Creasy will not be a spiritual "cast-away." He prints it at the end of the sermon, as he had with some of Katy's words in *Victorina*.[24]

Given the several times that Mather agonizes about Creasy's faltering religious convictions in the diary, and the fact that this manuscript profession of faith does not survive, one might wonder whether Mather invented it out of whole cloth to save face before his congregation. He does, however, mention the manuscript first in his private diary, prior to the more final death-notice that prompted him to deliver the sermon. Yet for whatever reason, Mather seems to have changed his mind about the efficacy of the "written Instrument" Creasy left behind. At some point, he crossed out references that specifically addressed the *Paterna* notebook to Creasy (such as mentions of Abigail as "your mother"), and legated the private notebook to Sammy. In a tiny hand he wrote, next to the narration of Creasy's birth: "a Son of Great *Hopes*, and One Son who Thousands and Thousands of *Prayers*, were employ'd for him; Yett after all, a Sovereign GOD would not Accept of him. He was Buried in the Atlantic Ocean." It is a cold note, and one that does not square with Mather's own theology, in which it was not given to humans to know for certain who God would save in the end.[25]

Mather would outlive Creasy, the object of those "Thousands and Thousands" of prayers, by only a few years. In many of the dwindling diary entries and letters of his decline, he would describe himself in letters to others as "a man of sorrows," and even admitted to himself that "I am afraid of all my Sorrows." If we are to believe his surviving son's account, he returned on his deathbed to the figure of shipwreck that *Tela Praevisa* had used with Creasy to describe his own fear of being cast off by God on his own deathbed. *Life of the Reverend and Learned Dr. Cotton Mather* (1728) was the first publication by the Reverend Samuel Mather, who graduated from Harvard after Creasy's death and inherited leadership of the congregation. This *Life* copies long stretches from *Paterna*, excising the secret parts like the account in Latin of seeing an angel: since Mather had written *Paterna* in the third person to begin with, it was a biography that practically wrote itself. When it reaches the point of recounting Mather's last words, Samuel comingles the final entry in *Paterna* with the last words his father uttered: "THESE passages the Doctor writ; but many of us heard most of them from his Lips."

> BUT! What if after all a Sovereign GOD will have me to be a Cast-away; and I shall be cast into an Hell where the Divine Justice will be for ever scourging of me?—I deserve it should be so!—Faulty Thot's! fiery Darts!—In the Horror of Darkness I now humble my self as Clay before the Potter.

Which of those familiar figures for judgment and salvation did Mather speak aloud, and to whom? Were his perceived sins ("Faulty Thot's! fiery Darts!") linked at all to Creasy's errand to do business, as the reiteration of the phrase "a Sovereign GOD" from that margin-note in *Paterna* might suggest? The eternal Puritan fear of being a spiritual "Cast-Away," or not counted among the Elect, is especially poignant in light of what survivors could never know about the fate of those presumed lost at sea, like Creasy and the millions of other ocean-traveling souls, both willing and unwillingly transported, during this period. Samuel's brief commentary does not admit any doubts of his own filiopiety. He dismisses Mather's self-indicting language ("I deserve it should be so!") as a sign of his sanctification.[26]

A Small Female Shrub

To some biographers, Creasy's life and early death represent not only a failed effort at patriarchal succession (he did not become another link in the chain of Reverends), but a proof of the very "Criolian degeneracy" that young Cotton Mather had warned about in 1689. Barrett Wendell, one of the first makers of a (US) American literary canon, wrote in his biography in 1891: "With his eldest son—and to the end his dearest—straying further and further towards perdition, with the New England churches ever straying further and further from the holy traditions they were founded to preserve, Cotton Mather was left alone." The passage seems a potential source of Perry Miller's famous phrase "Left alone with America": Wendell shared Miller's sentiment that Mather was thrown by his sense that the original Puritan social ideal was dead, if not Miller's deep antagonism toward Mather. There is, however, an alternate reading. Whatever his pledge may have been to his forefathers' God, Increase

Mather Junior, Gentleman of Boston, did what he could to protect his familial and tribal interests. He blended in (as his father had directed) to the social and financial world based on inter-American trade, including the traffic in kidnapped humans to be sold as slaves, as it propelled the city into global significance in the early eighteenth century.[27]

Samuel Mather, obediently keeping the faith of and in the family, went on to name one of his own sons Increase. That Increase also "affected the Sea" like his long-dead uncle, going for a soldier during the Seven Years' War against Spain (prompted, once again, by the perceived dangers of Spanish Florida to English settlements in the southeast). The third Increase Mather died in Havana in 1762, during the British siege and occupation of the city. The only thing of value Cotton Mather had legated to his heirs was his portion of the Mather library, the greatest in seventeenth-century Boston. By the terms of Increase Sr.'s will (the same instrument that declared Spaniard a "Free Negro" at last), the library was to be divided only among those men of the family who became ministers. When no male children survived Samuel, his share of the library went to his daughter Hannah Mather Crocker (1752–1859).

Both learned and religious, Crocker presented herself as the spiritual as well as temporal heir of her grandfather: "I am the only little limb and the only grand child of Cotton," she wrote, "one Small female Shrub" of the family tree. Surviving the births of ten children, she moved on from this labor on behalf of heteropatriarchy to advance her own writing and advocacy. An eager abolitionist, she sought out the company of Phillis Wheatley (her father and cousin had been on Wheatley's all-male examining committee). Unlike her Tory father, she founded a women's Masonic lodge and published verse and essays in favor of the revolutionary cause. She wrote a history of Boston and *Observations on the Real Rights of Women* (1818), an important treatise supporting women's education and defending Mary Wollstonecraft. Sometimes pushing against and sometimes evading the constraints of gender, Crocker experimented with various pseudonyms for her publications. One that she used on three treatises written around 1812–1815 was "Increase Mather Jun.[ior] of the Inner Temple." (The Inner Temple was a Masonic reference; she also advocated for women to have a part in that fraternal organization.) Why, of all names, raise that one again, not in homage to Increase Senior but to the nonreproducing "Juniors"? Crocker was only ten when her older brother died in the siege of Havana. Surely she had also heard of her uncle, the other Increase Mather Jr., who had died somewhere unmarked in the Caribbean. The last page of the American Antiquarian Society's copy of Cotton Mather's funeral sermons for Creasy, *The Words of Understanding*, is nearly half taken up with the inscription of a single name, in the large, loopy handwriting of a child: "Hannah, Her Book." This copy likely came through the family, and may well have been so inscribed by that same Hannah when she was young.[28]

When an older Hannah took ownership of her portion of the Mather library, she decided to leave it to a national family, not a genealogical one. In negotiations with Isaiah Thomas and with other book and manuscript collectors in the new nation, Crocker cagily navigated the terms under which that inheritance would be donated and sold to the American Antiquarian Society— the archive that Thomas had founded in 1812 and imagined as the new nation's collective patrimony. Without that infusion, the AAS would not be the world-class collection it is today. For better or worse, she helped shape the New England filiopietism of the mid-nineteenth century, and the selective collection practices that would come to be called (in an echo of many of Cotton Mather's titles) "Americana."[29]

· XI ·

Coda

Colonial Lessons in Latinidad

If this book helps unfold the caricature of Cotton Mather from a flat sheet of paper into a three-dimensional pop-up, scissoring in views of other worlds and lives beyond him, it is doing only part of its work. I want to claim for a moment a privilege Mather took for granted and exercised frequently: the privilege of interpreting present and future conditions through the record of the past. He could not have anticipated the formation of the United States as such, yet that nation's memory keepers, both reverent and irreverent—from his preservationist granddaughter Hannah Mather Crocker to the makers of anti-Puritan satires that circulate in mass media—have made enduring work and play of him. Mather was not the only Creole settler to craft a version of his colony's history that anointed men of his own *ethnos* as heroic founders, as he did for Protestant Englishmen in *Magnalia Christi Americana;* however, he made it easier for other such men to embrace his tribalism while ignoring his belief in the equality of souls. I am not interested in judging Mather but in drawing lessons from the profound conflict of interpretation that he represents. Although the heroic historical narrative of English Puritan origins has always had its dissenters, only in the past quarter-century has it decisively run aground. From every level of public education to popular culture, it has become harder to ignore the consequential fact that US nation building rested upon economies of slavery and Indigenous land theft begun during the colonial period. Out of these entwined forms of violence, and from preexisting European prejudices, were fashioned their ideological buttresses: anti-Blackness on the one hand, primitivism on the other. African American and Indigenous thinkers, artists, and activists, living in persistent states of unredressed injury stemming from those ancestral traumas, have led the call for material, territorial, and political reparations and, just as importantly, for a corrective course of *countermemory*. It is weighty, contested, and unfinished work.[1]

But where do Latinos, the largest minoritized population in the United States today, fit into this racial reckoning? The notion of inherited trauma seems ill-suited to the complexities of our ancestry: Spanish and Portuguese people pillaged, colonized, enslaved, and evangelized along with the English and other Europeans. Some families who identify as Latina/o/x can claim a longstanding presence in formerly Spanish territories that were later incorporated into the United States; numerically, however, most descend from migrants who left other nations in the hemisphere. Historians of the early Americas and the Atlantic have few points of contact with the interdisciplinary formation of Latino Studies, which tends to focus on social science and policy. Perhaps because Latino Studies grew out of civil rights demands for greater inclusion in state institutions, it applies a limited historical frame to such questions, rarely extending even as far back as 1776. Yet I want to bring the two fields into conversation by suggesting that directing our gaze to the period *before* the nation's founding offers a way to imagine US Latinos within that collective project of aligning national memory, restorative justice, and belonging through a logic other than that of descent.

Turning to the prenational past to speculate on the future of a group defined through its residence in a nation may seem counterintuitive. But it is precisely the central concern of Latino Studies to show how residency does not confer full belonging—to track the differential partitioning of rights among birthright and naturalized US citizens on the mainland, territorial citizens, and denizens of many sorts: both those whose presence is authorized by the government (always with an expiration date) and those who are unauthorized or undocumented. No other group exists along such a wide spectrum of inclusion and exclusion at the demographic scale of sixty million US Latinos. To understand this contemporary phenomenon primarily as a function of the way people have migrated between American nations, or of how national borders themselves have moved, is to miss the larger significance of the colonial fabric they have in common. Without attempting to narrate chronologically the three centuries following the story I have related here, I want to stitch a few motifs over that story as provocations that might suture past to present. I have suggested in this book that the modifier "Spanish" functioned ambiguously as *demonym, ethnonym,* and what I have called *loquonym,* identifying persons by their place of origin, their ethnicity, or the speech community to which they belonged. Like a three-stranded embroidery floss, these conceptual threads are sometimes separated, but are most often drawn together through the fabric of depictions of *latinidad*. Because a biological notion of race took hold at roughly the same time as the rise of modern nations, that newer concept became the needle that pulled this thread. The widespread uncertainty about whether or not Latinos constitute a racial group is a result of that late-eighteenth-century invention: a mistaking of the needle for the thread. It was a ruthless tool, and it is high time to break it.

§ *Spanish Indian was to the colonial period as LatinX is to the present moment.*

Much has been written about the unsatisfying options for naming the aggregate population of people of Latin American background who reside in the United States. "Hispanic," the pannational umbrella term used by the federal government beginning in the early 1970s, has been largely replaced by "Latino" and its variants—the most recent, "Latinx," abjuring the gendered choice between masculine or feminine endings. If there is confusion over terminology, there is even more confusion about whether that term names an ethnicity or a race. In most data-collection contexts, ethnicity wins: government forms offer Hispanic / Latino as a binary option (yes / no, sometimes followed by another selection of national-origin subgroup), accompanied by race as a separate option (Black / white, and sometimes other choices). At the same time, a Census Bureau fact sheet also designates Latinos "the largest *ethnic or racial* group in the U.S.," officially hedging the bet. The lack of fixity between such terms amplifies the lack of agreement about what kind of terms they are in the first place. Rather than prescribe a particular usage, I want to follow Claudia Milian's use of LatinX, with an upper-case X, to signal something more than the refusal of traditional gender binaries suggested by the lower-case letter. Milian positions the X as an unsolved algebraic equation, a crossing-point, a speculative orientation of thought that both rejects the fiction of a unified *latinidad* and insists on engaging with a people whose existence is unevenly recognized. In this sense, LatinX maintains the fluctuation between demonym, ethnonym, and loquonym in the colonial term "Spanish Indian."[2]

LatinX is not a demographic label but a conceptual frame, one that downgrades ethnicity as the principal rationale of the category. Crossing time periods to align Spanish Indian with LatinX does not propose that the persons called Spanish Indians in Mather's household, or elsewhere in the archive, were the genealogical forebears of people who identify as Latina/o/x today. In the seventeenth and eighteenth centuries, the modifier "Spanish" was piled onto both "Indian" and "Negro" to form new group nouns for those who hailed from a zone of the Spanish Empire such as the West Indies, Florida, or elsewhere in New Spain. Its users did not much care to parse their descent. The demonymic function was useful for those English settlers who thought their imposed distinction between Spanish and Carolina Indians could predict who could be more tractably enslaved. Spanish Indian could also be a loquonym, as we have seen. From the early sixteenth century forward, a significant number of Indigenous people moving through North America, already accustomed to their own trade and translation networks, found utility in adding Spanish to the other tongues they spoke. The record is full of them, including the Christianized Timucua. Its function as an ethnonym, however, was quite weak: there is no evidence that people at this time called *themselves* Spanish Indians. The unknown particularities of the peoples from whom they actually descended may be represented by an X: the same kind of X that propels LatinX away from an excessive emphasis on ethnicity and descent.

The loquonymic sense of the Spanish in Spanish Indian continued to be an extra sticky adhesive in English American usage. In 1910, well before "Hispanic" was borrowed from a few New Mexican *hispanos* to become a broad panethnic term of governmentality, the US Census began to record the home languages of non-English-speaking households as a way to track immigrant assimilation. Unlike the other loquonymic categories in the 1910 census— tracking Yiddish, Polish, and Chinese speakers—"Spanish-speaking" survived as a descriptor and was widely used through the middle of the twentieth century to describe both the longstanding populations of formerly Mexican and Spanish territories and the new wave of migrants spurred across the border by the Mexican Revolution. Carey McWilliams chose the loquonym for his 1948 *North from Mexico: The Spanish-Speaking People of the Southwest* despite his recognition that many of these people were proficient in English, and some no longer kept Spanish in active use. It wasn't accuracy McWilliams was after. Rather, he found "Spanish-speaking" to be the least derogatory of the available options, arguing that "Latin," "Mexican," and "Indian" had all been tainted by their local use as ethnoracial slurs. Anticipating the Chicano movement and its elevation of indigeneity, he clarified, "The people who are generically Spanish-speaking are more Indian in racial origin, and perhaps in culture, than they are Spanish."

McWilliams's text, which languished in its time but later became a cornerstone for revisionist Chicano history, focused on the Southwest yet briefly noted the rising number of other Spanish-speaking populations in Florida and greater New York City. The presence of multiple national-origin groups gave rise to the panethnic terms Hispanic and Latino, but the category that these terms seek to name remains strongly associated with language use. To understand why, this three-stranded thread of demonym, ethnonym, and loquonym must be untangled from the processes of relative racialization that occurred in the nineteenth and twentieth centuries.[3]

❧ Under the nation, language became a tool of racialization.

The Census Bureau fact sheet's blurry description of Latinos as an "ethnic or racial group" reflects a particularly modern problem. In Mather's time, the terms "race" and "nation" were near synonyms to indicate one's forebears and relations: what we now call the ties of ethnicity. "Ethnic" was not yet a common term in English when Mather used the Spanish version, *éthnico,* as the last word of *La Fe del Christiano,* lifting it from the Greek and Latin to mean someone outside the spiritual community (in English, the word is usually translated as *gentile*). The word's evolution is worth recalling. In Mather's theological view, the intentional community of the church transcended differences of tribe, family, descent, language; only an irresolvable rift would turn one into an outcast ("ten lo por un Ethnico," as he translates the verse). A theological commitment to monogenesis led him to reason that skin color, apparently a function of the zone of the globe to which a particular son of Noah had migrated, had nothing to do with the mind's capacity for intelligence or the soul's capacity to know God. The whole premise of his multilingual evangelizing was that non-English others were predetermined to take their place among God's Elect in the millennial kingdom: "The *Whites* are but the least part of Mankind; the majority are a sort of *Tawnies*," he wrote in *The Negro Christianized,* expanding a then prevalent reference to Amerindians as Tawnies to mean something like people of color. As Chapter IX argues, Mather's actions in the face of such an accurate summation of white minority were meaner than his words. There is no question that he fell prey to European perceptions and biases about African and Indigenous people that were based in skin color among other forms of difference. However, these biases were not grounded in the biologized idea of race that would take hold later in the eighteenth century.

The social, legal, and ideological framing of the United States as a nation did not limit the rights of its denizens according to their language or place of origin. But these systems did institutionalize and empower white supremacy, and over the course of the nineteenth century a bioracial pyramid scheme, grounded in pseudoscience, informed the treatment of both native-born and immigrant people. Certain religious and ethnic groups, in particular Jews, Muslims, Asians, Mexicans, and other Latin Americans, were classified and treated in terms of their relative relation to an existing Black/white racial paradigm; Michael Omi and Howard Winant influentially call these the state's racial projects. While some immigrant groups could assimilate into whiteness, others were perpetually subject to the consequences of being perceived as non-white: residential segregation, targeting for extrajudicial violence and disproportionate incarceration, and other forms of second-class citizenship. As Catherine S. Ramírez puts it in her critique of classical assimilation theory, "In a pluralist United States, ethnicity is the path to assimilation. In contrast, race—specifically, non-whiteness—is an obstacle." One's native language is not visible on the body in the same way as other racializing features such as skin pigment and hair texture, yet speech and gestural performance do have embodied features that were enlisted into these systems of relative racialization.[4]

The generic use of "Spanish-speaking" as a loquonym disregarded individual language proficiencies to classify a group whose ability to assimilate was often in doubt. Historian Rosina Lozano shows, for example, how Anglo-American views about the Spanish language in the Southwest shifted at precisely the moment in the 1920s when an influx of migrants from Mexico arrived: even in areas where Spanish had been used in the public sphere and in schools since the nineteenth century, the language was delegitimized and associated with a proletarian underclass. The "Spanish-speaking" label classified these new migrants as belonging to the same racialized group as the populations who had been living in Texas and California for many generations and who had already been targeted for dispossession of land, labor abuse, lynching, and other iterations of the violent inequities of white supremacy. Residential redlining according to the loquonym "Spanish-speaking" was so prevalent that a landmark court case of educational desegregation, *Méndez v. Westminster* (a ruling in Orange County, California, in 1947), hinged on the common practice of assigning certain children into "Mexican schools" for Spanish speakers, regardless of their individual English skills, based on their racialized appearance. The plaintiff was actually Puerto Rican, at a time when mainland Puerto Ricans were bureaucratically divided into white, Black, or "mulatto," but all Mexicans were classified as white: a temporary practice that, as Natalia Molina explains, aimed to mollify white-supremacist nativists while protecting the flow of temporary migrant workers, who were discouraged from staying permanently.[5]

Just as ideologies of race are relational, so are ideologies of language. Periodic efforts to legislate English as the sole official language of states or of the nation, along with practices of punishing schoolchildren and employees at a workplace for using other languages to communicate, correlate with moments of increasing migration from Latin America in particular. Spanish and Asian languages, as the educational policy scholar Ofelia García points out, are policed and proscribed in the United States far more than other languages because they are linked to this history of the differential treatment of racialized immigrants. Ethnographer Jonathan Rosa describes "the overdetermination of racial embodiment and communicative practice" that results in a particular vulnerability for Latina/o/x individuals: "looking like a language and sounding like a race." Whereas a British, French, or Norwegian accent keeps one in the unmarked terrain of whiteness, of an ethnicity that can be assimilated away, performative linguistic difference remains a potentially racializing feature for people of Latin American, Asian, and Middle Eastern origin—but no other language approaches Spanish in scale. As in McWilliams's time, the group noun *Spanish-speaking* is not an accurate index of *latinidad* today: some three-quarters of self-identified Latina/o/x people claim to speak some Spanish, but less than half use it as their primary language at home, and a significant minority are Anglophone Latinos who speak relatively little or no Spanish. Association, not accuracy, is the point here. The persistent attachment of Latinos with the Spanish language ignores individual differences in proficiency to become a marker of what Mather meant by *un éthnico:* an outsider, an outcast, one who does not belong.[6]

❧ Spanish Indian hints at the ethnogenesis that would later be embraced as Brown identity.

As Chapters V and IX have suggested, the term Spanish Indian could be used as demonym, ethnonym, or loquonym, but it also conveyed some perception about embodied features including one's dress and carriage. The case of Tuqui indicates that his personal appearance made him vulnerable to being rendered as chattel by the English captain who "meant to make a perpetual Slave of him" but was bested by Mather. English settlers were quite aware of the way parallel colonial projects in the hemisphere were deploying labor practices that produced new hierarchies of the human. The term Spanish Indian may also have expressed a concept like the colonial Mexican *castas* category of *mestizo:* the product of a genealogical crossing, Spaniard X Indian. Mather's and Sewall's readings of Acosta, Las Casas, and other available sources would have familiarized them with that term as well as with *mulato,* which had already traveled from Portuguese and Spanish into English, appearing in runaway ads in the later seventeenth century as well as in England with one or two *t*s. When Mather wrote that "The *Whites* are but the least part of Mankind; the majority are a sort of *Tawnies*" two decades after his encounter with Tuqui, did he grasp the way that ethnogenesis among Africans, Amerindians, and Europeans was already nullifying the ability of many people of color in the Americas to identify with a single ancestral origin or place?

Mather's "Tawny" would become one of many purported skin-color terms associated with racial inferiority as the bioracial taxonomies of Linnaeus, Blumenbach, Morton, and Agassiz were naturalized into intellectual, political, and cultural norms. The phrase "race mixture" grants the spurious idea of an essentialized race a solidity that it does not have, but this concept and its negative associations were central to that era's debates over slavery and expansion. During the hemispheric expansionism of the nineteenth century that brought large parts of Mexico, Central America, Cuba, Puerto Rico, and the Philippines under direct US governance or powerful indirect influence, a concern about the indeterminate ethnic origins of Mexicans and Latin Americans fueled intense debates about whether and how to admit the conquered subjects in these territories to the rights of citizenship. The figure of the *mestizo* in particular was associated with degeneracy, a fall from the greatness of the same Mesoamerican pyramid builders that Mather had read about. Only in the later twentieth century did the colonial history of ethnogenesis become the basis of collective claims to rights by repurposing *mestizaje* affirmatively.[7]

In the 1970s, the Chicano and Chicana movements launched a counterdiscourse to the negative construction of racial mixing. *Chicanismo* claimed simultaneous belonging to two places: the *madre patria,* or motherland of Mexico, and the US Southwest as the historically antecedent homeland of Aztlán, the origin-point from which the Mexica had apparently migrated. The most influential theorist to emerge from this movement, Gloria Anzaldúa, called for a new *mestiza* consciousness that would reject the Christian patriarchal legacy of the sex/gender system, as well as the internalized and structural racisms wrought by colonialism. The key Chicano concepts of Brown Pride and Brown Power translated and adapted the Mexican intellectual José Vasconcelos's notion of a *raza de bronce* (bronze or brown-colored race). Following the Mexican Revolution, Vasconcelos institutionalized a mythos of shared descent from the *castas* category of Spaniard X Indian, uplifting the figure of the *mestizo* to unify a deeply riven nation. Yet this profoundly influential ideology remained tethered to a racial pyramid in which Black and Indigenous bodies and beliefs were presented as the least desirable, linking the idea of race mixing to unsavory eugenicist policies that suppressed Indigenous languages and cultural practices and denied the very existence of Afro-Mexicans.[8]

Mexico was not the only modern American state to embrace official *mestizaje* and *mulatez* in order to deny the existence of structural racism. After centuries of practicing *blanqueamiento,* or whitening and lightening, many republics in Spanish America, Brazil, and across the Caribbean have pointed at the visual evidence of ethnogenesis to declare themselves race-blind societies, in some cases enshrining antiracism in their constitutions (as in Ecuador and Bolivia) while continuing to function, effectively, as pigmentocracies. Immigrants tend to bring the social hierarchies of their home countries with them. One of the master plots of the Latino literary canon follows a hemispheric migrant who grapples with the shock of being racially recognized in a different way upon arrival in the United States: for example, the protagonist realizes that what she has always considered *piel clara* (light skin) is not perceived as white here, while her Spanish-language use—no matter how proper its register at home—is the handicap of an underclass. At least in fiction, such a realization often opens the door for new forms of solidarity across national-origin groups. *Latinidad* develops as the affective glue that binds a Salvadoran to a Dominican on the basis that both are similarly racialized in the United States: casually mistaken as members of the same ethnic or national group, they eventually forge a new one. Instead of bureaucratic terms like Hispanic or Latino, many individuals informally adopt Brown as a way to identify with other marginalized populations in the United States and the Global South (in constructions such as "Black and Brown people").[9]

For some, this use of Brown sits uncomfortably close to what Jonathan Rosa calls "spectrum-based racial logics that problematically imagine Latinxs as an intermediary 'brown' population located between Blackness at one end and Whiteness at the other." Likewise, the apparent links between Anzaldúa's *mestiza* consciousness and the weaponization of *mestizaje* in postrevolutionary

Mexico have pushed conversations about the persistence of intragroup racism to the forefront of Latino Studies. Critical LatinX Indigeneities and Afro-LatinX Studies have become their own scholarly specialties. But some have argued that the metaphor of human reproduction and *mestizaje* as "whitening" can be discarded from the conceptual apparatus of Brown identity. Claiming Brownness can instead be a way of refusing the tradition by which those immigrants (and others) who could assimilate into the privileges of whiteness always did so. Being Brown, as theorists like Lázaro Lima and José Esteban Múñoz argue, inheres not in a genealogical, national, or ethnic identity but in an orientation of thought—aligning with Milian's nonessentialism, in which "the intellectual possibilities for an unapologetic and urgent X worldview are realized alongside a nascent and developing LatinXness."[10]

❧ *The binary distinction between two Americas is a dubious legacy of the modern nation/race system.*

The work of Chicana/o/x scholars in situating its subjects in transborder space also challenged a centerpiece assumption of intellectual history and comparative political science: the two-Americas theorem. As Chapter VI argued, it has been taken as conventional wisdom that North and South America followed divergent paths in two profoundly important senses. One was religious: Catholic culture had a different notion of the individual and was more hierarchical, so it developed a different approach to political economy than Protestant cultures. The second was racial: the United States understood race as a Black/white binary rigidly upheld by the one-drop rule and Jim Crow segregation, while Latin America took a relaxed attitude toward race mixing. Classism and caste, according to this view, replaced race as the basis of exclusion in Latin America, in contrast to the vaunted class mobility achievable in the United States. In such binary comparisons, Indigenous people were all but erased in the North, while persisting as a modernization challenge for democracies in the South. These are caricatures of assumptions that have been discredited by the recent histories of the Atlantic world and vast early America I have referenced in this book, yet they persist in contemporary political commentary.

The notion of two distinct Americas postdated Cotton Mather. Europeans referred to a singular America, their previously unknown fourth continent, well into the seventeenth century. If Mather's historical writing began to assert a belated place for *English* America within that Indigenous and Spanish-dominated space, if he helped transform the meaning of "American" from Native to Creole, he nonetheless understood this new English America not as a space apart from the rest of the western hemisphere but as a rising component of it. Mather sought less to evangelize than to *re-evangelize* in the Americas, bringing those who had already been Christianized as Catholics into the Reformed faith, as well as those who had not heard the Gospel. While he aimed his most ambitious English and Latin works across the Atlantic, his readership for the Little Books was logically American, and this was particularly true of the multilingual works—from the Algonquian and Iroquois translations he commissioned to the Spanish and French tracts he composed. While he identified some places in the hemisphere as godless, corrupted, or barbaric compared to Boston—places like Carolina, Maine, and Barbados—these spaces formed a patchwork, not a binary.

The reduction of the variegated, diverse Americas into two basic and opposing parts was, instead, a product of the nineteenth century. After a brief flirtation with a shared hemispheric republicanism, built into the fraternal rhetoric of the Monroe Doctrine if not its later application, the United States doubled down on its investment in the mythos of an Anglo-Saxon founder population. The imperial motives that cast both Spaniards and Latin Americans as a menacingly "off-white," when not outright "mongrel," population propelled thinkers from the South to define themselves *in contrast to* the grasping Yankee world: "el desdén del vecino formidable, que no la conoce, es el mejor peligro de nuestra América," as José Martí famously put it (the disdain of the formidable neighbor who knows nothing about it is the greatest danger faced by our America). The label of *Latin* America organized itself around an adversarial relationship toward the *yanqui* nation-state that had appropriated the name of the hemisphere for itself. At the same moment, pan-Hispanism celebrated the Iberian heritage and retrenched itself in a Catholic vision of unity across the former empire. Seeing two distinct Americas, in other words, has suited the purposes of many. Even recently, many synthetic and comparative histories of the Americas have upheld this nineteenth-century notion that the Reformation and Counter-Reformation created fundamentally different and contrasting intellectual, artistic, and political orientations. From the liberal-centrist Carlos Fuentes to the conservative Claudio Véliz in Spanish, from the liberals Richard Morse and Patricia Seed to the arch-conservatives Samuel P. Huntington and Victor Davis Hanson in English, the schism has offered irresistible contrasts. The Anglo / Latin divide plays out for pundits, speculating on the current and future state of inter-American relations, as a question of individualistic versus authoritarian tendencies, of cultures of the word versus cultures of the body, of free enterprise versus communitarianism—all mapped onto the seeming inevitability of geography.[11]

The past hundred years of extensive migration into the United States from within the hemisphere—the flows that reinforced a longstanding, enduring presence of what we will now call LatinX people within its national boundaries—demand a revisitation of this fundamental binary. What is missed when we continue to propagate such a division of the cultural and intellectual inheritances of the Americas based on the split between sects of Christianity? From the point of view of the Indigenous people, Africans, and their descendants, whose inscription as less than fully human—in what Sylvia Wynter calls the European concept of Man, as opposed to the Human—the Anglo and Latin spheres were far more alike than different. It was their exploitation, displacement, and deaths that made it possible for Creole settlers to, in large part, keep for themselves the privilege of carving out the particular contours of the thirty-five nations that now occupy what Europe once regarded as a singular space. Both Catholic and Protestant sects shared a powerful intention to evangelize nonbelievers into a Christian cosmology, which one can consider either an ideological feint or a potential escape hatch into liberation theologies that promote equality and justice. Every recapitulation of the idea that the sixteenth-century schism within Christianity pushed the Americas into irreconcilable visions of personhood and community amounts to a refusal to center the experience of those subjugated by the hemisphere's European settlement—the Indigenous peoples, Africans, and later the Asian laborers whose lives were forcibly disrupted to make those modern systems.[12]

I have argued that the loquonym *Spanish-speaking* remains latent in other demographic labels for the people signaled by LatinX. Ironically for the two-Americas concept and its extrapolation of different worldviews from the Catholic-Protestant schism, the religious sphere is one place in US culture where there is a wholehearted embrace of integrating Latinos through a widespread and affirmative use of Spanish. The contest between Reformation and Counter-Reformation that propelled so many expressions and actions during the colonial period has completely reshaped itself as a matter of theology, social and community organization, and practical ethics. On one end of the spectrum, progressive Catholics make alliances with mainline liberal Protestants and an ecumenical array of non-Christian partners. On the other end, dominionists promote a vision of prayerful wealth generation and of a godly nation run according to selectively amended biblical precepts. Across sectarian divides, however, Latinos are portrayed as the very future of Christianity in the United States. Being heard by the Spanish-speaking majority among them—"en lengua sabida a Vulgo," as Mather put it in *La Fe del Christiano*—remains essential to their project of expanding the numbers of the faithful.

❧ *LatinX makes a claim on US American memory as well as its futurity.*

This observation brings us back in closing to the vision of the two Boston churches I invoked in the Introduction. It would be easy to conclude from the story of *La Fe del Christiano* that Cotton Mather was a prophet who foresaw how an influx of Spanish-speaking migrants would revitalize evangelical Protestantism in North America today. It would also be wrong. For one thing, his own Congregationalist church evolved into a very liberal denomination, the United Church of Christ, with an offshoot into Unitarianism (although that has not stopped many waves of neo-Calvinists, in efforts to repurify the church, from reclaiming both Mathers). For another, the term *evangélico* in Spanish often carries the general meaning of "Protestant," not the more specific reference it has in English to the Pietist-Methodist-Baptist tradition of revivalism, which emphasizes the individual's active choice to seek salvation and be born again: those traditions largely, but not entirely, postdated Mather. Further, the charismatic movement within evangelicalism, often laced with a prosperity-gospel message, far outpaces other sectarian groups in the pace of adding Latina/o/x members. Despite his enthusiasm in the prayer closet, I suspect that Mather would barely recognize this twentieth-century charismatic formation, which puts comparatively little stress on the repeated reading and exegesis of the Bible that was an unshakable foundation of his practice. Finally, in contrast to the broad stereotype of being faithful Catholics, an increasing number of Latinos—as high as one in four—profess no religion at all. The implications of these demographic developments lie outside the scope of this book, although it is my hope that the provisional, nonessentialist, and in some ways utopian orientation toward LatinX thinking might have more to say in the future about spiritual and religious practice.[13]

The pedagogies of popular memory, illustrated in the Introduction by a walk along Boston's Freedom Trail, drove traditional teleological narratives of the United States from colony to nation, from Pilgrims and Puritans to Founders to Pioneers. Perhaps more than revisionist scholarship, it has been the social-justice movements protesting the occupation and misuse of Native land and the seemingly unending anti-Black violence produced by law and law enforcement that have propelled countermemory initiatives such as the "1619 Project." But futurity also ignites initiatives to reshape public memory. The prediction that nonwhite-identified people will become a majority in the United States at some point in the twenty-first century ("the majority are a sort of *Tawnies*") has been an important driver of current controversies around the way the national past is studied, taught, and popularly imagined. The arguments made in favor of establishing a Museum of the American Latino on the National Mall in Washington, DC, approved by Congress in 2021, appealed directly to this coming demographic curve. The museum's proponents cited the success of the National Museum of the American Indian (which opened in 2004) and the National Museum of African American Art and Culture (which opened in 2016) in expanding an awareness of Native and Black histories and perspectives among all visitors, regardless of their own ancestry. These physical sites, and the institutional recognition and investment they represent, concretize the controversies around new pedagogies of racial reckoning and countermemory.[14]

If the Latino Museum is ever realized as a countermemory project within the sacralized space of the National Mall, it will confront the same problems of heterogeneous origins that the other two museums did. How does such a site convey the truth that, in the process of nation making sketched above, many hundreds of distinct ethnic groups, of language-using, culture-creating, thought-generating *peoples*, were flattened into a category that was then systematically dehumanized as Indian or Black? Certain critics have always attacked such memory work as "divisive," as antithetical to the assimilative project of crafting a unified sense of national character. Yet these institutional spaces remain powerful and necessary for a functioning multiracial society, in whatever political shape the people of the future mold it.

If I had to choose one artifact to represent the linguistic difference of *latinidad* in the exhibits of this projected Museum of the American Latino—one element of what I've described as the loquonymic function of the various terms that seek imperfectly to label the people—it would be the deliberately damaged metal type in that Boston printer's case I describe in Chapter VIII. Physically altering an ff to make it an *ñ* did a kind of creative violence to the primacy of English letters, both in their metaphorical and their physical senses. I drew a parallel between this printer's hack and the special characters that were cast to represent the sounds of Indigenous languages in the evangelizing print projects of sixteenth- and seventeenth-century Mexico, Peru, Florida, and Boston— projects that, for all the destruction of Indigenous belief systems they threatened and achieved, also allowed linguist-activists to resuscitate the Wampanoag and Timucuan languages centuries later, and have aided the uninterrupted speech communities of modern Nahuatl, Mayan, and Zapotec languages to access their classical versions and their morphology. Institutions promoting the study, preservation, and cultural vitality of Indigenous languages in the United States (such as the well-established immersive educational programs in Diné / Navajo) now include Mesoamerican languages. In my California town, the Indigenous female secretary of a school bearing the name of an eighteenth-century grandee from New Spain helped start a Oaxacan mutual aid organization that now teaches and keeps alive the Zapotec variety spoken in the southeastern Sierra Norte. Perhaps that hacked, misshapen enye can represent, like the open-ended X in certain uses of LatinX, a state of semantic difference and unfixed possibility that goes beyond the binary of English / Spanish.[15]

National borders pose a different kind of binary that is not merely conceptual but has profound real-world consequences. Citizenship status determines people's rights in a way not anticipated in Mather's time. The twenty-first century has accelerated conditions that propel certain people out of the bounds of rights endowed by nations: the "universal" human rights promoted by the United Nations, including language rights, seem increasingly impossible to guarantee. Migrants and refugees from climate catastrophe and violence elsewhere in the hemisphere get shuffled into categories of unbelonging: the undocumented, the stateless, the people-in-waiting for whom the full rights of citizenship seem perpetually deferred, as they have been for Native and African American peoples. The lesson of this book for future-oriented projects such as the National Museum of the American Latino is that a notion of belonging based on ancestry and heritage, on the ethnonymic sense of Latina / o/x, does not suffice. Neither descent nor citizenship fills the cipher that is LatinX. How could such a museum, in thrall to congressional oversight, recognize the eleven million undocumented denizens of the country, not to mention the millions more who have passed through the detention and expulsion machine of its immigration-control system? Where in the halls of such a museum would one encounter the tens of thousands of such people who have been deported from the country, some of whom lived, worked, attended school, and served in the US military for years, even for decades?[16]

It is not descent, in the end, that has most greatly dehumanized migrant Latina/o/x persons as noncitizen outsiders; it is the demonymic function of their identities, the fact that they came from somewhere else in the Americas. This Coda has tried to wrest back the adjective *American* from its appropriation by the United States as a synonym for a single nation-state: one that expanded its territory and geopolitical influence through countless acts of interference in the sovereignty of other polities. Many Latino Studies scholars have argued that this history justifies reparations and restorative justice in the form of a right to migrate, to work, and to seek naturalization if desired. Returning, semantically and conceptually, to an earlier, prenational sense of *América* as a space with a shared history would make every migrant from this hemisphere, regardless of their origin or ethnicity, demonymically *American*.[17]

· XII ·

Transcription and Translation of
Cotton Mather's *La Fe del Christiano* (1699)

Three known physical copies of *La Fe del Christiano* exist: one each at the American Antiquarian Society, the Houghton Library of Harvard University, and the New York Public Library. The first has damage to the first leaf; the second has minor foxing and a hand-inked *virgulilla* above the N in SENORES on the title page; the third is a near-perfect copy with no markings. A microform of the Houghton Library copy was made for the Early American Imprints, 1639–1800 (Evans) series, and is the source for the digital images now gathered under the Evans Digital Library licensed by the Readex Corporation. I have used the printed copies as proof-texts for the transcription and have left intact idiosyncrasies of spelling, capitalization, and italicization, as well as apparent mistakes and typos, because they feature in the discussion of this little book's materiality as well as its content. The original page numbering is indicated in square brackets prior to each new page; pages 1 and 2 were not numbered in the original, but I add them here for clarity. The footer, by which typesetters indicated the lead line of the page that should come next when collating the large printed sheets, is also reproduced.

In 1967, Thomas E. Johnston published an English translation without a Spanish transcription. With the exception of one misleading error (he transcribed "viandas," meaning foods and especially meats, as "viudas" or widows, which made for a convoluted interpretive commentary), Johnston's is a useful translation that is based on a reconstruction of Mather's theological intentions. It silently corrects Mather's errors, and does not distinguish between the biblical citations and the sentences Mather composed on his own. Since one of my aims in this book has been to show how language attitudes and ideologies stemming from complex histories of intercultural contact can enter the speech produced by learners like Mather, erasing the signs of his struggles with Spanish would represent a lost opportunity to analyze his interlanguage: the interference from English, perhaps Latin and French. In addition, Mather's own translation theory, as I elaborate in Chapters VII and VIII, emphasized both scholarly accuracy and an acknowledgment of translation's inevitable failure—even a joyful embrace of that failure. Indeed, Mather's mystical reading of Babel is reminiscent of some of the most important documents of postmodern translation theory: Walter Benjamin's "Task of the Translator" and Jacques Derrida's "Des Tours de Babel," which dwell upon the impossibility of human language to reproduce a divine original. His branch of Protestantism did not revere any biblical translation as final and definitive; its practice was to study and apply the scriptures in a fresh and contemporary way.[1]

This translation is informed by both my scholarly findings here and the historical current of translation theory which embraces, rather than denies, the gap between original and translation. One source of the gap is temporal: more than three centuries separate Mather's time from ours; the textures and rhythms of literary language have changed along with the connotations of particular words. It seems most in keeping with Mather's own practice to reach for a contemporary idiom of US English rather than a deliberately antiquated one. In doing so, I attempt to give a sense of how *La Fe del Christiano* might have read to native Spanish speakers in Mather's time: a little off, a little foreign-sounding. His intermediate proficiency in Spanish, along with the limits of his available sources, moved him to make specific compositional choices. Like any beginning learner, Mather was thinking in English and "turning" (as he put it) his English into Spanish with the help of his reference texts, which were mostly in the already somewhat antiquated Castilian of the *Siglo de Oro* (as discussed in Chapters VII and VIII). However, it is also likely that he was exposed through conversation to other varieties of oral Spanish. Thus, my *Faith of the Christian* represents a diachronic back-translation of his seventeenth-century Spanish into twenty-first-century English. To emphasize Mather's interlanguage, I have chosen what Lawrence Venuti—following Friedrich Schleiermacher and José Ortega y Gasset—calls "foreignizing" translation, a practice that does not try to smooth out places where the source and target language may be out of joint in order to make the translation read smoothly, but rather allows the unassimilable difference of the source text to come through. The English here is a little misaligned, sometimes comically so, even when it was not Mather's intention to amuse (as in the case of the probable typo *comierdas*).[2]

Given these guiding principles, it should go without saying that this version does not promise perfect consistency with Mather's theology. Mather faced a special problem when addressing faraway, invisible Catholics in a language he was just learning: how much to simplify key concepts without losing either his audience or theological precision. He did not have the opportunity to explain to them the distinction between terms like "consecrated" and "holy," as he might do while standing in the pulpit in his own church. For example, he declines to include the term *publicano* (publican), a reference to the Jewish tax collectors working for the Roman Empire, suggesting that he wanted to be understood by ordinary people in *lengua sabida a Vulgo,* a language known to the layperson. Publican */publicano* is a good example of a biblical term that was not in use in everyday Spanish, and therefore less suited for seeding the hemisphere with a text "in the express words of *Sacred Scripture*" that would take root and survive until its flowering. Presuming that no Protestant Bible, evangelist, or community would be there to help the Spanish reader, it made sense to use terms that could be understood through self-study. Mather must have given some thought as to how to express the Calvinist term "election"—being predestined to be saved by God, with caveats—and its collective noun, the Elect. The expression he chooses in the title, "Suerte entre los Sanctificados," is not bad: "suerte" is a result of being sorted by someone, and the "sanctificados" were those made holy, sanctified, by God's grace. Elsewhere he chooses "Justificados," the justified, but puts it in the same sentence with "Justicia": intelligible as a process related to a legal system of some kind, but expressed in a tautology that uninitiated readers might have found mystifying rather than clarifying. Distinctions between the concepts of forgiveness, remission, redemption, salvation, sanctification, and justification are significant in theological contexts, but all I aim to do here is illustrate how the text itself—in its material form, complete with typos and missing accent marks—transmitted those nuances or, more often, did not have space to.

Most often, the lack of diacritical marks noted in Chapter VIII would not seriously confuse a Spanish reader, but in cases of ambiguity, such as *amo*—which can be a noun indicating "master" or a verb for "loved"—I replicate the aura of that ambiguity with an invented or puzzling word of my own. Capitalization conventions are another source of diachronic difference between original and translation: the usage in Mather's time tended toward hypercapitalization, but his Spanish contemporaries were more reserved about it. Thus, my translation includes some capitalizations in unexpected places that further reproduce the whiff of foreignness that it would have had to its original readership. When the text misspells in a way that goes beyond the kinds of orthographic variations that were common prior to the eighteenth-century standardization of Spanish, my English version misspells too.

As I explain in Chapter VIII, more than half of the total text consists of direct or abridged citations from the Bible, all from the New Testament except the Ten Commandments. Johnston chose to render these citations in the King James version, which was in wide circulation in colonial New England although the Geneva Bible, with its purer Calvinist pedigree, was preferred. Both of these early modern English versions cannot but help sound antiquated to readers today, and because the King James is so deeply integrated into English discourse even among Christians, citing from it would precisely fail to convey the freshness Mather's tract would have had to its first readers. However, the latest Bible translations today make use of biblical source texts that came into circulation only after Mather's time, so I have not borrowed from them either. (Early modern Protestant translations were based on Erasmus's 1516 *Textus Receptus*, but later biblical scholars have had access to fourth- and fifth-century codices as well as new archaeological discoveries of textual fragments.)

Mather had access to the 1602 Amsterdam edition of Cipriano de Valera's revision of the Casiodoro de Reina translation, likely Sewall's expensive and prized folio copy. Valera, like the Calvinist Puritans, was aiming for a "plain style" that I have tried to render here as well. Mather often abridged the Valera translation and sometimes substituted a word or two; likely he kept a polyglot Bible close at hand while composing and actively corrected Valera when it suited his purposes—or when he reckoned the available space on the printed page and tried to find ways to shorten the citation. Using a digital facsimile of the 1602 edition, I have described Mather's significant changes in the endnotes to the English translation, abbreviating references to the 1602 Spanish text with RVA for Reina-Valera Antigua, the acronym in common use today. His citations from it are often abridgments that occasionally contain errors that may be his own or errors that crept in during the printing process. This reader-focused translation replicates these errors. Thus, the Bible verses cited here should be understood as translative literary renderings, not intended in any way to conform to or contribute to biblical scholarship. It is a reasoned yet *irreverent* interpretation of the Reverend's work.[3]

Transcription

[1]
La Fe del Christiano: En Veyntequatro Articulos de la Institucion de *CHRISTO*. Embiada A LOS ESPANOLES, Paraque abran sus ojos, y paraque se Conviertan de las Tinieblas a la luz, y de la potestad de Satanas a Dios: Paraque reciban por la Fe que es en JESU CHRISTO, Remission de peccados, y Suerte Entre los *Sanctificados*.
Por C. MATHERO, *Siervo del Señor JESU CHRISTO*.
II Timoth. I. 13.
Reten la Forma de las Sanas palabras, que de mi oyste, en la Fe, y Charidad, que es en Christo Jesus.
BOSTON, 1699.

[2]
Apocalyp. cap. 18.4
Y oi otra boz del cielo, que dezia, Salid della [*i. e.* de la *Roma*] pueblo mio, porque no seays participantes de sus Peccados, y que no recibays de sus Plagas.

Atqui jus divinum Ecclesia tollere, aut immutare non potest. *A Costa* de procur. Indorum Salute, *p.* 530.

[3]
La Fe del Christiano: En Veyntiquatro Articulos de la Institucion de Christo.
    I.   *De las Escrituras.*
TOda Escriptura es inspirada divinamente.
    2. *Tim.* 3. 15.
    II. *De Dios.*
Nosotros no tenemos mas de un Dios, del qual son todas las cosas.
I *Cor.* 8.6
    III. *De las Personas en Dios.*
Dios es el Padre, y el Hijo, y el Espiritu Sancto.
Math. 28 19.
    IV. *De los Decretos de Dios.*
Dios Señalo algunos antes para Ser Adoptados en Hijos por Jesu Christo, en si mismo, por el buen Querer de su voluntad,—que haze todas las Cosas por el Arbitrio de su voluntad.

Eph. i. 5, 11.

V. *De la Criacion del Mundo.*

En el prencipio crio Dios los Cielos, y la Tierra. Y vido Dios todo lo que avia hecho, y heaqui que era bueno en gran manera.

Gen. I. I 31

[A2 // VI]

[4]

VI. *De la Providencia.*

Dios Sustienta todas las Cosas, con la palabra de su potencia.

Heb. 1.3

VII. *De los Angeles.*

Los Angeles son todos espiritus Servidores, Embiados en Servicio por causa de los, que seran Herederos de salud. Y Angeles que no guardaron su Origen, mas dexaron su habitacion, los Dios ha reservado, debaxo de escuridad en prisiones Eternas, hasta el Iuyzio de aquel gran dia.

Hebr. 1. 14.

Jud. 6.

VIII. *Del estado del Hombre delante del peccado.*

Crio Dios al Hombre a su Imagen; a Imagen de Dios lo crio.

Gen. 1. 27

IX. *Del estado del Hombre, despues del peccado.*

El peccado entro en el Mundo por un Hombre, y por el peccado la muerte; y la muerte ansi passo a todos los Hombres, en aquel en quien todos peccaron.

Rom. 5. 12

X. *De la Redemcion de peccadores.*

De tal manera amo Dios al Mundo que aya dado a su Hijo Unigenito: Paraque todo aquel que en el cree, no se pierda, mas aya vida Eterna.

Jean. 3.16

[XI]

[5]

XI. *De las Naturas en la persona de nuestro Redemptor.*

De los Israelitas, es Christo segun la carne, el qual es Dios sobre todas las cosas, Bendito por siglos.

Rom 9.5

XII. *De las Dos condiciones de nuestro Redemptor.*

Christo Jesus agotase a si mismo, tomando forma de siervo, hecho semejante a los Hombres: Y hallado como Hombre en la Condicion, se humillo a si mismo, hecho obediente hasta la muerte, y muerte de cruz. Por loqual Dios tambien lo ensalço, y le dio Nombre qe es sobre todo nombre.

Phil. 2.7, 8, 8

XIII. *De la Venida Segunda del Salvador nuestro Jesu Christo.*

Dios ha Establecido un Dia, en el qual, ha de Juzgar con Justicia a todo el mundo, por aquel Varon el qual determino, dando fe a todos, levantandolo de los muertos.

Acts 17. 31

XIV. *De la Resurreccion de los muertos.*

Vendra hora, quando todos los que estan en los sepulchros, oyran la Boz de Jesu Christo; y los que hizieron bienes, saldran a Resurrecion de Vida; mas los que hizieron males, a Resurrecion de Juyzio.

Joan 5 28, 29.

[A3] [XV]

[6]

XV. *Del camino que lleva a la salud.*

Por Gracia somos salvos, por la Fe; y esto no de nosotros, que Don de Dios es.

Eph. 2. 8.

XVI. *De la Justification de los Fieles.*

Por Jesu Christo es annunciada Remission de peccados; Y en El es Justificado todo aquel que creyere.

Acts 13. 38, 39.

XVII. *De la Obediencia de los Fieles.*

Palabra fiel es, que los que creen a Dios, procuren governarse en buenas obras; esto es lo bueno, y lo util a los hombres.

Tit. 3. 8.

XVIII. *De la perserverancia de los Fieles.*

El qui commenço en nosotros la buena obra, la perficionara hasta el Dia de Jesu Christo.

Phil. 1.6.

XIX. *De la Regla de la Vida.*

Hablo Dios todas estas palabras, diziendo.

 1. No tendras Dioses agenos delante de mi.

 2. No te haras Imagen, ni ninguna semejança, no te inclinaras a ellas, ni las honrraras.

 3. No tomaras el Nombre de Jehova tu Dios en vano.

Exod. 20

[4 Accor-]

[7]

 4. Acordartehas de Dia de Sabbado, para Sanctificarlo.

 5 Honrra a tu padre, y tu madre.

 6 No Mataras.

 7 No cometeras Adulterio.

 8 No Hurtaras.

 9 No hablaras contra tu proximo falso testimonio

 10 No cobdiciaras cosa alguna de tu proximo.

XX. *De la Regla del Ruego.*

Jesus Christo Enseñava sus Discipulos, diziendo, Orareys ansi.

 1. Padre nuestro, que estas en los cielos:

 2. Sea Sanctificado tu Nombre:

 3. Venga tu Reyno:

 4. Sea hecha tu Voluntad; como en el Cielo, ansi tambien en la Tierra:

 5. Danos oy nuestro Pan quotidiano:

 6. Y Sueltanos nuestras deudas, como tambien nosotros Soltamos a nuestros deudores:

 7. Y no nos metas en Tentacion,mas libra nos de mal:

 8. Porque Tuyo es el Reyno, y la Potencia, y la Gloria, por todos los Siglos. *Amen.*

Matth. 6:

[A 4] [XXI]

[8]

XXI. *De la Iglesia.*

Se dezia a JESUS, Tu eres el Christo,el Hijo del Dios Biviente: Entonces respondiendo Jesus, dixo, Sobre Esta piedra edificare mi Iglesia, y las puertas del Infierno no prevaleceran contra ella.

Matth. 16 16, 18

XXII. *De los Administradores en la Iglesia.*

Los Ancianos que goviernan bien, (en la Iglesia) Son dignos de Doblada Honrra; y mayormente los que Trabajan, en predicar y enseñar.

I Tim. 5 17.

Los Diaconos ansi mismo, que tengan el misterio de la Fe con limpia Consciencia, y que bien ministrase ganon para si buen Gradu.

I Tim. 3 8.

XXIII. *De los Sacramentos, en la Iglesia.*

Jesus hablo, diziendo, Id, Enseñad a todas las Gentes, Baptizandolos en Nombre del Padre, y del Hijo, y del Espiritu Sancto.

Matt. 28. 18, 19

El Señor Jesus, la noche, que fue entregado, tomo el pan: y aviendo hecho Gracias, lo partio, y dixo,

I Cor. 11 23, 24, 25, 26

[Tomad]

[9]

Tomad, comed, Esto es mi cuerpo, que por vosotros es partido; hazed Esto en memoria de mi

Ansimismo tomo tambien el vaso, despues de aver Cenado, diziendo, Este vaso es el Nuevo Testamento en mi Sangre: Hazed esto todas las vezes que bevereys, en memoria de mi. Si ansi lo haziendo, la muerte del Señor annun-ciamos hasta que venga.

XXIV. *De la Disciplina, en la Iglesia.*

Jesus dixo, si tu hermano peccare contra ti, ve y redarguyelo, entre Ti y el Solo: Si te oyere, ganado has a tu hermano. Mas si no te oyere, toma aun Contigo uno o dos; paraque en Boca de dos o de tres testigos, consista toda la cosa. Y si no oyere a ellos, di lo a la Congregacion; y si no oyere a la Congregacion, ten lo por un Ethnico.

Matth. 18 15, 16, 17

[La]

[10]

La Religion pura; En Doze Palabras Fieles, y dignas de ser recibidas de Todos.

I

LA Palabra de Cristo en sagrada Escritura, deve ser Gozada, Buscada, y Sabida par las Gentes de todas suertes: y es una grande Iniquitad, impedir el Vulgo de Leer de aquella preciosa palabra de la Vida.

JOAN. cap. 5, 39.

Escrudinad las Escrituras; porque ellas son las que dan testimonio de Mi.

ROMAN. cap. 15 4. *Las cosas que antes fueron escriptas, para nuestro enseña-miento fueron escriptas; para que por el padecer, y por la consolacion de las es-crituras ayamos espereança.*

[II]

[11]

II

La sagrada Escritura declara bastantamente todo que nosotros devemos creer, o hazer, al fin que consigamos Salvacion eterna.

2 *TIMOTH,* cap. 15, 16, 17.

Las sagradas Escrituras te pueden hazer sabio para la salud, por la fe, que es en Christo Jesus.

Toda Escritura inspirada divinamente es util para enseñar, para redarguyr, para corregir, para instituyr en justicia.

Para que el hombre de Dios sea perfecto, perfectamente instruydo, para toda buena obra.

MATH. 15. 9. *En vano Me honrran, enseñando doctrinas, mandamientos de hombres.*

III

Señor nuestro Jesu Christo es la sola Cabeça de su iglesia; y no ay ningun otro Soberano sobre las Conciencias de los Cristianos.

MATH. cap. 23. 8

Uno es buestro Maestro, el CHRISTO, y todos vosotros soys hermanos.

EPHES. cap. 1.22. *Sujetando le todas las cosas debaxo de sus pies, y poniendo le por Cabeça sobre todas las cosas a la Iglesia.*

[12]
IV
El Papa de *Roma* es el Antichristo, y el hombre de Peccado, descrivido y prenunciado en la Palabra del Señor nuestro JESU CHRISTO.
II THESSAL. cap. 2. 3, 4, 7, 8.
. . . *Se manifieste el hombre de Peccado, el Hijo de la Perdicion,*
Opponiendo se y levantando se contra todos loque se llama Dios, o divinidad: tanto que se assiente en el Templo de Dios como Dios, haziendo se parecer Dios.
Por que ya se obra el mysterio de Iniquitad, solamente que el que aora domina, domine hasta que sea quitado.
Y entonces sera manifestado aquel Iniquo, al qual el Señor matara con el Espiritu de su Boca, y con la CLARIDAD de su Venida lo DESTRUIRA.

V
En nuestros Oraciones no es licito invocar los Santos, o los Angeles: mas devemos Rezar solamente a Dios Todo poderoso, en nuestro Señor Jesu Christo.
[MAT

[13]
MATTH. cap. 4. 10
Jesus le dize—Escripto esta, Al Señor tu Dios adoraras, y a el solo serviras.
II CHRON. cap. 6 30. *Tu solo conoces coracon de los hijos de los hombres.*

VI
La Justificacion del Peccador es obtenida solamente por Fe en la Justicia de nuestro Señor Jesu Christo, que era el Fiador a Dios por nosotros: y no por las obras, o padeciamentos, o merecimientos de algunas Criaturas.

ROMAN. cap. 3.22, 24, 25, 28.
La Justicia de Dios, por la Fe de Jesu Christo, para todos, y sobre todos los que creen en el:
Justificados graciosamente por su Gracia, por la Redencion que es en Jesu:
Al qual Dios ha propuesto por aplacacion, por la Fe en su sangre.

Ainsi concluimos ser el hombre jusitificado por Fe, sin las obras de la Ley.

ROMAN. cap. 10. 3 *Ignorando la Justicia de Dios, y procurando de establecer la suya, no son sujetos a la Justicia de Dios.*

[VII]

[14]

VII

Baptismo, y la Cena del Señor son los solos Sacramentos del concierto de la Gracia, debaxo el Nuevo Testamento.

MATTH. cap. 28 19.

Enseñad a todas las Gentes: Baptizando los en Nombre del Padre, y del Hijo, y del Espiritu Sancto

I CORINT. cap. 11. 27. *Pruevese cada uno a si mismo, y coma ansi de aquel Pan, y beva de aqual Vaso.*

VIII

En Eucharistia no es Transubstanciacion del Pan consagrado, en Cuerpo de nuestro Señor: mas la adoracion del Pan en Eucharistia, es Idolotria criminal.

I CORINT. cap. 11. 23, 25, 26.

El Señor Jesus la noche que fue entregado, tomo el Pan: Ansi mismo tomo tambien el Vaso

Porque todas las vezes que comierdes este Pan, y bevierdes este Vaso, la Muerte del Señor annunciays hasta que Venga.

IX

El Detenimiento del Vaso de los Legos en Eucharistia, es Praesuncion y Sacrilegio Vedado par nuestro Señor Jesu Christo.

[15]

MATTH. cap. 26, 27, 28

Tomando el Vaso, y hechas gracias, dioles diziendo, Beved de el Todos.

Porque esto es mi Sangre del Nuevo Testamento, la qual es derramada por muchos, para Remission de los Peccados.

X.

Todos Exercicios de la Religion hechos en la Iglesia de Dios, deven ser hechos en Lengua sabida a Vulgo.

I CORINT. cap. 14, 16, 17, 26, 28.

————*El que occupa lugar de Idiota como dira, Amen, sobre tu bendicion!*
porque no sabe loque has dicho.——*El otro no es edificado.*

Todo se haga a Edificacion.

Si no uviere Interprete, Calle en la Iglesia.

PSALM. 47. 8. *Cantad Entendiendo.*

ROMAN. cap. 12. 1. *Es vuestro Racional culto.*

XI.

Doctrina que defende el Matrimonio, y aparta los hombres de la Viandas,
es la doctrina de la Apostacia.

I TIMOTH. cap. 4. 1, 2, 3.

El Espiritu dize manifiestamente, que en los postreros tiempos algunos aposta-
taran de Fe, escuchando a espiritus de Error, y a doctrinas de Demonios:

[Que

[16]

Que con Hypocracia hablaran mentira, teniendo cauterizada la Conciencia.

Que defenderan el Matrimonio, apartar se los hombres de las Viandas, que
Dios crio paraque con hazimiento de gracias participassen de ellas los fieles, y los
que han conocido la Verdad

XII

Los Espiritus de los Hombres, en la ora de la Muerte van o al Cielo, o al
Infierno: y Purgatorio es la ficion de los Engañadores en los postreros tiempos.

JOAN. cap. 3. 36

El que cree en el Hijo, tiene Vida eterna: mas el que al Hijo es incredulo, no
vera la Vida: mas la Yra de Dios esta sobre el.

LUC. cap. 16. 22, 23. *Acontecio que murio el mendigo, y fue llevado por los*
Angeles al seno de Abraham: y murio tambien el rico, y fue sepultado.

Y en el Infierno alcondo sus ojos, estando en los Tormentos.

ROMAN. cap. 8. 1. *Ninguna Condemnacion ay para los que estan en Christo*
Jesus.

PHILIP. cap. 1. 23.

Teniendo desseo de ser desetado, y estar con Christo.

ACTOS. cap. 7. 59.——*Dixiendo, Señor Jesus, Recibe mi espiritu.*

FINIS

English Translation

The Faith of the Christian: In Twenty-Four Articles of *CHRIST'S* Institution. Sent out TO THE SPANISH, so they might open their eyes, and turn from the darkness to the light, and from Satan's power to God's: So they may receive through the faith that is in JESUS CHRIST, remission of sins, and be sorted among the Elect.[4]

By C. MATHER, *Servant of the Lord JESUS CHRIST.*
II Timoth. I. 13.
Hold on to the Example of the Saving words, that you heard from me, in the Faith, and Caring, that is in Christ Jesus.
BOSTON, 1699.

Apocalyp. chap. 18.4
And I heard another voice from heaven, that was saying, Go out from her [*i.e.* from *Rome*] my people, that you all may not be participants in her Sins, and that you do not receive her Plagues.

Atqui jus divinum Ecclesia tollere, aut immutare non potest. *A Costa* de procur. Indorum Salute, *p.* 530.[5]

The Faith of the Christian: In Twenty-Four Articles of *CHRIST'S* Teaching.
   I. *On the Scriptures.*
All Scripture is divinely inspired.
   2. *Tim.* 3. 15.
   II. *On God.*
We have no more than one God, from whom all things come.
   I *Cor.* 8.6
   III. *Of the Persons of God.*
God is the Father, and the Son, and the Holy Spirit.
   Math. 28 19.
   IV. *On the Decrees of God.*
God Marked some people before to be Adopted Children through Jesus Christ, in himself, by the good Desire of his will,—[He] that does all Things according to the Discretion of his will.[6]

Eph. i. 5, 11.

V. *Of the Creation of the World.*

In the buh-ginning God created the Heavens and the Earth. And God sighted all that he had made, and look here, it was very good in a great way.[7]

Gen. I. 1 [*and*] 31

VI. *On Providence.*

God Sustains all Things by the word of his might.

Heb. 1.3[8]

VII. *On the Angels.*

The angels are all ministering spirits, sent forth to minister for the sake of those who shall be Heirs of salvation. And the angels who did not take care of their Original state, but left their home place, those God has reserved below the darkness eternal prisons, until the Judgment of that great day.

Hebr. 1. 14.

Jud. 6.[9]

VIII. *On the state of Man before sin.*

God created man after his image; in the image of God he created him.

Gen. 1. 27

IX. *On the state of Man, after sin.*

Sin entered into the World through a Man, and through sin, death; and so death passed into all men: in that in whom all of them have sinned.[10]

Rom. 5. 12

X. *On the redemption of sinners.*

In this way lovemaster God has given his only begotten son: in order that anyone who believes in him, should not be lost, but should have eternal life.[11]

Jonn. 3.16

XI. *On the natures within the person of our Redeemer.*

Out of the Israelites, it is Christ came, according to the flesh, who is God over all things, Blessed for centuries.

Rom 9.5[12]

XII. *On the dual conditions of our Redeemer.*

Christ Jesus humbled himself, taking the form of a servant, made like Men: And was found in Man in the Shape, he humbled himself, and made obedient up until death, even the death of the cross. For this God also has exalted him, and gave him a name tht is above every name.

Phil. 2.7, 8, 8[13]

XIII. *On the Coming Second of the Saviour Jesus Christ.*

God has Appointed a Day, in which he is going to Judge with justice the whole world, by that Male whom he decided on, giving faith to everyone, raisingupit from the dead.

Acts 17. 31[14]

XIV. *On the resurrection of the dead.*

The hour will come, when all those who are in the graves, will hear the Voice of Jesus Christ; and those who did goods will emerge to the Resurrection of Life: but those who did evils, to the resurrection of Judgment.

John 5 28, 29.[15]

XV. *On the road that leads to saving.*

By Grace we are saved, through Faith; and this is not from us, which is the Gift of God.

Eph. 2. 8.[16]

XVI. *On the Justification of the Faithful.*

Through Jesus Christ is preached the Remission of sins; And in Him is Justified every one who believes.

Acts 13. 38, 39.[17]

XVII. *On the Obedience of the Faithful.*

It is a true saying, that those who believe in God will be careful to devote themselves to good works; this is the good, and the profitable thing to men.

Tit. 3. 8.[18]

XVIII. *On the perseverance of the Faithful.*

The one who among us began the good work, will bring it to completion before the day of Jesus Christ.

Phil. 1.6.[19]

XIX. *On the Rule of Life.*

God spoke all these words, saying,

1. You will not have other Gods before me.

2. You will not make an Image, or any Semblance, you will not bow down to them, or worship them.

3. You will not take the Name of Jehovah your God in vain.

Exod. 20

4. You will remember the Day of Sabbath, to make it holy.

5 Honor your father, and your mother.

6 You will not kill.

7 You will not commit Adultery.

8 You will not Steal.

9 You will not speak false testimony against your neighbor

10 You will not cobet any thing of your neighbor's.[20]

XX. *On the rule of prayer.*

Jesus Christ Taught his Disciples, saying, you will Pray in this way.

1. Our father, who is in heaven:

2. Let your Name be made holy;

3. Let your Kingdom come;

4. Let your Will be done: as it is in Heaven, so also on Earth;

5. Give us today our daily Bread:

6. And Release us from our debts, as we release our debtors;

7. And do not put us into temptation, but liberate us from evil:

8. For yours is the kingdom, and the power, and the glory, for all the ages. Amen.[21]

Matth. 6:

XXI. *On the Church.*

He said to JESUS, You are the Christ, the son of the living God: Then Jesus said, responding, Upon This rock I will build my church, and the gates of hell will not prevail over it.

Matth. 16 16, 18

XXII. *On the ministers of the Church.*

The Elders who govern well; (in the Church), are worthy of twice the honor; and especially those who labor in preaching and teaching.

I Tim. 5 17.

The deacons also, let them keep the mystery of the Faith with a clean Conscience, and them what minister well gain for themselves good standin.[22]

I Tim. 3 8.

XXIII. *On the sacraments in the church.*

Jesus spoke, saying, Go, teach to all the people, baptizing them in the name of the father, and the son, and the holy spirit.

Matt. 28. 18, 19

The Lord Jesus, the night he was betrayed, took the bread: and having given Thanks, he broke it, and said,

I Cor. 11 23, 24, 25, 26

Take, eat: This is my body, that is broken for you; do this in memory of me.

In the same way he taketook the cup also, after having Dined, saying, This cup is the New Testament in my Blood: Do this every time you drink it, in memory of me. For in doing this, we proclaim the death of the Lord until he should come again.[23]

XXIV. *On Discipline, in the Church.*

Jesus said, if your brother sins against you, go and criticize, between You and him Alone. If he hears you, you have won over your brother. But if he does not hear you, take one or two persons With you, so that in the Mouths of two of three witnesses, the whole matter will become clear. And if he does not listen to them, tell it to the Congregation; And if he does not listen to the congregation, let him be considered an Outsider.[24]

Matth. 18 15, 16, 17

———

The Pure Religion. In Twelve Maxims That Are True And Worthy Of Being Received By Everyone.[25]

I

The Word of Christ in holy Scripture, should be Enjoyed, Sought out, and Known by People of all sorts: and it is a great Iniquity to keep the Common person from Reading out of that precious word of Life.

JOHN, chap. 5:39

Stoody the Scriptures; for these are what give testimony to me.[26]

ROMANS, *chap. 15:4.*

The things that were written before, were written for our teaching; so that through suffering and the consolation of the scriptures we might have hope.[27]

II

The holy Scripture states enoughly everything that we ought to believe, or to do, in order to gain eternal Salvation.[28]

2 *TIMOTH*, chap. 15, 16, 17.

The sacred Scriptures can make you knowledgeable about Salvation, by way of the faith, that is in Christ Jesus.

All Scripture divinely inspired is useful to teach, to criticize, to instruct in justice.[29]

So that the man of God should be perfect, perfectly taught to do every good work.

MATT. 15.9 *In vain they honor my teaching doctrines, human mandates.*

III

Our Lord Jesus Christ is the only Head of his church; and there is no other Sovereign over the Consciences of Christians.

MATH. chap. 23. 8

One is your Master, the CHRIST, and all of you are brothers.

EPHES. chap. 1.22. *Subjecting him everything under his feet, and putting him as Head over all things to the Church.*[30]

IV

The Pope in *Rome* is the Antichrist; and the man of Sin, described and predicted in the word of our Lord Jesus Christ.

II THESSAL. chap. 2. 3, 4, 7, 8.

He proves himself the man of Sin shows himself, the Son of Perdition, opposing him self and raising himself up against everything that is called God, or divinity; making himself seem God.

Because this is how the mystery of Iniquity will be shown, only that he who dominates now, dominates until he will be removed.

And then that Iniquity will be manifested, which the Lord will kill with the Spirit of his Mouth, and with the BRIGHTNESS of his Coming will DESTROY it.[31]

V

In our Prayers it is not proper to invoke the Saints or the Angels: instead we should pray only to All Mighty God, in our Lord Jesus Christ.

MATTH. chap. 4. 10
Jesus said to him—It's written that you will worship the Lord your God, and only him will you serve.
II *CHRON.* chap. 6 30. *You alone know heart of the sons of men.*[32]

VI

The Justification of the Sinner is obtained only through Faith in the Judgment of our Lord Jesus Christ, who was the Guarantor for us: and not by deeds, or sufferings, or by the merit of some Things.[33]

ROMAN. chap. 3.22, 24, 25, 28.
The Justice of God, by Faith in Jesus Christ, for everyone, and over everyone who believes in him:
Justified graciously by his Grace, by the Redemption that is in Jesus: Those whom God has set out for appeasing by Faith in his blood. Therefore we conclude that man is justified through Faith, without the works of the Law.
ROMAN. chap. 10. 3 *Ignoring the Justice of God, and managing to establish their own, they are not submitted to the Justice of God.*[34]

VII

Baptism, and the Lord's Supper are the only Sacraments that accord with the Grace explained in the New Testament.
MATTH. chap. 28 19.
Teach to all the People: Baptizing them in the Name of the Father, and the Son, and the Holy Spirit
I *CORINT.* chap. 11. 27. *Every person should test themselves, and then eat of that Bread, and drink of that Cup.*
VIII

The Eucharist is not the Transubstantiation of the sacred Bread, into the Body of our Lord; the adoration of the Bread in Eucharist is criminal idolatry.
I *CORINT.* chap. 11. 23, 25, 26.

The Lord Jesus the night that he was turned in, taketook the Bread: the same way taketook the Cup also

Because every time that you eatcrap this Bread, and dreenk this Cup, you Proclaim the Death of the Lord until he Comes Again.[35]

IX

Holding back the Cup from lay persons at Eucharist is a Presumption and a Sacrilege, Prohibited by our Lord Jesus Christ.[36]

MATTH. chap. 26, 27, 28

Taking the Cup, and having given thanks, he gave it to them saying, Drink from it Everyone.

Because this is my Blood in the New Testament, which is spilled out for many, for Remission of Sins.

X.

All religious Activities done in the Church of God should be done in a Language known to the common person.

I CORINT. chap. 14, 16, 17, 26, 28.

—He who plays the Idiot will say, Amen, over your blessing! because he does not know what you have said.—The other guy is not edified.

Let everything be done for Edification.

If there is no Translator, Don't Speak in the Church

PSALM. 47. 8. *Sing with Understanding.*

ROMAN. chap. 12. 1. *It's your Reasonable service.*[37]

XI.

A Doctrine that restricts marriage, and forbids men from eating Meat, is the doctrine of apostasy.

I TIMOTH. chap. 4. 1, 2, 3.

The Spirit says clearly, that in the end times some will turn away from the Faith, listening to the spirits of Error, and to the doctrines of Demons.

[16]

That with Hypocrisy they will speak lies, having cauterized their Conscience.

That they will restrict Marriage, sepa-rate men from Meats, that God create-ated so that with the giving of thanks all the faithful could participate in eating them, and those who have come to know the Truth[38]

XII

The Spirits of men in the hour of Death go either to Heaven, or to Hell; and Purgatory is a fiction of the Deceivers in the end times.

JOHN. chap. 3. 36

He who believes in the Son, has Life eternal: but he who is a disbeliever in the Son, will not see Life: but the Anger of God is over him.

LUKE. chap. 16. 22, 23. *It happened that the beggar died, and he was carried by the angels to the bosom of Abraham; and the rich man had died as well, and he was buried.*

And in Hell razin his eyes, being in the Torments.[39]

ROMAN. chap. 8. 1. *There is no Condemnation for those who are in Christ Jesus.*

PHILIP. chap. 1. 23.

Having the desire to be untyed, and be with Christ.[40]

ACTS. chap. 7. 59.—*Saying, Lord Jesus, Receive my spirit.*

FINIS

NOTES

ACKNOWLEDGMENTS

INDEX

Notes

Abbreviations

AAS	American Antiquarian Society, Worcester, MA
Diary	*Diary of Cotton Mather.* Edited by Worthington C. Ford, 2 vols. New York: Frederick Ungar, 1957.
Fe	Cotton Mather, *La Fe del Christiano.* Boston, 1699.
Letters	*Selected Letters of Cotton Mather.* Edited by Kenneth Silverman. Baton Rouge: Louisiana State University Press, 1971.
Paterna	*Paterna: The Autobiography of Cotton Mather.* Edited by Ronald Bosco. Delmar, NY: Scholars' Facsimiles and Reprints, 1976.
Quotidiana	Mather Family Papers, American Antiquarian Society
RVA	*La Biblia: Los sacros libros del viejo y nuevo testamento,* trans. Cipriano de Valera (Amsterdam: Lorenzo Jacobi, 1602), aka Reina-Valera Antigua.

I. Introduction

1. I use the term *Puritan* because it is recognizable to nonspecialist readers, but this is not the term preferred by the majority group of New England settlers. "Puritan" was originally a derogatory reference to those who challenged the practices of the Church of England. Some religious historians eschew the term because of its vagueness or because of the way it later became synonymous with the rejection of pleasure ("puritanical"). It's more accurate to call the Mathers Non-Separating or Nonconformist members of the Anglican Church who advocated for a cleansing of what they saw as vestigial Catholic tendencies within it—unlike the several branches of Dissenting or Separatist sects (such as the "Pilgrims" who came to Plymouth in 1620). This majority among English American Protestants favored self-governance at the local level of the congregation, rejecting the Anglican hierarchy; this belief lent Mather's church the

name Congregationalist. See Michael P. Winship, *Hot Protestants: A History of Puritanism in England and America* (New Haven, CT: Yale University Press, 2018); David D. Hall, *The Puritans: A Transatlantic History* (Princeton, NJ: Princeton University Press, 2019).

2. This is not to downplay the significance of present or historical migration patterns of other groups, particularly from China, India, and other sites in East and Southeast Asia, the Middle East, and Africa. However, media analyses indicate a persistent focus on the Latino body as the representative unauthorized migrant: see Otto Santa Ana, *Juan in a Hundred: The Representation of Latinos on Network News* (Austin: University of Texas Press, 2013), and José A. Cobas, Jorge Duany, and Joe R. Feagin, *How the United States Racializes Latinos: White Hegemony and Its Consequences* (Boulder, CO: Paradigm, 2009).

3. The scholarship on the history of whiteness and its intersection with critical race theory is vast; see Richard Delgado, ed., *Critical Race Theory: A Reader,* 3rd ed. (New York: New York University Press, 2017), and Michael Omi and Howard Winant, "Introduction," in *Racial Formation in the United States,* 3rd ed. (New York: Routledge, 2014). Lisa Marie Cacho, *Social Death: Racialized Rightlessness and the Criminalization of the Unprotected* (New York: New York University Press, 2012), makes the important connection between the reconstitution of anti-Black violence as a carceral regime following Reconstruction and the policing and punishment of nonwhite migrants, principally Chinese, Filipino, and Mexican, in the early twentieth century. I owe the phrase "Jews and other Others" to Jonathan Freedman, *Klezmer America: Jewishness, Ethnicity, Modernity* (New York: Columbia University Press, 2008).

4. "Hispanic," an anglicized version of *hispanoamericano* (itself a late nineteenth-century coinage), derives from the demonym *Hispania* for the Roman imperial hinterland on the Iberian peninsula. *Latino* moved that demonymic reference point to designate an origin in *Latin* America, gaining ground because of its ease of translation and its ability to assign linguistic gender—the same capacity that led to its transformation into a nonbinary form, Latinx or Latine. As with tribally specific Native identities, the people so designated overwhelmingly self-identify with more granular designations that sometimes pertain to their family's origin in a particular homeland (e.g., *dominicana, cubano,* or terms that are affectionate nicknames for the sending nation, such as *catracho* and *boricua*) and sometimes to a region (e.g., *michoacano, tejana,* or a pan-national alliance term such as *centroamericana*). These are demonyms that begin to serve an ethnonymic function when a community organizes as such to their collective benefit, as with transmigration networks and self-help organizations. The most long-lived neologisms for US resident Latinx populations, however, began as ethnonyms, emphasizing the group's evolution as a minoritized population within present US borders: *Chicano* is the best example, along with the less widespread *Nuyorican.* Skeptics of the utility of Latino / Hispanic (and there are many) emphasize the

bottom-up formation of such terms as opposed to the top-down panethnicity with a particular utility to governments and markets. See Clara E. Rodriguez, *Changing Race: Latinos, the Census, and the History of Ethnicity in the United States* (New York: New York University Press, 2000). Recognizing the unsettled nature of the term, I use "Latina/o/x" here to indicate the gender-identification possibilities for individuals while retaining "Latino" as an adjective and in the plural as a group noun for people of Latin American origin living in the United States, regardless of citizenship status. There is no standard onomastic term for members of the same speech community (a crucial concept in in sociolinguistics), but "loquonym" has been proposed in online forums as a logical combination of the Greco-Latin root for "speech" and the classifying suffix -onym. I use it here to highlight the strong association of Hispanic/Latina/o/x populations with a shared language.

5. Joanna Brooks, "Working Definitions: Race, Ethnic Studies, and Early American Literature," *Early American Literature* 41, no. 2 (2006): 313–320.

6. Bryce Traister, "Afterword," in *American Literature and the New Puritan Studies,* ed. Bryce Traister (Cambridge: Cambridge University Press, 2017), 220. Abram C. van Engen, *City on a Hill: A History of American Exceptionalism* (New Haven, CT: Yale University Press, 2020).

7. On the nineteenth-century formation of Puritan Studies, see Lawrence Buell, *New England Literary Culture: From Revolution through Renaissance* (Cambridge: Cambridge University Press, 1989); Christopher Felker, *Reinventing Cotton Mather in the American Renaissance: "Magnalia Christi Americana" in Hawthorne, Stowe, and Stoddard* (Boston: Northeastern University Press, 1994); and especially Lindsay DiCuirci, *Colonial Revivals: The Nineteenth-Century Lives of Early American Books* (Philadelphia: University of Pennsylvania Press, 2018). For recent summaries of the field, see Traister, *American Literature and the New Puritan Studies;* Sarah Rivett and Abram van Engen, eds., "Postexceptionalist Puritans," special issue, *American Literature* 90, no. 4 (2018); and Kristina Bross and Abram van Engen, eds., *A History of American Puritan Literature* (Cambridge: Cambridge University Press, 2020).

8. Kenneth Silverman, *The Life and Times of Cotton Mather* (New York: Harper and Row, 1984), 425. For new scholarship based on the *Biblia,* see Reiner Smolinski and Jan Stievermann, eds., *Cotton Mather and "Biblia Americana": America's First Bible Commentary—Essays in Reappraisal* (Tübingen: Mohr Siebeck, 2010).

9. William C. Spengemann, *A New World of Words: Redefining Early American Literature* (New Haven, CT: Yale University Press, 1994), 23. Mitchell Breitweiser, "All on an American Table: Cotton Mather's *Biblia Americana,*" *American Literary History* 25, no. 2 (2013): 381–405, at 389.

10. Sari Altschuler, *The Medical Imagination: Literature and Health in the Early United States* (Philadelphia: University of Pennsylvania Press, 2018). Although Altschuler's work focuses on a later period, her insistence on the imaginative and thus

literary dimensions of medical research and thought is useful in understanding Mather. Sarah Rivett, *The Science of the Soul in Colonial New England* (Chapel Hill: University of North Carolina Press for the Omohundro Institute of Early American History and Culture, Williamsburg, Virginia, 2011), treats the various dimensions of his natural philosophy work. A recent example of the periodic revival of Mather-Boylston-Onesimus in public discourse is Jess McHugh, "A Puritan Minister Incited Fury by Pushing Inoculation against a Smallpox Epidemic," *Washington Post,* March 8, 2020, https://www.washingtonpost.com/history/2020/03/07/smallpox-coronavirus -antivaxxers-cotton-mather/.

11. Robert E. Brown, "Hair Down to There: Nature, Culture, and Gender in Mather's Social Theology," in Smolinski and Stievermann, *Cotton Mather and "Biblia Americana,"* 495–514.

12. Jane Kamensky, reviewing a recent popular history of the crisis, notes that despite spawning some "500 books, nearly 1,000 dissertations and twice as many scholarly articles" in multiple languages, as well as such popular representations, "the Salem episode is more gripping than it was important" in the life of the colony ("*The Witches: Salem, 1692,* by Stacy Schiff," *New York Times,* October 27, 2015).

13. Lorenzo J. Greene, *The Negro in Colonial New England, 1620–1776* (Port Washington, NY: Kennikat, 1942). Ibram X. Kendi, *Stamped from the Beginning: The Definitive History of Racist Ideas in America* (New York: Nation Books, 2016); Jason Reynolds and Ibram X. Kendi, *Stamped: Racism, Anti-Racism, and You: A Remix of "Stamped from the Beginning" for Young Adults* (New York: Little, Brown, 2020); also Reynolds and Kendi, *Stamped (For Kids): Racism, Anti-Racism, and You* (New York: Little, Brown, 2021).

14. "Rules for the Society of Negroes, 1693" (Boston: B. Harris, repr. 1693), image 1; broadside held at the American Antiquarian Society, digitally displayed by the Library of Congress at https://www.loc.gov/resource/rbpe.03302600/?sp=1.

15. For an assessment of Sewall versus Mather on slavery, see Mark Peterson, *The City-State of Boston* (Princeton, NJ: Princeton University Press, 2019).

16. There is no indication in Increase Mather's papers of when Spaniard entered his household, but in Mather's will, written in 1719, he requests that upon his death (which occurred in 1723) Spaniard be manumitted and "esteemed a Free Negro" (Silverman, *Life and Times,* 369). Benjamin Wadsworth, president of the college from 1725 to 1737, held at least one enslaved woman, and his successor, Edward Holyoke, at least two more, counting them as property to be passed on to heirs; see https://www .wbur.org/edify/2017/04/24/harvard-slavery-exhibit.

17. Margaret Newell, *Brethren by Nature: New England Indians, Colonists, and the Origins of American Slavery* (Ithaca, NY: Cornell University Press, 2015); Wendy Warren, *New England Bound: Slavery and Colonization in Early New England* (New

York: Liveright, 2017); Andrés Reséndez, *The Other Slavery: The Uncovered Story of Indian Slavery in North America* (New York: Mariner, 2017).

18. See, e.g., Saidiya Hartman, "Venus in Two Acts," *Small Axe* 12, no. 2 (2008): 1–14; Marisa Fuentes, *Dispossessed Lives: Women, Slavery, and the Archive* (Philadelphia: University of Pennsylvania Press, 2016).

19. Stanley T. Williams, *The Spanish Background of American Literature*, 2 vols. (New Haven, CT: Yale University Press, 1968). For a summation of this post-1992 revisionism, see Ralph Bauer, "Early American Literature and American Literary History at the 'Hemispheric Turn,'" *American Literary History* 22, no. 2 (2010): 250–265, and *Early American Literature* 45, no. 2 (2010): 217–233.

20. Bell Gale Chevigny and Gari Laguardia, eds., *Reinventing the Americas: Comparative Studies of Literature of the United States and Spanish America* (New York: Cambridge University Press, 1986), x–xi. Carlos J. Alonso, "Spanish: The Foreign National Language," *ADFL Bulletin* 37, no. 2–3 (2006): 15–20. A recent analysis of languages other than English spoken in the home by people age five and up, based on data from the 2018 U.S. Census Bureau's American Community Survey, indicates that there are 41.5 million Spanish speakers in the U.S., while Chinese has 3.5 million. Karen Zeigler and Steven A. Camarota, "67.3 Million in the United States Spoke a Foreign Language at Home in 2018," Center for Immigration Studies (October 2019), 4.

21. Alicia Mayer, *Dos Americanos, Dos Pensamientos: Carlos de Sigüenza y Góngora y Cotton Mather* (Mexico City: Universidad Nacional Autónoma de México, 1998).

22. Eliga H. Gould, "Entangled Histories, Entangled Worlds: The English-Speaking Atlantic as a Spanish Periphery," *American Historical Review* 112, no. 3 (2007): 764–786, at 768. Jorge Cañizares-Esguerra, *Puritan Conquistadors: Iberianizing the Atlantic* (Stanford, CA: Stanford University Press, 2006), 215. Katherine Grandjean, *American Passage: The Communications Frontier in Early New England* (Cambridge, MA: Harvard University Press, 2015). Paul Gilroy, *The Black Atlantic: Modernity and Double-Consciousness* (Cambridge, MA: Harvard University Press, 1995), and Jace Weaver, *The Red Atlantic: American Indigenes and the Making of the Modern World, 1000–1927* (Chapel Hill: University of North Carolina Press, 2014). Karin Wulf, "For 2016, Appreciating #VastEarly America," *Uncommon Sense* (blog), Omohundro Institute of Early American History and Culture, https://blog.oieahc.wm.edu/for-2016-appreciating-vastearlyamerica/.

23. For continental recalibration, see Claudio Saunt, "Go West: Mapping Early American Historiography," *William and Mary Quarterly* 3rd ser., 65, no. 4 (2008): 745–778.

24. Mather on "American": Cotton Mather, *Biblia Americana: America's First Bible Commentary*, vol. 1, *Genesis*, ed. Reiner Smolinski (Tübingen: Mohr Siebeck, 2010), 75; see also Silverman, *Life and Times*, 425.

25. *Paterna* 42. The essential reference source to track Mather's publication activity at all scales, from broadsides to "Small Books" and beyond, is Thomas J. Holmes, *Cotton Mather: A Bibliography of His Works,* 3 vols. (Cambridge, MA: Harvard University Press, 1940).

26. For the field's origin in Isaiah Thomas, see Matt Cohen, "The History of the Book in New England: The State of the Discipline," *Book History* 11 (2008): 301–323. Examples of the way literary criticism on this period has been transformed by book-history methods include Hugh Amory and David D. Hall, eds., *A History of the Book in America,* vol. 1, *The Colonial Book in the Atlantic World* (Cambridge: Cambridge University Press, 2000); E. Jennifer Monaghan, *Learning to Read and Write in Colonial America* (Amherst: University of Massachusetts Press, 2005); Patricia Crain, *The Story of A: The Alphabetization of America from the New England Primer to the Scarlet Letter* (Stanford, CA: Stanford University Press, 2002); Matthew Brown, *The Pilgrim and the Bee: Reading Rituals and Book Culture in Early New England* (Philadelphia: University of Pennsylvania Press, 2007). On the influence of the communications circuit model, see Robert Darnton, "'What is the History of Books?' Revisisted," *Modern Intellectual History* 4, no. 3 (2007), 495–508.

27. See Paul Kroskrity, "Language Ideologies and Language Attitudes." *Oxford Bibliographies in Linguistics,* https://doi:10.1093/obo/9780199772810-0122.

28. The considerable bibliography on the use, study, and reclamation of Native-language practices in New England includes Edward G. Gray, *New World Babel: Languages and Nations in Early America* (Princeton, NJ: Princeton University Press, 1999); Hilary Wyss, *Writing Indians: Literacy, Christianity, and Native Community in Early America* (Amherst: University of Massachusetts Press, 2000); Phillip Round, *Removable Type: Histories of the Book in Indian Country, 1663–1880* (Chapel Hill: University of North Carolina Press, 2010); Jean O'Brien, *Firsting and Lasting: Writing Indians Out of Existence in New England* (Minneapolis: University of Minnesota Press, 2010); Sarah Rivett, *Unscripted America: Indigenous Languages and the Origins of a Literary Nation* (Oxford: Oxford University Press, 2017).

29. Jane Kamensky, *Governing the Tongue: The Politics of Speech in Early New England* (New York: Oxford University Press, 1998), 151.

30. The 1646 Westminster Confession, a key document of Reform Protestantism, had thirty-three articles of faith. Although Mather mentions in his *Diary* that he chose twenty-four because it was a "sacred number," he does not spell out why. There are twenty-four elders surrounding the throne of God in Revelation, and twenty-four letters in the Greek alphabet. Perhaps more importantly, twenty-four is twice twelve, the number of Christ's disciples and of the articles of faith in the Nicene Creed, the fourth-century statement about what Christians believe. The number of articles of faith in the shorter Apostle's Creed—which took its current form in the eighth century but by legend was dictated with one contribution from each of the Apostles—

is also twelve. Mather was not prone to conform his sermons or other writings to such numerological conceits, but he read extensively in Talmudic texts for the *Biblia Americana* and may have been influenced by that tradition of numerology.

31. Meredith Marie Neuman, *Jeremiah's Scribes: Creating Sermon Literature in Puritan New England* (Philadelphia: University of Pennsylvania Press, 2013).

II. The Global Designs of a Creole Family

1. A good reception history is Edward M. Griffin, "A Singular Man: Cotton Mather Reappraised," *Early American Literature* 50, no. 2 (2015): 475–494. The father-son psychologization is best seen in Robert Middlekauff, *The Mathers: Three Generations of Puritan Intellectuals, 1596–1728* (New York: Oxford University Press, 1971). For the currents of Puritan Studies over time, see Abram Van Engen, "Prologue: Pilgrims, Puritans, and the Origins of America," in *A History of American Puritan Literature*, ed. Kristina Bross and Abram Van Engen (Cambridge: Cambridge University Press, 2020), 17–34.

2. Aníbal Quijano and Immanuel Wallerstein, "Americanity as a Concept, or the Americas in the Modern World," *International Social Science Journal* 44, no. 4 (1992): 549–557.

3. Christopher Heaney, "Marrying Utopia: Mary and Philip, Richard Eden, and the English Alchemy of Spanish Peru," in *Entangled Empires: The Anglo-Iberian Atlantic, 1500–1830*, ed. Jorge Cañizares-Esguerra (Philadelphia: University of Pennsylvania Press, 2018), 85–104. Margaret Rich Greer, Walter Mignolo, and Maureen Quilligan, eds., *Rereading the Black Legend: The Discourses of Religious and Racial Difference in the Renaissance Empires* (Chicago: University of Chicago Press, 2007). Mather activates the Black Legend especially in *The Wonders of the Invisible World: Observations as Well Historical as Theological, Upon the Nature, the Number, and the Operations of the Devils (1693)*, ed. Reiner Smolinski (Lincoln: University of Nebraska Digital Commons, 1998), 33.

4. J. H. Elliott, *Empires of the Atlantic World* (New Haven, CT: Yale University Press, 2008).

5. Carla Gardina Pestana, *Protestant Empire: Religion and the Making of the British Atlantic World* (Philadelphia: University of Pennsylvania Press, 2009); Karen Ordahl Kupperman, *Providence Island, 1630–1641: The Other Puritan Colony* (Cambridge: Cambridge University Press, 1993).

6. Kenneth Silverman, *The Life and Times of Cotton Mather* (New York: Harper and Row, 1984), 70–74; Ian K. Steele, "Origins of Boston's Revolutionary Declaration of 18 April 1689," *New England Quarterly* 62, no. 1 (1989): 75–81.

7. A. W. Plumstead, ed., *The Wall and the Garden: Selected Massachusetts Election Sermons, 1670–1775* (Minneapolis: University of Minnesota Press, 1968), 137. See John

Canup, "Cotton Mather and 'Criolian Degeneracy,'" *Early American Literature* 24, no. 1 (1989): 20–34. On degeneracy debates, see Antonello Gerbi, *The Dispute of the New World: The History of a Polemic, 1750–1900*, trans. Jeremy Moyle (Pittsburgh, PA: University of Pittsburgh Press, 1973).

8. *Diccionario crítico etimológico de la lengua castellana*, ed. Joan Corominas, s.v. "Criollo" (Madrid: Gredos, 1954), 1:943–944. "Creole, n. and adj.," *OED Online*, September 2021, http://www.oed.com/view/Entry/44229. An excellent social overview is José Antonio Mazzotti, "Criollismo, Creole, and Créolité," in *Critical Terms in Caribbean and Latin American Thought*, ed. Yolanda Martínez-San Miguel, Benigno Sifuentes-Jáuregui, and Marisa Belausteguigoitia (New York: Palgrave, 2016), 87–99.

9. Mather is the source for the *OED*'s first usage citation of "American" as a stand-alone noun meaning a European settler. "American, n.," *OED Online*, September 2021, http://www.oed.com/view/Entry/6342. Quote from Mather in Reiner Smolinski, ed., *The Kingdom, the Power, and the Glory: The Millennial Impulse in Early American Literature* (Dubuque, IA: Kendall/Hunt, 1998), xi.

10. Stephanie E. Smallwood, "Reflections on Settler Colonialism, the Hemispheric Americas, and Chattel Slavery," *William and Mary Quarterly* 76, no. 3 (2019): 414; James Sidbury and Jorge Cañizares-Esguerra, "Mapping Ethnogenesis in the Early Modern Atlantic," *William and Mary Quarterly* 68, no. 2 (2011): 182. See also Ralph Bauer and José Antonio Mazzotti, *Creole Subjects in the Colonial Americas: Empires, Texts, Identities* (Chapel Hill: University of North Carolina Press, 2009).

11. See Teresa A. Toulouse, "'Reader . . . Behold One Raised by God': Religious Transformations in Cotton Mather's *Pietas in Patriam: The Life of His Excellency Sir William Phips, Knt.*," in *Religious Transformations in the Early Modern Americas*, ed. Stephanie Kirk and Sarah Rivett (Philadelphia: University of Pennsylvania Press, 2014), 231–251.

12. On comparative ethnodemonology across Catholic, Protestant, and Indigenous contexts, see Ralph Bauer, *The Alchemy of Conquest: Science, Religion, and the Secrets of the New World* (Charlottesville: University of Virginia Press, 2019).

13. Silverman, *Life and Times of Cotton Mather*, 123.

14. David Levin, *Cotton Mather: The Young Life of the Lord's Remembrancer, 1663–1703* (Cambridge, MA: Harvard University Press, 1978), 269; on his turn to authorship, 272–275. Cotton Mather, *Magnalia Christi Americana, Books I and II*, ed. Kenneth Ballard Murdock and Elizabeth W. Miller (Cambridge, MA: Belknap Press of Harvard University Press, 1977), 268, 172.

15. *Magnalia* 172. "Mighty convulsions": *Diary* 1:202, 205, 207–208, 212–214, 222–224, 239.

16. David D. Hall, *Worlds of Wonder, Days of Judgment: Popular Religious Belief in Early New England* (Cambridge, MA: Harvard University Press, 1990). *Paterna* 112–113; English translation, 395.

17. Elizabeth Reis argues that women in particular were warned away from claiming to have had contact with angels; see "Immortal Messengers: Angels, Gender, and Power in Early America," in *Mortal Remains: Death in Early America,* ed. Nancy Isenberg and Andrew Burstein (Philadelphia: University of Pennsylvania Press, 2012), 163–175.

18. "Wrestling" *Diary* 1:206; Spanish, 1:223–224. See also *Paterna* 148.

19. *Paterna* 157–158.

20. *Diary* 1:284–285.

21. *Diary* 1:284–285.

22. *Diary* 1:293–294.

23. *Diary* 1:293–294; 1:285–286, 1:295–296.

24. *Paterna* 148.

25. Helen K. Gelinas, "Regaining Paradise: Cotton Mather's 'Biblia Americana' and the Daughters of Eve," in *Cotton Mather and "Biblia Americana": America's First Bible Commentary—Essays in Reappraisal,* ed. Reiner Smolinski and Jan Stievermann (Tübingen: Mohr Siebeck, 2010), 474.

III. Telling the Future of *America Mexicana*

1. I have relied on the modern translation and commentary in José de Acosta, *Natural and Moral History of the Indies,* ed. Jane E. Mangan and Walter Mignolo, trans. Frances M. López-Morillas (Durham, NC: Duke University Press, 2002). For a provocative reception history across sects, see Jorge Cañizares-Esguerra, "José de Acosta, a Spanish Jesuit–Protestant Author: Print Culture, Contingency, and Deliberate Silence in the Making of the Canon," in *Encounters between Jesuits and Protestants in Asia and the Americas,* ed. Jorge Cañizares-Esquerra, Robert Aleksander Maryks, and Ronnie Po-Chia Hsia (Leiden: Brill, 2018), 185–227.

2. Ralph Bauer details different eschatological pressures on the "alchemy of conversion" between Jesuits and Puritans in *The Alchemy of Conquest: Science, Religion, and the Secrets of the New World* (Charlottesville: University of Virginia Press, 2019), especially 215–266. For other pan-American comparisons, see Frank Graziano, *The Millennial New World* (New York: Oxford University Press, 1999). The Puritan eschatological tradition is illustrated in the introduction and exemplary texts in Reiner Smolinski, ed., *The Kingdom, the Power and the Glory: The Millennial Impulse in Early American Literature* (Dubuque, IA: Kendall Hunt, 1998); Zachary McLeod Hutchins, *Inventing Eden: Primitivism, Millennialism, and the Making of New England* (New York: Oxford University Press, 2014). On Spanish versions, see Luís Filipe Silvério Lima and Ana Paula Torres Megiani, "An Introduction to the Messianisms and Millenarianisms of Early-Modern Iberian America, Spain, and Portugal," in *Visions, Prophecies and Divinations: Early Modern Messianism and Millenarianism in Iberian America,*

Spain and Portugal, ed. Luis Felipe Silvério Lima and Ana Paula Torres Megiani (Leiden: Brill, 2016), 1–40.

3. Reiner Smolinski, ed., *The Threefold Paradise of Cotton Mather: An Edition of "Triparadisus"* [1727] (Athens: University of Georgia Press, 1995), 57.

4. On experimenting with spoken Hebrew in contact situations, see Edward G. Gray, *New World Babel: Languages and Nations in Early America* (Princeton, NJ: Princeton University Press, 2000), 47. On Increase and Cotton Mather's eschatology over the years and their views on Menasseh, Thorowgood, and Mede, see Sarah Rivett, *Unscripted America: Indigenous Languages and the Origins of a Literary Nation* (Oxford: Oxford University Press, 2017), 52–53.

5. On Eliot and the New England Company, see Richard W. Cogley, *John Eliot's Mission to the Indians before King Philip's War* (Cambridge, MA: Harvard University Press, 1999); Kathryn N. Gray, *John Eliot and the Praying Indians of Massachusetts Bay: Communities and Connections in Puritan New England* (Lewisburg, PA: Bucknell University Press, 2015); Kristina Bross, *Dry Bones and Indian Sermons: Praying Indians in Colonial America* (Ithaca, NY: Cornell University Press, 2004). Lisa Brooks, *Our Beloved Kin: A New History of King Philip's War* (New Haven, CT: Yale University Press, 2018), chap. 4.

6. Michael P. Clark, ed., *The Eliot Tracts: With Letters from John Eliot to Thomas Thorowgood and Richard Baxter* (Westport, CT: Praeger, 2003), 138–139.

7. See Jill Lepore, *The Name of War: King Philip's War and the Origins of American Identity* (New York: Knopf, 1998); Brooks, *Our Beloved Kin.*

8. Cotton Mather, *The Triumphs of the Reformed Religion in America: The Life of the Renowned John Eliot* (Boston: Benjamin Harris and John Allen, 1691).

9. For English general knowledge of Spanish America, see J.N. Hillgarth, *The Mirror of Spain, 1500–1700: The Formation of a Myth* (Ann Arbor: University of Michigan Press, 2000). Mather, *Quotidiana,* boxes 43–48. Antonio de Herrera y Tordesillas's *Description of the Indies* in four volumes (Latin ed., 1601), known as the "Décadas" (Seville, 1615), gave more information about Mexico than other available sources at the time. On *Biblia Americana:* Zarate citation *Biblia* 1:598; Acosta on Peru 3:194. See Smolinski's editorial note on the presence of Acosta in Genesis, *Biblia* 1:508.

10. Cotton Mather, *The Wonders of the Invisible World: Observations as Well Historical as Theological, Upon the Nature, the Number, and the Operations of the Devils (1693),* ed. Reiner Smolinski (Lincoln: University of Nebraska Digital Commons, 1998), 103–104; quotation, "The Devil" at 105.

11. Jorge Cañizares-Esguerra, in *Puritan Conquistadors: Iberianizing the Atlantic* (Stanford University Press, 2006), catalogues the differences and striking similarities between Catholic (mainly Franciscan) and Reformed approaches to "the satanization of the American continent" (18).

12. Cotton Mather, *Magnalia Christi Americana, Books I and II,* ed. Kenneth Ballard Murdock and Elizabeth W. Miller (Cambridge, MA: Belknap Press of Harvard University Press, 1977).

13. Samuel Sewall, "Phaenomena quaedam Apocalyptica ad Aspectum Novi Orbis Configurata. Or, Some Few Lines towards a Description of the New Heaven (1697)," ed. Reiner Smolinski, *Electronic Texts in American Studies,* 2, https://digitalcommons.unl.edu/etas/25.

14. Samuel Sewall, *The Diary of Samuel Sewall, 1674–1729,* ed. M. Halsey Thomas (New York: Farrar, Straus and Giroux, 1973), 1:122. Samuel Lee's daughter Lydia would eventually become Mather's third wife, as Chapter X elaborates. Sewall, "Phaenomena," 2.

15. Barbara E. Mundy, *The Death of Aztec Tenochtitlan, the Life of Mexico City* (Austin: University of Texas Press, 2015), 122–127. Mather, *Quotidiana,* item 45.

16. Sewall, "Phaenomena," 2, 62.

17. Sewall, "Phaenomena," 3.

18. See Heather Miyano Kopelson, "Finding Nunnacôquis: A Tale of Online Catalogs, Marginalia, and Native Women's Linguistic Knowledge," *Commonplace* 18, no. 2 (2018), http://commonplace.online/article/vol-18-no-2-kopelson/; Mukhtar A. Isani, "The Growth of Sewall's 'Phaenomena Quaedam Apocalyptica,'" *Early American Literature* 7, no. 1 (1972): 64–75.

19. Sewall, "Phaenomena," 65, 64–65.

20. Sewall, "Phaenomena," 42–43. Michael Hoberman, *New Israel/New England: Jews and Puritans in Early America* (Amherst: University of Massachusetts Press, 2011), chap. 2.

21. For strictures against Jews in Boston see Hoberman, *New Israel/New England,* 30–32.

22. Sewall, *Diary,* 1:401–402. On Darién, see Karen Ordahl Kupperman, *Providence Island, 1630–1641: The Other Puritan Colony* (Cambridge: Cambridge University Press, 1993).

23. Sewall, *Diary,* 1: 380; 1:476. Other references to chocolate on 380, 476, 563, 570, 636.

24. Sewall, *Diary,* 1:401.

25. Sewall, *Diary,* 1:397.

26. For the significance of the 1692 Corn Riot, see Anna Herron More, *Baroque Sovereignty: Carlos Sigüenza y Góngora and the Creole Archive of Colonial Mexico* (Philadelphia: University of Pennsylvania Press, 2013), chapter 4. Alicia Mayer, in *Dos Americanos, Dos Pensamientos: Carlos de Sigüenza y Góngora y Cotton Mather* (Mexico City: Universidad Nacional Autónoma de México, 1998), makes the connection between this event and Sewall's diary entry (150). On Sigüenza y Góngora's use of *Mercurio*

volante to report of expeditions to the northern reaches of New Spain that are now part of the US, including Florida and New Mexico, see More, *Baroque Sovereignty,* 200–210.

27. Cotton Mather, *Triumphs of the Reformed Religion in America: The Life of the Renowned John Eliot* (Boston: Benjamin Harris and John Allen, 1691), 124.

28. On the evolution of Mather's eschatology, see Reiner Smolinski, "Israel Redivivus: The Eschatological Limits of Puritan Typology in New England," *New England Quarterly* 63, no. 3 (1990): 357–395.

IV. From Language Encounters to Language Rights

1. Lope de Vega's embrace of writing for the *vulgo,* the popular audience, famously expresses this shift in literary Spanish. See Antonio Sánchez Jiménez, "Vulgo, imitación y natural en el 'Arte nuevo de hacer comedias' (1609) de Lope de Vega," *Bulletin of Hispanic Studies* 88, No. 7 (2011), 727–742.

2. See Frances E. Karttunen, *Between Worlds: Interpreters, Guides, and Survivors* (New Brunswick, NJ: Rutgers University Press, 1994). Anna Brickhouse, *The Unsettlement of America: Translation, Interpretation, and the Story of Don Luis de Velasco, 1560–1945* (New York: Oxford University Press, 2015).

3. Edward G. Gray and Norman Fiering, *The Language Encounter in the Americas, 1492–1800* (New York: Berghahn, 2000).

4. Matt Cohen and Jeffrey Glover, eds., *Colonial Mediascapes: Sensory Worlds of the Early Americas* (Lincoln: University of Nebraska Press, 2014), 2. Key texts include Walter D. Mignolo, *The Darker Side of the Renaissance: Literacy, Territoriality, and Colonization* (Ann Arbor: University of Michigan Press, 1995); Elizabeth Hill Boone and Walter D. Mignolo, eds., *Writing without Words: Alternative Literacies in Mesoamerica and the Andes* (Durham, NC: Duke University Press, 1994); Elizabeth Hill Boone, *Stories in Red and Black: Pictorial Histories of the Aztecs and Mixtecs* (Austin: University of Texas Press, 2000); Camilla Townsend, *Annals of Native America: How the Nahuas of Colonial Mexico Kept Their History Alive* (Oxford: Oxford University Press, 2007). On the boundary-definition of text and writing, see Germaine Wonkentine, "Dead Metaphor or Working Model? 'The Book' in Native America," in Cohen and Glover, *Colonial Mediascapes,* 33–46, and Andrew Newman, "Early Americanist Grammatologies" in Cohen and Glover, *Colonial Mediascapes,* 47–57.

5. Major sources contrasting Catholic/Protestant missionary linguistics include Edward G. Gray, *New World Babel: Languages and Nations in Early America* (Princeton, NJ: Princeton University Press, 1999); Sarah Rivett, *Unscripted America: Indigenous Languages and the Origins of a Literary Nation* (Oxford: Oxford University Press, 2017); Sean P. Harvey and Sarah Rivett, "Colonial-Indigenous Language Encounters in

North America and the Intellectual History of the Atlantic World," *Early American Studies* 15, no. 3 (2017): 442–473.

6. Enrique Florescano, *Memory, Myth, and Time in Mexico: From the Aztecs to Independence,* (Austin: University of Texas Press, 1994), 508. On responses to Spanish assimilation, see David Eduardo Tavárez, *The Invisible War: Indigenous Devotions, Discipline, and Dissent in Colonial Mexico* (Stanford, CA: Stanford University Press, 2011).

7. In addition to Boone's and Townsend's work on reading Mesoamerican codices produced before and after contact, see Isabel Laack, *Aztec Religion and Art of Writing: Investigating Embodied Meaning, Indigenous Semiotics, and the Nahua Sense of Reality* (Leiden: Brill, 2019);

8. Carlos Alberto González Sánchez, *New World Literacy: Writing and Culture across the Atlantic, 1500–1700,* trans. Tristán Platt (Lewisburg, PA: Bucknell University Press, 2011), 45.

9. For a general overview of Spanish adaptation of imperial governance structures in New Spain and Peru, see J. H. Elliott, *Empires of the Atlantic World: Britain and Spain in America, 1492–1830* (New Haven, CT: Yale University Press, 2006). On education, see Pilar Gonzalbo Aizpuru, *Educación y colonización en la nueva España, 1521–1821* (Mexico City: Universidad Pedagógica Nacional, 2001). Jorge Cañizares-Esguerra, "Envoi: Whose Classical Traditions?," *Bulletin of Latin American Research* 37, no. S1 (2018): 199–200.

10. See David Rojinsky, *Companion to Empire: A Genealogy of the Written Word in Spain and New Spain, c.550–1550* (Leiden: Brill, 2010), chap. 3; Byron Ellsworth Hamann, *The Translations of Nebrija: Language, Culture, and Circulation in the Early Modern World* (Amherst: University of Massachusetts Press, 2015). Mignolo, in *Darker Side of the Renaissance* and other works, identifies Nebrija's grammar as a racial one; for a counterargument, see Andrew Laird, "Colonial Grammatology: The Versatility and Transformation of European Letters in Sixteenth-Century Spanish America," *Language and History* 61, no. 1–2 (2018): 52–59. On when Castilian became equivalent to Spanish and the post-Nebrija integration of Latin terms to purify the language, see David A. Pharies, *A Brief History of the Spanish Language* (Chicago: University of Chicago Press, 2007), 93.

11. On policy changes see González Sánchez, *New World Literacy,* 43–45.

12. See Gregory J. Shepherd, *José de Acosta's "De Procuranda Indorum Salute": A Call for Evangelical Reforms in Colonial Peru* (Bern: Peter Lang, 2015).

13. José de Acosta, *De Procuranda Indorum salute,* trans. G. Stewart McIntosh, 2 vols. (Tayport: Mac Research, 1996), 2:18.

14. Acosta, *Procuranda,* 2:16, 2:21.

15. See in general José Luis Suárez Roca, *Lingüística misionera española* (Oviedo: Pentalfa Ediciones, 1992), and for the orderliness of Nahuatl, Catherine Fountain,

"Transculturation, Assimilation, and Appropriation in the Missionary Representation of Nahuatl," in *Colonialism and Missionary Linguistics*, ed. Klaus Zimmermann and Birte Kellermeier-Rehbein (Berlin: De Gruyter, 2015), 177–198, at 184–185.

16. On myth and fact about Catholic print, see Natalia Maillard Álvarez, "Introduction," in *Books in the Catholic World during the Early Modern Period* (Leiden: Brill, 2013), ix–xlii; "Control and exuberance" cited on x. See also José Torre Revello, *El libro, la imprenta, y el periodismo en América durante la dominación española* (Buenos Aires: Talleres S. A. Casa Jacobo Peuser, 1940); Ma Pilar Gutiérrez Lorenzo, *Impresos y libros en la historia económica de México (siglos XVI–XIX)* (Guadalajara: Universidad de Guadalajara, 2007). On rationale, see Marina Garone Gravier, *Historia de la tipografía colonial para lenguas indígenas* (Mexico City: Centro de Investigaciones y Estudios Superiores en Antropología Social, Universidad Veracruzana, 2014), 17.

17. Statistics in Garone Gravier, *Historia de la tipografía*, 183. Ralph Bauer, *The Alchemy of Conquest: Science, Religion, and the Secrets of the New World* (Charlottesville: University of Virginia Press, 2019), 239.

18. See Ana Carolina Hosne, *The Jesuit Missions to China and Peru, 1570–1610: Expectations and Appraisals of Expansionism* (New York: Routledge, 2013). Acosta, *Procuranda*, 2:25, 2:17.

19. Sean P. Harvey, *Native Tongues: Colonialism and Race from Encounter to the Reservation* (Cambridge, MA: Harvard University Press, 2015); Gray, *New World Babel*, 30, 53. For detailed comparative studies of French Jesuit and English Protestant missionary linguistics, see Rivett, *Unscripted America;* on its influence upon Locke and eighteenth-century linguistic theory, see Sarah Rivett, *The Science of the Soul in Colonial New England* (Chapel Hill, NC: University of North Carolina Press for the Omohundro Institute of Early American History and Culture, Williamsburg, Virginia, 2011). The example of Roger Williams, an antagonist of the Puritans, among the Narragansett is an important element of comparative studies.

20. Thomas Gage, *A New Survey of the West Indies, 1648: The English-American* (New York: McBride, 1929), 298.

21. Eliot's proficiency in Algonquian is uncertain: Mather's biography makes grand claims about his eloquence in it, but Eliot's own self-assessment is modest. See Rivett, *Science of the Soul*, chap. 3, on epistemologies of conversion; *Unscripted America*, chap. 2; Gray, *New World Babel*, chap. 4. On Eliot's lack of proficiency, see Steffi Dippold, "The Wampanoag Word: John Eliot's *Indian Grammar*, the Vernacular Rebellion, and the Elegancies of Native Speech," *Early American Literature* 48, no. 3 (2013): 543–575. On the Native students at Harvard and Cheeshahteaumuck's poem, see Lisa Brooks, *Our Beloved Kin* (New Haven, CT: Yale University Press, 2018), chap. 2; for James Printer's later imprisonment and Mather's denunciation of him, see 194–200.

22. Brooks, *Our Beloved Kin*, chap. 2, makes this argument, as do Hilary E. Wyss, *Writing Indians: Literacy, Christianity, and Native Community in Early America* (Am-

herst: University of Massachusetts Press, 2000); Phillip H. Round, *Removable Type: Histories of the Book in Indian Country, 1663–1880* (Chapel Hill: University of North Carolina Press, 2010). Kristina Bross, *Dry Bones and Indian Sermons: Praying Indians in Colonial America* (Ithaca, NY: Cornell University Press, 2004); Matthew P. Brown, *The Pilgrim and the Bee: Reading Rituals and Book Culture in Early New England* (Philadelphia: University of Pennsylvania Press, 2007).

23. On the skull anecdote see Jill Lepore, *The Name of War: King Philip's War and the Origins of American Identity* (New York: Knopf, 1998). Cotton Mather, *The Triumphs of the Reformed Religion in America: The Life of the Renowned John Eliot* (Boston: Benjamin Harris and John Allen, 1691), 99.

24. For assessments of the [r] see Dippold, "Wampanoag Word"; for the demontalk see Gray, *New World Babel,* 47; for number of letters, see Rivett, *Unscripted America,* 92–93, and on the linguistic ministries of the Cottons, 108–114.

25. Samuel Sewall, *Letter-Book: 1685–1712* (Boston: Massachusetts Historical Society, 1886), 1:297.

26. The quote is from Acosta, *Procuranda,* Book 6, chapter 7 (trans. McIntosh), 2:122.

27. See Jaime Lara, "The Spanish New World," in *A Companion to the Eucharist in the Reformation,* ed. Lee Palmer Wendel (Leiden: Brill, 2013), 293–320.

28. See Pharies, *Brief History of the Spanish Language. Quotidiana* items 45 and 48.

V. Becoming a Spanish Indian

1. *Paterna* 223.

2. Michael Hoberman, *New Israel/New England: Jews and Puritans in Early America* (Amherst: University of Massachusetts Press, 2011), 83. Letter cited in Alejandra Dubcovsky, *Informed Power: Communication in the Early American South* (Cambridge, MA: Harvard University Press, 2016), 65.

3. *Diary* 1:22.

4. *Diary* 1:203. The volumes for 1693–1694, when the second encounter with Phips took place, are unfortunately missing, as they might have provided more background to this story. Some commentators have assumed that the man Sewall refers to as "Spaniard, Increase Mather's Negro" was in fact the "Spanish Indian" that the son gave the father in 1681. Since this occurred prior to Mather's financially advantageous marriage to Abigail Phillips, it is hard to imagine that Cotton Mather had the means for *purchasing* property in the form of an enslaved person, and there were still few persons of African ancestry in Boston at that time: perhaps the young minister was granted authority by a congregant or by the town selectmen over a person deemed a war captive or a vagrant. There is no documentation of Spaniard being in Increase Mather's household prior to 1702 (when his name appears in Sewall's diary), although he left little documentation about his personal business.

5. Saidiya Hartman, "Venus in Two Acts," *Small Axe* 12, no. 2 (2008): 1–14, 6. For an overview of the growth of speculative histories of the enslaved, see Brian Connolly and Marisa Fuentes, "Introduction: From Archives of Slavery to Liberated Futures?," *History of the Present* 6, no. 2 (2016): 105–116.

6. "ingenuous, adj.," *OED Online,* September 2021, https://www.oed.com/view /Entry/95769. The contemporary meaning of "ingenuous" as "innocent, guileless" (now more common in its antonym, "disingenuous") did not arise until the later eighteenth century. The term could, of course, be confused with the earlier-appearing word "ingenious," which has a different etymology and meant "clever and self-serving" in a negative sense. In tracking Mather's fairly frequent use of "ingenuous" in *Magnalia Christi Americana* and other writings, I have not noticed such a confusion with "ingenious," nor does his treatment of Tuqui, especially the offer of an "Instrument for his freedom," suggest that Mather viewed him as deceitful.

7. Wendy Warren, *New England Bound: Slavery and Colonization in Early America* (New York: Liveright, 2016); See Margaret Ellen Newell, *Brethren by Nature: New England Indians, Colonists, and the Origins of American Slavery* (Ithaca, NY: Cornell University Press, 2015).

8. On the translations of the early *Indias del poniente* into *Indias Occidentales* and West Indies, see Ricardo Padrón, *The Spacious Word: Cartography, Literature, and Empire in Early Modern Spain* (Chicago: University of Chicago Press, 2004). On the porous racial categories of *castas* in New Spain, see Matthew Restall, ed. *Beyond Black and Red: African-Native Relations in Colonial Latin America* (Albuquerque: University of New Mexico Press, 2005); Ben Vinson and Matthew Restall, eds., *Black Mexico: Race and Society from Colonial to Modern Times* (Albuquerque: University of New Mexico Press, 2009); María Elena Martínez, *Genealogical Fictions: Limpieza de Sangre, Religion, and Gender in Colonial Mexico* (Stanford, CA: Stanford University Press, 2008).

9. In Laura Arnold Leibman, ed., *Experience Mayhew's "Indian Converts": A Cultural Edition* (Amherst: University of Massachusetts Press, 2008), 213–214.

10. Jonathan Dickinson, *God's Protecting Providence: Man's Surest Help and Defence in the times of the greatest difficulty and most Imminent danger Evidenced in the Remarkable Deliverance of divers Persons, from the devouring Waves of the Sea, amongst which they Suffered Shipwrack* (Philadelphia, 1699), 7, 34, 48–49; on Spanish language "tests," see 23, 25, 27. See Lisa Voigt, *Writing Captivity in the Atlantic World: Circulations of Knowledge and Authority in the Iberian and English Imperial Worlds* (Chapel Hill: University of North Carolina Press, 2009), 328–329.

11. Dickinson, *God's Protecting Providence*, 73, 74.

12. Anna Brickhouse, *The Unsettlement of America: Translation, Interpretation, and the Story of Don Luis de Velasco, 1560–1945* (New York: Oxford University Press, 2015).

13. Amy Turner Bushnell, *Situado and Sabana: Spain's Support System for the Presidio and Mission Provinces of Florida* (Athens: University of Georgia Press, 1995); John E.

Worth, *The Timucuan Chiefdoms of Spanish Florida*, 2 vols. (Gainesville: University Press of Florida, 1998). Paul E. Hoffman, *Florida's Frontiers* (Bloomington: Indiana University Press, 2002). Jerald T. Milanich, *The Timucua* (Cambridge, MA: Blackwell, 1996).

14. Indoctrination estimate cited in Worth, *Timucua Chiefdoms of Spanish Florida*, 1:110; on the difficulty of demographic estimates, see 2:8–10, 138. On the rebellion see Worth, *Timucua Chiefdoms of Spanish Florida*, 2:46–50, and Dubcovsky, *Informed Power*.

15. Alejandra Dubcovsky and George Aaron Broadwell, "Writing Timucua: Recovering and Interrogating Indigenous Authorship," *Early American Studies* 15, no. 3 (2017): 409–441. See also Julian Granberry, *A Grammar and Dictionary of the Timucua Language* (Tuscaloosa: University of Alabama Press, 1984).

16. Francisco de Pareja, *Arte de la lengua Timuquana*, ed. Lucien Adam and Julien Vinson (Paris: Maisonneuve frères et C. Leclerc, 1886), 1.

17. The main clues we have about Pareja's movements are the permissions letters written by each level of functionary as Pareja brought the whole set of manuscripts to him for approval: these place Pareja in Santa Elena (the principal mission) in June 1610; in St. Augustine in August and in Havana in September 1610; and in Mexico City by February 1612 (one of the letters reads 1611, but since it is placed out of order, it may be a misprint). The 1612–1614 span of the publication dates for the first set of texts might suggest that he was gone from Florida for about five years; it is also possible that, after a first voyage where he secured these permissions, he delegated someone to bring the remaining texts back to Florida with new recruits as each one was published. The second set of letters, which precedes the 1627 imprint of the *Catecismo*, places him in Florida in December 1624 and in Mexico City by September 1625.

18. See Dubcovsky, *Informed Power*, 68–92, for the central role of Lucas, a *cacique* who was prosecuted for writing this seditious letter; as a "third-generation mission Indian," Dubcovsky writes, Lucas relied on a network of Timucua literates. William Sturtevant analyzes the 1688 letter in Timucua swearing allegiance to the King of Spain in "History of Research on the Native Languages of the Southeast," in *Native Languages of the Southeastern United States*, ed. Janine Scancarelli and Heather K. Hardy (Lincoln: University of Nebraska Press, 2005), 10.

19. See Dubcovsky and Broadwell, "Writing Timucua," 412–414.

20. On Spanish literacy among Apalachee as well as Timucua, see E. Thomson Shields Jr, "Negating Cultures, Saving Cultures: Franciscan Ethnographic Writings in Seventeenth-Century *la Florida*," in *Recovering the US Hispanic Literary Heritage*, vol. 3, ed. María Herrera-Sobek and Virginia Sánchez Korrol (Houston, TX: Arte Público, 1993), 218. See Jerald T. Milanich, *Laboring in the Fields of the Lord: Spanish Missions and Southeastern Indians* (Tallahassee: University Press of Florida, 2006), 143–148; on "Mexican Indians," 167. On the presence of enslaved Africans, see Worth, *Timucua Chiefdoms of Spanish Florida*, 2:46–50.

21. Pareja, *Confessionario en lengua castellana, y timuquana con algunos consejos para animar al penitente* (Mexico City: En la emprenta de la viuda de Diego Lopez Danalos, 1613), 47–48.

22. On the collapse of the missions, see Milanich, *Timucua*, 196–215, Dubcovsky, *Informed Power*, 99–145. On the larger context of how practices of slavery in the Southeastern Indigenous world were transformed by European notions of chatteldom, see Brett Rushforth, *Bonds of Alliance: Indigenous and Atlantic Slaveries in New France* (Chapel Hill: University of North Carolina Press for the Omohundro Institute of Early American History and Culture, Williamsburg, Virginia, 2012).

23. Estimate from Christina Snyder, *Slavery in Indian Country: The Changing Face of Captivity in Early America* (Cambridge, MA: Harvard University Press, 2010), 68–69. The worst of the slave raids on the Guale-Timucua missions fell between 1685 and 1706 (Worth, *Timucua*, 2:138); after that, most people carried off were Appalachee (Dubcovsky, *Informed Power*, 123).

24. See John E. Worth, "Creolization in Southwest Florida: Cuban Fishermen and 'Spanish Indians,' ca. 1766–1841," *Historical Archaeology* 46, no. 1 (2012): 142–160. William C. Sturtevant, "Chakaika and the 'Spanish Indians: Documentary Sources Compared with Seminole Tradition,'" *Tequesta* 13 (1953), 35–73.

25. See Ann Marie Plane, *Colonial Intimacies: Indian Marriage in Early New England* (Ithaca, NY: Cornell University Press, 2000), 96, for the story of "Maria," a "Spanish Indian" servant accused of infanticide in 1678, and for the story of a Mohawk woman classified as Spanish in 1743, Linford D. Fisher, "A 'Spanish Indian Squaw' in New England: Indian Ann's Journey from Slavery to Freedom," in *Hearing Enslaved Voices: African and Indian Slave Testimony in British and French America, 1700–1848,* edited by Sophie White and Trevor Burnard (New York: Routledge, 2020), 79–97.

26. Mission raids documented by year in Milanich, *Laboring in the Fields of the Lord,* 171–172, 184.

27. Milanich, *Timucua*, 188. Snyder, *Slavery in Indian Country*, 126, notes that some of these Creek-Catawban-Iroquoian people, who had come from far off, then practiced "becoming Spanish" as a survival strategy.

VI. Teaching by Catechism and Conversation

1. For an overview of the movement away from second-language instruction to acquisition, as influentially modeled by applied linguist Stephen Krashen in the 1980s and his theory of quality, level, order of second-language input, see Bill VanPatten, Megan Smith, and Alessandro G. Benati, *Key Questions in Second Language Acquisition: An Introduction,* (Cambridge: Cambridge University Press, 2019).

2. Mayhew cited in Sarah Rivett, *Unscripted America: Indigenous Languages and the Origins of a Literary Nation* (Oxford: Oxford University Press, 2017), 89–90. Mather's early Latin learning: David Levin, *Cotton Mather: The Young Life of the Lord's Remem-*

brancer, 1663–1703 (Cambridge, MA: Harvard University Press, 1978), 159, 259. "Daily Discourses," *Diary* 2:554.

3. Jürgen Leonhardt, *Latin: Story of a World Language,* trans. Kenneth Kronenberg (Cambridge, MA: Harvard University Press, 2013), 146. Barbara E. Mundy, *The Death of Aztec Tenochtitlan, the Life of Mexico City* (Austin: University of Texas Press, 2015), 209.

4. Leonhardt, *Latin,* 147–149. Kenneth Silverman, *The Life and Times of Cotton Mather* (New York: Harper and Row, 1984), 70.

5. *Paterna* 7. Samuel Eliot Morison, *Harvard College in the Seventeenth Century* (Cambridge, MA: Harvard University Press, 1936), 1:83–88, quote on 84; on spot-translations, 194–195. "Derision," Silverman, *Life and Times,* 16.

6. See, e.g., Patricia Crain's comment, "print was an alternative fluency to that of speech": "Print and Everyday Life in the Eighteenth Century," in *Perspectives on American Book History: Artifacts and Commentary,* ed. Scott E. Casper, Joanne D. Chaison, and Jeffrey D. Groves (Amherst: University of Massachusetts Press, 2002), 68. "You sitt alone," quoted in Stacey Dearing, "On Physical and Spiritual Recovery: Reconsidering the Role of Patients in Early American Restitution Narratives," *Journal of Medical Humanities* 42, no. 3 (2021): 11. Dearing usefully describes his treatment of the stammer.

7. *Diary* 1:206. "Ten Times": Silverman, *Life and Times,* 37.

8. Cotton Mather, *Manuductio ad Ministerium. Directions for a Candidate of the Ministry* (Boston: Thomas Hancock, 1726), 28. There is an annotation in Mather's handwriting in his copy of the *Philosophical Transactions of the Royal Society* 5, no. 61 (1670), held at the AAS: "A letter of Dr. John Wallis to Robert Boyle Esq; concerning the said doctor's essay of teaching a person dumb and deaf to speak, and to understand a language; together with the success thereof."

9. On the dominance of Brinsley and Lily in this period, see George Emery Littlefield, *Early Schools and School-Books of New England.* (Boston: Club of Odd Volumes, 1904), 241. Ezekiel Cheever, Mather's master at the Boston Latin School, later wrote his own *Accidence* (1709); it was the first American Latin text. On the Puritan use of Ramist catechisms, see Meredith Marie Neuman, *Jeremiah's Scribes: Creating Sermon Literature in Puritan New England* (Philadelphia: University of Pennsylvania Press, 2013).

10. See in general Lee Palmer Wandel, *Reading Catechisms, Teaching Religion* (Leiden: Brill, 2015). The Congregationalists mostly but not exclusively used the Westminster Catechism, approved in the mid-seventeenth century; see Wilberforce Eames, *Early New England Catechisms. A Bibliographical Account of Some Catechisms Published before the Year 1800, for Use in New England* (Worcester, MA: C. Hamilton, 1898).

11. John Cotton, *Milk for Babes. Drawn Out of the Breasts of Both Testaments. Chiefly, for the Spirituall Nourishment of Boston Babes in Either England: But May Be of Like*

Use for Any Children, ed. Paul Royster (London: J. Coe, for Henry Overton, 1646), http://digitalcommons.unl.edu/etas/18.

12. See Patricia Crain, *The Story of A: The Alphabetization of America from "The New England Primer" to "The Scarlet Letter"* (Stanford, CA: Stanford University Press, 2000), 38–52; Rivett *Unscripted America*, 65–69; and in general E. Jennifer Monaghan, *Learning to Read and Write in Colonial America* (Amherst: University of Massachusetts Press, 2005).

13. Mather, "An Essay on the Memory of My Venerable MASTER: Ezekiel Cheever" (1708), cited in Littlefield, *Early Schools and School-Books*, 231.

14. On the American Puritan adaptation of Locke, see Sarah Rivett, *The Science of the Soul in Colonial New England* (Chapel Hill: University of North Carolina Press for the Omohundro Institute of Early American History and Culture, Williamsburg, Virginia, 2011). On the many iterations of the claim to a "Natural Methods," see L. G. Kelly, *Twenty-Five Centuries of Language Teaching Methodology: 500 B.C.–1969* (Rowley, MA: Newbury House, 1969).

15. Ana Carolina Hosne, *The Jesuit Missions to China and Peru, 1570–1610: Expectations and Appraisals of Expansionism* (New York: Routledge, 2013), 114. Marina Garone Gravier, *Historia de la tipografía colonial para lenguas indígenas* (Mexico City: Centro de Investigaciones y Estudios Superiores en Antropología Social, Universidad Veracruzana, 2014), 186–194, describes these forms. She uses *catecismo* as "a generic term which refers to a series of books or manuals of an evangelical nature, designed to promote the faith, the sacraments, and religious life" (186, translation mine).

16. For different uses of catechisms among French Jesuits in the Americas, see Rivett, *Unscripted America*, 49; on sectarian differences, 120. An argument emphasizing differences is Edward G. Gray, *New World Babel: Languages and Nations in Early America* (Princeton, NJ: Princeton University Press, 1999), 42–45.

17. Cotton Mather, *Cares about the Nurseries. Two Brief Discourses. The One, Offering Methods and Motives for Parents to Catechise Their Children While yet under the Tuition of Their Parents. The Other, Offering Some Instructions for Children, How They May Do Well, When They Come to Years of Doing for Themselves.: [Three Lines from Luther]*, Early American Imprints, 1st series, no. 1065 (Boston: T. Green, for Benjamin Eliot, 1702), 20.

18. On the Catholic associations of parrots with Protestants, see Bruce Boehrer, *Animal Characters: Nonhuman Beings in Early Modern Literature* (Philadelphia: University of Pennsylvania Press, 2010), chap. 2. On the English fetish of insincere conversion derived from Las Casas, see E. Shaskan Bumas, "The Cannibal Butcher Shop: Protestant Uses of Las Casas's 'Brevísima Relación' in Europe and the American Colonies," *Early American Literature* 35, no. 2 (2000): 107–136. On alchemy and conversion among Franciscans especially, see Ralph Bauer, *The Alchemy of Conquest: Science, Religion, and the Secrets of the New World* (Charlottesville: University of Virginia Press, 2019).

19. Henry Bowden and James P. Ronda, eds., *John Eliot's Indian Dialogues: A Study in Cultural Interaction* (Westport, CT: Greenwood, 1980).

20. Allison Margaret Bigelow, *Mining Language: Racial Thinking, Indigenous Knowledge, and Colonial Metallurgy in the Early Modern Iberian World* (Chapel Hill: University of North Carolina Press for the Omohundro Institute of Early American History and Culture, Williamsburg, Virginia, 2020), 139.

21. See Barbara Mahlmann-Bauer, "Catholic and Protestant Textbooks in Elementary Conversation," in *Scholarly Knowledge: Textbooks in Early Modern Europe*, ed. Emidio Campi, Simone De Angelis, and Anja-Silvia Goeing, and Anthony T. Grafton (Geneva: Librairie Droz, 2008), 341–390.

22. E. Thomson Shields Jr, "Negating Cultures, Saving Cultures: Franciscan Ethnographic Writings in Seventeenth-Century La Florida," in *Recovering the US Hispanic Literary Heritage*, vol. 3, ed. María Herrera-Sobek and Virginia Sánchez Korrol (Houston, TX: Arte Público, 1993), 218. A modern edition of a later version can be found in Jerald T. Milanich and William C. Sturtevant, eds., *Francisco Pareja's "Confessionario": A Documentary Source for Timucuan Ethnography*, trans. Emilio F. Moran (Tallahassee, FL: Division of Archives, History, and Records Management, Department of State, 1972). Accessible examples from the *Confesionario* include Mikaela Perron, ed., "Francisco Pareja, Confessionario," Early Visions of Florida, http://earlyfloridalit.net/?page_id=94.

23. Alejandra Dubcovsky and George Aaron Broadwell, "Writing Timucua: Recovering and Interrogating Indigenous Authorship," *Early American Studies* 15, no. 3 (2017): 432. James C. Scott, *Domination and the Arts of Resistance: Hidden Transcripts*, rev. ed. (New Haven, CT: Yale University Press, 1992).

24. Pareja cited in Jerald T. Milanich, *The Timucua* (Cambridge, MA: Blackwell, 1996), 189–190.

25. Edmund Morgan, *The Puritan Family Religion and Domestic Relations in Seventeenth-Century New England* (New York: Harper and Row, 1966), 98. Mather Diary, I: 300.

Kenneth P. Minkema, "Introduction," *Biblia Americana, vol. 3: Joshua-2 Chronicles* (Tübingen: Mohr Sieback, 2014), 7–8.

26. Kennerly M. Woody, "Cotton Mather's *Manuductio ad Theologiam:* The 'More Quiet and Hopeful Way,'" *Early American Literature* 4, no. 2 (1969), 3–48, discusses Mather's maxim making as part of his turn to ecumenical Pietism, 17–20.

VII. Books as Keys to the Spanish Tongue

1. *Paterna* 90. On theories of language arising from Babel in the context of American language encounters, see Edward G. Gray, *New World Babel: Languages and Nations in Early America* (Princeton, NJ: Princeton University Press, 1999); Sarah Rivett,

Unscripted America: Indigenous Languages and the Origins of a Literary Nation (Oxford: Oxford University Press, 2017); Sean P. Harvey, *Native Tongues: Colonialism and Race from Encounter to the Reservation* (Cambridge, MA: Harvard University Press, 2015).

2. Paul V. Kroskrity, "Language Ideologies and Language Attitudes," *Oxford Bibliographies in Linguistics*, https://doi.org/10.1093/obo/9780199772810-0122. *Paterna* 99. *Paterna* is coded and unsigned, he explains, because he does not know "what Hands, besides *Yours*, this Work may fall into" (6).

3. The origin of the term "mock Spanish" is Jane H. Hill, "Hasta La Vista, Baby: Anglo Spanish in the American Southwest." *Critique of Anthropology* 13, no. 2 (1993): 145–176.

4. See Patsy M. Lightbown and Nina Spada, *How Languages Are Learned*, 3rd ed. (Oxford: Oxford University Press, 2009), chap. 4.

5. David A. Pharies, *A Brief History of the Spanish Language* (Chicago: University of Chicago Press, 2007), notes that the personal *a* to indicate persons or personified objects that are direct objects (a residue of the Latin *ad*, indicating direction) was "fully obligatory" by the sixteenth century (130; see also 162).

6. Anthony T. Grafton, "Textbooks and the Disciplines," in *Scholarly Knowledge: Textbooks in Early Modern Europe*, ed. Emidio Campi, Simone De Angelis, and Anja-Silvia Goeing, and Anthony T. Grafton (Geneva: Librairie Droz, 2008), 11–38, at 27. Of the vast bibliography on printing's effects on early modern Europe, see Adrian Johns, *The Nature of the Book: Print and Knowledge in the Making* (Chicago: University of Chicago Press, 1998); Fernando Bouza, *Communication, Knowledge, and Memory in Early Modern Spain,* trans. Sonia López and Michael Agnew (Philadelphia: University of Pennsylvania Press, 2004).

7. Samuel Sewall, *Letter-Book, 1685–1712* (Boston: Massachusetts Historical Society, 1886), 123. *Paterna* 42. See Julius Herbert Tuttle, "The Libraries of the Mathers," *Proceedings of the American Antiquarian Society* 20, no. 2 (1910): 269–356; and Joshua Gee, John Hancock, and James Diman, *Catalogus librorum Bibliothecae Collegij Harvardini: Quod est Cantabrigiae in Nova Anglia* (Boston: B. Green, 1723).

8. Vladimir Hansa, "Teaching of Spanish as a Foreign Language in the XVII Century," *Hispania* 43, no. 3 (1960): 343–346; Aquilino Sánchez, "Spanish as a Foreign Language in Europe: Six Centuries of Teaching Materials," *Language and History* 57, no. 1 (2014): 59–74.

9. Jason Lawrence, *Who the Devil Taught Thee so Much Italian? Italian Language Learning and Literary Imitation in Early Modern England* (Manchester: Manchester University Press, 2005); Marianne Montgomery, *Europe's Languages on England's Stages, 1590–1620* (Farnham: Ashgate, 2012). Dale B. J. Randall and Jackson C. Boswell, *Cervantes in Seventeenth-Century England: The Tapestry Turned* (Oxford: Oxford University Press, 2009). James Lea, "To the practitioners in the Spanish," in Richard Percyvall [Perceval], *Bibliotheca Hispanica: Containing a Grammar; with a Dictionarie*

in Spanish, English, and Latine; Gathered out of Diuers Good Authors: Very Profitable for the Studious of the Spanish Toong. By Richard Percyuall Gent. The Dictionarie Being Inlarged with the Latine, by the Aduise and Conference of Master Thomas Doyley Doctor in Physicke (London: John Jackson, for Richard Watkins, 1591), vii.

10. John Minsheu's *Ductor in Linguas* was republished in 1617, 1625, 1626, and 1627.

11. John Minsheu, *A Dictionarie in Spanish and English, first published ino the English tongue by Ric. Percevale Gent. now enlarged and amplified with many thousand words* (London: Edm. Bollifant, 1599). There is no way to tell for certain about which Spanish reference works Harvard held in 1698, since the first shelf list was not made for another quarter-century. Listed in this 1723 catalog were three imprints that could have been used for Spanish-language study and translation: *Bibliotheca Hispanica* (London, 1591) of Richard Parcyvall [Perceval], in quarto; John Minsheu's polyglot dictionary, *Ductor in Linguas* (London, 1617), and his *Spanish and English Dictionary* (London, 1599), both in folio; and several versions of Latin-Greek and polyglot dictionaries by, or inspired by, Ambrosio Calepino. It is possible that Sewall himself, or one of the heirs of Mather's personal library, donated or sold one of those titles to Harvard.

12. Antonio del Corro, *Reglas gramaticales para aprender la lengua española y Franceia, consiriendo la una con la otra, segun el order de las partes de la oration Latinas* (Oxford: Joseph Barnes, 1586). John Thorie [Thorius], *The Spanish grammer* [*sic*], *with certaine rules teaching both the Spanish and french tongues, by which those which have some knowledge in the French tongue, may the easier attain to the Spanish* (London: John Wolfe, 1590).

13. I am indebted to Jordan Alexander Stein for noticing Stepney's title on the library list in his perusal of the Sewall family papers at the Massachusetts Historical Society. William Stepney, *The Spanish Schoole-Master: Containing Seuen Dialogues, According to Euery Day in the Weeke, and What Is Necessarie Euerie Day to Be Done, Wherein Is Also Most Plainly Shewed the True and Perfect Pronunciation of the Spanish Tongue, toward the Furtherance of All Those Which Are Desirous to Learne the Said Tongue within This Our Realme of England* (London: R. Field for [J]ohn Harison, 1591), 29.

14. Stepney, *Spanish Schoole-Master*, 64–65, 112–113, iv.

15. César Oudin, *A Grammar Spanish and English: Or A briefe and compendious method, teaching to reade, write, speake, and pronounce the Spanish tongue, with dialogues translated from Juan de Luna's Dialogos Familiares* (Paris, 1622); Juan de Luna, *Arte breve, y compendiossa . . .* (London: William Jones, 1623). John Sanford, *Propylaion, or An Entrance to the Spanish Tongue . . .* (London: Thomas Haveland, 1611). Oudin's French-Spanish grammar (translated into English) "is the longest lived of all grammars in any modern language" from 1597 onward (Hansa, "Teaching of Spanish as a Foreign Language," 344), but it was based on his knowledge of Italian and French, copied from two Italian-Spanish grammar texts.

16. James Howell, *A new English grammar: prescribing as certain rules as the languages will bear, for forreners to learn English: ther is also another grammar of the Spanish or Castilian toung, with some special remarks upon* (London: for T. Williams, H. Brome, and H. Marsh, 1662); J. Smith, *Grammatica Quadrilinguis: Or Brief Instructions for the French, Italian, Spanish, and English Tongues: With the Proverbs of Each Language, Fitted for Those Who Desire to Perfect Themselves Therein* (London: Dorman Neuman, 1674), ii.

17. Lewis Owen, *The Key of the Spanish Tongue: Or a plaine and easie introduction whereby a man may in very short time attaine to the knowledge and perfection of that language* (London: 1605, 1606), 10. The copy of this text in Harvard's Houghton Library was legated by the hispanophile James Russell Lowell, but it is not clear whether he purchased it in London or whether the copy had been preserved in New England: it is not impossible that both he and Mather had touched this copy, which (given Lowell's harsh judgment on the Puritans and on Mather in particular) would be a sounding irony.

18. *Quotidiana* 44:138.

19. Owen, *Key of the Spanish Tongue*, 10.

20. Sewall, *Letter-Book*, 199.

VIII. Impressing the Word in Exotic Types

1. *Diary* 1:284–285.

2. On Puritan preferences among Bible translations, see Meredith Marie Neuman, *Jeremiah's Scribes: Creating Sermon Literature in Puritan New England* (Philadelphia: University of Pennsylvania Press, 2013), 149–152. On translation theory in New England, see Sarah Rivett, *The Science of the Soul in Colonial New England* (Chapel Hill: University of North Carolina Press for the Omohundro Institute of Early American History and Culture, Williamsburg, Virginia, 2011), chap. 2.

3. Valera's preface to the 1602 edition calls this a "second edition" of Reina's Bible, stating that 2,600 copies had been printed in Basel and were all quickly bought; presumably the Amsterdam edition had a similar print run. Cipriano de Valera, *La Biblia, que es, los Sacros Libros del Vieio y Nvevo Testamento: Revista y conferida con los textos Hebreos y Griegos y con diversas translaciones* (Amsterdam: En casa de Lorenço Iacobi, 1602), iii. For the translation's history, see Luis Rivera-Pagán, "La Biblia Reina-Valera (1569–1602) y La Cultura Española," *Palabra Viva: Revista de La Sociedad Biblica* 27 (2009): 19–20.

4. See Sergio Fernández López, "Las llamadas Biblias del Exilio en España," *Bibliothèque d'Humanisme et Renaissance* 73, no. 2 (2011): 293–301.

5. The Houghton Library at Harvard owns a copy, but it was obtained sometime after the 1723 library shelf list was made. That catalog does include Pérez de Piñeda's

translation of Psalms. Joshua Gee, John Hancock, and James Diman, *Catalogus librorum Bibliothecae Collegij Harvardini: Quod est Cantabrigiae in Nova Anglia* (Boston: B. Green, 1723). Carlos Alberto González Sánchez, *New World Literacy: Writing and Culture across the Atlantic, 1500–1700,* trans. Tristán Platt (Lewisburg, PA: Bucknell University Press, 2011), 109.

6. Cotton Mather, *Biblia Americana. America's First Bible Commentary: A Synoptic Commentary on the Old and New Testaments,* vol. 4, *Ezra—Psalms,* ed. Reiner Smolinski (Tübingen: Mohr Siebeck, 2014), 439, 536, 621, 733.

7. See Christopher N. Phillips, "Cotton Mather Brings Isaac Watts's Hymns to America; or, How to Perform a Hymn without Singing It," *New England Quarterly* 85, no. 2 (2012): 203–221.

8. Reiner Smolinski, "Introduction," in Mather, *Biblia Americana. America's First Bible Commentary: A Synoptic Commentary on the Old and New Testaments,* vol. 1, *Genesis,* ed. Reiner Smolinski (Tübingen: Mohr Siebeck, 2010), 6. Vladimir Nabokov, "Problems in Translation: 'Onegin' in English." *Partisan Review* 22, no. 4 (1955): 512.

9. On *suerte* as the early modern Spanish term for a printer's sort, see Marina Garone Gravier, *Historia de la tipografía colonial para lenguas indígenas* (Mexico City: Centro de Investigaciones y Estudios Superiores en Antropología Social, Universidad Veracruzana, 2014), 119.

10. Matthew P. Brown, *The Pilgrim and the Bee: Reading Rituals and Book Culture in Early New England* (Philadelphia: University of Pennsylvania Press, 2007), 23. Brown emphasizes the relationship of the gift and market economies in devotional reading (25). Hugh Amory, "Printing and Bookselling in New England, 1638–1713," Hugh Amory and David D. Hall, eds., *A History of the Book in America,* vol. 1, *The Colonial Book in the Atlantic World* (Cambridge: Cambridge University Press, 2000), 95. In addition to this definitive volume, see also Hugh Amory, *Bibliography and the Book Trades: Studies in the Print Culture of Early New England,* (Philadelphia: University of Pennsylvania Press, 2005).

11. David D. Hall, Ways of Writing: The Practice and Politics of Text-Making in Seventeenth-Century New England (Philadelphia: University of Pennsylvania Press, 2008), 138–146.

12. See Brown, *Pilgrim and the Bee,* 196–197; Lawrence C. Wroth, *The Colonial Printer* (Portland, ME: Anthoensen, 1938); Isaiah Thomas and Benjamin Franklin Thomas, *The History of Printing in America, with a Biography of Printers, and an Account of Newspapers,* 2 v. (Albany, NY: Joel Munsell for the American Antiquarian Society, 1874).

13. For a precise accounting of the equipment available to Boston printers, see John Bidwell, "Printers' Supplies and Capitalization," Amory and Hall, *The Colonial Book in the Atlantic World,* 163–182. Amory refers to Timothy Green as "the youngest and laziest" of the family, but emphasizes his extraordinarily close ties to his patrons:

of his eighty-two known productions, sixty-three were written by the Mathers, including most of Cotton Mather's imprints from 1704, which Amory refers to as "virtually an in-house press for the Second Church" ("Printing and Bookselling in New England, 1638–1713," 96).

14. Separately cast accented vowels appear in Ezechiel Carré's *Echantillon* (Boston: B. Green & J. Allen, 1690), discussed in Chapter IX; these were probably hand-me-downs from the cases ordered for printing in Algonquian. It has also been suggested that the makeshift [ç] could have been a *zeta* from the Greek case set backwards. My thanks to Meredith Neuman for assistance with a technical examination of an original print.

15. See José Torre Revello, *El libro, la imprenta, y el periodismo en América durante la dominación española* (Buenos Aires: Talleres S. A. Casa Jacobo Peuser, 1940); Lawrence S. Thompson, *Printing in Colonial Spanish America.* (Hamden, CT: Archon, 1962). Early Mexican printers were often similarly pushed by circumstance toward improvisation, turning an illuminated upper-case M upside down for a W, or placing a Greek letter sideways; see Garone Gravier, *Historia de la tipografía colonial.*

16. When starting his own shop, Timothy could have acquired what remained of the types brought by Harris and then used by Pierce, who had closed his shop by 1691. It can be difficult to distinguish between early Boston imprints based on design, since the types available were all Dutch-made. Some distinctions between the upper-case italic Q, T, and Y can, however, be observed between the Pierce-Harris imprints of the early 1690s, and the Green family imprints.

17. Robert Bringhurst and Peter Rutledge Koch, "The California Tradition in Type Design." San Francisco: Book Club of California Keepsake (enclosure), 2015. I am grateful to José Guerrero for bringing this to my attention.

18. Hall, *Ways of Writing*, 139. Amory, "Reinventing the Colonial Book" in Amory and Hall, *The Colonial Book in America*, 51. *Paterna* 42, 47.

19. *Diary* 1:300.

20. On the distribution of the 1704 tract see Katherine Grandjean, *American Passage: The Communications Frontier in Early New England* (Cambridge, MA: Harvard University Press, 2015), 193–194. "Books of Piety": *Diary* 1:26. Michael Hoberman, *New Israel/New England: Jews and Puritans in Early America* (Amherst: University of Massachusetts Press, 2011), chap. 2 is devoted to the Frazons, but edits out the connection with the Spanish text.

21. Grandjean, *American Passage*, 172, on dating of reliable English post.

22. On the Dutch, *Diary* 1:402; on putting tracts aboard ships, *Diary* 2:14, also 2:555. On Mather's ministry to sailors, see Steven J. J. Pitt, "Cotton Mather and New England's 'Seafaring Tribe,'" *New England Quarterly* 85, no. 2 (2012): 222–252; to pirates, Jason M. Payton, "Piracy, Piety, and Providence in Cotton Mather's *The Vial*

Poured Out upon the Sea," in *American Literature and the New Puritan Studies,* ed. Bryce Traister (Cambridge: Cambridge University Press, 2017), 142–156.

23. Samuel Sewall, *Letter-Book: 1685–1712* (Boston: Massachusetts Historical Society, 1886), 1:297, 386. Someone sent him an "Old Testament in Spanish" by way of Governor Dudley in 1702: this must be another Ferrara Bible, because there was no separately published Protestant translation of the Old Testament alone.

24. Alicia Mayer, *Dos Americanos, Dos Pensamientos: Carlos de Sigüenza y Góngora y Cotton Mather* (Mexico City: Universidad Nacional Autónoma de México, 1998), 122–123. González Sánchez, *New World Literacy,* 232. *Diary* 1:299.

IX. Racial Fears on Eighteenth-Century Frontiers

1. Cotton Mather, *Theopolis Americana: An Essay on the Golden Street of the Holy City: Publishing, a Testimony against the Corruptions of the Market-Place. With Some Good Hopes of Better Things to Be yet Seen in the American World. In a Sermon, to the General Assembly of the Massachusett-Province in New-England. 3 d. 9 m. 1709* (Boston: Printed by B. Green; sold by Samuel Gerrish at his shop, 1710).

2. Howard C. Rice, "Cotton Mather Speaks to France: American Propaganda in the Age of Louis XIV," *New England Quarterly* 16, no. 2 (1943): 203. Detailed comparisons of French and English missionizing can be found in Sarah Rivett, *Unscripted America: Indigenous Languages and the Origins of a Literary Nation* (Oxford: Oxford University Press, 2017); Gordon M. Sayre, *Les Sauvages Américains: Representations of Native Americans in French and English Colonial Literature* (Chapel Hill: University of North Carolina Press, 2000); Catherine Ballériaux, "'Tis Nothing but French Poison, All of It': Jesuit and Calvinist Missions on the New World Frontier," in *Encounters between Jesuits and Protestants in Asia and the Americas,* ed. Jorge Cañizares-Esguerra, Robert Aleksander Maryks, and Ronnie Po-Chia Hsia (Leiden: Brill, 2018), 275–301.

3. In 1697, Mather wrote an English address glorifying the sufferings of the Huguenots and inserted a letter he composed in French to the local French church; no copies have survived. See Rice, "Cotton Mather Speaks to France," 212–214, on this text and its relation to Elias Neau.

4. *Diary* 1:302. Cotton Mather, *La Vrai Patron des Saines Paroles* (Boston: T. Green[?], 1704). The sole known copy is held at the Boston Public Library.

5. See Teresa A. Toulouse, *The Captive's Position: Female Narrative, Male Identity, and Royal Authority in Colonial New England* (Philadelphia: University of Pennsylvania Press, 2013); Laura M. Chmielewski, *The Spice of Popery: Converging Christianities on an Early American Frontier* (Notre Dame, IN: University of Notre Dame Press, 2012); Evan Haefeli and Kevin Sweeney, eds., *Captive Histories: English, French, and*

Native Narratives of the 1704 Deerfield Raid (Amherst: University of Massachusetts Press, 2006).

6. Cotton Mather, *The Man of God Furnished* (1708), which contained three catechisms, one specifically aimed at Canada.

7. Cotton Mather, *Another Tongue Brought in, to Confess the Great Savior of the World. Or, some communications of Christianity, put into a tongue used among the Iroquois Indians in America and put into the hands of the English and the Dutch traders* (Boston: Benjamin Green, 1707). Samuel Mather, *The Life of the Late Reverend and Learned Dr. Cotton Mather: Of Boston, (New England.)* . . . (Philadelphia, PA: American Sunday School Union, 1829), 41–42.

8. For a discussion of the /r/, see Steffi Dippold, "The Wampanoag Word: John Eliot's Indian Grammar, the Vernacular Rebellion, and the Elegancies of Native Speech," *Early American Literature* 48, no. 3 (2013): 543–575.

9. See Rivett, *Unscripted America*, 119–120, for *Another Tongue*. Cotton Mather, *The Triumphs of the Reformed Religion in America the Life of the Renowned John Eliot* (Boston: Benjamin Harris and John Allen, 1691), 127–129.

10. *A Monitory, and Hortatory Letter to those ENGLISH, Who Debauch the Indians, by Selling Drink Among Them* (Boston, 1700), 22.

11. *Epistle to the Christian Indians* (1700), 4.

12. See M. Bianet Castellanos, Lourdes Gutiérrez Nájera, and Arturo J. Aldama, eds., *Comparative Indigeneities of the Américas: Toward a Hemispheric Approach* (Tucson: University of Arizona Press, 2012); Shari M. Huhndorf, *Mapping the Americas: The Transnational Politics of Contemporary Native Culture* (Ithaca, NY: Cornell University Press, 2009); María Josefina Saldaña-Portillo, *Indian Given: Racial Geographies across Mexico and the United States* (Durham, NC: Duke University Press, 2016).

13. Jan Stievermann, "The Genealogy of Races and the Problem of Slavery in Cotton Mather's 'Biblia Americana,'" in *Cotton Mather and "Biblia Americana"—America's First Bible Commentary: Essays in Reappraisal*, ed. Rainer Smolinski and Jan Stievermann (Tübingen: Mohr Siebeck, 2010), 515–576, at 545. On his connections to German Pietists, see Oliver Scheiding, "The World as Parish: Cotton Mather, August Hermann Francke, and Transatlantic Religious Networks," in Smolinski and Stievermann, *Cotton Mather and Biblia Americana*, 131–166,

14. *Letters* 127.

15. See Phillip H. Round, *Removable Type: Histories of the Book in Indian Country, 1663–1880* (Chapel Hill: University of North Carolina Press, 2010), chap. 1; Kristina Bross, *Dry Bones and Indian Sermons: Praying Indians in Colonial America* (Ithaca, NY: Cornell University Press, 2004); Lisa Brooks, *Our Beloved Kin* (New Haven, CT: Yale University Press, 2018), chap. 4; Hilary E. Wyss, *English Letters and Indian Literacies: Reading, Writing, and New England Missionary Schools, 1750–1830* (Phila-

delphia: University of Pennsylvania Press, 2012); Hilary E. Wyss, *Writing Indians: Literacy, Christianity, and Native Community in Early America* (Amherst: University of Massachusetts Press, 2000).

16. See *Diary* 2:379, 478, 500, on the "Charity-Schole."

17. Gregory E. O'Malley, *Final Passages: The Intercolonial Slave Trade of British America, 1619–1807* (Chapel Hill: University of North Carolina Press for the Omohundro Institute of Early American History and Culture, Williamsburg, Virginia, 2014). 11; see also 7, 189.

18. Samuel Sewall, *The Diary of Samuel Sewall, 1674–1729,* ed. M. Halsey Thomas (New York: Farrar, Straus and Giroux, 1973), 2:613–614. There is an enormous bibliography on race in the early modern period: on *castas,* see Ilona Katzew, *Casta Painting: Images of Race in Eighteenth-Century Mexico* (New Haven, CT: Yale University Press, 2004). For Afro-Indian complexities, see Matthew Restall, ed., *Beyond Black and Red: African-Native Relations in Colonial Latin America* (Albuquerque: University of New Mexico Press, 2005). One debate centers on when race and slave status became more or less coterminous. For a convincing case that this happened around 1680, see Michael Guasco, *Slaves and Englishmen: Human Bondage in the Early Modern Atlantic World* (Philadelphia: University of Pennsylvania Press, 2014), 162.

19. Margaret Ellen Newell, *Brethren by Nature: New England Indians, Colonists, and the Origins of American Slavery* (Ithaca, NY: Cornell University Press, 2015); Brett Rushforth, *Bonds of Alliance: Indigenous and Atlantic Slaveries in New France* (Chapel Hill: University of North Carolina Press for the Omohundro Institute of Early American History and Culture, Williamsburg, Virginia, 2012).

20. Newspaper advertisements: Narragansett, July 22, 1706; *New England Courant,* June 17, 1723; Boston *Gazette,* August 1764; *Boston News-Letter,* August 18, 1712; July 31, 1730. On language skills in runaway ads, see Sharon Block, *Colonial Complexions: Race and Bodies in Eighteenth-Century America* (Philadelphia: University of Pennsylvania Press, 2018). 116–117. I am grateful to Professor Block for sharing further items from her database. See also "Rediscovering the Stories of Self-Liberating People," Freedom on the Move, https://freedomonthemove.org/.

21. Sewall, *Diary* 2:695, 2:822, 2:852.

22. *Records Relating to the Early History of Boston* (Boston: Registry Department, 1876–) vol. 8, *Selectmens' Minutes 1700–1728,* 88. *Diary* 2:549–550.

23. Diary 1:180, 2: 200. The broadside with Sewall's annotation about Spaniard, from the collection of the American Antiquarian Society, can be seen at https://www.loc.gov/resource/rbpe.03302600/?st=gallery. Although the source citation is to the 1693 broadside, this must be a reprint, since it makes reference to *The Negro Christianized,* which was not published until 1706.

24. See Dana D. Nelson, *The Word in Black and White: Reading "Race" in American Literature, 1638–1867* (New York: Oxford University Press, 1992), chap. 1, and Elizabeth

Ceppi, *Invisible Masters: Gender, Race, and the Economy of Service in Early New England* (Hanover, NH: Dartmouth College Press, 2018).

25. Cotton Mather, *The Negro Christianized: An Essay to Excite and Assist the Good Work, the Instruction of Negro-Servants in Christianity. [Four Lines of Scripture Texts]* (Boston: Printed by B. Green, 1706), 4, 7, 20. Stievermann, "Genealogy of Races and the Problem of Slavery.'"

26. Ibram X. Kendi, *Stamped from the Beginning: The Definitive History of Racist Ideas in America* (New York: Nation Books, 2016), 48. Stievermann, "Genealogy of Races and the Problem of Slavery," 518, 519.

27. *Diary* 1:554.

28. On Philemon see Stievermann, "Genealogy of Races and the Problem of Slavery," 560.

29. Kathryn Koo, "Strangers in the House of God: Cotton Mather, Onesimus, and an Experiment in Christian Slaveholding," *Proceedings of the American Antiquarian Society* 117 (2007): 143–176. Koo guesses that the child who heard Onesimus recite "might have been Sammy," though he was only six at the time (160).

30. Koo offers a transcription of the crossed-out parts of the manumission agreement but assumes that all the crossed-out lines were a result of *Mather's* "revising and rethinking the ties of kinship upon which Christianized slavery rested" ("Strangers in the House of God," 168). This assumption takes agency away from Onesimus and does not allow us to imagine that there was a dialogic negotiation by which Onesimus heard and / or read the first draft of the agreement, then himself insisted on the better final terms. See Cerise L. Glenn and Landra J. Cunningham, "The Power of Black Magic: The Magical Negro and White Salvation in Film," *Journal of Black Studies* 40, no. 2 (2009): 135–152.

31. Mather, *The Negro Christianized*, 4.

32. *Diary* 2:32–39; 1:412.

33. Stievermann, "Genealogy of Races and the Problem of Slavery," 566.

X. The Shipwreck of the Family Design

1. Kenneth Silverman, *The Life and Times of Cotton Mather* (New York: Harper and Row, 1984), 271–273. *Diary* 2:259.

2. Samuel Mather, *The Life of the Late Reverend and Learned Dr. Cotton Mather: Of Boston, (New England.)* . . . (Philadelphia, PA: American Sunday School Union, 1829), 140. See Elizabeth Bancroft Schlesinger, "Cotton Mather and His Children," *William and Mary Quarterly* 10, no. 2 (1953): 181–189.

3. Cotton Mather, *The Best Ornaments of Youth. A Short Essay, on the Good Things, Which Are Found in Some, and Should Be Found in All, Young People,* Early American Imprints, 1st series, no. 1308 (Boston: Timothy Green, 1707). "Little birds": *Diary* 1:303; reading aloud, *Diary* 2:41.

4. See Helen K. Gelinas, "Regaining Paradise: Cotton Mather's *Biblia Americana* and the Daughters of Eve," in *Cotton Mather and "Biblia Americana": America's First Bible Commentary—Essays in Reappraisal,* ed. Rainer Smolinski and Jan Stievermann (Tübingen: Mohr Siebeck, 2010), 463–494. Gelinas proposes that he read Fénélon's radical *Instructions on the Education of Daughters* in French, 467. Cotton Mather, *Victorina: A sermon preach'd, on the decease and at the desire, of Mrs. Katharin Mather, by her father. Whereunto there is added, a further account of that young gentlewoman, by another hand* (Boston: B. Green, 1717), 50.

5. *Diary* 2:462 on French.

6. Jennifer Jordan Baker, "'It Is Uncertain Where the Fates Will Carry Me': Cotton Mather's Theology of Finance," *Arizona Quarterly* 56, no. 4 (2000): 2. Compare the readings of *Theopolis* in Perry Miller, *The New England Mind: From Colony to Province* (Boston: Beacon, 1961) and Mark A. Peterson, *The City-State of Boston: The Rise and Fall of an Atlantic Power, 1630–1865* (Princeton, NJ: Princeton University Press, 2019). Quote on *Theopolis, Diary* 2:19.

7. *Diary* 2:239.

8. On the "disposal" of Creasy, see *Diary* 2:233, 2:239. *Letters* 178–179.

9. See *Letters* 184–185.

10. The love letter concludes: "As a token of my own disconsolate condition, while the best creature I ever saw is out of my sight, I scarce allow Cuthbert once with his razor to render my face visible, till you return." (*Letters* 184). None of Mather's letters to Abigail or Elizabeth, if he wrote any, have survived.

11. "Much polished," *Letters* 192. "More finished Gentleman," *Diary* 2:606. "Lucriferous," *Diary* 2:220. Samuel Mather, *Life of Cotton Mather,* 90.

12. Mather, *Victorina:* "Killing thing," i; Katy's poem, 50; tribute poem 82.

13. A sampling of "scholarly" moral judgments against Creasy by biographers and editors: "the unhappily named boy . . . confirmed in his evil ways," Robert Middlekauff, *The Mathers: Three Generations of Puritan Intellectuals, 1596–1728* (New York: Oxford University Press, 1971), "Mather's scapegrace son," Kenneth Silverman, commentary in his edition of *Letters* 200; "a sorrow to his father and a disgrace to the Mather name," Ronald Bosco, in his edition of *Paterna,* iv; "a scapegrace," Kenneth Ballard Murdock, in Cotton Mather, *Magnalia Christi Americana, Books I and II,* ed. Kenneth Ballard Murdock and Elizabeth W. Miller (Cambridge, MA: Belknap Press of Harvard University Press, 1977), 20.

14. See *Diary* 2:480–485; there seems to have been a three-day course of prayer "that he may not go on in a Course of Impiety" even before the tribunal (*Diary* 2:484). Quote in *Diary* 2:485.

15. On betrothal, see *Letters* 192. On daughters, see Silverman, *Life and Times,* 400–401.

16. On the Howell estate, see *Letters* 282–283. The widowed stepdaughter had remarried a nephew of Samuel Sewall, and then she and Sewall both died, leaving two

children that Mather had to support as well. *Diary* 2:589; on "having nothing," see *Diary* 2:734.

17. On Mather and Onesimus, see Cristobal Silva, *Miraculous Plagues: An Epidemiology of Early New England Narrative* (New York: Oxford University Press, 2011), chap. 4.

18. "Lieutenant," *Diary* 2:663–664. "Man of Sorrows," *Diary* 2:613.

19. "Night-Riot," *Diary* 2:600–601. Moneylending is Silverman's interpretation of the letter; see *Letters* 284. Quote from *Letters* 308–309. From my perusal of the manuscript at the AAS, I would transcribe the line Silverman gives as "in the same view" as "in your sound view."

20. Unpublished manuscript letter at AAS. The words of the second sentence are especially difficult to make out, but Heidi Morse helped me arrive at this transcription and translation: "Mi Fili, Semper mihi dilectus es, et (quod ipse magis forsan desideras) non munus mihi. Et aliquando necessarius; quod hodie atque hac hora experior. Ideoque, Nil mihi reserebas, alternando ipse veni. C.M." (My Son, To me you were always beloved, and (perhaps because you yourself desire more) not [merely] a duty to me. And at some time or another it is inevitable [to feel] that which I am experiencing today, and even at this hour. Therefore, nothing that you were sowing [perhaps in the sense of investing] for me should, in turn, be sold itself.)

21. Check manuscript at Massachusetts Historical Society. Debt manuscript in AAS Mather papers. On Boston's "concentrated capital in shipping" at this time and a description of these practices in traders' offices, see John J. McCusker and Russell R. Menard, *The Economy of British America, 1607–1789* (Chapel Hill: University of North Carolina Press, 2014), 98.

22. L. Vernon Briggs, *History of Shipbuilding on North River, Plymouth County, Massachusetts,* by (Boston: Coburn Bros., 1889), 284–285, provides a partial sense of Frizzel's maritime holdings. Israel Hobart built the "brig't'on" [brigantine?] *Speedwell* for Frizzel in 1699 and the ship *Prudence & Dorothy* (co-owned by Frizzel with "John Phillips and John Trent of Barbadoes"); in 1700 he built the brig't'on *Dorothy* (co-owned by Frizzel and two other Bostonians). Samuel Sewall's diary reports that the Selectmen held "another Council about giving Liberty to Mr. Frizzel's Ship, from Salt-Tartuda [*Tortuga*] to come up." This would have been just before the smallpox outbreak. Samuel Sewall, *The Diary of Samuel Sewall, 1674–1729,* ed. M. Halsey Thomas (New York: Farrar, Straus and Giroux, 1973), 2:979. For mentions of Frazon in the 1700s, see *Diary* 2:62, 2:233, 2:500. Letter in manuscript at AAS.

23. O'Malley argues that English ships did in fact have some trade on these (purportedly off-limits) islands, including human cargo slipped into spare spaces in the hold. Gregory E. O'Malley, *Final Passages: The Intercolonial Slave Trade of British America, 1619–1807* (Chapel Hill: University of North Carolina Press for the Omohundro Institute of Early American History and Culture, Williamsburg, Virginia, 2014), 230.

24. *Diary* 2:720–25. Cotton Mather, *The Words of Understanding. Three Essays; I. The Philomela. With, The Notes of Morning-Piety.: II. The Ephemeron. Or, Tears Drop'd on Dust and Ashes.: III. Jonah: Or, The Dove in Safety.: Occasioned by Some Early Deaths Which Require Such Notice to Be Taken of Them.: [Three Lines of Quotation]*, Early American Imprints, 1st series, no. 2562 (Boston: S. Kneeland, for J. Edwards, 1724). Cotton Mather, *Tela Praevisa. A Short Essay, on Troubles to Be Look'd for. A Wise Expectation of, and Preparation for, Troublesome Changes, Recommended unto the Strangers and Pilgrims in This Present Evil World by Cotton Mather D.D. and F.R.S. [One Line from Matthew]* (Boston: B. Green, for Thomas Hancock, 1724). At least he said this publicly; privately, in the diary, he veered between near-wordless grief and a cool resignation, when he published one sermon, so that "he might do some good since he did none in life."

25. "Man of Sorrows," *Letters* 152, *Diary* 2:703. *Paterna* 158.

26. Samuel Mather, *Life of Cotton Mather*, 152.

27. Barrett Wendell, *Cotton Mather: The Puritan Priest* (New York: Harcourt, Brace and World, 1963); Perry Miller, *Errand into the Wilderness* (Cambridge, MA: Belknap Press of Harvard University Press, 1956).

28. It is also possible that the copy belonged to Crocker's mother, Hannah Huntington.

29. See Alea Henle, "The Widow's Mite: Hannah Mather Crocker and the Mather Libraries," *Information and Culture* 48, no. 3 (2013): 323–343; Hannah Mather Crocker, *Observations on the Real Rights of Women and Other Writings*, ed. Constance Post (Lincoln: University of Nebraska Press, 2011). On filiopietism and the nineteenth-century uses of Mather's *Magnalia* in particular, see Lindsay DiCuirci, *Colonial Revivals: The Nineteenth-Century Lives of Early American Books* (Philadelphia: University of Pennsylvania Press, 2018).

XI. Coda

1. On racial reckoning see, e.g., the *New York Times*'s "1619 Project," headed by Nikole Hannah-Jones, and the scores of rebuttals it has produced, as well as Ta-Nehisi Coates, "The Case for Reparations," *The Atlantic*, June 2014. A summary of recent Native scholarship that highlights reparations demands can be found in Roxanne Dunbar-Ortiz, *An Indigenous Peoples' History of the United States* (Boston: Beacon, 2014). Cognizant of the warning in the title of Eve Tuck and K. Wayne Yang, "Decolonization Is Not a Metaphor," *Decolonization: Indigeneity, Education, and Society* 1, no. 1 (2012): 1–40, I have avoided making a claim to be enacting decolonization in this writing.

2. See G. Cristina Mora, *Making Hispanics: How Activists, Bureaucrats, and Media Constructed a New American* (Chicago: University of Chicago Press, 2014). For many,

there is a crucial distinction between "Hispanic," which includes US residents originally from Spain itself but would culturally exclude Portuguese colonies such as Brazil, and "Latino," which as a demonym for Latin America would include Brazil as well as at least part of the Caribbean, although defining the Latin Caribbean is no simple task either. In practice, this careful distinction between Hispanic and Latino may be observed by individuals but rarely by US culture at large. For an argument that "Latinx" belongs to the LGBTQ+ individuals who coined it and that it loses critical power when used generically as a substitute group noun for all Latinos, see Richard T. Rodriguez, "X Marks the Spot," *Cultural Dynamics* 29, no. 3 (2017): 202–213. Claudia Milian, *LatinX* (Minneapolis: University of Minnesota Press, 2019), 1–7.

3. US census takers began to experiment in 1910 with ways of noting home languages of residents and classifying them ethnically according to that language. The census shifted to ethnonational categories rather than language-specific ones in 1930, marking "Mexican" for the only official time as a "race" option. See Jennifer Leeman, "Categorizing Latinos in the History of the US Census: The Official Racialization of Spanish," in *A Political History of Spanish: The Making of a Language,* ed. José del Valle (Cambridge: Cambridge University Press, 2013), 305–324. Carey McWilliams, *North from Mexico: The Spanish-Speaking People of the Southwest,* reprint ed. (New York: Monthly Review, 1961), 7.

4. Michael Omi and Howard Winant, "Introduction," in *Racial Formation in the United States,* 3rd ed. (New York: Routledge, 2014), 1–18. Catherine S. Ramírez, *Assimilation: An Alternative History* (Berkeley: University of California Press, 2020), 9. Natalia Molina blends the paradigm of "racial projects" with that of "racial scripts" in *How Race Is Made in America* (Berkeley: University of California Press, 2015). In her analysis of twentieth-century court cases, Molina shows how, in the 1930s, resident Mexicans were classified as "other" in order to deprive them of rights assigned to whites. Paradoxically, by appealing to the blood-quantum logic through which the federal government treated Native nations, some Mexicans improved their legal standing by identifying with Indigenous descent.

5. See in general Rosina Lozano, *An American Language: The History of Spanish in the United States* (Berkeley: University of California Press, 2018). On *Westminster,* see Molina, *How Race is Made in America,* chap. 2.

6. Ofelia García, "Racializing the Language Practices of US Latinos," in *How the United States Racializes Latinos: White Hegemony and Its Consequences,* ed. José A. Cobas, Jorge Duany, and Joe R. Feagin (Boulder, CO: Paradigm, 2009), 101–115. Jonathan Rosa, *Looking Like a Language, Sounding Like a Race* (Stanford, CA: Stanford University Press, 2018), 5, coins the term "raciolinguistic." The precise enumeration of Spanish speakers in the United States is a matter of some dispute due to the range of possible proficiencies that the term encapsulates. Data from the US Census Bureau yields lower numbers than surveys and studies performed by the Instituto Cervantes,

the Academia Norteamericana de la Lengua Española, and other globally oriented institutions. For an overview of these issues, see Humberto López Morales, *Enciclopedia del Español en los Estados Unidos* (Madrid: Instituto Cervantes, Editorial Santillana, 2009).

7. On the links between nineteenth-century racialization and imperial projects in the hemisphere, see Reginald Horsman, *Race and Manifest Destiny: The Origins of American Racial Anglo-Saxonism* (Cambridge, MA: Harvard University Press, 1986); María DeGuzmán, *Spain's Long Shadow: The Black Legend, Off-Whiteness, and Anglo-American Empire* (Minneapolis: University of Minnesota Press, 2005); Laura E. Gómez, *Manifest Destinies: The Making of the Mexican American Race* (New York: New York University Press, 2008).

8. On the culture-making aspects of the Chicana/o movement(s), see Maylei Blackwell, *¡Chicana Power! Contested Histories of Feminism in the Chicano Movement* (Austin: University of Texas Press, 2011); Randy J. Ontiveros, *In the Spirit of a New People: The Cultural Poilitics of the Chicano Movement* (New York: New York University Press, 2013). On Mexico's current racial reckoning, see Federico Navarrete, *México racista: Una denuncia* (Mexico City: Grijalbo, 2016).

9. See Edward Telles, *Pigmentocracies: Ethnicity, Race, and Color in Latin America* (Chapel Hill: University of North Carolina Press, 2014). On *blanqueamiento* in the major Latino-producing Caribbean countries, see Jorge Duany, *The Puerto Rican Nation on the Move: Identities on the Island and in the United States* (Chapel Hill: University of North Carolina Press, 2000), Ginetta E. B. Candelario, *Black Behind the Ears: Dominican Racial Identity from Museums to Beauty Shops* (Durham, NC: Duke University Press, 2007); Pedro Pérez Sarduy and Jean Stubbs, *Afro-Cuban Voices: On Race and Identity in Contemporary Cuba* (Gainesville: University Press of Florida, 2000). On the ways that Mexicans commonly refuse to identify with the Black/white/Native census categories for race, among other measures of their racial identification, see Julie A. Dowling, *Mexican Americans and the Question of Race* (Austin: University of Texas Press, 2014). Laura E. Gómez, *Inventing Latinos: A New Story of American Racism* (New York: New Press, 2020), documents by subgroup which US Latinos tend to choose "other" in the race category when forced to do so and which choose "white."

10. Rosa, *Looking Like a Language*, 2. For a critique of Chicana/o paradigms of the "new mestiza," see María Eugenia Cotera and María Josefina Saldaña-Portillo, "Indigenous but Not Indian? Chicana/os and the Politics of Indigeneity," in *The World of Indigenous North American*, ed. Robert Warrior (New York: Routledge, 2014), 549–568. See the foundational collection, Miriam Jiménez Román and Juan Flores, eds., *The Afro-Latin@ Reader: History and Culture in the United States* (Durham, NC: Duke University Press, 2010), and Maylei Blackwell, Floridalma Boj Lopez, Luis Urrieta Jr., eds., "Critical Latinx Indigeneities," special issue, *Latino Studies* 15, no. 2 (2017), as well as María Josefina Saldaña-Portillo, *Indian Given: Racial Geographies across*

Mexico and the United States (Durham, NC: Duke University Press, 2017). On the making of "Brown" as a pan-Latino identity, see José Esteban Muñoz, *The Sense of Brown,* ed. Joshua Chambers-Letson and Tavia Nyong'o (Durham, NC: Duke University Press, 2020), Lázaro Lima, *Being Brown: Sonia Sotomayor and the Latino Question* (Oakland: University of California Press, 2018). Milian, *LatinX,* 6.

11. "El desdén": José Martí, *Nuestra América,* ed. Juan Marinello, Hugo Achúgar, Cintio Vitier, Antonio Bastardo Casañas (Caracas: Biblioteca Ayacucho, 2005), 38. On the nineteenth-century invention, see Walter D. Mignolo, *The Idea of Latin America* (Malden, MA: Wiley-Blackwell, 2005). Carlos Fuentes, *The Buried Mirror: Reflections on Spain and the New World* (Boston: Mariner, 1999); Claudio Véliz, *The New World of the Gothic Fox: Culture and Economy in English and Spanish America* (Berkeley: University of California Press, 1994); Richard M. Morse, *New World Soundings: Culture and Ideology in the Americas* (Baltimore, MD: Johns Hopkins University Press, 1989); Patricia Seed, *American Pentimento: The Invention of Indians and the Pursuit of Riches* (Minneapolis: University of Minnesota Press, 2001); Samuel P. Huntington, *Who Are We? The Challenges to America's National Identity* (New York: Simon and Shuster, 2005); Victor Davis Hanson, *MexiFornia: A State of Becoming,* 2nd ed. (New York: Encounter, 2007).

12. Sylvia Wynter, "1492: A New World View," in *Race, Discourse, and the Origin of the Americas,* ed. Vera Lawrence Hyatt and Rex Nettleford (Washington, DC: Smithsonian Institution Press, 1995), 5–57. For an integration of Asian labor and trade patterns into the colonial Americas, see Lisa Lowe, *The Intimacies of Four Continents* (Durham, NC: Duke University Press, 2015).

13. Tony Tian-Ren Lin, *Prosperity Gospel Latinos and Their American Dream* (Chapel Hill: University of North Carolina Press, 2020). Pew Research Center, "The Shifting Religious Identity of Latinos in the United States," May 7, 2014, https://www.pewforum.org/2014/05/07/the-shifting-religious-identity-of-latinos-in -the-united-states/.

14. Peggy McGlone, "Congress Authorizes Smithsonian Museums Focused on American Latinos and Women's History," *Washington Post,* December 22, 2020. On the delicate balance of tribal identities and pan-ethnicities in the making of the National Museum of the American Indian, see Amy Lonetree, *Decolonizing Museums: Representing Native America in National and Tribal Museum* (Chapel Hill: University of North Carolina Press, 2012).

15. See https://scsenderos.org, and, for the University of California, Santa Cruz partnership, "Nido de Lenguas," https://wlma.ucsc.edu/nidodelenguas/.

16. Not all of these undocumented and deported migrants are from Latin America, but a substantial majority—approximately 85 percent—are. See Alicia Schmidt Camacho, "Hailing the Twelve Million: U.S. Immigration Policy, Deportation, and the Imaginary of Lawful Violence," *Social Text* 28, no. 4 (2010): 1–24, and *Migrant*

Imaginaries: Latino Cultural Politics in the U.S.-Mexico Borderlands (New York: New York University Press, 2008); Nicholas De Genova and Nathalie Peutz, eds., *The Deportation Regime: Sovereignty, Space, and the Freedom of Movement* (Durham, NC: Duke University Press, 2010); Lisa Marie Cacho, *Social Death: Racialized Rightlessness and the Criminalization of the Unprotected* (New York: New York University Press, 2012); Angela Naimou, *Salvage Work: U.S. and Caribbean Literatures and the Debris of Legal Personhood* (New York: Fordham University Press, 2015); Laura Briggs, *Taking Children: A History of American Terror* (Oakland: University of California Press, 2020).

17. For statistics on legal migration quotas, see Elliott Young, *Forever Prisoners: How the United States Made the World's Largest Immigrant Detention System* (New York: Oxford University Press, 2021). Joseph Nevins, "Migration as Reparations," NACLA, 24 May, 2016, https://nacla.org/blog/2016/05/24/migration-reparations, directed at El Salvador and its people in particular, was widely circulated on the Internet.

XII. Transcription and Translation of Cotton Mather's *La Fe del Christiano* (1699)

1. Thomas Johnston, "A Translation of Cotton Mather's Spanish Works: La Fe del Christiano and La Religion Pura," *Early American Literature Newsletter* 2, no. 2 (1967): 7–21. A good introduction to Western translation theory, including chapters dedicated to the Babel story and to each of the translation theorists mentioned here, is Daniel Weissbort and Ástráður Eysteinsson, *Translation: Theory and Practice: A Historical Reader* (Oxford: Oxford University Press, 2006).

2. See Lawrence Venuti, *The Translator's Invisibility: A History of Translation,* 2nd ed. (New York: Routledge, 2007).

3. Because the Reina-Valera Antigua (RVA) in common circulation is based on Valera's 1625 corrected version rather than the 1602, readers should be aware that the citations given here may not match other editions calling themselves Reina-Valera, even those that are designated Reina-Valera Antigua.

4. See Chapter VIII for a discussion of the title. The two subordinate clauses that follow "Españoles" refer to but do not cite Acts 26:18, where the Lord tells Paul that he is sending him out to his own people, "so that *you* [Paul] may open their eyes." Mather uses the same words as the RVA but changes the address to Spanish people in the plural, correctly changing the pronoun from *tus* to *sus.*

5. See Chapters III and IV on the Acosta epigraph: "For the Church cannot modify or take away what is a divine right."

6. Compare the Geneva translation of this sentence: "Who hath predestinated us, to be adopted through Jesus Christ in himself, according to the good pleasure of his will." The RVA translation is: "Habiéndonos predestinado para ser adoptados hijos por

Jesucristo á sí mismo, según el puro afecto de su voluntad." Since the term *predestinado* was available in the RVA, it is interesting that Mather simplified it, perhaps thinking it too technical for a reader without a nearby Protestant to explain this non-Catholic concept. He writes instead (in modern standard Spanish), "señaló algunos antes," or "pointed out some people before." He also substitutes "querer" for RVA's "afecto," to indicate pleasure.

7. The Spanish here copies exactly the RVA, except for the lack of a space between "he" and "aqui." The Spanish really did read "era bueno en gran manera," a phrase that sounds odd to a contemporary reader.

8. The RVA reads "y sustentando todas las cosas con la palabra de su potencia": here Mather correctly changed the verb form from the participle *sustentando* to the present indicative *sustienta*, an indicator of his grammatical understanding. The verse referenced represents only a few clauses of a longer utterance, so this is a major abridgement. Compare Geneva: "by his mighty word."

9. The first sentence corresponds to the first verse cited, but Mather changes an interrogative ("Are they not all ministering spirits . . . ?") into an indicative. The verse from Hebrews does not name the "spirits" as "angels": it is Mather who links them to the mysticism of Jude, adding the copula "y." He changes the RVA description of the angels slightly: "espiritus administradores enviados por servicio a favor de los que . . ." By preferring "servidores" to "administradores," perhaps he means to avoid a hierarchical notion of angels. The phrase "en servicio" seems to imagine them as agents who are actively serving fallen mankind (see Chapter II for angelic visions). He tinkered with the RVA's "a favor de los que" to "por causa de," perhaps to save space. He also tinkered with the Jude verse, adding "Dios" after "los" in order to clarify who was sequestering the fallen angels in hell. The "e" that begins "oscuridad" is an error.

10. The odd phrase "En aquel en quien" (literally "in that / he who in who") is not in RVA, which uses "pues que" ("since / thus / therefore"). Mather alters the RVA to stress that Adam's fall made all men sinners. Compare Geneva: "Wherefore, as by one man sin entered into the world, and death by sin, and so death went over all men: in whom all men have sinned." These two redundant phrases might represent two different tries at expressing the idea and are redundant: either "en aquel" or "en quien" could have been crossed out in the manuscript but not corrected before final printing.

11. The only change from RVA, aside from omitting the unnecessary first word for space, is that he uses *aya* (haya), the subjunctive form of *haber,* instead of *ha dado:* it is subjunctive in the Latin Vulgate, so he seems to be disagreeing with or correcting the RVA's indicative mood here. He also substitutes "aya" for the RVA "tenga."

12. The RVA verse says "de los padres" (of the fathers): Mather adds "De los Israelitas" to clarify the Jewish genealogy of Christ. This is surely related to his use of *La Fe del Christiano* to try to convert the Jewish Frazon brothers (see Chapters III

and IX). Grammatically, he again shows enough understanding of Spanish to interpolate for clarity, as he did in the verse from Revelation on the title-page verso (see Chapter III).

13. The source should read verses 7–9. Mather changed one verb in the RVA here: "agotase" instead of "se anonadó" to convey self-humbling or self-sacrifice. He also substituted "le dió" for "dióle," as if knowing it was an archaism. His textbook must have insisted that the indirect object could not be appended to an indicative verb (it still can, however, go at the end of an imperative).

14. I comment on the nonidiomatic word order of "Venida Segunda" in Chapter VII. Mather tinkered slightly with the RVA here, adding "God" at the start of the verse to clarify the subject and changing "al mundo" to "a todo el mundo" (perhaps making it more inclusive), muddying the RV's clearer "con haberle levantado" to the participle "levantandolo." Usually, his reference glosses use the Spanish abbreviation for books of the Bible ("Ioan") rather than the English ("John"). Today's Bibles call this book "Hechos de los Apóstoles," because the term *acto* has taken on a more exclusively theatrical significance, but in the seventeenth century it retained the sense of "deeds" or "works," and is translated "Actos" in RVA.

15. Mather makes two telling changes here. The RVA contrasts "los que hizieron bien" and "los que hizieron mal," and Mather changes them to "bienes" and "males": he seems to mistake the adverbs *bien* and *mal* for adjectives that should agree with their plural pronoun (*los*). Did he not recognize that *bueno y malo* are the adjectival forms? This could have been confusing to a native speaker, since *bien* can also be a noun; in particular, *bienes* means "goods." He makes another significant change: instead of "condenación," he writes "Juyzio," even though the cognate with the Geneva's "resurrection of condemnation" is right there in the RVA. Perhaps there was a philological reason for this, or perhaps it is a space-saver. There is also a clarifying insertion of "Boz [voz] de Jesu Christo" for the simpler "su voz" in RVA.

16. In this verse, one of the fundamental planks of Protestant theology, Mather changes the second-person address ("through grace you are saved") to a first-person plural address: "through grace *we* are saved." This "we" seems to be an adaptation to his audience, rather than a scholarly correction. It is as if he wanted to include himself and all his listeners as part of the same polity. Unaccountably, he also changes the word order from RVA's "pues es Don de Dios" to "que Don de Dios es." This could be a simple transcription error, but perhaps he liked the poetic effect.

17. Mather follows the cognates in the RVA's uses of both "remissión" and "justificación," where Geneva uses "forgiveness" instead of "remission," and "justification." As with his avoidance of "predestination," he may have realized that the finer points of distinction between these theological concepts were not vital to the message.

18. In all versions, the final clause indicates plural "things": "these things are good and useful." Mather uses the RVA's vocabulary, but changes "estas cosas son buenas"

to "esto es lo bueno," correctly using the abstract pronominal noun. This too seems like an economizing decision to save space.

19. As in Article XV, Mather changes "vosotros" to the more intimate "us." The minor mistake of "qui" for "que" may be a typo.

20. Mather does a little trimming of the language of the Second, Fourth, Fifth, and Tenth Commandments. In number 4, a space has been omitted between "Acordarte has," and Mather has changed the RVA's "reposo" (rest) to "Sabbado." This too might be a nod to his hoped-for Sephardic convert.

21. This rendition of the Lord's Prayer in Spanish solidifies the hypothesis about which edition Mather consulted. Mather's version includes two deviations from the best-known (1625) version known as the Reina-Valera Antigua: "sea sanctificado" instead of "sanctificado sea," and "suéltanos" instead of "perdónanos." Valera used the latter two in his 1596 New Testament, changed them to the former versions in the 1602 complete Bible, and then changed them *back* to ("santificado sea" and "perdónanos," which became ritualized for Spanish Protestant readers, in subsequent printings (1625 and after).

22. The convoluted syntax comes from Mather trying to compress three verses (1 Timothy 3:8, 9, 13, not all acknowledged in his gloss) into one. The RVA reads: "Los diáconos asimismo, deben ser honestos, no bilingües, no dados á mucho vino, no amadores de torpes ganancias, Que tengan el misterio de la fe con limpia conciencia. . . . Porque los que bien ministrasen, ganan para sí buen grado, y mucha confianza en la fe que es en Cristo Jesús." There is an agreement problem in Mather's Spanish: "ministrase" should be the plural "ministrasen" to go with the plural subject "diaconos." "Ganon" in the original should be "ganan"; "Gradu" should be "Grado." (RVA: "los que ministaren, ganan para si buen grado.") It is difficult to know whether these erroneous vowels were in Mather's original or whether they are errors that entered in the typesetting process and were not corrected in proof. A shortage of type is not out of the question, either.

23. As with the Lord's Prayer, the apparent differences from today's RVA are in the Valera 1602: "enseñad" instead of "Id y doctrinad"; "gentes" (peoples) for "Gentiles" (Gentiles). Valera also used "el vaso" rather than "la copa." The phrase "dióles diziendo" is also exclusively in Valera 1602. Mather, however, does abridge the RVA's long phrase, "Porque todas las veces que comiereis este pan y bebereis esta copa," into a simpler one: "Si ansi lo haziendo." In the RVA it is a collective "you" who does the proclaiming ("anunciáis"), which Mather changes to "we" ("anunciamos").

24. The most suggestive deviation from the RVA in this section is Mather's substitution of "Congregacion" for the RVA's "Iglesia." Moving away from the Church of England's administrative hierarchy was important for New England Congregationalists. Mather also leaves off the final line of Matthew 18:17, "let him be considered a heathen and a publican," even though there was plenty of room to add the RVA's "publicano."

A publican was a tax collector, often despised in the Roman Empire, though the sympathetic subject of a parable in the gospel of Luke. Perhaps he did not think it wise to confuse a reader with uncommon terms that required the layman to know something about the social structure of the Roman Empire—to know what a "publican/o" was. "Ethnico" was the RVA's choice for a term now translated as "gentile": an outsider, an outcast.

25. In this second tract within the book (the first that Mather composed), everything in roman type represents something composed in Spanish by Mather himself, while the sentences in italics are copied from the Reina-Valera translation, often with abridgments to make them more concise.

26. This is one enye that Mather or the printer misses, and the word is inverted: it should be "escudriñad." The verse is significantly abridged.

27. Mather's choice of "el padecer," suffering, for the Latin *patientam* is one of the most puzzling moves in this document (if it was not simply a transcription error). It was usually translated as "patience" or "endurance," and it is "la paciencia" in the RVA. If this was a deliberate choice on his part and not a hasty transcription error, the effect is to say that Christians must suffer for their faith. This certainly would have been the case for Protestants in Spanish America.

28. "Bastantamente": I have not found instances of this word in the RVA or in historical dictionaries. It may be an invention of Mather's.

29. Mather leaves out the "and" and moves the verb "is," hence my inverted translation.

30. RVA has "Sometió" for "sujetando le" and "diólo" for Mather's "poniendo le." In both cases he seems to want to make the verb reflexive, something Christ is doing to himself, but Mather uses an indirect pronoun instead.

31. Mather changes the RVA's "o que se adora" for the shorter "divinity," makes several condensations for space and improvises the upper-case emphasis for "CLARIDAD" and "DESTRUIRA." On the printer's use of Greek letters, see Chapter VIII.

32. Mather omits Christ's words to Satan, and misses an important article before "heart."

33. Despite "perdonar" being available in the Lord's Prayer, Mather uses cognates for justification/justice for both forgiveness and righteousness. Given that this was also a secular word, this choice may have been at cross-purposes with his seeming intention elsewhere to use simple language. In this phrase of Mather's own composition, "algunas Criaturas" is open to interpretation: it could signify creaturely beings or created things. Given the anti-Catholic context here, he could be thinking of indulgences or relics.

34. The phrase "sobre todos" is not in RVA. Mather changes RVA's "gratuitamente," freely, for "graciosamente," and "en propiciación" for "por aplacacion."

35. Mather changes the RVA's "copa" to "vaso" for unknown reasons. Both "comieres" and "bebiereis" have an extra "d" inserted, perhaps by the compositor. I approximate the unfortunate typo.

36. On Mather's use of the unusual term "Legos," see Chapter VI.

37. Supporting the concept of language rights, Mather abridges these verses heavily. He changes RVA's "un mero particular" to "Idiota." On Psalm singing, see Chapter VI. Mather changes "Cantad con inteligencia" to "cantad entendiendo."

38. For this argument against priestly celibacy and against the Catholic practice of abstaining from meat or from food altogether on designated holy days, Mather makes several changes to the RVA to make his points clearer. The original verse reads "prohibirán casarse," prohibiting marriage for ministers of the gospel altogether; Mather reframes this as a reservation. He also removes the verb "abstenerse" in discussing foods.

39. The RVA has "alzó sus ojos," raised his eyes; Mather probably intends "alzando," but without the cedilla, the word looks wrong.

40. Mather has "desetado" for RVA's "desatado."

Acknowledgments

The seed for this book was planted as I was sorting through early Spanish imprints at the Huntington Library in 2005–2006, supported by a Frederick Burkhardt Fellowship from the American Council of Learned Societies. I began writing it in earnest in 2015–2016, with the support of a Faculty Fellowship from the National Endowment for the Humanities. (Any views, findings, conclusions, or recommendations expressed in this publication do not necessarily reflect those of either organization.) If this seems like an unconscionably long time between an initial thought and its completion, it is because I originally intended the story of Cotton Mather and *La Fe del Christiano* to serve as a mere preface to what would have been a very different book about the history of language ideologies surrounding Spanish in the United States. The questions the story raised about "Spanish Indians" sent me back to refresh a neglected interest in the colonial period that I thought I had left behind in graduate school. As with Cotton Mather's own compositional practice, what I then decided to hive off as a "Small Book" kept growing in size as new ideas expanded the bellows and fanned the flame. Sometimes you write the book, sometimes the book writes you: at one point in the process I rented a house on Hanover Street in Santa Cruz, and only later realized that this was the name of the Boston street where Mather lived for most of his life. Also like Mather, I could not have done this in the absence of informants, supporters, and privileges that should not go unspoken. To begin with, the spaces where I lived and worked while writing this book are the traditional and unceded lands of the Awaswas-speaking Uypi tribe and other Ohlone peoples. Walking by the shore and in the forests here, tended and preserved by them and by some who came after, was always an accessory to my thinking.

For their warm welcome and for granting me access to original printed texts and the fragile manuscripts in Mather's own hand, including gems such as the unpublished *Quotidiana* notebooks, draft letters, and Onesimus's manumission document, I am deeply grateful to the librarians and archivists at the American Antiquarian Society, especially Elizabeth Pope. Likewise, I am indebted to the Houghton Library at Harvard University, not only for enabling my access to some of the rare editions Mather and Sewall perused, but for granting permission to share the beautiful images that appear in this book. The McGregor Library in Special Collections at the University of Virginia allowed me to examine the *Paterna* manuscript, and David Levin's typescript notes on it, in detail. In addition to the boon of their extensive digital collection, the Massachusetts Historical Society kindly helped with access to some nondigitized materials, even during a pandemic-restricted research period.

Audience members at the Dartmouth Futures of American Studies Institute, the University of Colorado, Emory University, the Center for Cultural Studies at the University of California Santa Cruz, the University of California Berkeley, the TransAmerican Studies Working Group at Stanford University, the University of Illinois at Urbana-Champaign, the McNeil Center for Early American Studies at the University of Pennsylvania, Rice University, and Pomona College made valuable comments on early versions of this material before it became a separate book. I am grateful to those gracious hosts, as well as to interlocutors at later stages, where I presented more polished work at the University of Notre Dame, Duke, Princeton, and Yale Universities. More than anything, I learned from listening to wonderful presentations at meetings sponsored by the Society of Early Americanists and the Onohumdro Institute of Early American History & Culture, especially the joint meetings with colonial Latin Americanists. My research and teaching are spread beyond this period, however, and I also gleaned invaluable ideas from conferences of the Latina/o Studies Association, the American Studies Association, C19: The Society of Nineteenth-Century Americanists, the Recovering the U.S. Hispanic Heritage Project, and the English Institute. Workshops and symposia sponsored by the American Antiquarian Society happily kept bringing me back under the dome, and I am grateful to Molly Hardy, Jim Moran, and Ashley Cataldo for organizing them.

It is a challenge to sort the people who have inspired and helped me with this project according to those collaborative communities of thought because so many of them overlap. My most profound debts accrue to the brilliant people with whom I have been exchanging thoughts about hemispheric and trans-american studies for decades and who have become dear and supportive friends. Rodrigo Lazo, Sara E. Johnson, and Jesse Alemán critiqued drafts of every chapter during our multi-year peripatetic writing workshop: they have each read enough about Mather for a lifetime. Sara's unmatched powers of perception and Jesse's fierce and penetrating humor kept me mindful, committed, and on task. Anna Brickhouse has been a treasured collaborator on many projects; her generosity as a reader is rightfully legendary. José Aranda, Laz Lima, Claudia Milian, and Ricky Rodriguez extended their intellectual and personal hospitality many times over the years as I worked around, and eventually through, this project. I am most grateful for repeated conversations and exchanges of material with Pedro Caro, Raúl Coronado, John Alba Cutler, Emily García, John Moran González, Carmen Lamas, Laura Lomas, Marissa López, Manuel Martín-Rodríguez, Yolanda Padilla, Alberto Varón, and other inspiring scholars I have met through the Recovery Project. In the broader LatinX orbit, I have enjoyed the fellowship and support of Mary Pat Brady, Debra Castillo, Gloria Chacón, Robert McKee Irwin, Curtis Márez, Desirée Martin, Paula Moya, Ramón Saldívar, Maritza Stanchich, Jennifer Harford Vargas, Maria Windell, and Karina Zelaya. Ralph Bauer, Jonathan Beecher Field, and Meredith Neuman were especially helpful in orienting me to the state of the field in early American studies; I also learned much from conversations with Allison Bigelow, Michelle Burnham, Patrick Erben, Sandra Gustafson, Len van Morze, Sarah Rivett, Ana Schwartz, Jonathan Senchyne, Cristobal Silva, and Theresa Toulouse. I am especially grateful to John Garcia, Heather Kopelson, and the incomparable Jordan Alexander Stein for sharing with me items they found in the course of their own research. Tilting toward those who specialize in later (pan-)American cultures, I am indebted to the late Lauren Berlant, Sara Blair, Deborah Cohn, Paul Erickson, Jonathan Freedman, Robert Gunn, Martin Harries, Peter Hulme, Gordon Hutner, Jeff Insko, Jennie Jackson, Dana Luciano, Gesa Mackenthun, Sarah Mesle, Meredith McGill, Lloyd Pratt, Sarah Salter, Shirley Samuels, Elisa Tamarkin, and Kyla Wazana Tompkins for sharing invitations, insights, and their own brilliant work over the years. As I was putting final touches on this book, I also enjoyed the virtual fellowship of the members of the "Archival Fragments, Experimental Modes" coffee-table workshop sponsored by the Omohundro Institute.

Long ago, Werner Sollors generously brought me onto the editorial board of the *New Literary History of America* with Harvard University Press, and introduced me to Lindsay Waters. Lindsay was responsible for placing this book with Harvard, bringing news of Mather and his interlocutors back to the place it belongs. Emily Silk has been a tremendous editor, reading versions of the manuscript in a way that uniquely combined sensitivity and practicality: I am indebted to her and to the Press's anonymous readers for their valuable revision suggestions. I am also grateful to the very professional editorial and production teams at the Press, including Emeralde Jensen-Roberts, and at Westchester Publishing Services, including Michael Durnin and Sherry Gerstein. My thanks especially to Graciela Galup for designing the palimpsestic cover, with its subtle reference to *in tlilli, in tlapalli*.

I know how fortunate I am to have a tenured position with occasional sabbaticals at the University of California Santa Cruz, a public Hispanic-Serving Institution whose mission I can still support. In the Literature Department, I have been nourished by a very caring Chair in Carla Freccero, and by my visionary, smart, and dedicated colleagues whom I thank collectively. Susan Gillman has been a cherished interlocutor in the longtime project of worlding the Americas. Juan Poblete gave me a crucial book from his Melquiadean library, while the clever Micah Perks kept me laughing. Vilashini Cooppan embodies the spirit of hospitality and grace. And Jody Greene has been my teacher in precious, uncountable ways over the years we've been tied together on the monkey-rope. I've learned an enormous amount from my undergraduate and graduate students over the years. I am especially grateful for the one-on-one time I shared with my advisees Heidi Morse, Lisa Schilz, Gabriela Ramírez-Chávez, Mariana Romero, and Matt Suazo. Elsewhere on campus, I have enjoyed the stimulation of programming sponsored by the Research Center for the Americas and The Humanities Institute. My accomplished and compassionate Mom's Night Out colleagues were a mutual aid society during the rocky times that each of us lived through. I cannot imagine Santa Cruz without the company of *mis queridas amigas* Cat Ramírez and Jennifer Gonzalez, whose brilliance, style, and wisdom I have secretly been trying to emulate for all these years. Joshua Dienstag, Hilary Hochman, and Nancy Watzman, my lifelong friends, have been unflagging supporters even from a distance.

My dear children, Teodoro and Elias Morrell, lived their childhoods throughout the making of this book; they participated in our experiment in dual linguistic immersion and tolerated my absence on many research trips. I come from a long line of *bordadoras* and creative people: ancestors, this word-stitching is the best I could do. Love and gratitude to my parents, Dave and Cheryle Gruesz; my brother Carl and sibkids Karina, Esther, and Sylvana; *mis primas-hermanas* Jennifer Silva Redmond and Maya de Silva Chafe and the rest of my Cal-Mex cousins and extended family. Finally, my life's companion Rodrigo Lazo has taught me what it is to be surprised by joy. Mi amor, I am grateful for you every day.

Index